zoom Deutsch 1

Teacher Book

Pat Dunn
Corinna Schicker
Marcus Waltl
Chalin Malz

OXFORD
UNIVERSITY PRESS

OXFORD
UNIVERSITY PRESS

Great Clarendon Street, Oxford OX2 6DP

Oxford University Press is a department of the University of Oxford.
It furthers the University's objective of excellence in research,
scholarship, and education by publishing worldwide in

Oxford   New York

Auckland Cape Town Dar es Salaam Hong Kong Karachi
Kuala Lumpur Madrid Melbourne Mexico City Nairobi
New Delhi Shanghai Taipei Toronto

With offices in

Argentina Austria Brazil Chile Czech Republic France Greece
Guatemala Hungary Italy Japan Poland Portugal Singapore
South Korea Switzerland Thailand Turkey Ukraine Vietnam

Oxford is a registered trade mark of Oxford University Press
in the UK and in certain other countries

© Oxford University Press 2011

The moral rights of the author have been asserted

Database right Oxford University Press (maker)

First published 2011

All rights reserved. No part of this publication may be reproduced,
stored in a retrieval system, or transmitted, in any form or by any means,
without the prior permission in writing of Oxford University Press, or as
expressly permitted by law, or under terms agreed with the appropriate
reprographics rights organization. Enquiries concerning reproduction
outside the scope of the above should be sent to the Rights Department,
Oxford University Press, at the address above

You must not circulate this book in any other binding or cover
and you must impose this same condition on any acquirer

British Library Cataloguing in Publication Data

Data available

ISBN-13: 978-0-19-912775-7

10 9 8 7 6

Printed in Great Britain by Bell & Bain Ltd, Glasgow

Paper used in the production of this book is a natural, recyclable product
made from wood grown in sustainable forests. The manufacturing process
conforms to the environmental regulations of the country of origin.

Acknowledgements
The authors and publishers would like to thank the following people for
their help and advice: Julie Green, Angelika Libera

Contents

Summary of Unit Contents	4
Long Term Plan	6
Introduction	7
The components of *Zoom Deutsch 1*	7
Student Book	7
Teacher Book	7
Audio CDs and MP3 files	7
Copymasters	8
Workbooks	8
OxBox CD-ROMs	8
Video	9
Course progression	9
PLTS in *Zoom Deutsch 1*	10
The Renewed MFL Framework	10

Teaching notes for *Zoom Deutsch 1*		
Los geht's!		11
Unit 0	Hallo!	16
Unit 1A	Meine Familie	38
Unit 1B	Meine Schule	59
Unit 2A	Freizeit und Hobbys	82
Unit 2B	Wo wohnst du?	105
Unit 3A	Guten Appetit!	128
Unit 3B	Mein Zuhause	154
Unit 4A	Modestadt Berlin!	179
Unit 4B	Zu Besuch	202

Symbols used in this Teacher's Book:

- a pairwork activity
- a groupwork activity
- a video activity
- a listening activity – audio on accompanying CD
- AT X.X reference to a National Curriculum Attainment Level
- L&S 1.1 reference to a Framework objective
- core activities are highlighted in pale grey (see Course progression, page 9)

# Summary of Unit Contents

	Contexts	Grammar	Skills	Pronunciation	Culture	Framework
Los geht's!	• Greetings • Introduction to Germany and German-speaking countries; names of towns and countries • Symbols of Germany • Classroom language	• *Das ist …* • Gender: *ein, eine*	• Use German to communicate in class	• Compare German and English sounds and spellings • *ß, ä, ö, ü*	• Germany and German-speaking countries	L&S 1.4 IU 3.1, 3.2 KAL 4.1, 4.3 LLS 5.2, 5.3, 5.4
Unit 0 Hallo!	• Greetings; introduce yourself and spell your name • Numbers up to 31; months • Say your age and birthday • Say which country you're from, where you live and what languages you speak	• The German alphabet • *Ich bin, du bist; ich habe, du hast* • Word order in simple sentences • Ordinal numbers • **Extra Plus:** Masc. and fem. forms of nationalities	• Identify language patterns and words from the same family • Learning tips: regular revision • Work out meaning (cognates, visuals)	• *w* • *ei, ien* • *ä, ö, ü* • Letter combinations	• Germany, Austria and Switzerland	L&S 1.1, 1.2, 1.4, 1.5 R&W 2.1, 2.2, 2.4 IU 3.1, 3.2 KAL 4.1, 4.2, 4.3, 4.4, 4.5 LLS 5.1, 5.2, 5.3, 5.4, 5.5, 5.6, 5.7
Unit 1A Meine Familie	• Family, brothers and sisters • Pets and zoo animals • Colours • Descriptions of self and others	• *Mein(e), dein(e)* • *Ich habe (k)ein(e)(n) …* • *Er, sie, es* • Noun plurals • *Ich bin, du bist, er/sie/es ist* + adjectives	• Use a bilingual dictionary • Learn words and their plurals • Work out meaning • Identify language patterns	• *ü* • *sch* • *v* • *ei*	• Popular pets in Germany; names of pets • A German pop rock band	L&S 1.1, 1.2, 1.3, 1.5 R&W 2.1, 2.2, 2.4, 2.5 KAL 4.1, 4.2, 4.3, 4.4, 4.6 LLS 5.1, 5.2, 5.3, 5.4, 5.5, 5.7, 5.8
Unit 1B Meine Schule	• Classroom objects; items in a school bag • Opinions of school subjects • Ask and say what time it is; talk about school timetables • Days of the week	• Gender: *der, die, das* • *Ich habe (k)ein(e)(n) …* • *Ich habe, du hast, er/sie hat, wir haben* • "Verb second" word order	• Work out meaning (cognates, context, component parts of a word, visuals) • Ask questions	• *ö*	• School routine in Germany	L&S 1.1, 1.2, 1.3, 1.4 R&W 2.1, 2.2, 2.3, 2.4, 2.5 IU 3.1, 3.2 KAL 4.1, 4.2, 4.3, 4.4, 4.5, 4.6 LLS 5.1, 5.3, 5.4, 5.5, 5.7
Unit 2A Freizeit und Hobbys	• Sports and musical instruments • Hobbies: talk about what you like doing and prefer doing, and what your favourite hobby is • Talk about computer games • Say how often you do something	• *Gern, nicht gern, lieber, am liebsten* • Present tense of a regular verb (*spielen*) and irregular verbs (*fahren, lesen, sehen*) • *Denn* • How to say "them" (*sie*) • Word order with time phrases	• How to keep a record of new language • Deduce meaning from intonation • Use known language to work out meaning of new words • Adapt language to create new language	• *a* and *ä* • Pronounce words that look alike in English and German	• Internet habits of German teenagers • A German pop singer	L&S 1.1, 1.2, 1.3, 1.4 R&W 2.1, 2.2, 2.4 KAL 4.1, 4.2, 4.3, 4.4, 4.5, 4.6 LLS 5.1, 5.2, 5.3, 5.4, 5.5, 5.8

Unit	Topics	Grammar	Skills/Strategies	Phonics	Cultural content	Framework references
Unit 2B **Wo wohnst du?**	• Countries, regions and the weather • Types of neighbourhood; types of house; rooms in a house or flat; bedroom descriptions • Numbers up to 100	• Present tense of *wohnen* • Prepositions + dative *(einem/einer/einem, dem/der/dem)* • *Es gibt* + accusative *(einen/eine/ein)*	• Learning techniques • Adapt language to create new language • Work out meaning of compound nouns • Work out language patterns	• *ch*	• Facts and figures about Germany • Life in an area of Germany	L&S 1.1, 1.2, 1.4, 1.5 R&W 2.1, 2.2, 2.3, 2.4, 2.5 IU 3.1, 3.2 KAL 4.1, 4.2, 4.3, 4.4, 4.5 LLS 5.1, 5.2, 5.3, 5.4, 5.5, 5.6, 5.7, 5.8
Unit 3A **Guten Appetit!**	• Food: likes, dislikes and what you eat for different meals • Order a snack • Numbers up to 1000; quantities and packaging; food shopping • Healthy eating • Order a meal in a restaurant	• "Verb second" word order • *Ich möchte* + noun • Singular and plural nouns (units of quantity) • *Man soll* + infinitive • *Ich esse* + *kein(e)(n)* …	• Use linking words • Use familiar language in a new context • Use polite language • Work out language patterns • Use different strategies to work out meaning	• Long *u* and short *u*	• Typical German meals • German food specialities	L&S 1.1, 1.2, 1.3 R&W 2.1, 2.2, 2.4, 2.5 IU 3.1, 3.2 KAL 4.1, 4.2, 4.3, 4.4, 4.5, 4.6 LLS 5.1, 5.3, 5.4, 5.5, 5.6, 5.7, 5.8
Unit 3B **Mein Zuhause**	• Places in a town • Talk about what you can do in a place and express your opinions • Ask for and give directions • Buy tickets and presents • Tourist information	• *Es gibt* + *(k)ein(e)(n)* … • Modal verbs (*können, wollen*) • The imperative (*du, Sie*) • *Ich möchte/nehme* + accusative • Subject–verb inversion in questions	• Ask questions • Evaluate and improve written work • Identify language patterns • Listening strategies	• *v* and *w*	• Places of interest in Berlin and other German towns	L&S 1.1, 1.2, 1.3, 1.5 R&W 2.1, 2.2, 2.3, 2.4, 2.5 IU 3.1, 3.2 KAL 4.1, 4.2, 4.3, 4.4, 4.5, 4.6 LLS 5.1, 5.2, 5.4, 5.5, 5.6, 5.7, 5.8
Unit 4A **Modestadt Berlin!**	• Clothes: descriptions and opinions • Say what you usually wear and what you'd like to wear • Go shopping for clothes • Explain problems with clothes; say what you're going to buy • Talk about designer clothing and school uniform	• Singular noun + *ist*, plural + *sind* • The accusative case (*ich trage einen/eine/ein* + adjective + noun; *der* changes to *den*; object pronouns: *ihn, sie es*) • Present tense of *tragen* • *Ich möchte* + infinitive • Future tense • The comparative	• Evaluate and improve written work • Identify cognates and false friends • Apply previously learned language in a new context • Identify language patterns	• *isch, ich, ig*	• German fashion designers	L&S 1.1, 1.2, 1.3, 1.4, 1.5 R&W 2.1, 2.2, 2.4, 2.5 IU 3.1, 3.2 KAL 4.1, 4.2, 4.3, 4.4, 4.5 LLS 5.1, 5.3, 5.5, 5.6, 5.7, 5.8
Unit 4B **Zu Besuch**	• Holidays: destination, means of travel, accommodation, duration of stay • Talk about things you can do on holiday and what you're going to do • Talk about past holidays • A visit to an amusement park	• Prepositions *in* and *auf* + dative • Modal verbs (*können, wollen*) • Future tense • Perfect tense (auxiliaries *haben* and *sein* + past participle) • Use a range of structures	• Listening strategies • Language patterns • Compound nouns • Express opinions • Recycle familiar words/phrases in different tenses	• Word endings	• Places of interest in Germany, Austria and Switzerland	L&S 1.1, 1.2, 1.4 R&W 2.1, 2.2, 2.4, 2.5 IU 3.1, 3.2 KAL 4.1, 4.2, 4.3, 4.4, 4.5, 4.6 LLS 5.1, 5.2, 5.3, 5.4, 5.5, 5.7, 5.8

Long Term Plan

Zoom Deutsch Long Term Plan

	Year 7 objectives							Year 8 objectives*		
	Los geht's!	Unit 0	Unit 1A	Unit 1B	Unit 2A	Unit 2B	Unit 3A	Unit 3B	Unit 4A	Unit 4B
Strand 1: Listening and speaking (L&S)										
L&S 1.1: Understanding and responding to the spoken word		•	•	•	•	•	•	•	•	•
L&S 1.2: Developing capability and confidence in listening		•	•	•	•	•	•	•	•	•
L&S 1.3: Being sensitive to the spoken word		•	•	•	•		•	•	•	
L&S 1.4: Talking together	•	•	•	•	•	•				
L&S 1.5: Presenting and narrating		•	•			•		•		
Strand 2: Reading and writing (R&W)										
R&W 2.1: Understanding and responding to the written word		•	•	•	•	•	•	•	•	•
R&W 2.2: Developing capability and confidence in reading		•	•	•	•	•	•	•	•	•
R&W 2.3: Being sensitive to the written word			•			•		•		
R&W 2.4: Adapting and building text		•	•	•	•	•	•	•	•	•
R&W 2.5: Writing to create meaning		•	•	•	•	•	•	•	•	•
Strand 3: Intercultural understanding (IU)										
IU 3.1: Appreciating cultural diversity	•	•		•		•		•	•	•
IU 3.2: Recognising different ways of seeing the world	•	•		•		•		•	•	•
Strand 4: Knowledge about language (KAL)										
KAL 4.1: Letters and sounds	•	•	•	•	•	•	•	•	•	•
KAL 4.2: Words		•	•	•	•	•	•	•	•	•
KAL 4.3: Gender, number and other inflections	•	•	•	•	•	•	•	•	•	•
KAL 4.4: Sentence structure		•	•	•	•	•	•	•	•	•
KAL 4.5: Verbs and tenses		•	•	•	•	•	•	•	•	•
KAL 4.6: Questions and negatives			•	•	•		•	•		•
Strand 5: Language learning strategies (LLS)										
LLS 5.1: Identifying patterns in the target language		•	•	•	•	•	•	•	•	•
LLS 5.2: Memorising	•	•	•	•		•	•	•		
LLS 5.3: Using knowledge of English or another language	•	•	•	•	•	•	•		•	•
LLS 5.4: Working out meaning	•	•	•	•	•	•	•	•	•	•
LLS 5.5: Using reference materials		•	•	•	•	•	•	•	•	•
LLS 5.6: Reading aloud		•					•	•	•	
LLS 5.7: Planning and preparing		•	•	•		•	•	•	•	•
LLS 5.8: Evaluating and improving			•			•	•	•	•	•

* Year 8 objectives continue in *Zoom Deutsch 2*

Introduction

The course

Welcome to *Zoom Deutsch 1*.

Zoom Deutsch 1
- is a broad-ability German course for 11–14 year olds with a fully-integrated video drama
- is fully flexible for all abilities with opportunities for reinforcement and extension throughout
- delivers the revised Key Stage 3 Programme of Study, PLTS and the Renewed Framework for Languages.

The components of Zoom Deutsch 1

Student Book
The 176-page Student Book consists of nine main units, plus two introductory spreads (*Los geht's!*). Two clear routes through the book are suggested, one for students following a two-year course, and one for students following a three-year course. Depending on the route followed, one unit represents either four or six weeks' work.

The Student Book contains the following sections:

Los geht's!
This four-page starter unit raises students' awareness of the German language and introduces them to some basic German phrases and greetings, as well as to aspects of the German-speaking world. Page 6 of the *Los geht's!* section introduces some key classroom language.

Einheiten 0–4B
There are nine 16-page units set in different contexts. Each unit has been planned to be interesting and motivating, as well as to provide a coherent and systematic approach to language development in terms of grammar, pronunciation and study skills. An outline of the content of each unit is given on pages 4–5 of this book.

Each unit is divided into:
- four core spreads, each of which includes activities in all four skills, language learning tips and grammar explanations
- a fifth spread, offering more in-depth coverage of the topic areas specifically intended for students following a three-year Key Stage 3
- a grammar and skills spread (*Sprachlabor*) which is divided into three sections:
Grammar (focusing on the key grammar points from the core spreads), Skills (promoting language learning strategies) and Pronunciation
- two pages of reinforcement and extension material, one for lower- and one for higher-ability students (*Extra Star* and *Extra Plus*), which are ideal for independent work – these can be used in class by students who finish other activities quickly or as alternative homework material

- a test page (*Testseite*), which revises the language and structures of the unit, and can also be used as a quick formative test of all four skills
- a vocabulary list and checklist
- a page of extra reading and homework material (*Lesen*).

Lesen
Zoom Deutsch 1 has a nine-page reading section for students to attempt once they are confident with the core language of the unit. These pages are designed to encourage independent reading and help students develop reading strategies. There is one reading page per unit, providing activities suitable for students of all abilities. The material can be used in class by students who finish other activities quickly or for homework.

Grammatik
The key grammar points taught in each unit are consolidated in a detailed grammar reference section at the back of the Student Book. This section also provides extra practice activities focusing on selected grammar points, with answers at the end of the grammar section for self-checking. Further grammar practice is provided in the Copymasters and Workbooks, and on the *Interactive OxBox CD-ROM*.

Vokabular
A German–English glossary contains the words in the Student Book for students' reference.

Teacher Book
Each unit contains the following detailed teaching notes:
- a Unit Overview Grid, providing a summary of the unit: contexts and objectives, language learning, grammar, key language, renewed Framework objectives and NC levels for each spread
- a Week-by-Week overview, providing details of the two- and three-year routes through each unit
- a Planner section for each core teaching spread for ease of lesson planning, providing cross-references to other course components and including suggestions for starter, plenary and homework activities
- ideas for presenting and practising new language
- detailed notes on all the Student Book material, including answers to all activities
- suggestions for further activities to reinforce and extend the content of the Student Book
- transcripts for all listening material and video clips
- answers and transcripts for the Workbook activities.

Audio CDs and MP3 files
The CDs provide the listening material to accompany the Student Book, Copymasters, Workbooks and assessment material. The listening material was recorded by native German speakers. Sound files are also available in MP3 format on the *Interactive OxBox CD-ROM*.

Introduction

Copymasters
The Copymasters provide opportunities for further practice and extension of the language of the Student Book units. All the Copymasters, together with answers and transcripts, are provided on the *Interactive OxBox CD-ROM*. Each unit has the following Copymasters:
- *Vokabular*: a list of key vocabulary from the unit, which students can use as a reference or as an aid to learning
- *Checklist*: a checklist of the core language of the unit, providing an opportunity for students to review their progress and reflect on areas for improvement
- *Starters and plenaries*: one page of starter and plenary activities
- *Hören Star* and *Plus*: one page of listening activities suitable for lower-ability students and one page for higher-ability students
- *Sprechen*: speaking activities
- *Lesen und schreiben Star* and *Plus*: two pages of reading and writing activities, one page suitable for lower-ability students and one page for higher-ability students
- *Grammatik*: consolidation and practice of key grammar points
- *Kompetenzen*: language learning strategies
- *Extra Star* and *Plus*: extra material for students covering *Zoom Deutsch* in three years.

Workbooks
Reinforcement and extension activities are provided in the *Zoom Deutsch 1* Foundation and Higher Workbooks. There is one page to accompany spreads 1–5 of each unit of the Student Book, followed by:
- *Sprachlabor*: extra grammar practice
- *Think*: skills practice and language learning strategies
- *Vokabular*: a list of key vocabulary from the unit
- *Checklist*: a checklist of the core language of the unit

The Workbooks are designed for students to write in, so are ideal for setting homework. Rubrics are provided in English throughout so that students can work independently.

OxBox CD-ROMs
The *Zoom Deutsch* course is accompanied by two CD-ROMs: the *Zoom Deutsch1 Interactive OxBox* and the *Zoom Deutsch 1 Assessment OxBox*.
- The *Interactive OxBox* is a CD-ROM of teacher and student-oriented resources which parallel the topic coverage of *Zoom Deutsch1* Student Book.
- The *Assessment OxBox* offers a suite of interactive and paper-based tests to accompany the Student Book.

OxBox also contains a "User Management" folder, into which you can import class registers and create user accounts for your students. OxBox provides two separate environments, one for teachers and one for students. Teachers have access to all of the resources; students can complete interactive activities and take tests that you have assigned to them.

OxBox is compatible with all standard Microsoft Office programs so, as well as being able to create new plans and assessments using the OxBox interface, you can also import your own Word or Excel-based lesson plans and materials into OxBox and file them in one centralised location. Many of the resources included in OxBox are themselves fully editable Word and PowerPoint files, permitting you to adapt them to the needs of a particular class or combine them with your own materials as you see fit.

The *Zoom Deutsch 1 Interactive OxBox* contains:
Lesson planning:
- Course overviews and unit plans
- Lesson plans offering ideas and strategies for delivering the *Zoom Deutsch* course, and suggestions on how you can combine the different resources available in the *Zoom Deutsch* Student Book and on OxBox
- The lesson planner provides a simple template in which you can write additional lesson plans which link to resources in OxBox. Using the lesson planner, you can also customise existing plans, tailoring them to different classes by changing the materials used in the lesson.

Teaching materials:
- The video clips that are used throughout the *Zoom Deutsch 1* Student Book
- Audio clips: the audio for the *Zoom Deutsch 1* Student Book and Copymasters
- Copymasters together with answers and transcripts
- An interactive activity accompanying each unit of the *Zoom Deutsch 1* Student Book. These consist of a foundation screen (NC levels 1–4) and a higher screen (NC levels 2–5/6) and practise listening, reading and writing. Interactive activities include the following activity types:
  – drag and drop
  – fill the gap
  – linking lines
  – ordering
  – multiple choice
  – sorting (putting things into categories)
- A record and playback activity and a pronunciation activity to practise speaking
- Pelmanism games
- Grammar presentations which are PowerPoint adaptations of the *Sprachlabor* spread
- An eBook of the *Zoom Deutsch 1* Student Book.

The *Zoom Deutsch 1 Assessment OxBox* contains:
- A diagnostic test to help assess students' level of language awareness and prior knowledge of German going into Year 7 or 8.
- Formative tests, designed to be completed by students as they progress through the course, helping them to master what they have learned and improve any areas of weakness. There are four formative tests for each unit of the course, one for each skill, each consisting of two questions (one at foundation level, and one at higher level). Question types for the listening, reading and writing are as for the interactive activities above. Speaking tests are in the form of record and playback activities. Students have two chances to answer each

Introduction

question, after which they can see a full breakdown of which bits they got right and which wrong.
- Summative tests intended to help you assess students' progress and provide them with a snapshot of the level they have reached at the end of each unit. There are four summative tests for each unit of the course, one for each skill. These are supplied in interactive form and as Word documents that can be printed out if you don't have access to the ICT suite. In a summative assessment, students may only attempt each question once and will not receive any feedback until they see their final result at the end of the test. Once all the members of a class have sat a summative test, the results are aggregated automatically enabling you to identify areas of strength and weaknesses.
- Summative end-of-term and end-of-year tests customised according to the route you are taking (two-year or three-year). These end-of-term and end-of-year tests will be made up of summative test questions for each skill for each unit. Depending on the route you are following, one suggestion of how to use the questions is as follows:

Test	Test	2-year pathway	3-year pathway
1st year	End of term 1	Book 1 Units 0–1B	Book 1 Units 0–1A
	End of term 2	Book 1 Units 2A–3A	Book 1 Units 1B–2A
	End of year 1	Book 1 Units 3B–4B	Book 1 Units 2B–3A
2nd year	End of term 1	Book 2 Units 0–1B	Book 1 Units 3B–4A
	End of term 2	Book 2 Units 2A–3A	Book 1 Unit 4B, Book 2 Unit 0
	End of year 2	Book 2 Units 3B–4B	Book 2 Units 1A–1B
3rd year	End of term 1		Book 2 Units 2A–2B
	End of term 2		Book 2 Units 3A–3B
	End of year 3		Book 2 Units 4A–4B

- Summative assessment guidance notes including answers, the marks available for each question and a breakdown of the National Curriculum levels that particular overall percentage scores equate to.

Video

A key feature of **Zoom Deutsch 1** is a video drama focusing on four teenagers. It is available as part of the *Interactive OxBox* package. The function of the video is threefold:
- it serves to provide an authentic view of life in a German-speaking country
- it introduces four aspirational German-speaking characters, providing students with added motivation for learning German
- it provides examples of key language in use, translating language learning from theory into practice.

There are two video clips per unit:
- an episode of the **video drama** featuring four teenagers, which ties in with activities on one or more of the four core spreads
- a **video blog**, in which one of the four teenagers talks about the unit topic from his or her personal perspective.

Each **video drama** can be used in its entirety to set the scene for the corresponding unit.

Excerpts from it are then used again later in the unit to focus on specific language points. A synopsis of the plot is provided at the beginning of the teaching notes for each unit.

When using the video drama as a unit starter, try to concentrate initially on visual content rather than on an understanding of the script. This helps to boost students' confidence in their ability to cope with authentic speech: it shows that even without understanding everything that is said, it is still possible to work out quite a lot by focusing on visual information, body language, tone of voice, etc.

Set students other visual challenges, e.g. ask them to spot German signs on buildings, Berlin landmarks, film posters outside a cinema, etc. – a few suggestions are given at the start of the teaching notes for each unit. Students will enjoy showing how sharp-eyed they are! In later units, challenge them to identify familiar language in the clip before you move on to focus on the new language points.

The *Sprachpunkt* section at the end of each video drama is a useful tool for highlighting and clarifying key language. Captions are shown on-screen to facilitate oral practice.

The **video blog** is usually used with the fifth spread of each unit, although occasionally it comes up on one of the other four spreads. In addition to offering extended listening practice, it provides a model for students to produce their own video blog, enabling them to personalise the language of the unit.

The level of language in the video drama and video blog is challenging but is made accessible for all via the activities and support provided in the Student Book and suggested in the teaching notes. This approach enables students of all abilities to experience authentic material at a higher level.

Course progression

Zoom Deutsch is a two-part course, consisting of two Student Books of nine units each. It caters both for schools following a two-year Key Stage 3 and for those following a three-year Key Stage 3 by offering different "routes" through each unit:

- For the three-year Key Stage 3, we suggest that you cover each unit in its entirety, including core spreads 1–4, the optional spread 5 (which provides more in-depth coverage of the unit themes) and spread 6

Introduction

(grammar and skills), selecting additional material from the Extra and *Lesen* pages as appropriate. This provides sufficient material for a half-term's teaching per unit. Following this route, two units are covered per term.
- For the two year Key Stage 3, we suggest that your main focus should be core spreads 1–4 and spread 6 (grammar and skills), but that you may wish to use additional material selectively if time permits. On the core spreads themselves, certain activities are optional, so you may wish to use these selectively too. In the teaching notes, we have used pale grey highlighting to identify core activities on the core spreads, so that it is easy to see what is optional and what is essential. Following this "accelerated" route, three units are covered per term.

The Week-by-Week overviews, which can be found at the beginning of each unit's teaching notes in this book, give a detailed breakdown of which activities and spreads to cover each week according to the route you are following.

PLTS in *Zoom Deutsch 1*

A key aim of **Zoom Deutsch 1** is that students should be able to learn in a meaningful way, thinking flexibly, analysing language, problem solving, justifying answers and making predictions based on previous knowledge. As a guide, the following features and types of activity in *Zoom Deutsch 1* help to promote the six PLTS:

- **Independent enquirers**
  - Video drama, video blog, *Lesen* section: provide stimulus material prompting students to explore aspects of German lifestyle and culture and to consider different attitudes and perspectives.
- **Creative thinkers**
  - *Think* boxes throughout, *Sprachlabor*: encourage students to think creatively about language, e.g. by identifying and explaining language patterns, working out meaning and developing language learning strategies.
  - *Challenge* (on spreads 1–5 of each unit) and other open-ended activities: provide opportunities for students to give a creative or personal response to the unit themes.
- **Reflective learners**
  - Spread objectives: clearly state the focus of each spread, so that students know what they are about to learn and can review their progress afterwards.
  - NC levels shown for key activities in the Student Book: this helps students to evaluate their progress and set goals. Some of the Think boxes encourage sharing of assessment criteria with students, so that they understand what needs to be done in order to achieve a particular NC level.
  - *Testseite* and "I can …" checklist (end of each unit): opportunity for students to review what they've learned and reflect on areas for improvement.
- **Team workers**
  - Opportunities throughout for students to work together in pairs and groups.

- **Self-managers**
  - *Think* boxes, *Sprachlabor*: encourage students to take responsibility for their own learning.
  - *Vokabular* (end-of-unit, end-of-book), *Grammatik* (end-of-book): encourage independent use of reference materials.
  - *Testseite* and "I can …" checklist: opportunity for students to review what they've learned and set their own goals for improvement.
  - *Extra Star*, *Extra Plus*, *Lesen* section: ideal for independent work.
  - Workbooks: designed for self-study.
- **Effective participators**
  - Opportunities throughout for students to engage with issues of interest to young people and to consider different attitudes and perspectives.

The Renewed MFL Framework

Zoom Deutsch has been carefully planned to ensure that all Framework objectives are covered in familiar contexts.

- The **Long Term Plan** on page 6 of this book provides an overview of the objectives to be covered in **Zoom Deutsch 1**. The Year 8 objectives continue into **Zoom Deutsch 2**.
- The **Summary of Unit Contents** grid on page 4 shows the objectives covered in each unit of **Zoom Deutsch 1**.
- The **Unit Overview grids** which can be found at the beginning of the teaching notes for each unit in this book show which objectives are covered in each spread of each unit.
- The **Planner** section at the beginning of the teaching notes for each spread includes a list of the objectives covered in that spread.
- Framework icons beside activities in the teaching notes show clearly which activities are associated with particular objectives.

Zoom Deutsch reflects the focus of the Renewed MFL Framework on key areas of teaching and learning. These include:
- Starters – suggestions for starter activities for each core spread are given in the Planner sections in this Teacher Book and are given in the lesson plans on the OxBox Interactive CD-ROM. Additional starter activities are provided on the *Starters and plenaries* Copymasters.
- Setting lesson objectives – the Planner sections provide a clear list of objectives for each spread.
- Modelling – **Zoom Deutsch** provides clear examples for all activities where appropriate.
- Questioning
- Practice
- Plenaries – suggestions for plenary activities for each core spread are given in the Planner sections in this Teacher Book and are given in the lesson plans on the OxBox Interactive CD-ROM. Additional plenary activities are provided on the *Starters and plenaries* Copymasters.

Los geht's!

Willkommen! Seite 4–5

Planner

Objectives
- Vocabulary: greetings; names of towns and countries
- Grammar: *das ist ...*
- Skills: learn words by listening and repeating; work out meaning; compare German and English sounds and spellings

Resources
- Student Book, pages 4–5
- CD 1, tracks 2–3

Key language
Das ist ...
Hallo! Guten Tag! Wie geht's?
Deutschland, Österreich, die Schweiz

Framework references
L&S 1.4; IU 3.2; KAL 4.1; LLS 5.3

AT 1.1 | AT 3.1 — **1 Hör zu und lies.**
This activity introduces the four recurring characters from the video. Students listen, read along and repeat.

🎧 **CD 1, track 2** Seite 4, Übung 1 und 2
- Das ist Nina.
- Hallo!
- Das ist Ali.
- Guten Tag!
- Das ist Kathi.
- Wie geht's?
- Das ist Nico.
- Hallo!

Think
Students work out (from the ex. 1 texts) how to say "This is ..." in German (*Das ist ...*).

AT 1.1 | AT 3.1 — **2 Hör noch einmal zu.**
Students read and listen again and identify three different greetings.

Answers: *Hallo! Guten Tag! Wie geht's?*

L&S 1.4 — **Follow-up**
Set up a chain around the class: each student introduces the person next to them, who gives a greeting in German then introduces the next person, e.g.
Ben: *Das ist James!*
James: *Guten Tag! Das ist Emma.*
Emma: *Hallo! Das ist ...*

IU 3.2 — **Deutschland, Österreich und die Schweiz**
Read through the information box about Germany and other German-speaking countries. Compare Germany and the UK in terms of their size and position in Europe, e.g. the UK is an island on the edge of Europe, whereas Germany is right at the centre of Europe. Do students think this influences the perspectives of people living in the two countries? Do they think Germans are likely to feel "more European" than their UK counterparts?

AT 1.1 | AT 3.1 | KAL 4.1 — **3 Hör zu und wiederhole.**
Students look at the map of Germany, Austria and Switzerland. They listen and repeat the names of key towns, pointing to each one on the map as they say it.

🎧 **CD 1, track 3** Seite 5, Übung 3

Deutschland	Österreich
Berlin	Wien
München	Salzburg
Frankfurt	Innsbruck
Bonn	
Köln	**Die Schweiz**
Stuttgart	Bern
Düsseldorf	Zürich
Hamburg	Basel
Hannover	Genf
Leipzig	
Dresden	
Hollfeld	
Bayreuth	

11

Los geht's!

KAL 4.1
LLS 5.3
Follow-up
- Play the ex. 3 recording again and focus on differences between German and English pronunciation: point out that although some place names are spelled the same in English and German, they sound different. Look at the umlauts and compare the effect they have on pronunciation, e.g. compare the *ü* in *München* with the *u* in *Frankfurt*.

- Elicit the English names for the countries and towns, e.g. *München* – Munich. For a competitive challenge, display a list of the place names in German and English and ask students to match them up.

Was ist das? Seite 6–7

Planner

Objectives
- Vocabulary: symbols of Germany; classroom language
- Grammar: gender (*ein*, *eine*)
- Skills: compare German and English spellings; use German for classroom communication; pronounce *ä*, *ö*, *ü* and *ß*

Resources
- Student Book, pages 6–7
- CD 1, tracks 4–6
- Foundation and Higher Workbooks, pages 4–7
- Workbook audio: CD 3 and 4, tracks 2–30

Key language
Das ist England / Deutschland / London / Berlin / Fußball / Hockey. Das ist ein Auto / ein Bus / ein Sportschuh / eine CD. Wie sagt man „biro" auf Deutsch? Wie bitte? „Biro" heißt Kuli auf Deutsch. Wie schreibt man das? Kuli – was bedeutet das? Ich weiß es nicht. Ich verstehe nicht. Bitte schön. Danke schön. Ruhe, bitte!

Framework references
L&S 1.4; IU 3.1; KAL 4.1, 4.3; LLS 5.2, 5.3, 5.4

AT 3.1
KAL 4.3
LLS 5.3, 5.4
1 Lies die Fragen. Was ist richtig?
Students complete a picture quiz about Germany. Afterwards, talk about what helped them to understand the quiz, e.g. similarity between German and English words, visuals as clues, process of elimination.
Read through the quiz, emphasising the pronunciation of words that look the same as or similar to English words, e.g. *England*, *Auto*, *Bus*. Read through the *Grammatik* box on gender. Ask students to identify the different words for "a" in the quiz.

Answers: **1** *b;* **2** *a;* **3** *b;* **4** *a;* **5** *a*

AT 1.1
2 Ist alles richtig? Hör zu. (1–5)
Students listen to check their answers to ex. 1.

CD 1, track 4 Seite 6, Übung 2
1 Das ist Deutschland.
2 Das ist ein Auto.
3 Das ist ein Sportschuh.
4 Das ist Fußball.
5 Das ist Berlin.

LLS 5.3 **Think**
Students are encouraged to identify a key difference between German and English orthography. They should notice that all the German nouns in the quiz are written with an initial capital (*Auto*, *Bus*, etc.) whereas in English only proper nouns are written with a capital.

Los geht's!

IU 3.1 **Follow-up**
Talk about the images of Germany that feature in the picture quiz. Can students suggest anything else that is associated with Germany? For example, they might think of food stereotypes (sausages, beer, sauerkraut), German engineering, efficiency, Christmas markets and other images such as Bavarian *Lederhosen* and German holidaymakers claiming the best places by the pool with their beach towels.
Talk about stereotypical images of other nationalities. Invite students to suggest what people from other countries might associate with the British.

AT 1.1–2
AT 3.1–2
L&S 1.4
3 Hör zu und lies. (1–10)
This cartoon introduces some useful classroom language. Students listen and read along. Encourage them to repeat each question or statement, imitating the pronunciation and intonation.

🎧 **CD 1, track 5**   Seite 7, Übung 3
1 Wie sagt man „biro" auf Deutsch?
2 „Biro" heißt „Kuli" auf Deutsch.
3 Wie schreibt man das?
4 Ich verstehe nicht.
5 Wie bitte?
6 Ich weiß es nicht.
7 „Kuli?" Was bedeutet das?
8 Bitte schön.
9 Danke schön!
10 Ruhe, bitte!

AT 3.1–2
L&S 1.4
4 Was passt zusammen?
Students match the English expressions a–j to the captions in the cartoon.

Answers: **a** 7; **b** 3; **c** 6; **d** 8; **e** 5; **f** 10; **g** 1; **h** 2; **i** 9; **j** 4

L&S 1.4
LLS 5.2
Follow-up
- Students play a dice game to practise the classroom language. The dots on the dice represent the numbers of the German expressions 1–10. Students take turns to throw the dice and say the corresponding expression together with its English equivalent – two throws of the dice will be needed for numbers 7–10, e.g.
A: (throws a 3) *Wie schreibt man das?* – How do you spell that?
B: (throws a 6 and a 3 = 9) *Danke schön!* – Thank you!
The first person to say all ten expressions is the winner.

- Students stage their own version of the cartoon. Ask them to use a different word instead of "biro" – they could choose something from the quiz on page 6, e.g. *Wie sagt man „car" auf Deutsch?* Challenge each member of the group to learn their line by heart so that they can perform the scene without reading from the book.

- Talk about different ways to learn the classroom expressions, e.g. writing them down and reading them aloud, listening and repeating while doing an appropriate mime.

- Students could write out the expressions as signs to display around the classroom as an aide-memoire. Encourage them to try to use German as much as possible for routine classroom communication. Each week, you could choose a "phrase of the week" and challenge students to use it as much as they can. New expressions can be added gradually, as you progress through the course.

KAL 4.1 **Think**
This section introduces some letters and sounds that don't exist in English: umlauts and the ß. Students listen and practise pronunciation.

🎧 **CD 1, track 6**   Seite 7, *Think*
sagen – sägen
rufen – üben
schon – schön

At this stage you may wish to focus on some of the pronunciation points covered on pages 4–7 of the Foundation and Higher Workbooks: see transcripts beginning on next page.

Los geht's!

Foundation and Higher Workbook

Pronunciation
Consonants

🎧 **CD 3 and 4, track 2** — Seite 4

Consonants / Konsonanten

b	Berlin	l	lustig
d	Deutsch	m	Mutter
f	Fisch	n	nein
h	Haus	p	Polen
k	klein	t	Timo

🎧 **CD 3 and 4, track 3** — Seite 4

g / g
grün   Giraffe   Morgen

🎧 **CD 3 and 4, track 4** — Seite 4

j / j
Joghurt   Jahr   jetzt

🎧 **CD 3 and 4, track 5** — Seite 4

r / r
rot
Rhein
Regen
Trier
tragen

🎧 **CD 3 and 4, track 6** — Seite 4

s / s
sieben   sechs   singen

🎧 **CD 3 and 4, track 7** — Seite 4

st – sp / st – sp
Straße   Sturm   spielen

🎧 **CD 3 and 4, track 8** — Seite 4

s / s
lustig   Maske   fast

🎧 **CD 3 and 4, track 9** — Seite 5

v / v
viel
Vater
vierzig
Vogel
Verboten

🎧 **CD 3 and 4, track 10** — Seite 5

w / w
will   weiß
Löwe   Wolke

🎧 **CD 3 and 4, track 11** — Seite 5

z / z
Zoo   Zeitung
Zeit   Zürich

🎧 **CD 3 and 4, track 12** — Seite 5

ß / ß
Straße   groß   Fuß

🎧 **CD 3 and 4, track 13** — Seite 5

ss / ss
muss   lass
Schluss   Schloss

Combinations of consonants

🎧 **CD 3 and 4, track 14** — Seite 5

ch / ch
acht   lachen
Achtung   Loch

🎧 **CD 3 and 4, track 15** — Seite 5

sch / sch
schade   Fisch   Schule

14

Los geht's!

Vowels

🎧 **CD 3 and 4, track 16** — Seite 6

short a / kurzes a
hat   Mann
machen   Klasse
kann

🎧 **CD 3 and 4, track 17** — Seite 6

long a / langes a
Straße   haben
baden   malen

🎧 **CD 3 and 4, track 18** — Seite 6

short e / kurzes e
England essen frech

🎧 **CD 3 and 4, track 19** — Seite 6

long e / langes e
Esel sehen leben

🎧 **CD 3 and 4, track 20** — Seite 6

i / i
in   billig
Interview   ich

🎧 **CD 3 and 4, track 21** — Seite 6

short o / kurzes o
toll doppel Pommes

🎧 **CD 3 and 4, track 22** — Seite 6

long o / langes o
Mode Cola Hallo

🎧 **CD 3 and 4, track 23** — Seite 7

short u / kurzes u
Hund muss lustig

🎧 **CD 3 and 4, track 24** — Seite 7

long u / langes u
Stuhl Schule Buch

Combinations of vowels

🎧 **CD 3 and 4, track 25** — Seite 7

ie / ie
viel   sie
Liebe   vier

🎧 **CD 3 and 4, track 26** — Seite 7

ei / ei
mein   kein
dein   heiße

🎧 **CD 3 and 4, track 27** — Seite 7

au / au
Haus Maus blau

Umlauts

🎧 **CD 3 and 4, track 28** — Seite 7

a → ä
Vater / Väter   Hand / Hände
hatte / hätte

🎧 **CD 3 and 4, track 29** — Seite 7

o → ö
Post / hören   schon / schön
rot / Löwe

🎧 **CD 3 and 4, track 30** — Seite 7

u → ü
muss / müssen   pur / für
Gruß / grüßen

0 Hallo!

Unit 0 Hallo!	Unit overview grid					
Page reference	Objectives	Grammar	Skills and pronunciation	Key language	Framework	AT level
Pages 8–9 **0.1 Wie heißt du?**	Greetings; say your name and spell it	The German alphabet	Compare German and English words; use visuals to work out meaning; imitate German sounds	Guten Morgen! Guten Abend! Hallo! Auf Wiedersehen! Tschüs! Wie heißt du? Ich heiße Alex. Wie schreibt man das? Das schreibt man …	L&S 1.1, 1.2, 1.4 R&W 2.2 IU 3.1, 3.2 KAL 4.1 LLS 5.2, 5.3, 5.4, 5.7	1.1–2, 2.1–2, 3.1–2
Pages 10–11 **0.2 Wie alt bist du?**	Use numbers 1–20; say how old you are	Ich bin … Du bist …	Understand the importance of regular revision; use existing knowledge to work out language rules	Numbers 1–20 Wie alt bist du? Ich bin (zwölf) Jahre alt. Wie geht's? Mir geht's fantastisch/(sehr) gut/ nicht so gut/schlecht.	L&S 1.1, 1.2, 1.4 KAL 4.2 LLS 5.1, 5.2, 5.6, 5.7	1.1–2, 2.1–2, 3.1–2, 4.1
Pages 12–13 **0.3 Ich habe Geburtstag!**	Use numbers 21–31; learn the months in German; say which month your birthday is in	Ich habe … Du hast …	Use cognates to work out meaning; use existing knowledge to work out language rules	Numbers 21–31 Januar, Februar, März, April, Mai, Juni, Juli, August, September, Oktober, November, Dezember Wann hast du Geburtstag? Ich habe im Mai Geburtstag.	R&W 2.2, 2.4 KAL 4.1, 4.2 LLS 5.1, 5.3, 5.4	1.1–2, 2.1–2, 3.1–2, 4.1–2
Pages 14–15 **0.4 Mein Land, meine Sprache**	Learn the names of some countries and languages; say where you come from, where you live and what language(s) you speak	Das ist … Ich komme aus … Ich wohne in … Ich spreche …	Identify links between spelling and pronunciation (w, ei, ien)	Das ist … Deutschland, Frankreich, Großbritannien, Italien, Österreich, Polen, die Schweiz, Spanien, die Türkei. Ich wohne in Deutschland/in der Schweiz/in der Türkei. Ich komme aus Deutschland/aus der Schweiz/aus der Türkei. Ich spreche … Deutsch, Englisch, Französisch, Italienisch, Polnisch, Spanisch, Türkisch.	L&S 1.1, 1.2, 1.4 R&W 2.1, 2.2, 2.4 KAL 4.1 LLS 5.3, 5.4, 5.5, 5.7	1.1–2, 2.1–2, 3.1–2, 4.1–2
Pages 16–17 **0.5 Kathis Videoblog**	Say what date your birthday is; give personal information	Ordinal numbers	Identify language patterns	Wann hast du Geburtstag? Ich habe am ersten Mai Geburtstag. Wie ist dein Nachname? Mein Nachname ist … Was ist deine Telefonnummer? Meine Telefonnummer ist …	L&S 1.1, 1.2, 1.4, 1.5 R&W 2.4 LLS 5.1, 5.7	1.1–3, 2.1–2, 3.2, 4.1–2

0 Hallo!

Unit 0: Week-by-week overview
(Three-year KS3 Route: assuming six weeks' work or approximately 10–12.5 hours)
(Two-year KS3 Route: assuming four weeks' work or approximately 6.5–8.5 hours)

About Unit 0, Hallo!: In this unit, students learn how to greet people and introduce themselves: they say their name, age and birthday, where they come from, where they live and what language(s) they speak. They learn the German alphabet, numbers 1–31, months, and the names of some countries and languages, and there are opportunities to find out about German-speaking countries and places in Berlin.

Students also begin using some key verb forms (*ich bin/du bist, ich habe/du hast*). There is a strong focus on thinking skills, e.g. using visual clues and cognates to deduce meaning, working out language rules and identifying language patterns, and students are encouraged to revise regularly to help them remember what they've learned. They practise pronunciation of umlauts, letter combinations (*ei, ie, sp*) and the letter *w*.

Three-Year KS3 Route

Week	Resources	Objectives
1	0.1 Wie heißt du?	Greetings; say your name and spell it The German alphabet Compare German and English words Use visuals to work out meaning Imitate German sounds
2	0.2 Wie alt bist du? 0.6 Sprachlabor ex. 1	Use numbers 1–20; say how old you are *Ich bin, du bist* Understand the importance of regular revision; use existing knowledge to work out language rules
3	0.3 Ich habe Geburtstag! 0.6 Sprachlabor ex. 2	Learn the months and numbers 21–31; say which month your birthday is in *Ich habe, du hast* Use cognates to work out meaning; use existing knowledge to work out language rules
4	0.4 Mein Land, meine Sprache 0.6 Sprachlabor ex. 3–8	Learn the names of some countries and languages; say where you come from, where you live and what language(s) you speak *Das ist …; ich komme aus …, ich wohne in …, ich spreche …* Identify links between spelling and pronunciation (*w, ei, ien*)

Two-Year KS3 Route

Week	Resources	Objectives
1	0.1 Wie heißt du? (*Omit ex. 8*)	Greetings; say your name and spell it The German alphabet Compare German and English words Use visuals to work out meaning Imitate German sounds
2	0.2 Wie alt bist du? (*Omit ex. 5*) 0.6 Sprachlabor ex. 1	Use numbers 1–20; say how old you are *Ich bin, du bist* Understand the importance of regular revision; use existing knowledge to work out language rules
3	0.3 Ich habe Geburtstag! (*Omit ex. 5 and 8*) 0.5 Kathis Videoblog *selective use of ordinal numbers (if appropriate)* 0.6 Sprachlabor ex. 2	Learn the months and numbers 21–31; say which month your birthday is in *Ich habe, du hast* Use cognates to work out meaning; use existing knowledge to work out language rules
4	0.4 Mein Land, meine Sprache (*Omit ex. 4 and Challenge*) 0.6 Sprachlabor ex. 5–8 0.8 Vokabular 0.8 Testseite	Learn the names of some countries and languages; say where you come from, where you live and what language(s) you speak *Das ist …; ich komme aus …, ich wohne in …, ich spreche …* Identify links between spelling and pronunciation (*w, ei, ien*) Key vocabulary and learning checklist Assessment in all four skills

17

0.1 Hallo!

Three-Year KS3 Route				Two-Year KS3 Route		
Week	Resources	Objectives	Week	Resources	Objectives
5	0.5 Kathis Videoblog	Say what date your birthday is; give personal information Ordinal numbers Identify language patterns			
6	0.7 Extra (Star/Plus) 0.8 Vokabular 0.8 Testseite 0 Lesen	Reinforcement and extension of the language of the unit Key vocabulary and learning checklist Assessment in all four skills Further reading to explore the language of the unit and cultural themes			

0.1 Wie heißt du? Seite 8–9

Planner

Objectives
- Vocabulary: greetings; say your name and spell it
- Grammar: the German alphabet
- Skills: compare German and English words; use visuals to help work out meaning; imitate German sounds

Video
- Video clip 0

Resources
- Student Book, pages 8–9
- CD 1, tracks 7–11
- Foundation and Higher Workbooks, page 8
- Workbook audio: CD 3 and 4, track 31
- Copymasters 4 (ex.2), 6 (ex.1)
- Interactive OxBox, Unit 0

Key language
Guten Morgen! Guten Abend! Hallo! Auf Wiedersehen! Tschüs!
Wie heißt du? Ich heiße Alex.
Wie schreibt man das? Das schreibt man …

Framework references
L&S 1.1, 1.2, 1.4; R&W 2.2; IU 3.1, 3.2; KAL 4.1; LLS 5.2, 5.3, 5.4, 5.7

Starters
- Student Book page 8, ex. 1. Set a time limit for this activity: students race against the clock to match the English expressions to their German equivalents, using the pictures to help them.
- To begin a lesson once the alphabet has been taught, play hangman (as a whole class or with students working in pairs) using names of famous people or language from this spread and the *Los geht's!* section.

Plenaries
- Separate out the names of some famous couples and write the individual names on small pieces of paper, e.g. Batman / Robin, Romeo / Juliet, film star couples and other double acts. Put them in a "hat" and ask students to pick one piece of paper each. Students circulate around the class asking *Wie heißt du?* until they find their other half.
- Word tennis in pairs. Student A has first "serve" and calls out a question, greeting or other expression; B returns A's serve by responding appropriately and without hesitation; A continues the rally by calling out another expression, e.g.
A: *Tschüs!*
B: *Auf Wiedersehen!*
A: *Wie schreibt man …?*
B: *Das schreibt man …*
Make sure they swap over so that B has a turn at serving.

Homework
- Students memorise the German alphabet, ready to recite it to their partner next lesson. Talk about ways of learning it, e.g. chanting it aloud using the chart you prepared in class (see teaching notes for ex. 4).
- *When … met …* Students work with a partner to write a dialogue in which two famous people greet each other, introduce themselves and spell their names.

0.1 Hallo!

Provide some ideas, e.g. imagine the first meeting of two people who later became a famous couple (David and Victoria Beckham), two well-known sporting rivals (a German footballer and a player from the England team), two fictional / cartoon characters, or some other implausible or amusing combination. Invite pairs to perform their dialogues in a following lesson.
- Students research one of the places in Berlin (from the video clip). They could design a poster about it in English and / or give a presentation to the class in a subsequent lesson.

Video clip 0: Kathi kommt nach Berlin!
Synopsis:
Kathi is the daughter of an Austrian businessman from an affluent background. She and her family have just arrived in Berlin from Vienna and are moving into their new flat. Outside, Kathi meets a local girl, Nina, who lives in the same building. Nina takes Kathi on a cycling tour of famous Berlin sights. The girls become friends and exchange phone numbers.

Play the video through a couple of times and ask questions to help students work out the gist of it. At this stage, concentrate on visual content rather than on an understanding of the script. (The clip will be used again later in the unit for work on specific language points.) Suggested focus:
- Can students see any clues that the action is taking place in Germany rather than the UK? (German flags, famous places in Berlin, German number plate on the van)
- Talk about the Berlin monuments: do students recognise them or know anything about them? Has anyone in the class visited Berlin or Germany?
- Ask students if they are surprised by what they see of Berlin. Did they have any expectations about what it would be like?
- Can students work out the gist of what is happening? They may be able to deduce from the removal van (Rent-a-Car) and Kathi's suitcase that she has just arrived in Berlin and is moving in to her new home.

Video clip 0

(Kathi meets Nina outside the block of flats)
Vater: Kathi!
Kathi: Ja, ja, ich komme schon! … Also, hier bin ich! Willkommen in Berlin!
Nina: Hi! Ich bin Nina. Wohnst du auch hier?
Kathi: Hi, Nina! Ich heiße Kathi. Ja, ich wohne jetzt auch hier. Ich komme aus Österreich.
Nina: Du kommst aus Österreich?
Kathi: Ja, ich komme aus Wien.
Nina: Ach, Wien! Wow, wie schön!
Kathi: Ja. Berlin ist auch super! Kommst du aus Berlin?
Nina: Ja, ich bin Deutsche und ich komme aus Berlin. Wollen wir eine Tour durch Berlin machen?
Kathi: Ja, toll! Aber mein Koffer …
Nina: Ich helfe dir.

(touring Berlin by bicycle)
Nina: Das ist der Reichstag.
Kathi: Super! …
Nina: Und das ist das Brandenburger Tor.
Kathi: Ja klar! …
Nina: Und das ist die Staatsoper.
Kathi: Toll! …
Kathi: Und was ist das?
Nina: Das ist der Fernsehturm …

Kathi: Und wie heißt du?
Nina: Sorry? Ich heiße Nina, also ich bin Nina.
Kathi: Nein, nein, der ganze Name.
Nina: Ach so. Nina *Neumann*.
Kathi: Wie bitte?
Nina: Nina, N-I-N-A, Neumann, N-E-U-M-A-N-N.
Kathi: Ach, *Neumann*. Klar!
Nina: Und du?
Kathi: Ich?
Nina: Wie heißt du?
Kathi: Ach so … ich … auch der ganze Name?
Nina: Äh, ja …
Kathi: Also gut, ich heiße Katharina Viktoria Bettina von Hohenstein. K-A-T-H …
Nina: K-A-T-H-I … Kathi. Das reicht schon!

Nina: Wie alt bist du? Bist du auch vierzehn Jahre alt?
Kathi: Ja.
Nina: Und dein Bruder?
Kathi: Karl? Er ist elf Jahre alt.
Nina: Elf? Ach, so jung!

(back at the flats)
Kathi: Hey Nina, das war fantastisch!
Nina: Schön!
Kathi: Wie ist deine Telefonnummer?
Nina: Warte einen Moment: 0176 29 04 07 11.
Kathi: Okay.
Nina: Und deine Nummer?
Kathi: Warte kurz … 0181 98 87 63 22.
Nina: Fantastisch!

0.1 Hallo!

Sprachpunkt

Hi! Ich bin Nina.
Wie heißt du?
Ich heiße Kathi.
Ich komme aus Österreich.
Wie alt bist du?

R&W 2.2 / LLS 5.3, 5.4 — **Think**
Point out the reading tips before students begin ex. 1. Two strategies are suggested for working out meaning: identify German words that are similar to English; look for clues provided by visuals (as in ex. 1).

AT 3.1 — **1 Finde die Paare.**
Students match the English expressions to their German equivalents.

Answers: **a** 3; **b** 4; **c** 6; **d** 2; **e** 5; **f** 1

AT 1.1 — **2 Hör zu (a–f). Welches Bild?**
Students listen and identify the corresponding German expressions in ex. 1.

Answers: **a** 4; **b** 2; **c** 6; **d** 5; **e** 1; **f** 3

🎧 **CD 1, track 7** — Seite 8, Übung 2

a Guten Abend.
b Ich heiße Alex.
c Wie heißt du?
d Tschüs!
e Guten Morgen.
f Auf Wiedersehen.

AT 2.1 / L&S 1.4 — **3 Macht zwei Dialoge.**
Students greet their partner and introduce themselves.

KAL 4.1 — **Think**
Students are introduced to the German alphabet, including umlauts and ß. They consider which letters might be the most difficult to pronounce, then listen to the ex. 4 recording to check whether they were correct.

KAL 4.1 / LLS 5.2 — **4 Hör zu und wiederhole.**
Students listen to the alphabet and repeat it. Work with them to produce an alphabet chart showing the sound of each letter, e.g. *A – ah, B – bay, C – say*, etc. Encourage students to copy this out in their exercise books, so that they can use it when learning the alphabet for homework.

🎧 **CD 1, track 8** — Seite 8, Übung 4

A, B, C, D, E, F, G, H, I, J, K, L, M, N, O, P, Q, R, S, T, U, V, W, X, Y, Z, Ä, Ö, Ü, scharfes S

5 Was folgt?
Students take turns to say a letter of the alphabet. Their partner responds by saying the next letter.

IU 3.1 — **Think**
Students look at the German computer keyboard and compare it with an English version: what is the same and what is different? Are there any additional keys? Why might this be?

6 Hör zu (1–8). Was fehlt?
Students listen to the letter sequences and supply the missing letters.

Answers: **1** C; **2** I; **3** J; **4** L, N; **5** O, R; **6** Q, S; **7** U, W; **8** V, X, Z

🎧 **CD 1, track 9** — Seite 9, Übung 6

1 A, B, …, D, E
2 F, G, H, …, J
3 H, I, …, K, L
4 K, …, M, …, O
5 M, N, …, P, Q, …
6 P, …, R, …, T
7 T, …, V, …, X
8 U, …, W, …, Y, …

Think
Before listening to the ex. 7 recording, point out the reminder about how to pronounce ß.

AT 1.1–2 / AT 3.1–2 — **7 Hör zu und lies.**
Students read and listen to the short conversation between Nico and Kathi. This activity provides a model for asking and saying how to spell something.

20

0.2 Hallo!

CD 1, track 10 — Seite 9, Übung 7

– Hallo! Wie heißt du?
– Hallo! Ich heiße Kathi.
– Wie schreibt man das?
– Das schreibt man K-A-T-H-I.

8 Sieh dir das Video an. Schreib Ninas Nachnamen auf.

AT 1.1–2
L&S 1.1, 1.2
LLS 5.7

Play the section of the video in which Nina and Kathi exchange surnames. Students note down Nina's surname as she spells it out.

Before watching the clip, reassure students that they don't need to worry about understanding everything that is said. The question asks them to identify Nina's surname, so encourage them to think ahead to the sort of familiar phrases they need to listen out for, e.g. *Wie heißt du? Ich heiße …*, the word *Nachname* (from ex. 8 rubric) and of course spellings. To prepare for listening, allow time for students to rehearse the German alphabet to themselves.

As a follow-up, spell out Kathi's full name (Katharina Viktoria Bettina von Hohenstein) and challenge students to note it down.

Answer: Neumann

Video clip 0
CD 1, track 11 — Seite 9, Übung 8

Kathi: Und wie heißt du?
Nina: Sorry? Ich heiße Nina, also ich bin Nina.
Kathi: Nein, nein, der ganze Name.
Nina: Ach so. Nina *Neumann*.
Kathi: Wie bitte?
Nina: Nina, N-I-N-A, Neumann, N-E-U-M-A-N-N.
Kathi: Ach, *Neumann*. Klar!
Nina: Und du?
Kathi: Ich?
Nina: Wie heißt du?
Kathi: Ach so … ich … auch der ganze Name?
Nina: Äh, ja …
Kathi: Also gut, ich heiße Katharina Viktoria Bettina von Hohenstein. K-A-T-H …
Nina: K-A-T-H-I … Kathi. Das reicht schon!

Challenge

AT 2.1–2
L&S 1.4

Using the model provided, students greet their partner, introduce themselves and spell their name.

0.2 Wie alt bist du? — Seite 10–11

Planner

Objectives
- Vocabulary: use numbers 1–20; say how old you are
- Grammar: *ich bin, du bist*
- Skills: understand the importance of regular revision; use existing knowledge to work out language rules

Video
- Video clip 0

Resources
- Student Book, pages 10–11
- CD 1, tracks 12–15
- Foundation and Higher Workbooks, page 9
- Workbook audio: CD 3 and 4, track 32
- Copymasters 3 (ex. 2), 4 (ex. 1)
- Interactive OxBox, Unit 0

Key language
Numbers 1–20
Wie alt bist du? Ich bin (zwölf) Jahre alt.
Wie geht's? Mir geht's fantastisch / (sehr) gut / nicht so gut / schlecht.

Framework references
L&S 1.1, 1.2, 1.4; KAL 4.2; LLS 5.1, 5.2, 5.6, 5.7

Starters
- Copymaster 3 (ex. 2).
- Use the mobile phone on Student Book page 10 as the basis for quick revision of the alphabet. In pairs, students take turns to "text" a short message to their partner by calling out the individual letters, e.g. H-A-L-L-O! Their partner notes down the letters and reads back the message.
- Once the numbers have been introduced, begin a lesson with a quick numbers game, e.g.
  – noughts and crosses
  – bingo
  – invisible writing: students draw a number on their partner's back with their finger, for their partner to guess
  – telepathy: write down a number – students try to guess what it is
  – hold your breath: students try to say a sequence of numbers as quickly as possible without taking a breath

0.2 Hallo!

- human calculators: students take turns to call out a number between 1 and 20 – their partner responds instantly with the number needed to make it up to 20. (This activity can be adapted when students learn higher numbers, because the number range can be whatever you want it to be, e.g. 1–31, or 1–70, or 70–100, etc.)
- Counting games, e.g.
  - count to a specified number saying odd numbers or even numbers only
  - count backwards
  - count in multiples of two, three, four, five, etc.
  - replace multiples of two (or three, four, etc.) with an agreed word or phrase, e.g. *eins, zwei, Tschüs!, vier, fünf, Tschüs!* …

Plenaries

- The number games and counting games suggested as starters (see above) can also be used as plenaries.
- Bring to the lesson some photos of people, animals or cartoon characters, taken from magazines or newspapers. Be sure to include a range of age groups, from young children (or young animals / birds) up to the age of 20. Divide the class into teams and hold up a couple of photos. Team A take on the identity of one photo, team B the other, then they build a dialogue around them. E.g. teacher holds up a photo of a toddler (team A) and an old-looking dog (team B):
  A: *Hallo! Wie alt bist du?*
  B: *Ich bin zwölf Jahre alt. Wie alt bist du?*
  A: *Ich bin zwei Jahre alt!*
  Continue with the remaining photos. The dialogues can be extended to include names and spellings.

Homework

- Students prepare a puzzle to test their partner on numbers 1–20. Provide them with some ideas, e.g. gap-fill sums with numbers written in words (*zehn + … = zwölf*), incomplete number sequences (*fünf – zehn – fünfzehn – …*), anagrams, a crossword puzzle, wordsearch, matching pairs game, word snake, etc. Prompt them to prepare an answer sheet. They exchange their puzzles with a partner in the following lesson.
- Students find photos of people, animals and cartoon characters of different ages (as in the second plenary above) and write dialogues or speech bubbles to accompany the photos. They could limit this to asking and saying how old their characters are, or they could make up extended dialogues in which they aim to use as much as possible of the language they've learned so far: greetings, names, spellings, asking how someone is, etc.

AT 1.1
AT 2.1

1 Hör zu und wiederhole.
Students listen and repeat numbers 0–10. Before listening, point out the pronunciation tip on the *ü* and *ch* sounds.

CD 1, track 12 Seite 10, Übung 1
null, eins, zwei, drei, vier, fünf, sechs, sieben, acht, neun, zehn

AT 2.1
LLS 5.2

2 A sagt eine Zahl. B sagt die Buchstaben.
Before students begin ex. 2, you may wish to revise the alphabet from spread 0.1 (see first starter listed in the *Planner* above). Take this opportunity to invite feedback on how students went about learning the German alphabet, e.g. by chanting it aloud, or by spelling familiar words in their head. Point out the importance of regular revision, and explain that they will need to keep going back regularly over what they've learned, to help them remember it.

Students then take turns to call out a number from the mobile phone. Their partner responds by saying which letters appear on that button of the phone, e.g.
A: *Fünf.*
B: *J, K, L.*

AT 2.1

3 A buchstabiert eine Zahl. B schreibt die Zahl auf.
Students take turns to spell out numbers; their partner listens and notes down the corresponding figure, e.g.
A: *Z-W-E-I.*
B: *2.*

AT 1.1

4 Hör zu (1–6). Welches Handy ist das?
Students listen as six people call different phone numbers. They choose a mobile phone to correspond with each number.
Point out the language box on *Wie geht's?* and the information about dialling codes for Germany, Austria and Switzerland.

Answers: **1** *d;* **2** *a;* **3** *c;* **4** *b;* **5** *f;* **6** *e*

0.2 Hallo!

🎧 **CD 1, track 13** — Seite 10, Übung 4

1 eins … drei … zwei
2 vier
3 eins … eins
4 zwei … neun
5 sechs … drei … zwei
6 vier … drei … fünf

Follow-up
For further practice of *Wie geht's?* and the responses, set up a chain around the class: each student asks the person next to them how they are feeling; the person responds (in an appropriate tone of voice) then asks the next person, e.g.
A: *Wie geht's?*
B: *Mir geht's schlecht! … Wie geht's?*
C: *Mir geht's sehr gut! … Wie geht's?*
D: *Mir geht's …*

5 Sieh dir das Video an. Schreib die Telefonnummern auf.

[AT 1.2] [L&S 1.1, 1.2] [LLS 5.7]

Ask students to keep their books closed so that they don't have a chance to read ex. 5 rubric. Play the section of the video in which Nina and Kathi exchange phone numbers, and ask students if they can work out the gist of what is happening. Students then open their books, look at ex. 5 and prepare for listening by rehearsing to themselves the first eight figures of each person's phone number (*null, eins, sieben*, etc.). Play the clip again. Students focus on noting down the final four figures of each person's phone number.

Answers: **a** … 07 11; **b** … 63 22

Video clip 0
🎧 **CD 1, track 14** — Seite 11, Übung 5

Kathi: Hey Nina, das war fantastisch!
Nina: Schön!
Kathi: Wie ist deine Telefonnummer?
Nina: Warte einen Moment: 0176 29 04 07 11.
Kathi: Okay.
Nina: Und deine Nummer?
Kathi: Warte kurz … 0181 98 87 63 22.
Nina: Fantastisch!

[LLS 5.1] **Think**
Students apply their knowledge of numbers 1–10 in German to work out the rule for forming 13–19. They identify the pattern in the number words beside ex. 6, then fill in the gaps in the English instructions.

Answers: You form the numbers 13 to 19 by taking the first <u>four</u> letters of the numbers <u>drei</u> to <u>neun</u> and adding the word <u>zehn</u> on the end.

[AT 3.1] [AT 4.1] **6 Was passt zusammen?**
Students match the figures 11–20 with the corresponding German words and copy them out in order.

Answers: **11** elf; **12** zwölf; **13** dreizehn; **14** vierzehn; **15** fünfzehn; **16** sechzehn; **17** siebzehn; **18** achtzehn; **19** neunzehn; **20** zwanzig

[AT 1.1] [AT 2.1] **7 Hör zu und wiederhole.**
Students listen and repeat the numbers 11–20.

🎧 **CD 1, track 15** — Seite 11, Übung 7

elf, zwölf, dreizehn, vierzehn, fünfzehn, sechzehn, siebzehn, achtzehn, neunzehn, zwanzig

[LLS 5.2] **Think**
To help them memorise the numbers, students are encouraged to count backwards from 20, then to try counting even numbers only. See also the counting games suggested in the *Planner* above.

[AT 3.2] [KAL 4.2] [LLS 5.6] **8 Lies den Dialog.**
This dialogue introduces how to ask someone's age and say how old you are. Point out the *Grammatik* box and the two high-frequency phrases *ich bin* and *du bist*.
Read the dialogue aloud with students. Encourage them to repeat after you, imitating the pronunciation and intonation. Allow students to practise in groups of three, then invite confident groups to read aloud to the class.

Follow-up
Play the section of the video in which Nina and Kathi talk about their ages. Ask students to note down Nina's and Kathi's age (both 14) and Kathi's brother Karl's age (11).

0.3 Hallo!

Video clip 0 (excerpt)

Nina: Wie alt bist du? Bist du auch vierzehn Jahre alt?
Kathi: Ja.
Nina: Und dein Bruder?
Kathi: Karl? Er ist elf Jahre alt.
Nina: Elf? Ach, so jung!

Challenge (AT 2.1–2, L&S 1.4)

Students make up mini-dialogues based on the ages of the cartoon people. For each person, they introduce themselves, give their age and say goodbye. Show them how to adapt the model dialogue. Point out that the only items they need to change are the name and the age. Encourage students to extend their dialogues using *Wie geht's? Mir geht's (sehr) gut / schlecht*, etc. Remind them of the *Follow-up* to ex. 4 (see teaching notes above).

0.3 Ich habe Geburtstag!   Seite 12–13

Planner

Objectives
- Vocabulary: learn the months and numbers 21–31; say which month your birthday is in
- Grammar: *ich habe*, *du hast*
- Skills: use cognates to work out meaning; use existing knowledge to work out language rules

Resources
- Student Book, pages 12–13
- CD 1, tracks 16–19
- Foundation and Higher Workbooks, page 10
- Workbook audio: CD 4, track 33
- Copymaster 4 (ex. 3)
- Interactive OxBox, Unit 0

Key language
Numbers 21–31
Januar, Februar, März, April, Mai, Juni, Juli, August, September, Oktober, November, Dezember
Wann hast du Geburtstag? Ich habe im Mai Geburtstag.

Framework references
R&W 2.2, 2.4; KAL 4.1, 4.2; LLS 5.1, 5.3, 5.4

Starters
- Student Book page 12, *Think* and ex. 1.
- Call the register; students answer by saying the month of their birthday.
- Student Book page 13, *Think*: students work out the pattern for forming numbers 21–31, then use this knowledge to work out numbers 32–39.
- The number games and counting games suggested in the *Planner* for spread 0.2 may be used as starters or plenaries.

Plenaries
- Discuss the pronunciation of the months: although many of them look similar to their English names, they sound very different. Ask students to suggest any sounds they've noticed in particular, e.g. *j* (in *Januar, Juni, Juli*) sounds like English *y*, and *z* (in *März, Dezember*) sounds like *ts*.
- Rolling question-and-answer around the class: student A begins by asking B *Wann hast du Geburtstag?* Student B answers (*Ich habe im … Geburtstag*) then asks C the question; and so on, around the class. The final student asks A the question, so that the sequence has come full circle.
- Number games and counting games: see fourth starter above.

Homework
- Students learn the months and prepare to recite them to their partner in the next lesson. Tell them they will be awarded two points per month: one point for remembering the name and a second point for pronunciation. (If it sounds like English, they won't get the second point!)
- Students research the birthdays and ages of their favourite celebrities. They find photos and write speech bubbles, e.g. *Hallo! Ich heiße Daniel Radcliffe. Ich bin … Jahre alt. Ich habe im … Geburtstag.*
- Student Book page 13, *Challenge*.

0.3 Hallo!

R&W 2.2 / LLS 5.3, 5.4 — Think
This reading tip points out that it is often possible to work out the meaning of new German words because of their similarity to English words. Students try this out on the months.

AT 3.1 / AT 4.1 / KAL 4.1 — 1 Was ist die richtige Reihenfolge?
Students copy out the months in the correct order. Read them aloud and ask students to repeat. Emphasise the difference in pronunciation between German and English.

Answers: Januar, Februar, März, April, Mai, Juni, Juli, August, September, Oktober, November, Dezember

AT 1.1–2 / AT 3.1–2 — 2 Hör zu. Wann hast du Geburtstag?
Students listen while focusing on the anagrams of the months in sentences a–e. They use the recording to help them solve the anagrams. As an extra challenge, ask them to listen out for the ages of Seema (12) and Silvia (13).

Answers: a Dezember; b März; c Mai; d Juli; e Februar

🎧 **CD 1, track 16** Seite 12, Übung 2
- Ich habe im Dezember Geburtstag.
- Hallo. Ich habe im März Geburtstag.
- Guten Tag. Ich habe im Mai Geburtstag. Ich bin zwölf Jahre alt.
- Ich habe im Juli Geburtstag. Ich bin dreizehn.
- Guten Morgen! Ich habe im Februar Geburtstag.

AT 1.2 — 3 Hör zu. Ein Interview im Radio.
Students listen and identify the month of each person's birthday.

Answers: 1 Claudia: October; 2 Julian: August; 3 Rebecca: January; 4 Klaus: June; 5 Martina: April

🎧 **CD 1, track 17** Seite 12, Übung 3
- Hallo Claudia. Wann hast du Geburtstag?
- Ich habe im Oktober Geburtstag.
- Und du, Julian. Wann hast du Geburtstag?
- Ich habe im August Geburtstag.
- Rebecca, wann hast du Geburtstag?
- Ich habe im Januar Geburtstag.
- Hallo Klaus. Wann hast du Geburtstag?
- Ich habe im Juni Geburtstag.
- Und jetzt Martina. Martina, wann hast du Geburtstag?
- Ich habe im April Geburtstag.

AT 2.1–2 / KAL 4.2 — 4 Macht Dialoge.
Students practise asking and answering the question *Wann hast du Geburtstag?* Point out the two high-frequency phrases in the model dialogue: *ich habe* and *du hast*.

AT 4.2 / R&W 2.4 — 5 Schreib die Dialoge auf.
Students write out their dialogues from ex. 4. They are encouraged to extend them by adding language from earlier in the unit, e.g. greetings, introducing themselves and spelling their name, asking and saying their age.

Follow-up
If your students would like to be able to say the date of their birthday, note that ordinal numbers are presented on spread 0.5. They are not core language for this stage in the course and are taught in *Zoom Deutsch 2*.

AT 1.1 / AT 2.1 — 6 Hör zu und wiederhole.
This activity introduces the numbers 21–31: students listen, read and repeat.

🎧 **CD 1, track 18** Seite 13, Übung 6
einundzwanzig, zweiundzwanzig, dreiundzwanzig, vierundzwanzig, fünfundzwanzig, sechsundzwanzig, siebenundzwanzig, achtundzwanzig, neunundzwanzig, dreißig, einunddreißig

LLS 5.1 — Think
Students work out the meaning of *und* and the pattern for forming numbers 21–31 in German, e.g. "one and twenty", "two and twenty", etc. Challenge them to work out how to say numbers 32–39.

AT 1.1 — 7 Welche Zahl hörst du? (a–f)
Students listen and identify the numbers.

Answers: a 28; b 21; c 22; d 27; e 31; f 24

🎧 **CD 1, track 19** Seite 13, Übung 7
a achtundzwanzig   d siebenundzwanzig
b einundzwanzig   e einunddreißig
c zweiundzwanzig   f vierundzwanzig

AT 2.1 — 8 A schreibt eine Zahl von 21–31 auf.
Number telepathy: students take turns to secretly write down a number between 21 and 31; their partner tries to guess what it is.

25

0.4 Hallo!

AT 4.1–2
R&W 2.4

Challenge
Students write a sentence for each cartoon person, saying how old they are and when their birthday is. Point out that the same framework is used for each sentence (*Ich heiße __. Ich bin __ Jahre alt. Ich habe im __ Geburtstag*), so all they need to do is to copy out the framework and fill in the names, ages and months.

Answers:
a *Ich heiße Anna. Ich bin achtzehn Jahre alt. Ich habe im Januar Geburtstag.*
b *Ich heiße Lars. Ich bin neunzehn Jahre alt. Ich habe im Oktober Geburtstag.*
c *Ich heiße Sabine. Ich bin siebzehn Jahre alt. Ich habe im Mai Geburtstag.*
d *Ich heiße Christian. Ich bin fünfzehn Jahre alt. Ich habe im Dezember Geburtstag.*
e *Ich heiße Lili. Ich bin sechzehn Jahre alt. Ich habe im März Geburtstag.*

0.4 Mein Land, meine Sprache

Seite 14–15

Planner

Objectives
- Vocabulary: learn the names of some countries and languages; say where you come from, where you live and what language(s) you speak
- Grammar: *das ist …; ich komme aus…, ich wohne in …, ich spreche …*
- Skills: identify links between spelling and pronunciation (*w, ei, ien*)

Video
- Video clip 0

Resources
- Student Book, pages 14–15
- CD 1, tracks 20–21
- Foundation and Higher Workbooks, page 11
- Copymasters 3 (ex. 3), 6 (ex. 3), 7, 8
- Interactive OxBox, Unit 0

Key language
Das ist … Deutschland, Frankreich, Großbritannien, Italien, Österreich, Polen, die Schweiz, Spanien, die Türkei.
Ich wohne in Deutschland / in der Schweiz / in der Türkei.
Ich komme aus Deutschland / aus der Schweiz / aus der Türkei.
Ich spreche … Deutsch, Englisch, Französisch, Italienisch, Polnisch, Spanisch, Türkisch.

Framework references
L&S 1.1, 1.2, 1.4; R&W 2.1, 2.2, 2.4; KAL 4.1; LLS 5.3, 5.4, 5.5, 5.7

Starters
- Copymaster 3, ex. 3.
- Student Book page 14, ex. 1: students identify countries and languages in the Europe text and list them in German and English.
- See first homework suggestion: students swap with a partner and complete each other's puzzles.

Plenaries
- Matching pairs. Working with a partner, students take turns to say they live in (or come from) a country; their partner responds by saying they speak the language, e.g.
  A: *Ich wohne in Polen.*
  B: *Ich spreche Polnisch.*
  Make sure they swap over so that B names the country and A responds with the corresponding language.
- Divide the class into teams. Call out key words or phrases from the unit; teams take turns to build them into any appropriate sentence. They win a point per correct sentence:
  Teacher: *Polnisch.*
  Team A: *Ich spreche Polnisch.* (= 1 point)
  Teacher: *November.*
  Team B: *Ich habe im November Geburtstag.* (= 1 point)

Homework
- Students make up a puzzle to test their partner on the German words for countries and languages, e.g. this could be a wordsearch, a crossword puzzle, anagrams, matching countries to languages, matching the names of countries to the outline of the country, etc. Tell them to prepare an answer sheet. The puzzles can be used as a starter activity in a following lesson.
- Student Book page 15, ex. 5 or *Challenge*.

26

0.4 Hallo!

AT 3.2
AT 4.1
R&W 2.1, 2.2
LLS 5.3, 5.4

1 Lies den Text. Mach eine Liste.
Students look at the Europe map and photos of eight teenagers: each person explains where they live and / or which country they come from, and which languages they speak. Students identify the countries and languages and list them in German and English.
Challenge them to find in the texts the German for "I speak ...", "I come from ..." and "I live in ..." (*ich spreche ..., ich komme aus ..., ich wohne in ...*).
Afterwards, ask students what helped them to understand the texts, e.g. similarities between German and English words, the map and visuals plus their own knowledge of Europe, process of elimination.

Answers: **Länder:** Deutschland (Germany), die Schweiz (Switzerland), Spanien (Spain), Österreich (Austria), Frankreich (France), die Türkei (Turkey), Großbritannien (Britain), Polen (Poland); **Sprachen:** Deutsch (German), Französisch (French), Italienisch (Italian), Spanisch (Spanish), Türkisch (Turkish), Englisch (English), Polnisch (Polish)

AT 1.1
AT 3.1
KAL 4.1

2 Hör zu. Wiederhole.
Students listen, read and repeat the country names. Point out the pronunciation tip on *w* and *ei* and encourage them to focus on these sounds. Compare the *ei* sound with the *ien* sound in *Großbritannien* and *Spanien*.

CD 1, track 20 Seite 15, Übung 2

a	Deutschland	e	Türkei
b	Österreich	f	Polen
c	Frankreich	g	Schweiz
d	Großbritannien	h	Spanien

AT 3.2
AT 4.2

3 Füll die Lücken aus.
Students copy out Nina's paragraph and fill in the gaps using the words provided.

Answers: **a** heiße; **b** Deutschland; **c** wohne; **d** 14; **e** Geburtstag; **f / g** Deutsch / Englisch

AT 1.2
L&S 1.1, 1.2
LLS 5.7

4 Sieh dir das Video an. Wähle die richtige Antwort.
Play the first section of the video, in which Kathi and Nina introduce themselves to each other. Students identify where each girl comes from.

Encourage them to prepare for the activity by looking at the answer options in a–b and working out what they need to listen for: *Ich komme aus Deutschland / Österreich / Berlin*. Point out that they can probably complete sentence b already, without even needing to watch the video, by using their answers to ex. 3. Encourage them to stay focused on the information they need and to disregard anything irrelevant.

Video clip 0
CD 1, track 21 Seite 15, Übung 4

Nina: Hi! Ich bin Nina. Wohnst du auch hier?
Kathi: Hi, Nina! Ich heiße Kathi. Ja, ich wohne jetzt auch hier. Ich komme aus Österreich.
Nina: Du kommst aus Österreich?
Kathi: Ja, ich komme aus Wien.
Nina: Ach, Wien! Wow, wie schön!
Kathi: Ja. Berlin ist auch super! Kommst du aus Berlin?
Nina: Ja, ich bin Deutsche und ich komme aus Berlin. Wollen wir eine Tour durch Berlin machen?
Kathi: Ja, toll! Aber mein Koffer ...
Nina: Ich helfe dir.

AT 2.1–2
L&S 1.4

Follow-up
In advance of the lesson, prepare small cards or pieces of paper with the name of a country or language written on each. Make sure each country card has a matching language card. Give a card to everyone in the class. They move around telling each other which country they come from or which language they speak, until they find their matching country / language. Once they've found their partner, encourage them to try keeping the conversation going, e.g.

A: (approaches student B) *Ich spreche Türkisch.*
B: (to A) *Ich wohne in Polen.*
A: (approaches student C) *Ich spreche Türkisch.*
C: (to A) *Ich komme aus Italien.*
A: (approaches student D) *Ich spreche Türkisch.*
D: (to A) *Ich komme aus der Türkei!*
A: *Wie geht's?*
D: *Gut ... Wie geht's?*
A: *Fantastisch! Wie heißt du?*
D: *Ich heiße ...*

0.5 Hallo!

AT 4.2
R&W 2.4

5 Schreib Sätze.
Students write a few sentences about themselves, giving details of their name, age, the month of their birthday, where they live, where they come from and the languages they speak. Point out that they can use Nina's text (ex. 3) as a model, copying out the key phrases and replacing Nina's details with their own. To support them, display a copy of Nina's text and highlight the words they need to change.

AT 4.2
R&W 2.4
LLS 5.5

Challenge
Students research five more countries and languages in a dictionary. They write a short text (as in ex. 3) on behalf of a famous person, using one of their new countries and languages.

0.5 Kathis Videoblog   Seite 16–17

Planner

Objectives
- Vocabulary: say what date your birthday is; give personal information
- Grammar: ordinal numbers
- Skills: identify language patterns

Video
- Video blog 0

Resources
- Student Book, pages 16–17
- CD 1, tracks 22–23
- Foundation and Higher Workbooks, page 12
- Workbook audio: CD 3 and 4, track 34
- Interactive OxBox, Unit 0

Key language
Wann hast du Geburtstag? Ich habe am ersten Mai Geburtstag.
Wie ist dein Nachname? Mein Nachname ist …
Was ist deine Telefonnummer? Meine Telefonnummer ist …

Framework references
L&S 1.1, 1.2, 1.4, 1.5; R&W 2.4; LLS 5.1, 5.7

Starters
- Student Book page 16, *Think* activity: students work out the pattern for forming ordinal numbers in German.
- Student Book page 17, ex. 4: before students watch the video, encourage them to prepare for the activity by trying to predict the missing words in Kathi's text. See teaching notes for ex. 4 below.

Plenaries
- Student Book page 16, ex. 3: class survey on birthdays.
  Alternatively, set up a question-and-answer chain around the class. Student A begins by asking the person next to them (B) when his / her birthday is; B answers, then asks C; C answers and asks D; and so on around the class. The final person completes the circle by asking A the question:
  A: *Wann hast du Geburtstag?*
  B: *Ich habe am achten Juni Geburtstag. Wann hast du Geburtstag?*
  C: *Ich habe am neunzehnten Februar Geburtstag. Wann hast du Geburtstag?*
  D: *Ich habe am …*
- Teacher versus the class. Tell students to close their books, then start talking about Heidi Klum and Kathi, giving a mixture of true and false information. Challenge the class to spot the false details. They win one point for each error they spot and an extra point if they can correct it; you win a point for each error they fail to spot, e.g.
  Teacher: *Ich heiße Heidi und ich wohne in Österreich.*
  Class: *Falsch … ich wohne in Amerika.* (= 2 points)

Homework
- Students find or draw pictures to represent different times of the year, then write sentences about birthdays to correspond with the pictures, e.g. *Ich habe am vierzehnten Februar Geburtstag* (beside a picture of hearts, to represent St Valentine's Day), *Ich habe am einunddreißigsten Oktober Geburtstag* (beside a picture of a Halloween lantern). Alternatively, ask them to keep the pictures and the sentences separate; then, in the next lesson, they swap with a partner and try to match each other's sentences to the corresponding pictures.
- Student Book page 17, *Challenge*. Students write and record their own video blogs, and play them back to the class.

0.5 Hallo!

LLS 5.1

Think
Students look at the language grid and try to work out the pattern for forming ordinal numbers in German. They fill in the gaps in the English explanation.
Point out the full stop in 1., 2., 3., 4., etc. and compare with English 1st, 2nd, 3rd, 4th.

Answers: When I say the date of my birthday, I usually add the letters -ten to the numbers 1–19. The exceptions are the numbers eins, drei, sieben and acht. For the numbers 20–31, I add -sten.

AT 4.1-2 **R&W 2.4**

1 Schreib Sätze.
Students look at the photos and dates. They choose words from each column of the language grid to help them build a sentence saying when each person's birthday is.

Answers: a Ich habe am vierten Januar Geburtstag. b Ich habe am achtundzwanzigsten Juni Geburtstag. c Ich habe am fünfzehnten August Geburtstag. d Ich habe am dritten Oktober Geburtstag.

AT 1.1-2

2 Hör zu (1–5). Wähle den richtigen Geburtstag.
Students listen and identify each person's birthday.

Answers: 1 d; 2 e; 3 a; 4 c; 5 b

CD 1, track 22 Seite 16, Übung 2

1 Ich habe am siebten Mai Geburtstag.
2 Ich habe am achten Oktober Geburtstag.
3 Ich habe am dritten Januar Geburtstag.
4 Ich habe am zwölften November Geburtstag.
5 Ich habe am dreißigsten Juli Geburtstag.

AT 2.1-2 **L&S 1.4**

3 Macht eine Umfrage in der Klasse: „Wann hast du Geburtstag?"
Students carry out a class survey to find out when everyone's birthday is, asking and answering the question *Wann hast du Geburtstag?*
Suggest that they prepare for the survey by listing the months, then all they need to do is to jot down the dates (and names, if you wish) beside the corresponding month, e.g. *Januar*: 3 (Sam), 28 (Lily), 29 (Emma); *Februar*: 9 (Tom), …
Talk about the results: does anyone share a birthday? Do some months have more birthdays than others? Are there some months in which nobody has a birthday?

AT 1.3 **L&S 1.1, 1.2** **LLS 5.7**

4 Sieh dir das Video an. Füll die Lücken aus.
Students watch Kathi's video blog and fill in the gaps in sentences a–g.
Before playing the video, discuss listening strategies, e.g. using questions and visuals as clues, predicting answers, using logic, sensible guesswork, etc. Make sure students realise that they can do a lot of preparation for this activity, e.g. they know before they start listening what Kathi's name is, which gives them the answer to a and b; they can see her age and birthday listed in her profile, so this provides the answers to c and d; they should remember the answer to e from video clip 0; and they can make a sensible guess at the answers to f. Once students have tried to anticipate all this, they should find it much easier to focus on key information when listening.

Answers: a Kathi; b K-A-T-H-I; c 14; d Mai; e Berlin; f Deutsch, Englisch, Französisch; g 52 937

Video blog 0
CD 1, track 23 Seite 17, Übung 4

Hallo. Wie geht's? Ich heiße Kathi. Das schreibt man K-A-T-H-I. Und mein Nachname ist von Hohenstein. Von: V-O-N. Hohenstein: H-O-H-E-N-S-T-E-I-N. Kompliziert, nicht! Und wie heißt du? Wie ist dein Nachname?
Ich bin vierzehn Jahre alt und ich habe am vierten Mai Geburtstag. Wann hast du Geburtstag?
Ich wohne in Berlin. Berlin ist total super. Und du? Wo wohnst du?
Ich spreche Deutsch, Englisch und Französisch. Und du?
Meine Telefonnummer zu Hause? Moment …
Die Nummer ist 030 38 52 937. Und wie ist deine Telefonnummer?
Tschüs!

AT 3.2

5 Füll die Lücken aus.
Students copy out Heidi Klum's text and fill in the gaps using the words provided.

Answers: a geht's; b heiße; c Geburtstag; d Jahre; e wohne; f Deutsch; g gut

AT 2.2 **AT 4.2** **L&S 1.5**

Challenge
Students answer the questions asked by Kathi in her video blog. They write and record their own video blog.

29

0.6 Hallo!

0.6 Sprachlabor
Seite 18–19

Planner

Objectives
- Grammar: word order in simple sentences; *ich bin, du bist; ich habe, du hast*
- Skills: identify words from the same family; pronounce umlauts (*ä, ö, ü*), letter combinations and *w*

Resources
- Student Book, pages 18–19
- CD 1, tracks 24–26
- Foundation and Higher Workbooks, pages 13–14
- Workbook audio: CD 3 and 4, tracks 35
- Copymasters 9, 10
- Interactive OxBox, Unit 0

Framework references
KAL 4.1, 4.2, 4.3, 4.4, 4.5; LLS 5.1

Word order, *sein* and *haben*

KAL 4.2, 4.3, 4.4, 4.5 This grammar section focuses on word order in simple sentences, and the *ich* and *du* forms of *sein* and *haben*.

1 Put the words in the right order.

Answers: **a** Hallo Franziska. Wie alt bist du? / Hallo Natalie. Ich bin zwölf Jahre alt. **b** Hallo Martin. Wie alt bist du? / Hallo Klaus. Ich bin vierzehn Jahre alt. **c** Hallo Sabrina. Wie alt bist du? / Hallo Bernd. Ich bin dreizehn Jahre alt.

2 Fill in the gaps with the correct form of *haben*.

Answers: **a** habe; **b** hast; **c** Hast; **d** habe

Identifying words from the same family

KAL 4.2 / LLS 5.1 This activity encourages students to focus on similarities between words belonging to the same family (e.g. *Türkei – Türkisch, Italien – Italienisch*) and language patterns (all the words for languages here end in -*isch* or -*sch*).

3 Match the flag (a–g) with the country (1–7) and the language (i–vi).

Answers: **a** 3 vi; **b** 7 iii; **c** 2 ii (also iii in north of Italy); **d** 4 i; **e** 6 v; **f** 1 i, ii, iii; **g** 5 iv

4 Look at the numbers for the countries in activity 3 and roll a dice.
Students play a dice game based on the countries and languages in ex. 3, e.g.
A: (rolls a two = country 2 = *Italien*) *Das ist Italien. Ich spreche Italienisch.*
B: *Richtig!* (then rolls the dice) *Das ist …*
They will need to roll the dice twice for country 7 (*Deutschland*). Who is the first to name all seven countries and their languages?

Pronunciation of umlauts (*ä, ö, ü*), letter combinations and *w*

KAL 4.1 Ex. 5–8 and the pronunciation tips focus on the sound of some letter combinations (*sp, ei, ie*), umlauts and *w*.

5 Listen carefully to the following words.
Students listen and repeat the words.

🎧 **CD 1, track 24** — Seite 19, Übung 5

a	fünf	g	Griechenland
b	zwölf	h	schlecht
c	Bär	i	gute Nacht
d	ich	j	tschüs
e	heiße	k	wie?
f	dreißig	l	wann?

6 A says a word in activity 5. B points at the word.
Students practise reading aloud the list of words from ex. 5.

7 Listen to the words (a–f) and try to spell them correctly.
Be prepared to pause the recording after each item to give students time to note down the spelling.

🎧 **CD 1, track 25** — Seite 19, Übung 7

a	heiße	d	Frankreich
b	Türkei	e	spreche
c	Eisbär	f	wann?

0.7 Hallo!

8 First try to pronounce these words. Then listen to check.

🎧 CD 1, track 26   Seite 19, Übung 8

a Spanien   d wie
b Wien   e dreißig
c zwei   f schreiben

0.7 Extra Star   Seite 20

Planner

Objectives
- Vocabulary: practise language from the unit
- Grammar: *ich bin, du bist; ich habe, du hast*
- Skills: use visuals and other clues to work out meaning

Resources
- Student Book, page 20
- Copymaster 11

AT 4.1   **1 Fill in the gaps to complete the numbers.**
Students copy out the numbers and fill in the missing letters.

Answers: **a** *eins*; **b** *sieben*; **c** *acht*; **d** *zehn*; **e** *elf*; **f** *siebzehn*; **g** *neunzehn*; **h** *zwanzig*

AT 3.1   **2 Which are positive and which are negative?**
Students copy out the list of words. They draw a smiley face or a sad face beside each one to show whether it is positive or negative.

Answers: <u>Positive</u>: *gut, super, fantastisch, sehr gut*; <u>Negative</u>: *schlecht, nicht gut, nicht so gut*

AT 3.1–2   **3 Match the questions and answers and write out the dialogue.**

AT 4.2   Point out that although each question has only one possible answer, the question-and-answer pairs can be sequenced differently.

Answers:
– Wie heißt du?
– Ich heiße Claudia Schiffer.
– Wie geht's?
– Sehr gut. Danke.
– Wie alt bist du?
– Ich bin 41 Jahre alt.
– Wann hast du Geburtstag?
– Ich habe im August Geburtstag.

AT 3.1–2   **4 Match the calendar pages with the phrases.**
Students choose an appropriate picture to represent each birthday.

Answers: **a** 4; **b** 1; **c** 6; **d** 2; **e** 5; **f** 3

0.8 Hallo!

0.7 Extra Plus
Seite 21

Planner

Objectives
- Vocabulary: practise language from the unit
- Grammar: masculine and feminine forms of nationalities
- Skills: use knowledge of grammar to work out meaning

Resources
- Student Book, page 21
- Copymasters 5, 12

Key language
Ich bin Engländer(in), Österreicher(in), Schweizer(in), Deutsche(r)

Framework references
R&W 2.1, 2.2; KAL 4.3; LLS 5.1, 5.4

AT 3.1 / AT 4.1 — **1 Was ist die Lösung?**
Students calculate the sums and write the answers in words.

Answers: **a** sechzehn; **b** elf; **c** einundzwanzig; **d** dreiundzwanzig; **e** fünfzehn; **f** siebzehn

KAL 4.3 / LLS 5.1, 5.4 — **Think**
Read through the information about masculine and feminine forms of nationalities. Point out to students that knowledge of German grammar can help with working out meaning, e.g. if they hear or read the word *Engländerin*, the *-in* ending shows that the person being referred to is female rather than male.

AT 4.2 — **2 Schreib Sätze für die Bilder.**
Supported by the information on masculine and feminine forms of nationalities, students write a sentence for each picture stating each person's nationality.

Answers: **a** Ich bin Engländerin. **b** Ich bin Schweizer. **c** Ich bin Österreicher. **d** Ich bin Schweizerin. **e** Ich bin Engländer. **f** Ich bin Deutsche. **g** Ich bin Deutscher.

AT 3.3 / R&W 2.1, 2.2 / LLS 5.1, 5.4 — **3 Lies den Text. Richtig oder falsch?**
Students read a text about the actress Franka Potente and decide whether the statements in English are true or false. Encourage them to correct the false statements.
Ask students to imagine this text without the accompanying photo and with Franka's name missing: how would they know whether the writer is male or female? Challenge them to find a clue in the text. (*Schauspielerin* has the feminine *-in* ending.)

Answers: **a** richtig; **b** falsch (from Germany); **c** falsch (22 July); **d** richtig; **e** falsch (says it's super)

AT 4.3 — **4 Schreib einen kurzen Absatz.**
Students write a paragraph about themselves, similar to the text in ex. 3.

0.8 Testseite
Seite 22

Planner

Resources
- Student Book, page 22
- CD 1, track 27
- Foundation and Higher Workbooks, page 15
- Copymasters 1, 2
- Assessment, Unit 0

AT 1.2 — **1 Listen (1–6). Who speaks about a–f?**
Students identify the gist (a–f) of what each person is talking about.
For an extra challenge, ask students to note down the details of a–f in English.

Answers: **1** d; **2** a; **3** e; **4** b; **5** f; **6** c (The details of a–f are: **a** 12; **b** May; **c** English and French; **d** Germany; **e** Tina; **f** not good)

32

0 Hallo!

CD 1, track 27 — Seite 22, Übung 1

1 Ich komme aus Deutschland.
2 Ich bin zwölf Jahre alt.
3 Das schreibt man T-I-N-A.
4 Ich habe im Mai Geburtstag.
5 Ach, nicht gut.
6 Ich spreche Englisch und Französisch.

AT 4.2 **2 Unscramble the word order in these sentences.**

For an extra challenge, ask students to write statements c and f as questions (*Wie heißt du? Wo wohnst du?*).

Answers: a Wann hast du Geburtstag? b Ich habe im Juni Geburtstag. c Ich heiße Karin. d Ich spreche Italienisch und Deutsch (Deutsch und Italienisch). e Ich komme aus Frankreich. f Ich wohne in England.

AT 3.2 **3 Match sentences 1–6 in the box below with a–f.**

Students identify the gist of each German sentence. For an extra challenge, ask students to note down the details of a–b and d–f in English.

Answers: a 4; b 1; c 6; d 2; e 5; f 3 (The details are: a German, Turkish, French; b 13; d March; e Turkey; f Berlin, Germany)

AT 2.2 **4 Make up an interview with a partner, asking the following questions (a–e). Match up the answers (1–5) first to help you.**

For an extra challenge, ask students to use their answers from ex. 4 as the basis for giving a short presentation about themselves.

Answers: a 5; b 1; c 2; d 3; e 4

0 Lesen
Seite 152

Planner

Resources
- Student Book, page 152

Framework references
R&W 2.1, 2.2; IU 3.1, 3.2

Deutschsprachige Länder

R&W 2.1, 2.2 / IU 3.1, 3.2 This reading page provides some key information about Germany, Austria and Switzerland. Three teenagers (one from each country) introduce themselves.

AT 3.3 **1 Answer the questions in English about Richard, Tanja and Thomas.**

Students answer questions about three German-speaking teenagers and search their texts for key words.
Afterwards, talk about Thomas's text. Ask students what is unusual about him – he's English but he lives in Germany. Ask students to consider possible reasons for this, e.g. his family might have moved there because of his parents' jobs.

Answers: a 1 Tanja; 2 Thomas; 3 Richard. B 1 cities in Austria, Switzerland and Germany; 2 Guten Tag; 3 toll, sehr gut

2 What do the words *Sprachen* and *Hauptstadt* mean?
Students work out the meaning of two key words. They may recognise *Sprache* and *ich spreche* as being from the same word family, and *Hauptstadt* can be deduced from the context.

Answers: languages, capital city

Follow-up
- Students use the information about German-speaking countries to make up a quick-fire quiz for their partner.
- Students write some questions or true / false statements about the three teenagers' texts, to exchange with their partner.
- Ask students to find out a few more things about one of the countries, which they feed back to the class in the next lesson.
- If anyone in the class has visited one of these countries, invite them to talk about their visit and to bring in some photos or souvenirs to show to the class.

0 Hallo!

Foundation Workbook

0.1 Wie heißt du? (Seite 8)

AT 1.1 **1** Listen to some German names being spelled out. Write down the names.

Answers: *a* Katja; *b* Stefan; *c* Natalie; *d* Moritz; *e* Janinn; *f* Fabian; *g* Lady Gaga; *h* Michael Ballack; *i* Nicole Seibert; *j* Arjen Robben

🎧 **CD 3, track 31** Seite 8, Übung 1

a Ich heiße Katja. Das schreibt man K-A-T-J-A.
b Ich heiße Stefan. Das schreibt man S-T-E-F-A-N.
c Ich heiße Natalie. Das schreibt man N-A-T-A-L-I-E.
d Ich heiße Moritz. Das schreibt man M-O-R-I-T-Z.
e Ich heiße Janinn. Das schreibt man J-A-N-I-N-N.
f Ich heiße Fabian. Das schreibt man F-A-B-I-A-N.
g Ich heiße Lady Gaga. Das schreibt man L-A-D-Y G-A-G-A.
h Ich heiße Michael Ballack. Das schreibt man M-I-C-H-A-E-L B-A-L-L-A-C-K.
i Ich heiße Nicole Seibert. Das schreibt man N-I-C-O-L-E S-E-I-B-E-R-T.
j Ich heiße Arjen Robben. Das schreibt man A-R-J-E-N R-O-B-B-E-N.

AT 2.1 **AT 4.1** **2** How do you say these things in German? Write them in and say them out loud.

Answers: *a* Guten Morgen! *b* Wie schreibt man das? *c* Wie heißt du? *d* Guten Abend! *e* Ich heiße … *f* Auf Wiedersehen!

3 Say these English words out loud. What German letters do they represent?

Answers: *a* H; *b* B; *c* K; *d* C; *e* J; *f* D

0.2 Wie alt bist du? (Seite 9)

AT 1.1 **1** Listen to these people giving you their ages. Write the ages in the bubbles.

Answers: *a* 18; *b* 3; *c* 12; *d* 20; *e* 15; *f* 6

🎧 **CD 3, track 32** Seite 9, Übung 1

a Ich bin achtzehn Jahre alt.
b Ich bin drei Jahre alt.
c Ich bin zwölf Jahre alt.
d Ich bin zwanzig Jahre alt.
e Ich bin fünfzehn Jahre alt.
f Ich bin sechs Jahre alt.

AT 3.1 **2** Add the prices to the labels.

Answers: *a* 2 €; *b* 1,15 €; *c* 2,20 €; *d* 3,10 €; *e* 14 €; *f* 16,15 €

AT 4.1–2 **3** These people are giving their ages. Write down what they are saying.

Answers: *a* Ich bin elf Jahre alt. *b* Ich bin siebzehn Jahre alt. *c* Ich bin neun Jahre alt. *d* Ich bin neunzehn Jahre alt. *e* Ich bin sieben Jahre alt. *f* Ich bin zwanzig Jahre alt.

0.3 Ich habe Geburtstag! (Seite 10)

AT 3.1 **1** Solve the clues and write in the German names of the months. The highlighted letters spell another month.

Answers: *a* Juli; *b* Februar; *c* Juni; *d* August; *e* Mai; *f* April (The highlighted letters spell: Januar.)

AT 3.1 **2** Do the sums, then write the answers, first the number, then the German word. Some words will be left over.

Answers: *a* 21 einundzwanzig; *b* 30 dreißig; *c* 24 vierundzwanzig; *d* 27 siebenundzwanzig; *e* 22 zweiundzwanzig; *f* 28 achtundzwanzig

AT 1.1 **3** Listen and work out how old these people are.

Answers: *a* 21; *b* 31; *c* 27; *d* 20; *e* 25; *f* 26

🎧 **CD 3, track 33** Seite 10, Übung 3

a Ich bin einundzwanzig Jahre alt.
b Ich bin einunddreißig Jahre alt.
c Ich bin siebenundzwanzig Jahre alt.
d Ich bin zwanzig Jahre alt.
e Ich bin fünfundzwanzig Jahre alt.
f Ich bin sechsundzwanzig Jahre alt.

0.4 Mein Land, meine Sprache (Seite 11)

AT 3.1 **1** Find the names of eight countries in this grid. The words can be horizontal, vertical or diagonal.

0 Hallo!

Answers:

	G								
	R	D	E	U	T	S	C	H	L	A	N	D
	P	O	L	E	N		C		
			ß			I			
			B	F	E				
				R					
			R	A	I			S	
		E		N		T		C	S
		T		K			A	H	P
	S	Ü		R			N	W	A
Ö		R		E			N	E	N
		K		I				I	I
		E		C			Z	E	E
		I		H					N

AT 3.1
AT 4.1
2 Unjumble the countries and insert the language.

Answers: **a** Deutschland, Deutsch; **b** Österreich, Deutsch; **c** Frankreich, Französisch; **d** Polen, Polnisch; **e** Spanien, Spanisch; **f** Großbritannien, Englisch

AT 4.1
3 Fill in the gaps with information about yourself.

Answers: students' own answers

0.5 Kathis Videoblog (Seite 12)

AT 3.1
AT 4.1
1 Complete these sentences to show what Nüssi the squirrel thinks of the seasons. The information is given below in English.

Answers: **a** schlecht; **b** sehr gut; **c** super; **d** fantastisch; **e** gut; **f** nicht gut

AT 1.1–2
2 When are these people's birthdays? Write down the month in English.
If you are following the three-year Key Stage 3 route and have done the work on ordinal numbers (spread 0.5 of the Student Book), ask students to note down the date as well as the month.

Answers: **a** (3) January; **b** (23) August; **c** (14) May; **d** (8) March; **e** (7) September; **f** (30) April

🎧 **CD 3, track 34**   Seite 12, Übung 2

a Ich habe am dritten Januar Geburtstag.
b Ich habe am dreiundzwanzigsten August Geburtstag.
c Ich habe am vierzehnten Mai Geburtstag.
d Ich habe am achten März Geburtstag.
e Ich habe am siebten September Geburtstag.
f Ich habe am dreißigsten April Geburtstag.

AT 2.1–2
3 Say the month of each person's birthday.
If you are following the three-year Key Stage 3 route and have done the work on ordinal numbers (spread 0.5 of the Student Book), challenge students to say the date as well as the month.

Answers: Ich habe im Juni (am zweiundzwanzigsten Juni) Geburtstag. Ich habe im März (am vierzehnten März) Geburtstag. Ich habe im August (am dritten August) Geburtstag. Ich habe im Juli (am zwölften Juli) Geburtstag. Ich habe im November (am sechsundzwanzigsten November) Geburtstag. Ich habe im Dezember (am vierten Dezember) Geburtstag.

0.6A Sprachlabor (Seite 13)

1 Put these words into the correct column.

Answers: Italien – Italienisch; Spanien – Spanisch; Türkei – Türkisch; Polen – Polnisch; Deutschland – Deutsch; Frankreich – Französisch; Großbritannien – Englisch; Schweiz – Deutsch, Französisch, Italienisch

2 Using your knowledge of German pronunciation, say these German words out loud. Then check the recording to see how accurate you were.

🎧 **CD 3, track 35**   Seite 13, Übung 2

ich … Wien … zwei … zwölf … schlecht … dreißig … Frankreich … tschüs … wie … Griechenland … fünf

3 Insert the correct form of *haben* (to have) or *sein* (to be).

Answers: **a** hast; **b** habe; **c** bist; **d** bin; **e** Hast; **f** habe

0.6B Think (Seite 14)

1 👥 **Take it in turns to say numbers between twenty and thirty to a partner. If you want to hear them again, say *Wie, bitte?***

2 👥 **Read these words aloud and get a partner to write them down accurately.**
Students practise *ei* and *ie* sounds.

Keeping a vocabulary list
Tips on how to keep a record of new language.

Learning vocabulary
Tips on different ways to learn new language.

0 Hallo!

Higher Workbook

0.1 Wie heißt du? (Seite 8)

AT 1.1 **1** Listen to some German names being spelled out. Write down the names.

Answers: **a** Katja; **b** Stefan; **c** Natalie; **d** Moritz; **e** Janinn; **f** Fabian; **g** Lady Gaga; **h** Michael Ballack; **i** Nicole Seibert; **j** Arjen Robben

🎧 **CD 4, track 31** Seite 8, Übung 1

a Ich heiße Katja. Das schreibt man K-A-T-J-A.
b Ich heiße Stefan. Das schreibt man S-T-E-F-A-N.
c Ich heiße Natalie. Das schreibt man N-A-T-A-L-I-E.
d Ich heiße Moritz. Das schreibt man M-O-R-I-T-Z.
e Ich heiße Janinn. Das schreibt man J-A-N-I-N-N.
f Ich heiße Fabian. Das schreibt man F-A-B-I-A-N.
g Ich heiße Lady Gaga. Das schreibt man L-A-D-Y G-A-G-A.
h Ich heiße Michael Ballack. Das schreibt man M-I-C-H-A-E-L B-A-L-L-A-C-K.
i Ich heiße Nicole Seibert. Das schreibt man N-I-C-O-L-E S-E-I-B-E-R-T.
j Ich heiße Arjen Robben. Das schreibt man A-R-J-E-N R-O-B-B-E-N.

AT 2.1 **AT 4.1** **2** How do you say these things in German? Write them in and say them out loud.

Answers: **a** Guten Morgen! **b** Wie schreibt man das? **c** Wie heißt du? **d** Guten Abend! **e** Ich heiße … **f** Auf Wiedersehen!

3 Say these English words out loud. What German letters do they represent?

Answers: **a** H; **b** B; **c** K; **d** C; **e** J; **f** D

0.2 Wie alt bist du? (Seite 9)

AT 1.1 **1** Listen to these people giving you their ages. Write the ages in the bubbles.

Answers: **a** 18; **b** 3; **c** 12; **d** 20; **e** 15; **f** 6

🎧 **CD 4, track 32** Seite 9, Übung 1

a Ich bin achtzehn Jahre alt.
b Ich bin drei Jahre alt.
c Ich bin zwölf Jahre alt.
d Ich bin zwanzig Jahre alt.
e Ich bin fünfzehn Jahre alt.
f Ich bin sechs Jahre alt.

AT 3.1 **2** Add the prices to the labels.

Answers: **a** 2 €; **b** 1,15 €; **c** 2,20 €; **d** 3,10 €; **e** 14 €; **f** 16,15 €

AT 4.1–2 **3** These people are giving their ages. Write down what they are saying.

Answers: **a** Ich bin elf Jahre alt. **b** Ich bin siebzehn Jahre alt. **c** Ich bin neun Jahre alt. **d** Ich bin neunzehn Jahre alt. **e** Ich bin sieben Jahre alt. **f** Ich bin zwanzig Jahre alt.

0.3 Ich habe Geburtstag! (Seite 10)

AT 4.1 **1** Solve the clues and write in the German names of the months. The highlighted letters spell another month.

Answers: **a** Juli; **b** Februar; **c** Juni; **d** August; **e** Mai; **f** April (The highlighted letters spell: Januar.)

AT 4.1–2 **2** Do the sums, then write the answers, first the number, then the German word.

Answers: **a** 21 einundzwanzig; **b** 30 dreißig; **c** 24 vierundzwanzig; **d** 27 siebenundzwanzig; **e** 22 zweiundzwanzig; **f** 28 achtundzwanzig

AT 1.1 **3** Listen and work out how old these people are.

Answers: **a** 21; **b** 31; **c** 27; **d** 20; **e** 25; **f** 26

🎧 **CD 4, track 33** Seite 10, Übung 3

a Ich bin einundzwanzig Jahre alt.
b Ich bin einunddreißig Jahre alt.
c Ich bin siebenundzwanzig Jahre alt.
d Ich bin zwanzig Jahre alt.
e Ich bin fünfundzwanzig Jahre alt.
f Ich bin sechsundzwanzig Jahre alt.

0.4 Mein Land, meine Sprache (Seite 11)

AT 3.1 **1** Find the names of eight countries in this grid. The words can be horizontal, vertical or diagonal. Write them out below.

Answers: Deutschland, Polen, Großbritannien, Österreich, Frankreich, Türkei, Schweiz, Spanien (See wordsearch grid above for Foundation Workbook 0.4 ex. 1.)

AT 3.1 **AT 4.1** **2** Unjumble the countries and insert the language.

Answers: **a** Deutschland, Deutsch; **b** Österreich, Deutsch; **c** Frankreich, Französisch; **d** Polen, Polnisch; **e** Spanien, Spanisch; **f** Großbritannien, Englisch

0 Hallo!

AT 4.2 **3 Write down, in full German sentences…**

Answers: students' own answers

0.5 Kathis Videoblog (Seite 12)

AT 4.1–2 **1 What is the nationality of these people? If you don't recognise any of the town names, look them up.**

This activity practises masculine and feminine forms of nationalities, so students will need to have worked on page 21 of the Student Book (0.7 *Extra Plus*) before they attempt it.

Answers: a Engländerin; b Deutscher; c Österreicherin; d Schweizer; e Deutsche; f Engländer; g Schweizerin; h Österreicher

AT 1.2–3 **2 Listen to this girl and circle the correct answers.**

Answers: a Austria; b Seefeld; c May; d German and French; e great; f not so good

🎧 **CD 4, track 34** Seite 12, Übung 2

Hallo! Na, wie geht's? Ich heiße Anne Blick und ich komme aus Österreich. Ich wohne in Seefeld. Ich habe am ersten Mai Geburtstag. Ich spreche Deutsch und ich spreche auch Englisch und Französisch. Französisch ist super, aber Englisch ist nicht so gut. Na, also, tschüs.

AT 4.2–3 **3 Write a paragraph about yourself.**

Answers: students' own answers

0.6A Sprachlabor (Seite 13)

1 Translate these countries and languages into German and write the German words in the correct column.

Answers: Italien – Italienisch; Spanien – Spanisch; Türkei – Türkisch; Polen – Polnisch; Deutschland – Deutsch; Frankreich – Französisch; Großbritannien – Englisch; Schweiz – Deutsch, Französisch, Italienisch

2 Using your knowledge of German pronunciation, say these German words out loud. Then check the recording to see how accurate you were.

🎧 **CD 4, track 35** Seite 13, Übung 2

ich … Wien … zwei … zwölf … schlecht … dreißig … Frankreich … tschüs … wie … Griechenland … fünf

3 Translate these sentences into German, using the correct form of *haben* or *sein*. Don't translate each word individually, otherwise it won't be correct.

Answers: a Wann hast du Geburtstag? b Ich habe im Dezember Geburtstag. c Wie alt bist du? d Ich bin zwölf Jahre alt. e Hast du im Januar Geburtstag? f Nein, ich habe im Dezember Geburtstag!

0.6B Think (Seite 14)

1 Take turns to dictate numbers between 20 and 30 to a partner. If you want to hear them again, say *Wie, bitte?*

2 Read these words aloud and get a partner to write them down accurately.
Students practise *ei* and *ie* sounds.

Keeping a vocabulary list
Tips on how to keep a record of new language.

Learning vocabulary
Tips on different ways to learn new language.

1A Meine Familie

Unit 1A Meine Familie			Unit overview grid			
Page reference	Objectives	Grammar	Skills and pronunciation	Key language	Framework	AT level
Pages 24–25 **1A.1 Das ist meine Familie!**	Say who there is in your family	*Mein(e), dein(e)*	Think about language patterns and the relationship between words	*Wer ist das? Das ist … mein/dein Vater, Opa, Bruder, Onkel. Das ist meine/deine Familie, Mutter, Oma, Schwester, Tante. Das sind … meine/ deine Eltern, Großeltern. Er/Sie heißt … Sie (pl.) heißen …*	L&S 1.1, 1.3 R&W 2.4 KAL 4.3 LLS 5.1	1.1–2, 2.1–2, 3.1–3, 4.1–3
Pages 26–27 **1A.2 Ich habe einen Bruder**	Talk about brothers and sisters	*Ich habe + eine(n)/keine(n) …*	Work out new language and plural patterns	*Hast du Geschwister? Hast du einen Bruder/ eine Schwester? Ja, ich habe einen Bruder/eine Schwester. Ja, ich habe zwei Brüder/Schwestern. Nein, ich habe keinen Bruder/keine Schwester/keine Geschwister. Nein, ich bin Einzelkind.*	L&S 1.1, 1.2 R&W 2.4, 2.5 KAL 4.3, 4.6 LLS 5.1, 5.4, 5.7	1.2–3 2.1–2, 3.2, 4.2
Pages 28–29 **1A.3 Hast du ein Haustier?**	Talk about pets and colours	*Ich habe + einen/eine/ein … Er, sie, es* Noun plurals	Strategies for learning new words and their plurals	*Ich habe einen Hund, einen Fisch, einen Wellensittich, einen Hamster, eine Katze, eine Maus, eine Schildkröte, eine Schlange, ein Meerschweinchen, ein Pferd, ein Kaninchen, ein Huhn. Er/Sie/Es ist … blau, braun, gelb, grau, grün, orange, rot, schwarz, weiß.*	KAL 4.3, 4.6 LLS 5.1, 5.2, 5.5	1.1–2, 2.1–2, 3.1–2, 4.2–3
Pages 30–31 **1A.4 Wie bist du?**	Describe yourself, your friends and family	*Ich bin/Du bist/ Er ist/Sie ist +* adjectives	Work out meaning; pronounce *ü* and *sch*	*Wie bist du? Ich bin/Er ist/Sie ist … faul, fleißig, frech, groß, intelligent, klein, laut, musikalisch, nett, romantisch, schüchtern, sportlich gar nicht, nicht, ziemlich, sehr*	L&S 1.1 KAL 4.2, 4.4, 4.6 LLS 5.3, 5.4, 5.5, 5.8	1.2, 2.2, 3.1–2, 4.1–2
Pages 32–33 **1A.5 Nicos Videoblog**	Talk about brothers, sisters and pets; describe zoo animals	*Ich habe (k)ein(e)(n) … Das ist ein(e) … Er/Sie/Es ist +* adjective	Pronounce *v* and *ei*	*ein Affe, ein Bär, ein Delfin, ein Elefant, eine Giraffe, ein Löwe, ein Nashorn, ein Papagei, ein Tiger, ein Vogel*	L&S 1.1, 1.2, 1.5 R&W 2.4, 2.5 KAL 4.1 LLS 5.7	1.1–3, 2.1–2, 3.1, 4.2

1A Meine Familie

Unit 1A: Week-by-week overview
(Three-year KS3 Route: assuming six weeks' work or approximately 10–12.5 hours)
(Two-year KS3 Route: assuming four weeks' work or approximately 6.5–8.5 hours)

About Unit 1A, *Meine Familie*: In this unit, students learn how to say who is in their family, and what brothers, sisters and pets they have. They learn colours and some adjectives to describe themselves and others, and begin to discover the effect that gender has on other words in a sentence, e.g. *mein(e), dein(e), Ich habe + ein(e)(n) …* and *er/sie/es*. They also meet the negative *kein* and learn how to form noun plurals.
In terms of language learning skills, students find out how information is presented in a bilingual dictionary. They think about language patterns and the relationship between words, and are encouraged to try working out meaning without using a dictionary. The pronunciation focus is *ü*, *sch*, *v* and *ei*.

Three-Year KS3 Route

Week	Resources	Objectives
1	1A.1 Das ist meine Familie! 1A.6 Sprachlabor ex. 1	Say who there is in your family *Mein(e), dein(e)* Think about language patterns and the relationship between words
2	1A.2 Ich habe einen Bruder 1A.6 Sprachlabor ex. 2–3	Talk about brothers and sisters *Ich habe eine(n)/keine(n) …* Work out new language and plural patterns
3	1A.3 Hast du ein Haustier? 1A.6 Sprachlabor ex. 4 and 5–7	Talk about pets and colours *Ich habe ein(e)(n) …; er/sie/es;* noun plurals Strategies for learning new words and their plurals
4	1A.4 Wie bist du? 1A.6 Sprachlabor ex. 8–9	Describe yourself, your friends and family *Ich bin/du bist/er ist/sie ist* + adjectives Work out meaning Pronounce *ü* and *sch*
5	1A.5 Nicos Videoblog	Talk about brothers, sisters and pets; describe zoo animals *Ich habe ein(e)(n)/kein(e)(n) …; das ist ein(e) …; er/sie/es ist* + adjective Pronounce *v* and *ei*
6	1A.7 Extra (Star/Plus) 1A.8 Vokabular 1A.8 Testseite 1A Lesen	Reinforcement and extension of the language of the unit Key vocabulary and learning checklist Assessment in all four skills Further reading to explore the language of the unit and cultural themes

Two-Year KS3 Route

Week	Resources	Objectives
1	1A.1 Das ist meine Familie! *(Omit ex. 4)* 1A.6 Sprachlabor ex. 1	Say who there is in your family *Mein(e), dein(e)* Think about language patterns and the relationship between words
2	1A.2 Ich habe einen Bruder *(Omit ex. 6)* 1A.6 Sprachlabor ex. 2–3	Talk about brothers and sisters *Ich habe eine(n)/keine(n) …* Work out new language and plural patterns
3	1A.3 Hast du ein Haustier? *(Omit ex. 8)* 1A.6 Sprachlabor ex. 4 and 5–7	Talk about pets and colours *Ich habe ein(e)(n) …; er/sie/es;* noun plurals Strategies for learning new words and their plurals
4	1A.4 Wie bist du? *(Omit ex. 2, ex. 4)* 1A.8 Vokabular 1A.8 Testseite	Describe yourself, your friends and family *Ich bin/du bist/er ist/sie ist* + adjectives Work out meaning Pronounce *ü* and *sch* Key vocabulary and learning checklist Assessment in all four skills

1A.1 Meine Familie

1A.1 Das ist meine Familie!

Seite 24–25

Planner

Objectives
- Vocabulary: say who there is in your family
- Grammar: *mein(e) / deine(e)* (my / your)
- Skills: think about language patterns and the relationship between words

Video
- Video clip 1A

Resources
- Student Book, pages 24–25
- CD 1, tracks 28–29
- Foundation and Higher Workbooks, page 16
- Workbook audio: CD 3 and 4, track 36
- Copymaster 15 (ex. 1), 20 (ex. 3–4)
- Interactive OxBox, Unit 1A

Key language
Wer ist das?
Das ist …
mein / dein Vater, Opa, Bruder, Onkel
meine / deine Familie, Mutter, Oma, Schwester, Tante
Das sind …
meine / deine Eltern, Großeltern
Er / Sie heißt …
Sie (pl.) heißen …

Framework references
L&S 1.1, 1.3; R&W 2.4; KAL 4.3; LLS 5.1

Starters
- Copymaster 15, ex. 1
- Before beginning work on this spread, show students a list of the German words for family members. Give them a few minutes, in pairs, to try to work out the English equivalents. Suggest that it might help if they think about the pronunciation of the words as well as the spelling. Allow time for feedback and ask students how they were able to work out the words, e.g. looks like English, sounds like English, or looks like the same word in another language (*Tante* is spelled the same as French *tante*, although it sounds completely different).
- Students exchange their puzzles (see first homework suggestion) with a partner and try to solve them.

Plenaries
- Word tennis. In pairs, students take turns to say members of the family; their partner adds the other half of the pair, e.g.
Student A: *Mein Onkel.*
Student B: *Meine Tante.*
Student A: *Meine Schwester.*
Student B: *Mein Bruder.*
If one partner says *meine Eltern* or *meine Großeltern*, the other names both of the people who make up the pair:
Student A: *Meine Eltern.*
Student B: *Mein Vater und meine Mutter.*
- Using their family trees (see ex. 4) and / or their own family photos, students give a mini-presentation introducing their family. They could do this to the whole class, in small groups or with a partner. Encourage members of the class or group, or their partner, to ask questions:
Student A: *Das ist mein Vater. Er heißt David.*
Student B: *Ist das deine Mutter?*
Student A: *Nein, das ist meine Tante …*

Homework
- Students prepare a puzzle to test their partner on the German words for family members, e.g. a wordsearch, a word snake, anagrams, mirror writing, or mismatched word halves (*Schw-uder, Br-utter, M-ester = Schwester, Bruder, Mutter*). Tell them to make a note of the answers, as a way of double-checking that the activity works. The puzzles are then used as a starter in a subsequent lesson.
- Students imagine they are a well-known cartoon character, celebrity, member of a TV soap family or historical figure. They invent and write a Facebook-style message (modelled on ex. 6) about their family, e.g. *Ich heiße Lisa Simpson. Mein Vater heißt Homer und meine Mutter heißt Marge …*

Video clip 1A: Kathi und die Jungs!
AT 1.1, 1.3
Synopsis:
Nina and Kathi chat while waiting to meet up with Nina's friend Nico, and we find out that Nina is crazy about Nico's brother Ralf. Nico arrives and is introduced to Kathi: the pair are instantly attracted to each other. Later, Kathi bombards Nina with questions about Nico and we find out all about his family. The two girls then meet Nina's other friend, Ali. After introducing Kathi to Ali, Nina has to rush home, leaving them to get to know each other.

Play the video through a couple of times and ask questions to check that students understand the gist of it. Talk about the German signs we see (DB, Potsdamer Platz, Arkaden).

Focus on the relationship between the characters and challenge students to work out from their body

1A.1 Meine Familie

language and tone of voice what their mood is and what they think of each other, e.g.
- When the two girls are waiting for Nico at the beginning of the clip, what does Nina's expression tell us? (She checks her watch and looks annoyed – Nico is probably late.)
- What do Nico and Kathi think of each other? (It is clear from their body language that it's love at first sight!)
- What does Nina think of Ralf? (The photo and her tone of voice when she talks about him suggest that she's besotted with him.)
- Can we tell what the relationship is between Nina, Nico and Ali? (They are all good friends.)

Once students have been introduced to the family vocabulary (via the first starter activity and ex. 1), play the clip again and ask them to raise their hand whenever a family member is mentioned.

Video clip 1A

(the girls wait for Nico in the shopping centre)

Kathi: Also, wie sind sie, Nico und Ali?
Nina: Also, Ali … er ist einfach Ali. Und Nico ist auch sehr cool. Aber sein Bruder Ralf … er ist so wundervoll … so schön, so sportlich, so intelligent …
Nico: Er ist langweilig … sehr, sehr langweilig.
Nina: Hallo Nico! Kathi, das ist Nico.
Kathi: Hallo!
Nico: Hallo!
Nina: Wo ist Ali?
Nico: Wer?
Nina: Ali der Große! Ali! Unser bester Freund?
Nico: Keine Ahnung.

(later, when the two girls are alone again)

Kathi: Also, hat er nur einen Bruder?
Nina: Nein, nein, er hat zwei … aber Ralf, er ist so intelligent, so sportlich, so schön …
Kathi: Ja, ja, ja, er ist fantastisch! Aber was sonst? Andere Brüder? Schwestern?
Nina: Er hat noch einen Bruder, Ulli, und eine Schwester, Britta.
Kathi: Und wie alt sind die?
Nina: Also, Ulli ist 19 und Britta ist 9. Ich bin 14 und Ralf ist 16. Das ist doch perfekt, oder?
Kathi: Ja, perfekt!

Nina: Ali, hi! Was machst du denn hier? Warte, du kennst Kathi noch gar nicht. Kathi, das ist Ali. Ali, der Große! Ali, das ist Kathi.

Ali: Hallo. Wie geht's? Gut!
Kathi: Hallo. Wie geht's? Gut!
Nina: Oh, nein … Es ist schon fünf Uhr! Ich muss nach Hause! Meine Mutter ist total streng. Aber, wir sehen uns später, okay? Tschüs.
Ali: Tschüs!
Kathi: Tschüs!

Ali: So, du kommst aus Wien.
Kathi: Ja, und du kommst aus Berlin.
Ali: Ja, ich bin ein Berliner Türke.
Kathi: Und … hast du auch so eine große Familie wie Nico?
Ali: Nein, ich habe keine Geschwister. Nur ich und meine Eltern.
Kathi: Ach, du bist Einzelkind.
Ali: Ja, und du?
Kathi: Ich habe einen Bruder, Karl. Karl Alexander Peter von Hohenstein III!
Ali: Der dritte?
Kathi: Ja … Er ist 11. Sehr frech! Und so faul!
Ali: Echt?
Kathi: Nein. Eigentlich ist er ziemlich nett.
Ali: Cooles iPhone. Du bist ziemlich reich, oder?
Kathi: Ja, ziemlich.
Ali: Cool.
Kathi: Und du?
Ali: Normal.
Kathi: Ali … normal bist du wirklich nicht!

Sprachpunkt
Hat er nur einen Bruder?
Ich habe einen Bruder, Karl.
Ich habe keine Geschwister.
Du bist Einzelkind.

1 Hör zu. Was passt zusammen?

AT 1.1–2
AT 3.1–2

The action has now moved on from Nico's and Kathi's first meeting in the video clip. Here, they are looking at Nico's family photos.
Students listen to the dialogue and match the photos to the corresponding sentences.

Answers: **a** 4; **b** 1; **c** 7; **d** 3; **e** 2; **f** 5; **g** 6

CD 1, track 28   Seite 24, Übung 1

- Wer ist das?
- Das ist meine Mutter.
- Und ist das dein Vater?
- Ja, das ist mein Vater.
- Und wer ist das?
- Meine Oma – das ist meine Oma.
- Aha – und das ist dein Opa?

1A.1 Meine Familie

- Ja, das ist mein Opa.
- Wer ist das, Nico?
- Das ist meine Schwester, Britta.
- Und das? Ist das dein Bruder?
- Ja, das ist mein Bruder Ulli. Er ist 19 …
- Und das ist dein Bruder Ralf – ich weiß!

AT 2.1–2

2 Wer ist das?
In pairs, students take turns to question each other about Nico's family, e.g.
A: (points to photo 2) *Wer ist das?*
B: *Das ist meine Schwester.*

LLS 5.1

Think
Students find the odd one out in each set of three family words.
This sort of activity encourages students to think about language patterns and relationships between words and phrases. Point out that there are no definitive answers, but that students must be able to explain their choices. Allow time for feedback and accept all answers that can be justified.

Answers: **1** mein Bruder *(because it's the only masculine noun)* or meine Mutter *(not a sibling);* **2** meine Mutter *(because it's the only feminine noun)* or mein Opa *(a grandparent, not a parent);* **3** meine Tante *(not a grandparent)* or meine Großeltern *(it's the only plural)*

AT 1.2

3 Hör zu. Welcher Name passt?
Kathi shows Nico her album of family photos. Students listen and match the family members to their corresponding names.

Answers: meine Oma: Elisabeth; mein Opa: Franz; meine Mutter: Anna; mein Vater: Peter; mein Bruder: Karl; meine Tante: Sandra; mein Onkel: Markus

🎧 **CD 1, track 29**   Seite 25, Übung 3

- Ist das deine Familie, Kathi?
- Ja, das sind meine Eltern. Meine Mutter heißt Anna und mein Vater heißt Peter.
- Und sind das deine Großeltern?
- Ja. Meine Oma heißt Elisabeth und mein Opa heißt Franz.
- Ah, und das ist dein Bruder …
- Ja, das ist mein Bruder Karl Alexander.
- Und wer ist das? Deine Tante?
- Ja, das ist meine Tante. Sie heißt Sandra.
- Und das – wer ist das?
- Das ist mein Onkel. Er heißt Markus.

AT 2.1–2

Follow-up
Students take turns to question each other about Kathi's family tree, e.g.
A: *Wer ist Karl?*
B: *Das ist mein Bruder.*

AT 2.1–2
AT 4.1

4 Mein Stammbaum.
Students draw and label their own family tree, then take turns to question each other about it (as in ex. 3 and the *Follow-up* activity).

KAL 4.3
LLS 5.1

5 Mein oder meine?
Students fill in the missing word (*mein* or *meine*) for each family member, using the language box for support.

Answers: **1** meine; **b** mein; **c** meine; **d** meine; **e** mein; **f** meine; **g** mein

KAL 4.3
LLS 5.1

Think
Students work out when to use *mein / meine* and *dein / deine* in the context of family members. They should be able to spot that *mein* and *dein* are used with male family members, whereas *meine* and *deine* are used with female family members and with plurals (parents, grandparents).

AT 3.2–3

6 Lies Toms Nachricht.
Students read Tom's message about his family and answer questions in English.

Answers: **1** Uwe and Vera; **b** Sebastian and Klara; **c** Walter and Ruth

AT 4.2–3
R&W 2.4

Challenge
Students write about their own family, using Tom's message as an example. They are encouraged to write three sentences.
As support, display Tom's message and show students how to use key structures in his text as a framework for their own writing. Highlight any words and phrases that students can replace with their own details, e.g. *Ich heiße (Tom) und ich bin (vierzehn) Jahre alt. (Mein Vater) heißt (Uwe) und …*

1A.2 Meine Familie

1A.2 Ich habe einen Bruder
Seite 26–27

Planner

Objectives
- Vocabulary: talk about brothers and sisters
- Grammar: *ich habe eine(n) / keine(n) …*
- Skills: work out new language and plural patterns

Video
- Video clip 1A
- Video blog 1A

Resources
- Student Book, pages 26–27
- CD 1, tracks 30–32
- Foundation and Higher Workbooks, page 17
- Workbook audio: CD 3 and 4, track 37
- Copymaster 16 (ex. 1), 17 (ex. 2)
- Interactive OxBox, Unit 1A

Key language
Hast du Geschwister?
Hast du einen Bruder / eine Schwester?
Ja, ich habe einen Bruder / eine Schwester.
Ja, ich habe zwei Brüder / Schwestern.
Nein, ich habe keinen Bruder / keine Schwester / keine Geschwister.
Nein, ich bin Einzelkind.

Framework references
L&S 1.1, 1.2; R&W 2.4, 2.5; KAL 4.3, 4.6; LLS 5.1, 5.4, 5.7

Starters
- Display a list of anagrams of the family vocabulary. Students race against the clock to solve them and write out the list with either *mein* or *meine*, e.g.
  redrub = mein Bruder
  termut = meine Mutter
  To make this activity easier, capitalise the initial letter of each word, e.g. *redruB*.
- See first plenary and first homework suggestion. In pairs, students check their partner's homework task.

Plenaries
- Tell students they are going to prepare a homework task for each other. They each write a few sentences about brothers and sisters (e.g. *Ich habe eine Schwester und zwei Brüder*), which they keep hidden from their partner. Then, on a separate piece of paper or in their partner's exercise book, they draw stick figures to represent each sentence. For homework, each student writes captions for their partner's drawings.
- When students are familiar with the family situation of the video characters, display the characters' names together with the names of their brothers and sisters, jumbled up together. Include a few additional names, as distractors. Challenge students, in pairs, to match up the names and write sentences describing the relationships. Warn them that one of the names doesn't have any matches (this is Ali, because he's an only child) but that they must still come up with a suitable sentence for it. Solution:
Ich heiße Kathi. Ich habe einen Bruder, Karl.
Ich heiße Nico. Ich habe zwei Brüder, Ralf und Ulli, und eine Schwester, Britta.
Ich heiße Ali. Ich habe keine Geschwister / Ich bin Einzelkind.

Homework
- See the first plenary activity: students do the homework task set by their partner.
- Students draw out a chart or graph of the survey results (ex. 5). If you wish them to summarise the results in writing, provide a model, e.g.

| 1 Person hat | einen Bruder / eine Schwester. |
| 2 / 3 / 4 / 5 / etc. Personen haben | zwei Brüder / zwei Schwestern / etc. keine Geschwister. |

- Students write a few gap-fill sentences, as in ex. 7, from the point of view of celebrities, historical figures, members of TV soap families, fictional or cartoon characters. Tell them to keep a note of the answers. The sentences can then be used in a following lesson: students swap with a partner, fill in the missing words, then check against the answers.

1A.2 Meine Familie

1 Sieh dir Nicos Videoblog an. Was passt für Nico?

AT 1.3
L&S 1.1, 1.2
LLS 5.7

Students watch Nico's video blog, focusing on how many brothers and sisters he has. They choose a set of photos to represent his family situation.

Point out that the photos provide a clue: students may recognise Nico's family from spread 1A.1 so can predict that set 1 is the answer. They can then watch the video blog to confirm their prediction. Encourage them to listen out for familiar key words (*Bruder, Schwester*) to help them identify the information they need, and to disregard anything irrelevant.

Answer: set 1

Video blog 1A
CD 1, track 30   Seite 26, Übung 1

Hallo! Ich heiße Nico, ich bin 14 Jahre alt und ich wohne in Berlin.
Ich habe drei Geschwister: ich habe zwei Brüder und eine Schwester. Meine Brüder heißen Ulli und Ralf. Ulli ist 19 Jahre alt. Er ist sehr groß und sehr musikalisch. Aber er ist ziemlich schüchtern. Ralf ist 16 Jahre alt. Und, ja, er ist sehr intelligent und sehr sportlich … ja, und noch sehr fleißig. Meine kleine Schwester Britta ist neun Jahre alt. Sie ist sehr frech und oft ziemlich laut. Sie ist nicht sehr nett – leider!
Wie ist deine Familie? Hast du auch Geschwister?

2 Sieh dir das Video an. Was passt für Ali und Kathi?

AT 1.3
AT 3.2
L&S 1.1, 1.2

Play the end section of video clip 1A, focusing on Ali's family and Kathi's family. Students choose one sentence (from a–f) to represent each person's situation.

Answers: Ali: e; Kathi: a

Video clip 1A
CD 1, track 31   Seite 26, Übung 2

Ali: So, du kommst aus Wien.
Kathi: Ja, und du kommst aus Berlin.
Ali: Ja, ich bin ein Berliner Türke.
Kathi: Und … hast du auch so eine große Familie wie Nico?
Ali: Nein, ich habe keine Geschwister. Nur ich und meine Eltern.
Kathi: Ach, du bist Einzelkind.
Ali: Ja, und du?
Kathi: Ich habe einen Bruder, Karl. Karl Alexander Peter von Hohenstein III!

Ali: Der dritte?
Kathi: Ja … Er ist 11. Sehr frech! Und so faul!
Ali: Echt?
Kathi: Nein. Eigentlich ist er ziemlich nett …

3 Hör zu. Geschwister. Was passt?

AT 1.2
L&S 1.1

Four young people talk about their brothers and sisters.
Students listen and choose a picture to represent how many brothers and sisters each person has.

Answers: Maren 4; Alex 3; Sandra 1; Carsten 2

CD 1, track 32   Seite 26, Übung 3

– Hallo Maren. Hast du Geschwister?
– Ja, ich habe einen Bruder und zwei Schwestern.
– Und du, Alex? Hast du Geschwister?
– Ich habe einen Bruder, aber ich habe keine Schwester.
– Hast du Geschwister, Sandra?
– Nein, ich habe keine Geschwister. Ich bin Einzelkind.
– Hallo Carsten. Hast du Geschwister?
– Ja, ich habe zwei Brüder und eine Schwester.

Follow-up
Challenge students, in pairs, to reconstruct the dialogue (orally and in writing) using their answers to ex. 3:
Student A: *Hast du Geschwister, Maren?*
Student B: *Ja, ich habe einen Bruder und zwei Schwestern.*
Play the recording again so that they can check their own version against the original.

Think

KAL 4.3
LLS 5.1, 5.4

Students use their knowledge of *eine* and *ein* to work out the meaning of *einen*.

4 Füll die Lücken aus.

KAL 4.3, 4.6
LLS 5.1

Students fill in the missing words (*eine / einen* or *keine / keinen*), using the *Grammatik* box on page 26 for support.

*Answers: **a** keine; **b** einen; **c** keine; **d** eine; **e** keinen*

Think

KAL 4.3
LLS 5.1, 5.4

Before students begin ex. 5, challenge them to work out the difference between *Bruder* and *Brüder*, and between *Schwester* and *Schwestern*. Point out *einen Bruder / zwei Brüder* and *eine*

44

1A.3 Meine Familie

Schwester / zwei Schwestern in the vocabulary box. This should provide a clue that the second word in each pair is a plural.

AT 2.2 **5 Umfrage: Hast du Geschwister?**
Students carry out a survey, in groups, to find out how many brothers and sisters their classmates have.
They make a note of each person's response, for use in ex. 6.

AT 2.1–2 **6 Ratespiel: Wer ist das?**
In groups, students play a guessing game based on the survey results, e.g.
A: (looking at the results) *Ich habe zwei Schwestern*.
B: (tries to remember) *Das ist Sarah!*

AT 3.2 **7 Füll die Lücken aus.**
Students fill in the missing words to complete three captions about the brothers and sisters of famous people.

Answers: **a** *zwei Brüder*; **b** *eine Schwester*; **c** *keine Geschwister, Einzelkind*

AT 4.2
R&W 2.4, 2.5 **Challenge**
Students write a speech bubble (modelled on the captions in ex. 7) about themselves and their own brothers and sisters. Alternatively, they write their text from the point of view of their favourite celebrity. For a variation, see the third homework suggestion in the Planner above.
Remind them of how to adapt a text by keeping the key structures but changing the details (see teaching notes for spread 1A.1 *Challenge*). Encourage students to read out their text to the class.

1A.3 Hast du ein Haustier? Seite 28–29

Planner

Objectives
- Vocabulary: talk about pets and colours
- Grammar: *ich habe + einen / eine / ein ...; er, sie, es*; noun plurals
- Skills: strategies for learning new words and their plurals

Resources
- Student Book, pages 28–29
- CD 1, tracks 33–36
- Foundation and Higher Workbooks, page 18
- Workbook audio: CD 3 and 4, track 38
- Copymaster 16 (ex. 4), 17 (ex. 3), 19 (ex. 1–3)
- Interactive OxBox, Unit 1A

Key language
Ich habe ...
einen Hund, einen Fisch, einen Wellensittich, einen Hamster
eine Katze, eine Maus, eine Schildkröte, eine Schlange
ein Meerschweinchen, ein Pferd, ein Kaninchen, ein Huhn
er / sie / es ist ...
blau, braun, gelb, grau, grün, orange, rot, schwarz, weiß

Framework references
KAL 4.3, 4.6; LLS 5.1, 5.2, 5.5

Starters
- Copymaster 15, ex. 3–4.
- Before listening to the ex. 1 recording, challenge students to identify the animal vocabulary: they may recognise *Hund, Fisch, Katze* and *Maus* because of their similarity to English. Provide a German–English breakdown of the components of the compound words and challenge students to work out the English, e.g. *Schild + Kröte* = shield + toad: which animal looks a bit like a toad with a shield? (tortoise)
- Play animal mimes or Pictionary, in pairs, groups or as a whole class. One student mimes or begins drawing an animal; the others try to guess what it is, e.g.
A: mimes or draws a fish.
B: *Ich habe einen Fisch*.
Colours could be indicated too:
A: mimes a fish and points to something orange in the classroom, or draws an orange fish.
B: *Ich habe einen Fisch. Er ist orange.*

Plenaries
- Display a grid with the squares numbered 1–9 (representing animals 1–9 on page 28). Divide the class into two teams for a game of noughts and crosses, e.g. to win square 3 (= cat), teams must say *Ich habe eine Katze*. To practise negatives, add a large X to some squares so that teams have to say *Ich habe keinen / keine / kein* + animal.

1A.3 Meine Familie

- Display a jumble of singular and plural animal words, e.g. *Hunde, Meerschweinchen, Schlange, Katze, Fische, Pferde, Schildkröte, Hamster*, etc. Students race against the clock to sort them into three categories: singular nouns, plural nouns, nouns that are spelled the same in the singular and plural.
- When students have learned colours and *er / sie / es*, play an extended version of noughts and crosses (see first plenary), e.g. to win square 3, teams would say *Ich habe eine Katze. Sie ist schwarz und weiß*. Or, to incorporate plurals, add an additional figure to each square, e.g. square 3 with figure 2 added = *Ich habe zwei Katzen*.

Homework
- Student Book page 28, ex. 5.
- Students choose a few fictional or cartoon characters and describe their pets, e.g. *Ich heiße Bart Simpson. Ich habe einen Hund, Santa's Little Helper. Er ist braun.* Alternatively, they could imagine and describe appropriate pets for celebrities or historical figures.

AT 1.1 **1 Hör zu. Was passt zusammen?**
Students listen to the recording and match the animal vocabulary (a–i) to the corresponding pictures (1–9). The sound effects help with identification.

Answers: **a** 7; **b** 8; **c** 5; **d** 3; **e** 1; **f** 2; **g** 6; **h** 4; **i** 9

CD 1, track 33 Seite 28, Übung 1
a Ich habe einen Hund.
b Ich habe einen Fisch.
c Ich habe einen Wellensittich.
d Ich habe eine Katze.
e Ich habe eine Maus.
f Ich habe eine Schildkröte.
g Ich habe ein Meerschweinchen.
h Ich habe ein Pferd.
i Ich habe ein Kaninchen.

AT 2.1–2 **2 Was hast du?**
Students take turns to give the number of a picture; their partner responds by saying they have this animal, e.g.
A: *Nummer 3!*
B: *Ich habe eine Katze.*

KAL 4.6 **Think**
This activity reminds students how to form negatives. They consider which letter of the alphabet is added to *ein(e)(n)* to make it negative.

Answer: k (*Ich habe keine Katze*)

AT 1.1 / AT 3.1 **3 Hör zu und lies. Farben.**
Students listen, read and repeat the colours.

CD 1, track 34 Seite 28, Übung 3
blau … braun … gelb … grau … grün … orange … rot … schwarz … weiß

AT 1.1–2 / AT 3.1–2 / KAL 4.3 **4 Hör zu und lies.**
Students listen, read and repeat the sentences. This activity introduces how to say "it" in German (*er, sie, es*). Before or after listening to the recording, look at the *Grammatik* box.

CD 1, track 35 Seite 28, Übung 4
a Das ist ein Huhn. Es ist gelb.
b Das ist ein Hamster. Er ist braun.
c Das ist eine Schlange. Sie ist grün.

AT 4.2–3 **5 Schreib Sätze.**
Students choose six pets from ex. 1 and write sentences explaining what colour they are.

Answers: any six of: **1** Das ist eine Maus. Sie ist grau. **2** Das ist eine Schildkröte. Sie ist grün. **3** Das ist eine Katze. Sie ist weiß und schwarz. **4** Das ist ein Pferd. Es ist braun. **5** Das ist ein Wellensittich. Er ist gelb. **6** Das ist ein Meerschweinchen. Es ist orange. **7** Das ist ein Hund. Er ist braun und weiß. **8** Das ist ein Fisch. Er ist blau / rot. **9** Das ist ein Kaninchen. Es ist weiß.

AT 1.2 / AT 3.2 / KAL 4.3 / LLS 5.1, 5.2 **6 Hör zu und lies.**
To introduce the work on plurals, ask students to consider the different ways of forming noun plurals in English, e.g. add -s or -es, change -y to -ies (lady – ladies), change -f to -ves (calf – calves, knife – knives), words that don't change (sheep), other irregular forms (man – men, woman – women, child – children, mouse – mice, tooth – teeth). Point out that, like English, German has several ways of forming noun plurals.

1A.4 Meine Familie

Before or after playing the recording, read through the *Grammatik* box. Emphasise that when learning new nouns it is always worth learning the plural too.

CD 1, track 36 Seite 29, Übung 6

Ich habe zwei Hunde, drei Katzen, vier Kaninchen, fünf Schildkröten, sechs Wellensittiche, sieben Hamster, acht Mäuse und neun Fische!

LLS 5.5 7 Finde die Pluralformen.
Students refer to the *Vokabular* page or the Glossary to find some noun plurals.
If you have not yet done any work on dictionary use, this might be an appropriate point to work on ex. 5–7 of spread 1A.6 (*Sprachlabor*), in which students identify the different types of information provided at entries in a bilingual dictionary, e.g. parts of speech, gender, plural.

Answers: **a** Hühner; **b** Meerschweinchen; **c** Schlangen; **d** Pferde

8 Was ist die Pluralform?
In pairs, students take turns to name pets in the singular; their partner responds with the plural form:
A: *Ein Hund!*
B: *Zwei Hunde!*

AT 2.1–2 Challenge
Students play a memory game in which they list as many pets as possible, e.g.
A: *Ich habe einen Hund.*
B: *Ich habe einen Hund und eine Katze.*
A: *Ich habe einen Hund, eine Katze und …*
Encourage them to include some plurals.

1A.4 Wie bist du?
Seite 30–31

Planner

Objectives
- Vocabulary: describe yourself, your friends and family
- Grammar: *ich bin / du bist / er ist / sie ist* + adjectives
- Skills: work out the meaning of new words; pronounce the *ü* and *sch* sounds

Resources
- Student Book, pages 30–31
- CD 1, tracks 37–41
- Foundation and Higher Workbooks, page 19
- Workbook audio: CD 3 and 4, track 39
- Copymasters 15 (ex. 3–4), 16 (ex. 2–3), 17 (ex. 1), 18, 19 (ex. 4), 20 (ex. 1–2)
- Interactive OxBox, Unit 1A

Key language
Wie bist du? Ich bin / Er ist / Sie ist …
faul, fleißig, frech, groß, intelligent, klein, laut, musikalisch, nett, romantisch, schüchtern, sportlich
gar nicht, nicht, ziemlich, sehr

Framework references
L&S 1.1; KAL 4.2, 4.4, 4.6; LLS 5.3, 5.4, 5.5, 5.8

Starters
- Copymaster 15, ex. 3–4.

- In pairs, students try to work out the meanings of the adjectives (page 30, ex. 1). Can they suggest ways to remember the adjectives that don't look like their English equivalents? E.g. *schüchtern* begins with a *sh* sound, as does its English equivalent "shy"; *frech* is a bit like the word "fresh", which is used informally especially in American English to mean "impertinent" – hence the link to "naughty". Encourage students to share their ideas but point out that there are no right or wrong ways – what works for one person may not make any sense at all to someone else.
- Start writing one of the adjectives on the board. As soon as someone recognises it, he / she names the adjective and puts it into a sentence about a well-known person or someone familiar to the class, e.g.
Teacher: starts to write: *in …*
Student: *Intelligent! Ich heiße* + name of teacher. *Ich bin intelligent.*
Continue with the rest of the adjectives.

Plenaries
- Students test each other in pairs to see how many of the twelve adjectives (from Student Book page 30) they can remember: one partner checks against the book while the other recites as many as possible (with their English translations, if you wish), then they swap over. Who remembers the most?

1A.4 Meine Familie

- Divide the class into teams. Call out the names of a few well-known people, cartoon characters or historical figures. Set a time limit for teams to build a description of each person, e.g.
  Teacher: *Homer Simpson.*
  Team: *Das ist Homer Simpson. Er ist sehr faul und gar nicht intelligent …*
  At the end of the time limit, each team reports back. Award points for the most impressive sentences, focusing on correct use of adjectives, *sehr*, *ziemlich*, *nicht* and *gar nicht*, and longer sentences using *und* and *aber*.

Homework
- Ask students to use a dictionary to find three additional adjectives. Tell them that in the next lesson they will have to convey the meanings of the new words to their partner (or to the class) without using English, e.g. by showing visuals to represent the words (like in ex. 1), by miming, or by suggesting some well-known people who share these characteristics. Set aside some time for this in a following lesson.
- Students write descriptions of their favourite cartoon characters, sporting personalities, musicians, celebrities, etc. Encourage them to use *sehr*, *ziemlich*, *nicht* and *gar nicht*, and to build longer sentences using *und* and *aber*.

LLS 5.3, 5.4, 5.5

Think
Students are encouraged to work out the meaning of the new adjectives by comparing them with English words, e.g. *romantisch* – romantic. They look up any words they can't work out on the *Vokabular* page or in the Glossary.

AT 3.1–2

1 Wie heißt das auf Englisch?
Students translate descriptions a–f into English.

Answers: **a** klein – small, nett – nice, romantisch – romantic; **b** intelligent – intelligent, fleißig – hard-working; **c** musikalisch – musical, laut – noisy / loud; **d** sportlich – sporty; **e** faul – lazy, frech – naughty / cheeky; **f** groß – tall / big, schüchtern – shy

2 Positiv oder negativ?
Students list the adjectives as positive or negative, then compare their lists with a partner: do they agree?
Point out that some may be neutral (e.g. *groß*, *klein*) or may be either positive or negative depending on the context – these are indicated in brackets in the answers.

Answers: **Positiv:** fleißig, intelligent, musikalisch, nett, romantisch, sportlich; **Negativ:** faul, frech, (laut, schüchtern); **Neutral:** klein, groß

AT 1.2

3 Hör zu. Wie bist du?
Kathi, Ali, Nina and Nico are doing a personality quiz in a magazine. Students listen and note the adjectives that they use to describe themselves.

Answers: **Kathi:** groß, nett, laut; **Ali:** intelligent, schüchtern, fleißig; **Nina:** musikalisch, frech, faul; **Nico:** romantisch, faul, sportlich

CD 1, track 37 — Seite 30, Übung 3

Ali:	Schaut mal – ein Quiz – der Persönlichkeitstest: Wie bist du?
Alle:	Hey, super!
Ali:	Also Kathi – wie bist du?
Kathi:	Ich bin groß. Ich bin nett – ja, ich bin nett. Und ich bin laut!
Nina:	Okay, Ali, du bist dran. Wie bist du?
Ali:	Hmm … ich bin intelligent. Ich bin schüchtern. Und ich bin fleißig.
Nico:	Und du, Nina – wie bist du?
Nina:	Also, ich bin musikalisch. Ich bin frech. Ja, und ich bin faul.
Kathi:	Und jetzt noch Nico. Wie bist du?
Nico:	Tja, also … ich bin romantisch. Und ich bin faul. Und ich bin sportlich!

AT 2.2

4 Ist alles richtig?
In pairs, students take turns to pretend to be Kathi, Ali, Nina and Nico. They describe themselves, referring to their answers from ex. 3, e.g.
A: *Kathi, wie bist du?*
B: *Ich bin groß …*

5 Wörter mit ü.
Students listen and repeat the words, focusing on pronunciation of the *ü* sound.

CD 1, track 38 — Seite 31, Übung 5

a grün
b Brüder
c tschüs
d fünf
e Hühner

1A.4 Meine Familie

6 Wörter mit *sch*.
Students practise the *sch* sound.

7 Hör zu und lies.
Students listen to check their pronunciation of the sentences in ex. 6.

CD 1, track 39 — Seite 31, Übung 7
a Das ist eine Schildkröte.
b Das ist eine Schlange.
c Susi Schuhmann ist schüchtern.
d Meine Schwester ist schrecklich!

AT 4.1–2
8 Wie bist du?
Students describe themselves using three adjectives from ex. 1.

AT 1.2 / AT 3.2 / KAL 4.2, 4.6
9 Hör zu und lies.
Students read and listen to two descriptions. Point out the words *sehr*, *ziemlich*, *nicht* and *gar nicht* in the language box, and explain that words like this help to make descriptions more interesting and precise, e.g. *Sie ist ziemlich sportlich* gives more information than *Sie ist sportlich*. Make sure students understand the difference between the two negatives *nicht* and *gar nicht*.

CD 1, track 40 — Seite 31, Übung 9
a Das ist meine Freundin Lisa. Sie ist nicht romantisch – aber sie ist ziemlich sportlich!
b Das ist mein Freund Andi. Er ist sehr laut – und er ist gar nicht musikalisch …

KAL 4.2, 4.4 / LLS 5.8
Think
Students work out the meaning of the linking word *aber* (but). Point out that words like *und* and *aber* help to improve speaking and writing because they allow you to join words, phrases and simple sentences to build more complex sentences.
Show students the following two short texts and invite them to choose which one they think seems more interesting and impressive:
1 *Sam ist sportlich. Sam ist nett. Sam ist intelligent. Sam ist nicht romantisch.*
2 *Sam ist sehr sportlich, nett und ziemlich intelligent, aber ist gar nicht romantisch.*

AT 1.2 / L&S 1.1
10 Hör zu und mach Notizen. (a–d)
Students listen to the descriptions and make notes about each person. Point out the suggested shorthand: ✓✓ = *sehr*; ✓ = *ziemlich*; ✗ = *nicht*; ✗✗ = *gar nicht*.
This activity could be tackled in two stages: on the first listening, students note the adjectives; on the second listening, they identify additional details (*sehr, ziemlich, nicht, gar nicht*).

Answers: **a** Sven: klein ✓, faul ✗✗; **b** Anne: sportlich ✗, intelligent ✓✓; **c** Markus: frech ✗, schüchtern ✓; **d** Tanja: fleißig ✓✓, groß ✗

CD 1, track 41 — Seite 31, Übung 10
a Mein Freund heißt Sven. Wie ist Sven? Also, er ist ziemlich klein. Aber er ist gar nicht faul!
b Meine Freundin heißt Anne. Anne ist nicht sehr sportlich. Aber sie ist sehr intelligent!
c Mein Freund heißt Markus. Markus ist nicht frech. Nein, er ist ziemlich schüchtern.
d Meine Freundin heißt Tanja. Sie ist sehr fleißig. Und Tanja ist nicht groß.

AT 2.2
Challenge
Students talk about their families, e.g.
A: *Wie ist deine Mutter?*
B: *Sie ist sehr nett, aber …*
Encourage them to be more precise in their descriptions by using *sehr, ziemlich, nicht* and *gar nicht*, and to build longer sentences using *und* and *aber*.

1A.5 Meine Familie

1A.5 Nicos Videoblog

Seite 32–33

Planner

Objectives
- Vocabulary: talk about brothers, sisters and pets; describe zoo animals
- Grammar: *ich habe ein(e)(n) / kein(e)(n) …; das ist ein(e) …; er / sie / es ist* + adjective
- Skills: pronounce *v* and *ei*

Video
- Video blog 1A

Resources
- Student Book, pages 32–33
- CD 1, tracks 42–44
- Foundation and Higher Workbooks, page 20
- Workbook audio: CD 3 and 4, track 40
- Copymaster 15 (ex. 2)
- Interactive OxBox, Unit 1A

Key language
ein Affe, ein Bär, ein Delfin, ein Elefant, eine Giraffe, ein Löwe, ein Nashorn, ein Papagei, ein Tiger, ein Vogel

Framework references
L&S 1.1, 1.2, 1.5; R&W 2.4, 2.5; KAL 4.1; LLS 5.7

Starters
- Copymaster 15, ex. 2.
- Before students watch Nico's video blog, challenge them to respond to the true / false statements (ex. 1) by referring to his profile box and by trying to remember what they've learned about Nico in the course so far. Once they've had a go at predicting the answers, play the video so that they can check whether they were right.
- Before beginning ex. 2, challenge students (working in pairs) to list the animals they already know. Can any pairs remember all twelve animals from spread 1A.3, including genders and plural forms?

Plenaries
- Teacher versus the class. Read out the text of Nico's blog but introduce a few errors and challenge students to spot them. The class win one point for each error they spot and an extra point if they can correct it; you win a point for each error they fail to spot, e.g.
Teacher: *Hallo! Ich heiße Nico und ich bin 16 Jahre alt.*
Class: *Falsch … 14 Jahre alt.* (= 2 points)
- When students are familiar with the zoo picture, ask them to close their books and to work with a partner to reconstruct a description of the animals from memory, including not only personality but also colours, e.g.
A: *Ein Delfin. Er ist grau und … äh …*
B: *… Ist er sportlich?*
A: *Ja, richtig, grau und sportlich!*
B: *Ein Bär – er ist …*

Homework
- Students write and record their own video blog about their family: see *Follow-up* to ex. 1.
- Students write five questions to test their partner's knowledge of Unit 1A. Encourage them to include questions about vocabulary, grammar and information about the main characters from the video, and to compile a separate answer sheet. Students exchange their questions with their partner in the next lesson. Alternatively, collect in everyone's questions and use them in a class quiz.

---

1 Sieh dir das Video an. Richtig (✓) oder falsch (✗)?

AT 1.3
L&S 1.1, 1.2
LLS 5.7

Students watch Nico's video blog and work out whether sentences a–h are true or false. Ask them to correct the false sentences.
Point out to students that they can prepare for this activity by trying to predict some of the answers, e.g. they can find out the answer to a by looking at Nico's profile, they know the answer to b from video clip 1A, and the photos provide a clue about Nico's brothers and sister. Encourage them to go through a–h making sure they know the German for any key words (e.g. *groß, musikalisch, schüchtern*, etc.) – this gives them a focus for listening and helps to improve concentration.

Answers: **a** ✓; **b** ✗ (Berlin); **c** ✓; **d** ✗ (19); **e** ✓; **f** ✗ (not lazy but very hard-working); **g** ✗ (9); **h** ✓

> **Video blog 1A**
> **CD 1, track 42**   Seite 32, Übung 1
>
> Hallo! Ich heiße Nico, ich bin 14 Jahre alt und ich wohne in Berlin.
> Ich habe drei Geschwister: ich habe zwei Brüder und eine Schwester. Meine Brüder heißen Ulli und Ralf. Ulli ist 19 Jahre alt. Er ist sehr groß und sehr musikalisch. Aber er ist ziemlich schüchtern. Ralf ist 16 Jahre alt. Und, ja, er ist sehr intelligent und sehr sportlich … ja, und noch sehr fleißig. Meine kleine Schwester Britta ist neun Jahre alt. Sie ist sehr frech und oft ziemlich laut. Sie ist nicht sehr nett – leider!
> Wie ist deine Familie? Hast du auch Geschwister?

1A.6 Meine Familie

L&S 1.5
R&W 2.4, 2.5

Follow-up
Students produce a mock-up blog profile for themselves, similar to Nico's, consisting of a personal information section and a photo of themselves. Encourage them to write and record their own video blog about their family: these can then be played back to the class in a following lesson.

KAL 4.1

2 Wie sagt man das?
Students work out how to pronounce the animal vocabulary. Point out the tips on pronunciation of v and *ei*.

AT 3.1

3 Was passt zusammen?
Students match the animal vocabulary to the corresponding pictures.

Answers: **a** 9; **b** 6; **c** 7; **d** 1; **e** 2; **f** 5; **g** 4; **h** 8; **i** 3; **j** 10

AT 1.1

4 Hör zu (1–10). Ist alles richtig?
Students listen to check their pronunciation (ex. 2) and their answers to ex. 3.

🎧 **CD 1, track 43**   Seite 33, Übung 4
1 Das ist ein Delfin.
2 Das ist ein Elefant.
3 Das ist ein Papagei.
4 Das ist ein Löwe.
5 Das ist eine Giraffe.
6 Das ist ein Affe.
7 Das ist ein Bär.
8 Das ist ein Nashorn.
9 Das ist ein Vogel.
10 Das ist ein Tiger.

AT 1.1–2
LLS 5.7

5 Hör zu (1–10). Wie ist er / sie / es?
Before playing the recording, challenge students to predict which adjective from page 31 might be used to describe each animal, e.g. *ein Delfin – er ist sportlich*. They then listen to the recording to check their predictions.

Answers: see transcript

🎧 **CD 1, track 44**   Seite 33, Übung 5
1 Das ist ein Delfin. Er ist sportlich!
2 Das ist ein Elefant. Er ist frech!
3 Das ist ein Papagei. Er ist musikalisch!
4 Das ist ein Löwe. Er ist laut!
5 Das ist eine Giraffe. Sie ist groß!
6 Das ist ein Affe. Er ist intelligent!
7 Das ist ein Bär. Er ist fleißig!
8 Das ist ein Nashorn. Es ist schüchtern!
9 Das ist ein Vogel. Er ist klein!
10 Das ist ein Tiger. Er ist faul!

AT 2.1–2

6 Macht Dialoge!
In pairs, students take turns to describe the animals, e.g.
A: *Nummer 1!*
B: *Das ist ein Delfin. Er ist sportlich!*

AT 4.2

Challenge
Students write descriptions of their own pets. If they don't have any, they could describe their ideal pets or those of famous people. Remind them to use *sehr, ziemlich, nicht* and *gar nicht* (see 1A.4) and to build longer sentences using *und* and *aber*.

1A.6 Sprachlabor   Seite 34–35

Planner

Objectives
- Grammar: possessive adjectives (*mein / meine, dein / deine*), gender and negatives
- Skills: use a bilingual dictionary; pronounce *ü* and *sch*

Resources
- Student Book, pages 34–35
- CD 1, tracks 45–46
- Foundation and Higher Workbooks, pages 21–22
- Copymasters 21, 22
- Interactive OxBox, Unit 1A

Framework references
KAL 4.1, 4.3, 4.6; LLS 5.5

51

1A.7 Meine Familie

Possessive adjectives: *mein / meine, dein / deine*

KAL 4.3 1 Fill in the gaps with the correct forms of *mein(e)* or *dein(e)*.

Answers: **a** meine; **b** dein; **c** meine; **d** deine; **e** mein; **f** deine

Gender and negatives

KAL 4.3 2 Choose the correct form of *ein(e)(n)*.

Answers: **a** einen; **b** eine; **c** ein; **d** einen; **e** einen; **f** ein

KAL 4.3, 4.6 3 Fill in the gaps with the correct negatives.

Answers: **a** keine; **b** keinen; **c** keinen; **d** kein

KAL 4.3 4 Write down *er*, *sie* or *es* for these nouns.

Answers: **a** sie; **b** es; **c** es; **d** er

Using a bilingual dictionary

LLS 5.5 This section focuses on the different types of information provided at entries in a bilingual dictionary, e.g. parts of speech, gender, plural, etc.

5 Look at extract a from a bilingual dictionary. Where does it say (a) what the gender of the noun is? (b) what the plural of the noun is?

Answers: **a** der Stiefvater (*der* shows that it is masculine); **b** die Stiefväter

6 Now look at b. Where does it say (a) if the word is a verb? (b) if the word is an adjective?

Answers: the parts of speech (verb and adjective) are shown immediately after the headwords "schön" and "spielen"

7 Use a dictionary to translate the underlined words.

Answers: **a** Eisbär; **b** schlank, dünn; **c** Ratte

Pronunciation of *ü* and *sch*

KAL 4.1 8 The German sound *ü* is called an umlaut. Listen carefully: do you hear *ü* or not? (1–8)

Answers: 1, 3, 6 and 8 contain ü sounds

🎧 CD 1, track 45   Seite 35, Übung 8

– ü … ü … ü
1 Brüder
2 Opa
3 Hühner
4 Mutter
5 Susi
6 müde
7 Hund
8 grün

KAL 4.1 9 Listen. How many *sch* sounds can you hear – more than two?

🎧 CD 1, track 46   Seite 35, Übung 9

Ich habe eine Schwester – sie ist sehr schüchtern. Ich habe auch eine Schildkröte und eine Schlange.

1A.7 Extra Star   Seite 36

Planner

Objectives
- Vocabulary: recognise and use the words for colours and other adjectives, family members and pets
- Grammar: practise key grammar points from the unit
- Skills: practise reading skills

Resources
- Student Book, page 36
- Copymaster 23

1A.7 Meine Familie

AT 3.1 — **1 Match the colours.**

Answers: *a* 4; *b* 1; *c* 5; *d* 2; *e* 3; *f* 6

AT 4.1 — **2 Write out these words correctly.**
Students solve the animal anagrams.

Answers: *a* eine Katze; *b* ein Hamster; *c* ein Pferd; *d* ein Kaninchen; *e* ein Hund; *f* ein Fisch

AT 3.1 — **3 Match the pictures.**
Students match the descriptions of appearance and personality to the corresponding pictures.

Answers: *a* 5; *b* 2; *c* 1; *d* 4; *e* 6; *f* 3

AT 3.1–2 / AT 4.1–2 — **4 Look at Anja's family tree and read her statements. Can you fill in the gaps?**

Answers: *a* Uwe; *b* Mutter; *c* Heinz; *d* Schwester; *e* Brüder

1A.7 Extra Plus   Seite 37

Planner

Objectives
- Vocabulary: recognise and use the words for colours and other adjectives, family members and pets
- Grammar: *das ist ein(e) …; er / sie / es ist …; ich habe eine(n) / keine(n) …*

- Skills: use knowledge of grammar and other strategies to work out meaning

Resources
- Student Book, page 37
- Copymaster 24

AT 3.2 — **1 Was passt zusammen?**
Students match questions about family and pets to their corresponding answers.
Students need to use different strategies to complete this activity, e.g. use their knowledge of grammar to work out that the answer to d will begin with the third person singular (*Er ist …*) and that the answer to f will begin with the first person singular (*Ich bin …*), identify familiar language and relationships between words.

Answers: *a* 3; *b* 4; *c* 6; *d* 2; *e* 1; *f* 5

AT 4.2–3 — **2 Haustiere und Farben – schreib Sätze.**
Students write sentences to describe the animal pictures.

Answers: *a* Das ist ein Wellensittich. Er ist blau. *b* Das ist eine Maus. Sie ist weiß. *c* Das ist ein Meerschweinchen. Es ist braun. *d* Das ist ein Huhn. Es ist orange. *e* Das ist eine Schlange. Sie ist rot. *f* Das ist eine Schildkröte. Sie ist grün.

AT 4.2 — **3 Geschwister – Ich habe eine(n) / keine(n) …**
Students write sentences about brothers and sisters, based on the stick figures.

Answers: *a* Ich habe keine Schwester. *b* Ich habe zwei Brüder. *c* Ich habe eine Schwester. *d* Ich habe keinen Bruder. *e* Ich habe zwei Schwestern.

AT 3.3 — **4 Richtig oder falsch?**
Students read David's text and decide whether statements a–d are true or false.
Instead of just identifying key words, they need to use their knowledge of grammar here, e.g. if they fail to identify the word *kein(e)* in statements a and b, it's likely that they will answer incorrectly.

Answers: *a* falsch (er hat eine Oma und einen Opa); *b* richtig; *c* richtig; *d* falsch (er hat zwei Haustiere: einen Wellensittich und eine Maus)

1A Meine Familie

1A.8 Testseite Seite 38

Planner

Resources
- Student Book, page 38
- CD 1, track 47
- Foundation and Higher Workbooks, page 23
- Copymasters 13, 14
- Assessment, Unit 1A

AT 1.1–2 **1 Listen (a–f) and match the pictures.**
Students listen to a girl's description of her family. They choose a picture to match each statement.

Answers: **a** 4; **b** 3; **c** 1; **d** 2; **e** 6; **f** 5

CD 1, track 47 Seite 38, Übung 1

a Das ist meine Mutter.
b Das ist mein Hund.
c Das sind meine Großeltern.
d Das ist meine Schwester.
e Das ist mein Vater.
f Das sind meine Brüder.

AT 4.2 **2 Unscramble the word order in these sentences.**

Answers: **a** Ich habe keine Geschwister. **b** Das ist meine Schwester Tanja. **c** Ich habe einen Bruder. **d** Das ist ein Meerschweinchen. **e** Mein Vater ist sehr nett. **f** Ich habe einen Wellensittich.

AT 2.2 **3 A asks questions a–e. B looks at the pictures and answers in full sentences.**
Students ask and answer questions about family and pets.

Answers: **a** Ja, ich habe einen Bruder und eine Schwester. **b** Er ist musikalisch. **c** Sie ist sportlich. **d** Ja, ich habe eine Katze. **e** Es ist gelb und braun.

AT 3.3 **4 Read the email and answer the questions.**

Answers: **a** none; **b** one brother and two sisters; **c** very naughty; **d** very nice; **e** a hamster and a cat; **f** the hamster is called Karli and is very shy, the cat is called Pauli and is white

1A Lesen Seite 153

Planner

Resources
- Student Book, page 153

Framework references
R&W 2.1, 2.2

Top Ten Haustiere

AT 3.1 **1 Which is the most common name for a cat in Germany – and which for a dog?**
Students read a magazine-style survey about favourite pets in Germany.

Answers: Mieke (cat), Hasso (dog)

AT 3.3 **2 Read the text about Tokio Hotel and answer the questions in English.**
Students read about the German band Tokio Hotel.

Answers: **a** Germany; **b** both are 21; **c** September; **d** twins; **e** German and English

Follow-up

- Students carry out a class survey to find the Top Ten pets and their names. They list the results and compare with the German Top Ten.
- Students research Tokio Hotel on the internet. Suggest that they find out five things about the band and their music to share with the class in the next lesson.
- Students produce a short magazine-style text about their own favourite band or musician, to be used in a class display.

1A Meine Familie

Foundation Workbook

1A.1 Das ist meine Familie! (Seite 16)

AT 3.1 **1** Emine is introducing her family. Fill in the gaps with a name.

Answers: **a** Mehmet; **b** Suzan; **c** Ayse; **d** Hassan; **e** Ahmed; **f** Rafat

AT 1.2 **2** Listen to Sascha describing his family. Who is who?

Answers: <u>father</u>: Boris; <u>mother</u>: Susanne; <u>sister</u>: Maria; <u>brother</u>: Klaus

> 🎧 **CD 3, track 36**   Seite 16, Übung 2
>
> Hi! Ich heiße Sascha und ich bin zwölf. Mein Vater heißt Boris und meine Mutter heißt Susanne. Das ist meine Schwester Maria und hier ist mein Bruder Klaus.

3 Add in an -e if required. If it's not required, leave it blank.

Answers: mein Bruder; meine Schwester; meine Oma; mein Vater; mein Opa; meine Großeltern; meine Mutter

1A.2 Ich habe einen Bruder (Seite 17)

AT 3.1–2 **1** Match the sentences to the pictures.

Answers: **a** 6; **b** 1; **c** 3; **d** 2; **e** 5; **f** 4

AT 1.2 **2** Listen to these people (a–f). How many brothers and sisters do they have?

Answers: **a** no brothers, two sisters; **b** no brothers, no sisters; **c** three brothers, no sisters; **d** no brothers, one sister; **e** one brother, one sister; **f** two brothers, two sisters

> 🎧 **CD 3, track 37**   Seite 17, Übung 2
>
> **a** Ich habe zwei Schwestern, aber keinen Bruder.
> **b** Ich habe keine Geschwister.
> **c** Ich habe keine Schwester, aber ich habe drei Brüder.
> **d** Ich habe eine Schwester, aber keinen Bruder.
> **e** Ich habe einen Bruder und eine Schwester.
> **f** Ich habe zwei Brüder und zwei Schwestern.

AT 4.1–2 **3** Translate these sentences.

Answers: **a** Ich habe zwei Brüder. **b** Ich habe eine Schwester. **c** Ich habe zwei Schwestern. **d** Ich habe einen Bruder. **e** Ich habe drei Brüder. **f** Ich bin Einzelkind / Ich habe keine Geschwister.

1A.3 Hast du ein Haustier? (Seite 18)

AT 3.1–2 **1** Colour in these animals correctly.

Answers: **a** brown; **b** black; **c** grey; **d** brown and white; **e** white; **f** yellow

AT 1.1–2 **2** Listen to these people. What pets do they have? Write the answers in English.

Answers: **a** two cats; **b** four fish; **c** three budgies; **d** a horse; **e** five mice; **f** two dogs, three hamsters

> 🎧 **CD 3, track 38**   Seite 18, Übung 2
>
> **a** Ich habe zwei Katzen.
> **b** Ich habe vier Fische.
> **c** Ich habe drei Wellensittiche.
> **d** Ich habe ein Pferd.
> **e** Ich habe fünf Mäuse.
> **f** Ich habe zwei Hunde und drei Hamster.

3 Decide whether these words are singular or plural.

Answers: **a** plural; **b** plural; **c** singular; **d** singular; **e** plural; **f** plural

1A.4 Wie bist du? (Seite 19)

AT 4.1 **1** Write in the adjectives. What is the mystery word down?

Answers: **a** faul; **b** romantisch; **c** klein; **d** sportlich; **e** schüchtern. The mystery word down is <u>frech</u>. It means <u>naughty</u> (or: <u>cheeky</u>).

AT 1.2 **2** Kalle Klug is a cool guy. Which adjectives apply to him?

Answers: **a** schüchtern: nein; **b** intelligent: ja; **c** sportlich: ja; **d** klein: nein; **e** groß: ja; **f** musikalisch: ja

> 🎧 **CD 3, track 39**   Seite 19, Übung 2
>
> – Toll! Kalle ist so musikalisch und intelligent!
> – Ja, und schau, wie groß und sportlich er ist!
> – Und er ist absolut nicht schüchtern!

1A.5 Nicos Videoblog (Seite 20)

AT 1.3 **1** Listen and answer these questions in English.

Answers: **a** 13; **b** Dortmund; **c** 8; **d** musical, intelligent; **e** 16; **f** small, shy

1A Meine Familie

🎧 **CD 3, track 40**   Seite 20, Übung 1

Hi! Ich heiße Tim. Ich bin dreizehn Jahre alt. Ich wohne in Dortmund.
Ich habe zwei Geschwister. Meine Schwester heißt Katrin. Sie ist acht Jahre alt. Sie ist musikalisch und intelligent.
Mein Bruder heißt Dennis. Er ist sechzehn Jahre alt. Er ist klein und schüchtern.

AT 4.1   **2 Unjumble the words to make animals. Write out the German word and its English translation.**

Answers: **a** Delfin (dolphin); **b** Affe (monkey); **c** Nashorn (rhino); **d** Löwe (lion); **e** Vogel (bird); **f** Elefant (elephant)

AT 3.1–2   **3 Write down these animals and their characteristics in English.**

Answers: **a** A dolphin is sporty, intelligent and hard-working. **b** A lion is noisy, lazy and cheeky / naughty.

1A.6A Sprachlabor   (Seite 21)

1 Write full sentences like the example provided.

Answers: **a** Das ist mein Bruder. Er heißt Klaus. **b** Das ist mein Opa. Er heißt Helmut. **c** Das ist meine Katze. Sie heißt Schnurri. **d** Das ist meine Tante. Sie ist sportlich. **e** Das ist mein Pferd. Es ist braun. **f** Das sind meine Eltern.

2 Complete the sentence using *kein* or *keine*.

Answers: Ich habe keinen Hund, keine Katze, kein Pferd und keine Geschwister.

1A.6B Think   (Seite 22)

1 👥 **Say these words out loud. Get a partner to assess how well you have pronounced them.**
Students practise pronunciation of *u / ü*, *o / ö* and *a / ä*.

2 Decide whether these words are nouns or adjectives. Write them in the correct column.

Answers: <u>Nouns</u>: Affe, Tiger, Schwester, Opa, Schlange, Einzelkind; <u>Adjectives</u>: nett, blau, romantisch, schwarz, faul, grün

3 Use the vocabulary page to work out the plural of these nouns.

Answers: Hunde, Mütter, Giraffen, Schlangen, Brüder, Katzen, Papageien, Schwestern, Väter

4 Look up these nouns, which you may not know. Write down the meaning and show you understand the gender by writing *der*, *die* or *das*.

Answers: das Geld (money); die Polizei (police); die Tür (door); das Boot (boat); die Arbeit (work); das Auto (car); das Fenster (window); der Wald (wood, forest)

5 Find the infinitive and the meaning of these new verbs in the dictionary.

Answers: ich laufe – laufen – to run; er bringt – bringen – to bring; wir bleiben – bleiben – to stay; ich lerne – lernen – to learn

1A Meine Familie

Higher Workbook

1A.1 Das ist meine Familie! (Seite 16)

AT 3.1 / AT 4.1 **1 Who are these relatives? Fill in the gaps with a German word.**

Answers: **a** Vater; **b** Mutter; **c** Schwester; **d** Bruder; **e** Opa; **f** Oma

AT 1.2–3 **2 Listen to Sascha describing his family. Who is who?**

Answers: Mein Vater heißt Boris. Meine Mutter heißt Susanne. Meine Schwester heißt Maria. Mein Bruder heißt Klaus.

> 🎧 **CD 4, track 36** Seite 16, Übung 2
>
> Hi! Ich heiße Sascha. Ich bin 12 Jahre alt und ich habe eine große Familie. Mein Vater heißt Boris und meine Mutter heißt Susanne. Ich habe zwei Geschwister. Das ist meine Schwester Maria und hier ist mein Bruder. Er heißt Klaus.

3 Write in *mein* or *meine*.

Answers: **a** mein; **b** meine; **c** meine; **d** mein; **e** mein; **f** meine; **g** meine

1A.2 Ich habe einen Bruder (Seite 17)

AT 3.1–2 **1 Write in the words for these relatives.**

Answers: **a** einen Bruder; **b** zwei Brüder; **c** zwei Schwestern; **d** eine Schwester; **e** Einzelkind; **f** einen Bruder und eine Schwester

AT 1.2 **2 Listen to these people (a–f). How many brothers and sisters do they have? Write the answers in English.**

Answers: **a** two sisters, no brothers; **b** no brothers, no sisters; **c** no sisters, three brothers; **d** one sister, no brothers; **e** one brother, one sister; **f** two brothers, two sisters

> 🎧 **CD 4, track 37** Seite 17, Übung 2
>
> a Ich habe zwei Schwestern, aber keinen Bruder.
> b Ich habe keine Geschwister.
> c Ich habe keine Schwester, aber ich habe drei Brüder.
> d Ich habe eine Schwester, aber keinen Bruder.
> e Ich habe einen Bruder und eine Schwester.
> f Ich habe zwei Brüder und zwei Schwestern.

AT 4.1–2 **3 Translate these sentences.**

Answers: **a** Ich habe zwei Brüder. **b** Ich habe eine Schwester. **c** Ich habe zwei Schwestern. **d** Ich habe einen Bruder. **e** Ich habe drei Brüder. **f** Ich bin Einzelkind / Ich habe keine Geschwister.

1A.3 Hast du ein Haustier? (Seite 18)

AT 4.1–2 **1 Describe these animals.**

Answers: **a** Das ist ein Pferd. Es ist braun. **b** Das ist ein Hund. Er ist schwarz. **c** Das ist eine Schildkröte. Sie ist grau. **d** Das ist eine Katze. Sie ist braun und weiß. **e** Das ist eine Maus. Sie ist weiß. **f** Das ist ein Wellensittich. Er ist gelb.

AT 1.1–2 **2 Listen to these people. What pets do they have? Write the answers in English.**

Answers: **a** two cats, a snake; **b** four chickens; **c** three budgies; **d** a horse, a dog; **e** five mice, a rabbit; **f** two dogs, a guinea pig, three hamsters

> 🎧 **CD 4, track 38** Seite 18, Übung 2
>
> a Ich habe zwei Katzen und eine Schlange.
> b Ich habe vier Hühner.
> c Ich habe drei Wellensittiche.
> d Ich habe ein Pferd und einen Hund.
> e Ich habe fünf Mäuse und ein Kaninchen.
> f Ich habe zwei Hunde, ein Meerschweinchen und drei Hamster.

AT 4.1 **3 Write in the numbers and the correct plural forms.**

Answers: **a** zwei Mäuse; **b** drei Pferde; **c** sechs Fische; **d** vier Kaninchen; **e** fünf Katzen; **f** zwei Hühner

1A.4 Wie bist du? (Seite 19)

AT 4.1 **1 Write in the adjectives. What is the mystery word down?**

Answers: **a** faul; **b** romantisch; **c** klein; **d** sportlich; **e** schüchtern. The mystery word down is <u>frech</u>. It means <u>naughty</u> (or: <u>cheeky</u>).

AT 1.2 **2 Kalle Klug is a cool guy. Which sentences are true and which are false? Write *richtig* (true) or *falsch* (false).**

Answers: **a** falsch; **b** richtig; **c** falsch; **d** falsch; **e** richtig; **f** richtig

57

1A Meine Familie

> 🎧 **CD 4, track 39** — Seite 19, Übung 2
>
> – Toll! Kalle ist so musikalisch und intelligent!
> – Ja, und schau, wie groß und sportlich er ist!
> – Und er ist absolut nicht schüchtern!

1A.5 Nicos Videoblog (Seite 20)

AT 1.3 **1 Listen and answer these questions in English.**

Answers: **a** 13; **b** Dortmund; **c** 8; **d** musical, intelligent; **e** 16; **f** small, shy

> 🎧 **CD 4, track 40** — Seite 20, Übung 1
>
> Hi! Ich heiße Tim und ich bin dreizehn Jahre alt. Ich wohne in Dortmund und ich habe zwei Geschwister. Meine Schwester heißt Katrin und sie ist acht Jahre alt. Sie ist musikalisch und intelligent.
> Mein Bruder heißt Dennis. Er ist sechzehn Jahre alt und er ist klein und schüchtern.

AT 4.1 **2 Unjumble the words to make animals. Write out the German word and its English translation.**

Answers: **a** Delfin (dolphin); **b** Affe (monkey); **c** Nashorn (rhino); **d** Löwe (lion); **e** Vogel (bird); **f** Elefant (elephant)

AT 3.1–2 **3 Write down these animals and their characteristics in English.**

Answers: **a** A dolphin is sporty, intelligent and hard-working. **b** A lion is noisy, lazy and cheeky / naughty.

1A.6A Sprachlabor (Seite 21)

1 Write full sentences like the example provided.

Answers: **a** Das ist mein Bruder. Er heißt Klaus. **b** Das ist mein Opa. Er heißt Helmut. **c** Das ist meine Katze. Sie heißt Schnurri. **d** Das ist meine Tante. Sie ist sportlich. **e** Das ist mein Pferd. Es ist braun. **f** Das sind meine Eltern.

2 Complete the sentence using *keinen*, *kein* or *keine*.

Answers: Ich habe keinen Hund, keine Katze, kein Pferd und keine Geschwister.

1A.6B Think (Seite 22)

1 👥 Say these words out loud. Get a partner to assess how well you have pronounced them.

Students practise pronunciation of *u / ü*, *o / ö* and *a / ä*.

2 Decide whether these words are nouns or adjectives. Write them in the correct column.

Answers: <u>Nouns</u>: Affe, Tiger, Schwester, Opa, Schlange, Einzelkind; <u>Adjectives</u>: nett, blau, romantisch, schwarz, faul, grün

3 Use the vocabulary page to work out the plural of these nouns.

Answers: Hunde, Mütter, Giraffen, Schlangen, Brüder, Katzen, Papageien, Schwestern, Väter

4 Look up these nouns, which you may not know. Write down the meaning and show you understand the gender by writing *der*, *die* or *das*.

Answers: das Geld (money); die Polizei (police); die Tür (door); das Boot (boat); die Arbeit (work); das Auto (car); das Fenster (window); der Wald (wood, forest)

5 Find the infinitive and the meaning of these new verbs in the dictionary.

Answers: ich laufe – laufen – to run; er bringt – bringen – to bring; wir bleiben – bleiben – to stay; ich lerne – lernen – to learn

1B Meine Schule

Unit 1B Meine Schule — **Unit overview grid**

Page reference	Objectives	Grammar	Skills and pronunciation	Key language	Framework	AT level
Pages 40–41 **1B.1 Mein Klassenzimmer**	Say what's in your classroom and what you have in your school bag	*Der, die, das* *Ich habe + einen/eine/ein …* *Ich habe + keinen/keine/ kein …*	Use question words	*Wer ist das? Was ist das?* *der Lehrer, der Schüler, der Schreibtisch, der Stuhl, die Lehrerin, die Schülerin, die Tafel, das Klassenzimmer* *der Bleistift, der Füller, der Kuli, der Ordner, der Taschenrechner, die Federtasche, die Schultasche, das Heft, das Lineal, das Schulbuch,*	L&S 1.4 R&W 2.4, 2.5 IU 3.1, 3.2 KAL 4.3, 4.6 LLS 5.1	1.1–3, 2.1–2, 3.1–2, 4.2
Pages 42–43 **1B.2 Schulfächer**	Say which school subjects you have; give opinions of school subjects	*Ich finde (+ subject + adjective), du findest* *Ich mag (+ subject), du magst*	Work out meaning; pronounce the ö sound	*Deutsch, Englisch, Erdkunde, Französisch, Geschichte, Informatik, Kunst, Latein, Mathe, Musik, Naturwissenschaften (Biologie, Chemie, Physik), Religion, Spanisch, Sport* *doof, einfach, fantastisch, furchtbar, gut, interessant, langweilig, prima, schwer, super* *Wie findest du Mathe? Ich finde Mathe toll/ nicht toll. Magst du Sport? Ich mag Sport. Ich mag Sport nicht. Was ist dein Lieblingsfach? Mein Lieblingsfach ist Deutsch.*	L&S 1.1, 1.2, 1.3, 1.4 R&W 2.2, 2.3, 2.4, 2.5 LLS 5.3, 5.4, 5.5	1.1–4, 2.1–3, 3.1, 3.3 4.2–3
Pages 44–45 **1B.3 Wie spät ist es?**	Ask and say what time it is; ask and say when you have different subjects	*Ich habe, du hast, er/sie hat, wir haben*	Use question words; use existing knowledge to work out new language	*Wie spät ist es? Es ist neun Uhr. Es ist halb neun. Es ist Viertel vor neun. Es ist Viertel nach neun. Es ist Mittag. Es ist Mitternacht. Wann haben wir Deutsch? Um wie viel Uhr haben wir Englisch? Um wie viel Uhr beginnt Mathe? Wir haben um zehn Uhr Sport. Kunst beginnt um halb zwölf.*	R&W 2.4 IU 3.1 KAL 4.3, 4.5, 4.6 LLS 5.4	1.1–3, 2.1–2, 3.2, 4.2

1B Meine Schule

Page reference	Objectives	Grammar	Skills and pronunciation	Key language	Framework	AT level
Pages 46–47 **1B.4 Mein Schultag**	Say the days of the week; ask and say on what day you have different subjects	"Verb second" word order	Work out meaning; identify language patterns	Montag, Dienstag, Mittwoch, Donnerstag, Freitag, Samstag, Sonntag *Am Montag habe ich Musik.*	R&W 2.3, 2.4 IU 3.1 KAL 4.4 LLS 5.3, 5.4	1.1–2, 2.2, 3.1, 4.2–3
Pages 48–49 **1B.5 Ninas Videoblog**	Talk about school subjects and times	"Verb second" word order	Work out meaning from context; recognise the importance of high-frequency words	*Am Montag habe ich Deutsch. Um zehn Uhr haben wir Pause/Mittagspause. Medienwissenschaften, Turnen, Kochen*	L&S 1.2 R&W 2.3, 2.4 KAL 4.2, 4.4 LLS 5.4, 5.7	1.2–4, 2.2, 4.2–3

Unit 1B: Week-by-week overview
(Three-year KS3 Route: assuming six weeks' work or approximately 10–12.5 hours)
(Two-year KS3 Route: assuming four weeks' work or approximately 6.5–8.5 hours)

About Unit 1B, *Meine Schule*: In this unit, students work in the context of school: they name classroom items, say what they have in their school bag, and give opinions of school subjects. They also ask and say what time it is, learn the days of the week and talk about school timetables, and there are opportunities to compare school life in Germany and the UK. Work on gender continues (*der/die/das*) and students are reminded of *Ich habe ein(e)(n)/kein(e)(n)*, which was taught in Unit 1A in the context of family/pets and is recycled here to talk about school equipment. Students are also introduced to "verb second" word order and the *wir* form of the verb (*wir haben*). There is chance for a recap of all the question words met so far (*Wie? Wann?* etc.), and students develop their range of strategies for working out the meaning of unfamiliar language. The pronunciation focus is the ö sound.

Three-Year KS3 Route

Week	Resources	Objectives
1	1B.1 Mein Klassenzimmer 1B.6 Sprachlabor ex. 1–2	Say what's in your classroom and what you have in your school bag *Der/die/das; ich habe einen/eine/ein …; ich habe keinen/keine/kein …* Use question words
2	1B.2 Schulfächer 1B.6 Sprachlabor ex. 5–8	Say which school subjects you have; give opinions of school subjects *Ich finde* (+ subject + adjective), *du findest; ich mag* (+ subject), *du magst* Work out the meaning of unknown words Pronounce the ö sound

Two-Year KS3 Route

Week	Resources	Objectives
1	1B.1 Mein Klassenzimmer (*Omit ex. 8*) 1B.6 Sprachlabor ex. 1–2	Say what's in your classroom and what you have in your school bag *Der/die/das; ich habe einen/eine/ein …; ich habe keinen/keine/kein …* Use question words
2	1B.2 Schulfächer 1B.6 Sprachlabor ex. 5–7	Say which school subjects you have; give opinions of school subjects *Ich finde* (+ subject + adjective), *du findest; ich mag* (+ subject), *du magst* Work out the meaning of unknown words Pronounce the ö sound

1B Meine Schule

	Three-Year KS3 Route			Two-Year KS3 Route	
Week	Resources	Objectives	Week	Resources	Objectives
3	1B.3 Wie spät ist es? 1B.6 Sprachlabor ex. 3	Ask and say what time it is; ask and say when you have different subjects *Ich habe, du hast, er/sie hat, wir haben* Use question words; use existing knowledge to work out new language	3	1B.3 Wie spät ist es? (*Omit Challenge*) 1B.6 Sprachlabor ex. 3	Ask and say what time it is; ask and say when you have different subjects *Ich habe, du hast, er/sie hat, wir haben* Use question words; use existing knowledge to work out new language
4	1B.4 Mein Schultag 1B.6 Sprachlabor ex. 4	Say the days of the week; ask and say on what day you have different subjects Use "verb second" word order Work out meaning; identify language patterns	4	1B.4 Mein Schultag (*Omit ex. 5 and 7*) 1B.6 Sprachlabor ex. 4 1B.8 Vokabular 1B.8 Testseite	Say the days of the week; ask and say on what day you have different subjects Use "verb second" word order Work out meaning; identify language patterns Key vocabulary and learning checklist Assessment in all four skills
5	1B.5 Ninas Videoblog	Talk about school subjects and times Use "verb second" word order Work out meaning from context Recognise the importance of high-frequency words			
6	1B.7 Extra (Star/Plus) 1B.8 Vokabular 1B.8 Testseite 1B Lesen	Reinforcement and extension of the language of the unit Key vocabulary and learning checklist Assessment in all four skills Further reading to explore the language of the unit and cultural themes			

1B.1 Meine Schule

1B.1 Mein Klassenzimmer

Seite 40–41

Planner

Objectives
- Vocabulary: say what's in your classroom and what you have in your school bag
- Grammar: der / die / das; ich habe einen / eine / ein …; ich habe keinen / keine / kein …
- Skills: use question words

Video
- Video clip 1B

Resources
- Student Book, pages 40–41
- CD 1, tracks 48–49
- Foundation and Higher Workbooks, page 24
- Workbook audio: CD 3 and 4, track 41
- Copymasters 27 (ex. 3), 28 (ex. 3), 30 (ex. 3)
- Interactive OxBox Unit 1B

Key language
Wer ist das? Was ist das?
der Lehrer, der Schüler, der Schreibtisch, der Stuhl
die Lehrerin, die Schülerin, die Tafel
das Klassenzimmer
der Bleistift, der Füller, der Kuli, der Ordner, der Taschenrechner
die Federtasche, die Schultasche
das Heft, das Lineal, das Schulbuch

Framework references
L&S 1.4; R&W 2.4, 2.5; IU 3.1, 3.2; KAL 4.3, 4.6; LLS 5.1

Starters
- Copymaster 27, ex. 3.
- Student Book page 40, ex. 1: students match the classroom vocabulary to the corresponding pictures. Afterwards, discuss any clues that helped them do this, e.g. the example answer tells them that *ein Lehrer* is a male teacher so *eine Lehrerin* is likely to be a female teacher, *Klasse* looks like English "class" so *Klassenzimmer* is likely to be a classroom.
- Display the eight classroom words from page 40 with their vowels missing, e.g. L_hr_r, Schr_ _bt_sch. Students race against the clock to copy out the words, fill in the missing letters and add the correct articles (der / die / das).
- Working in pairs, each student secretly notes down four items (from page 41) in an imaginary school bag. They take turns to guess what is in their partner's bag, e.g.
A: *Hast du ein Lineal?*
B: *Ja, ich habe ein Lineal.* (or *Nein, ich habe kein Lineal.*)
A: *Hast du …?*
Who is the first to guess all four items?

Plenaries
- Students play a memory game in pairs to see how many of the eight classroom words from page 40 they can recall:
A: *Das ist ein Schreibtisch.*
B: *Das ist ein Schreibtisch und das ist ein Lehrer.*
A: *Das ist ein Schreibtisch, das ist ein Lehrer und das ist …*
They point to each item (in the book or in the classroom) as they mention it. Which pairs succeed in remembering all eight words?
- Kim's game. Show a selection of items from a school bag and give students a few moments to memorise the display. Hide it, then challenge students to recall what was there, e.g.
Student A: *Ich habe ein Heft.*
Teacher: *Ja, richtig!* (or *Nein, ich habe kein Heft!*)
Student B: *Ich habe …*
This game can be played as a whole class, in groups or pairs.
- Variation on Kim's game. Give students a few moments to memorise a selection of items from a school bag. Hide the display temporarily while you remove an item, then reveal it again and ask students what is missing. Students respond using a full sentence: *Ich habe keinen / keine / kein* + missing item.

Homework
- Student Book page 40, ex. 4: students fill in the correct articles (der / die / das).
- Student Book page 41, *Challenge*.
- Students prepare their own version of ex. 7 as a puzzle to swap with a partner: they draw two school bags containing different items, then write a text describing one of the bags. In the next lesson, their partner identifies the bag that matches the text.

1B.1 Meine Schule

Video clip 1B: Rund um die Schule!

Synopsis:
On the way to school, Kathi quizzes Nina about Nico's favourite school subjects. Meanwhile, Ali and Nico have already arrived at school and are discussing school subjects too. As the action moves back and forth between the two conversations, we discover that Nina is mistaken about Nico – she gives Kathi a completely false impression of his likes and dislikes! … Suddenly, Nico realises he's left his school bag at home. Ali lends him everything he needs but ends up with nothing for himself!

Play the video through a couple of times and ask questions to check that students understand the gist of it. Ask what they notice about the four teenagers' clothes: they are on their way to school but are not wearing school uniform. Explain that school uniform is not generally worn in German schools.

Draw attention to the mural that Nina and Kathi walk past on their way to school, and point out that there is lots of graffiti and street art to be seen all over Berlin. This street art culture dates back to the 1980s, when the Western side of the Berlin Wall was covered extensively in paintings and graffiti. Only a few sections of the Wall remain, the longest being the East Side Gallery, a 1.3 kilometre stretch of the former Wall with its original murals.

Video clip 1B

(Kathi and Nina on the way to school)
Kathi: Also, was mag er denn?
Nina: Wer?
Kathi: Boris Becker! Nein. Wer wohl?
Nina: Ach so, Nico … ja … keine Ahnung … also … er mag Mathe … ja, er findet Mathe ganz toll!
Kathi: Super! Ich mag Mathe auch! Das ist mein Lieblingsfach. Und was noch?
Nina: Ähm … er mag Erdkunde überhaupt nicht.
Kathi: Hey! Ich hasse Erdkunde auch! Ich finde es langweilig. Langweilig und … was ist ein anderes Wort für langweilig?
Nina: Ja, finde ich auch!
Kathi: Und welche Fächer mag er noch nicht?
Nina: Sport mag er auch überhaupt nicht.

(Nico and Ali outside school)
Nico: Weißt du, eigentlich finde ich Erdkunde sehr interessant. Und du?
Ali: Natürlich! Ich finde alle meine Schulfächer interessant.

Nico: Na klar!
Ali: Mathe und Physik sind total interessant … und Latein und Englisch finde ich auch klasse … und natürlich Geschichte … und Deutsch mag ich sehr, aber …
Nico: Stop! Halt! Wann haben wir eigentlich Sport?
Ali: Um zwölf.
Nico: Super, Sport ist mein Lieblingsfach!
Ali: Echt?
Nico: Ja!

(Kathi and Nina still on the way to school)
Kathi: Ich hasse Sport auch! Ich finde es furchtbar. Bälle, Bälle, Bälle … groß, klein – immer dasselbe!
Nina: Verstehe. Sportlich bist du nicht: nett und elegant, aber nicht sportlich …

(Nico and Ali outside school)
Nico: Oh nein! Ich bin so doof!
Ali: Nein, bist du nicht. Was ist?
Nico: Meine Schultasche … Ich habe keine Schultasche … Meine Schultasche ist zu Hause!
Ali: Oh Nico! … Kein Problem – ich helfe dir. Hier … ich habe einen Bleistift.
Nico: Danke! Hast du auch ein Lineal für mich?
Ali: Nein, ich habe kein Lineal, aber ich habe einen Kuli … und auch einen Füller.
Nico: Danke. Und hast du auch einen Taschenrechner? Ich brauche einen Taschenrechner. Wir haben um zehn Uhr Mathe …
Ali: Ja, keine Panik. Ich habe auch einen Taschenrechner, und ich habe das Schulbuch.
Nico: Super, Ali! Und hast du ein Heft? Ich brauche noch ein Heft.
Ali: Ja, ich habe ein Heft.
Nico: Danke, Ali. Und hast du einen Ordner für mich?
Ali: Ja, ich habe einen Ordner.
Nico: Danke, Ali … *(he sees the girls arriving)* Oh, da sind die Mädchen!

Sprachpunkt
Er mag Mathe.
Mathe und Physik sind total interessant.
Sport ist mein Lieblingsfach.
Ich hasse Sport. Ich finde es furchtbar.

1 Was passt zusammen?
This activity introduces some key classroom vocabulary. Students match the words to the pictures.

Answers: **a** 2; **b** 6; **c** 5; **d** 7; **e** 4; **f** 8; **g** 1; **h** 3

1B.1 Meine Schule

AT 1.1 — **2 Hör zu (1–8). Ist alles richtig?**
Students listen to check their answers to ex. 1.

CD 1, track 48 — Seite 40, Übung 2

1 Das ist die Tafel.
2 Das ist der Lehrer.
3 Das ist das Klassenzimmer.
4 Das ist die Lehrerin.
5 Das ist der Schüler.
6 Das ist der Schreibtisch.
7 Das ist der Stuhl.
8 Das ist die Schülerin.

Think
Students are reminded that *ein* and *eine* mean "a". Can they work out what *der*, *die* and *das* mean?

AT 2.1 — **3 Wer / Was ist das?**
Students question each other about the key vocabulary. Student A says the number of a picture and asks *Wer* (or *Was*) *ist das?* Student B answers: *Das ist der / das / die …*

KAL 4.6 — **Think**
Point out the question words *Wer?* and *Was?* in the language box and in ex. 3 rubric. Suggest that students make a list of all the question words they know, e.g. *Wie? Wann? Wo?* They can add to this list as they work through the course.

KAL 4.3 — **4 Füll die Lücken aus.**
Before students begin ex. 4, read through the *Grammatik* box on gender. Students fill in the missing words (*der / die / das*) in the list of classroom vocabulary.

Answers: **a** die; **b** der; **c** der; **d** die; **e** das; **f** der

AT 1.2–3 — **5 Sieh dir das Video an. Was ist die richtige Reihenfolge?**
Play the final section of video clip 1B again: Ali goes through the contents of his school bag and lends everything to Nico. Students list the items a–i in the order they are mentioned. Ask them to identify the item that Nico asks for but Ali doesn't have (*ein Lineal*).

Answers: h, a, f, e, c, i, b, d, g

Video clip 1B
CD 1, track 49 — Seite 41, Übung 5
See final section of video clip 1B above: Nico and Ali outside school.

KAL 4.3, 4.6 / LLS 5.1 — **Grammatik**
Before students begin ex. 6, read through the *Grammatik* box on *Ich habe ein(e)(n) …* and *Ich habe kein(e)(n) …* Ask students where they have met this structure before: in Unit 1A, when talking about brothers, sisters and pets.

AT 2.2 / L&S 1.4 — **6 Was hast du?**
Students take turns to ask and answer the question *Hast du ein(e)(n) …?* Encourage them to go through their own school bags, comparing what they have and don't have. In future, if students arrive in the lesson without equipment, insist that they say so in German!

AT 3.2 — **7 Lies den Text. Was passt zusammen?**
Students work out which bag (1 or 2) represents Ben's text about school equipment. Point out the new word *eine Federtasche* (a pencil case).

Answer: bag 2

AT 4.2 / KAL 4.6 — **8 Was hat Ben nicht?**
Students write a few sentences (similar to the text in ex. 7) for picture 1, explaining which items Ben doesn't have in his bag.

Answer: *Ich habe keinen Füller. Ich habe keinen Kuli. Ich habe keinen Taschenrechner.*

AT 4.2 / R&W 2.4, 2.5 — **Challenge**
Students write six sentences explaining what they do and don't have in their school bag today. Suggest that they draw their bag (as in ex. 7) to illustrate their description.
For a more creative variation, see the third homework suggestion in the *Planner* above.

1B.2 Meine Schule

1B.2 Schulfächer

Seite 42–43

Planner

Objectives
- Vocabulary: say which school subjects you have; give opinions of school subjects
- Grammar: *ich finde* (+ subject + adjective), *du findest*; *ich mag* (+ subject), *du magst*
- Skills: work out the meaning of unknown words; pronounce the ö sound

Video
- Video clip 1B

Resources
- Student Book, pages 42–43
- CD 1, tracks 50–53
- Foundation and Higher Workbooks, page 25
- Workbook audio: CD 3 and 4, track 42
- Copymasters 30 (ex. 1–2), 32
- Interactive OxBox, Unit 1B

Key language
Deutsch, Englisch, Erdkunde, Französisch, Geschichte, Informatik, Kunst, Latein, Mathe, Musik, Naturwissenschaften (Biologie, Chemie, Physik), Religion, Spanisch, Sport
doof, einfach, fantastisch, furchtbar, gut, interessant, langweilig, prima, schwer, super
Wie findest du Mathe? Ich finde Mathe toll / nicht toll. Magst du Sport? Ich mag Sport. Ich mag Sport nicht. Was ist dein Lieblingsfach? Mein Lieblingsfach ist Deutsch.

Framework references
L&S 1.1, 1.2, 1.3, 1.4; R&W 2.2, 2.3, 2.4, 2.5; LLS 5.3, 5.4, 5.5

Starters
- Students look at the German names of school subjects on page 42 and identify any that look similar to English (e.g. *Mathe*) or are spelled the same (e.g. *Religion*). Challenge them, in pairs, to try pronouncing the words. They should realise by now that although some German and English words look very similar, they sound different. Play the ex. 1 recording so that they can check their pronunciation.
- See first homework suggestion: students complete each other's puzzles.

- Students note down two subjects that they think their partner likes, and two subjects that they think their partner doesn't like. They then ask each other questions to check whether they guessed correctly, e.g. one of A's guesses is that B doesn't like physics:
A: *Wie findest du Physik?*
B: *Ich mag Physik nicht. Es ist schwer.*
A has guessed correctly so wins a point. Who wins most points?

Plenaries
- Pictionary. Start drawing a symbol to represent a school subject; students compete to name the subject and say what they think of it, e.g.
Teacher: starts drawing a skeleton on the board.
Student: *Ich mag Biologie. Es ist interessant.*
This can be played as a whole class or in pairs / groups.
- Word tennis. Student A has first "serve" and says he or she likes or dislikes a subject; B returns A's serve by adding an appropriate comment – either positive or negative depending on whether A likes or dislikes the subject; A continues the rally by saying what he / she thinks of another subject:
A: *Ich mag Englisch.*
B: *Es ist interessant.*
A: *Ich mag Biologie nicht.*
B: *Ich finde Biologie langweilig.*
Make sure they swap over so that B has a turn at serving.

Homework
- Students make a puzzle to test their partner on the school subjects and / or opinions, e.g. a wordsearch, crossword, word snake, anagrams, matching pairs, mirror writing, mismatched word halves (e.g. *Latisch, Engl-ein*). Prompt them to prepare an answer sheet. They exchange puzzles with their partner in a following lesson.
- Student Book page 43, *Challenge*.
- As an alternative to *Challenge*, ask students to write opinions of school subjects on behalf of famous people, cartoon or fictional characters, or historical figures, e.g. Bill Gates: *Ich finde Informatik fantastisch. Informatik ist interessant …*; Van Gogh: *Mein Lieblingsfach ist Kunst …*

1B.2 Meine Schule

AT 1.1–2
AT 3.1

1 Hör zu und lies.
Students listen while reading the names of school subjects. This recording can be used first as a model for pronunciation of the subjects, then to focus on the opinion adjectives (ex. 2–3).

🎧 **CD 1, track 50** — Seite 42, Übung 1 und 3

a Deutsch. Deutsch ist gut.
b Englisch! Englisch ist interessant.
c Erdkunde. Erdkunde ist schwer.
d Französisch. Französisch ist prima.
e Geschichte! Geschichte ist einfach.
f Informatik. Informatik ist super!
g Kunst. Kunst ist doof.
h Latein. Latein ist langweilig.
i Mathe! Mathe ist fantastisch.
j Musik. Musik ist super.
k Religion. Religion ist interessant.
l Spanisch. Spanisch ist prima!
m Sport. Sport ist gut!
n Naturwissenschaften (Biologie, Chemie, Physik). Naturwissenschaften sind furchtbar.

R&W 2.2
LLS 5.3, 5.4, 5.5

Think
Before students do ex. 2, point out the reading tips: identify words that are similar to English, make sensible predictions, use the Glossary to check any words that you can't work out.

AT 3.1

2 Was passt zusammen?
Students apply the reading tips to help them match the English adjectives to their German equivalents.

Answers: interessant – interesting; einfach – easy; fantastisch – fantastic; gut – good; prima – great; super – super; langweilig – boring; schwer – difficult; furchtbar – awful; doof – stupid

AT 1.1–2
L&S 1.3

3 Hör noch einmal zu (a–n). Positiv oder negativ?
Play the ex. 1 recording again. Students note down whether each opinion is positive or negative. Can they work some of them out from the tone of voice? For example, compare the way the speaker says *Französisch* (upbeat) with the way she says *Latein* (gloomy-sounding).

Answers: **Positiv:** *a, b, d, e, f, i, j, k, l, m;* **Negativ:** *c, g, h, n*

AT 2.1–2
L&S 1.3

4 Partnerarbeit.
Students say what they think of the school subjects. They take turns to point to the subjects in ex. 1; their partner responds by giving his / her opinion, e.g.
A: points to art.
B: *Kunst ist prima!*
Encourage them to speak with appropriate intonation, depending on whether their opinion is positive or negative.

5 Hör zu und wiederhole: ö.
Students practise pronunciation of the ö sound.

🎧 **CD 1, track 51** — Seite 42, Übung 5

Ich höre zwölf Schildkröten auf Französisch – schön!

AT 1.3
AT 3.3

6 Hör zu und lies.
Students read and listen to Kathi's text in which she gives her opinions of school subjects.

🎧 **CD 1, track 52** — Seite 43, Übung 6

Ich finde Erdkunde sehr langweilig. Ja, Erdkunde ist schlecht! Ich mag Deutsch. Deutsch ist prima! Mein Lieblingsfach ist Mathe. Mathe ist super! Aber Sport … Sport ist furchtbar! Und ich finde Biologie nicht gut.

Think
Students identify in Kathi's text and in the key language box three ways to say they like a subject (*Ich finde … toll, Ich mag …, Mein Lieblingsfach ist …*) and how to say they don't like a subject (*Ich finde … nicht toll, Ich mag … nicht*).

AT 1.3
L&S 1.1, 1.2

7 Hör zu. Mach Notizen.
A group of teenagers are doing a survey on opinions of school subjects. Students copy out the grid and note down (in English) the subjects, likes and dislikes, and opinions.
If appropriate, tackle this activity in three stages: on the first listening, students fill in the subjects column; on the second listening, they focus on whether each person likes (✓) or dislikes (✗) the subject; finally, they note the comments and opinions.

66

1B.2 Meine Schule

Answers: **a** David: history, ✗, boring; **b** Bianca: IT, ✓, super / interesting; **c** Jens: Spanish, ✗, teacher is awful; **d** Jana: art, ✓, teacher is very nice; **e** Thomas: biology, ✗, very difficult; **f** Suse: PE, ✓, she's very sporty / it's her favourite subject

CD 1, track 53 — Seite 43, Übung 7

- Ich mache eine Umfrage: „Was ist dein Lieblingsfach?"
- Okay! Super!
- David, wie findest du Geschichte?
- Ich mag Geschichte nicht – Geschichte ist langweilig.
- Und du, Bianca – magst du Informatik?
- Ja, ich finde Informatik super. Informatik ist interessant.
- Jens, wie findest du Spanisch?
- Ich mag Spanisch nicht. Der Lehrer ist furchtbar.
- Magst du Kunst, Jana?
- Ja, ich finde Kunst prima. Die Lehrerin ist sehr nett.
- Thomas, wie findest du Biologie?
- Ich mag Biologie nicht. Biologie ist sehr schwer.
- Und du, Suse? Magst du Sport?
- Ja, ich mag Sport – ich bin sehr sportlich! Mein Lieblingsfach ist Sport.

Follow-up

AT 1.3–4
L&S 1.1, 1.2, 1.3

Play the first few scenes of the video clip again, in which Kathi, Nina, Nico and Ali discuss school subjects. Provide the following questions for students to focus on, and ask them to use facial expressions and tone of voice to help them understand the comments and opinions.

Conversation 1 between Nina and Kathi:
1. What are the three subjects mentioned?
2. What (according to Nina) is Nico's opinion of these subjects?
3. What does Kathi think of two of these subjects?

Conversation 1 between Nico and Ali:
4. What does Nico say about geography and PE?
5. What subjects does Ali mention?

Conversation 2 between Nina and Kathi:
6. What does Kathi think of PE?

And finally:
7. Explain the two mistakes made by Nina.

Answers: **1** maths, geography, PE; **2** maths – great, geography – doesn't like it, PE – doesn't like it; **3** maths – favourite subject, geography – boring; **4** geography – interesting, PE – favourite subject; **5** maths, physics, Latin, English, history, German; **6** she hates it; **7** Nina thinks Nico doesn't like geography and PE, but Nico says geography is interesting and PE is his favourite subject

Video clip 1B (excerpt)

(Kathi and Nina on the way to school)
Kathi: Also, was mag er denn?
Nina: Wer?
Kathi: Boris Becker! Nein. Wer wohl?
Nina: Ach so, Nico … ja … keine Ahnung … also … er mag Mathe … ja, er findet Mathe ganz toll!
Kathi: Super! Ich mag Mathe auch! Das ist mein Lieblingsfach. Und was noch?
Nina: Ähm … er mag Erdkunde überhaupt nicht.
Kathi: Hey! Ich hasse Erdkunde auch! Ich finde es langweilig. Langweilig und … was ist ein anderes Wort für langweilig?
Nina: Ja, finde ich auch!
Kathi: Und welche Fächer mag er noch nicht?
Nina: Sport mag er auch überhaupt nicht.

(Nico and Ali outside school)
Nico: Weißt du, eigentlich finde ich Erdkunde sehr interessant. Und du?
Ali: Natürlich! Ich finde alle meine Schulfächer interessant.
Nico: Na klar!
Ali: Mathe und Physik sind total interessant … und Latein und Englisch finde ich auch klasse … und natürlich Geschichte … und Deutsch mag ich sehr, aber …
Nico: Stop! Halt! Wann haben wir eigentlich Sport?
Ali: Um zwölf.
Nico: Super, Sport ist mein Lieblingsfach!
Ali: Echt?
Nico: Ja!

(Kathi and Nina still on the way to school)
Kathi: Ich hasse Sport auch! Ich finde es furchtbar. Bälle, Bälle, Bälle … groß, klein – immer dasselbe!
Nina: Verstehe. Sportlich bist du nicht: nett und elegant, aber nicht sportlich …

8 Umfrage: Schulfächer.

AT 2.2–3
L&S 1.4

Students carry out a survey to find out the favourite and least liked subject in the class. A model question-and-answer sequence is provided. Ask them to note down the responses in a grid, as in ex. 7.
You may wish to return to these results later to compare the preferences of boys and girls: see *Follow-up* activities in the teaching notes for *Lesen 1B*.

67

1B.3 Meine Schule

AT 4.2–3
R&W 2.3, 2.4, 2.5

Challenge
Using the text provided as a model, students explain in writing what their favourite subject is and which subjects they like and dislike. Look at the model and ask students to identify the variety of structures used to express likes, dislikes and opinions, plus one example of a rhetorical question (*Und was ist mein Lieblingsfach?*). Point out that features like this help to make the text more interesting and appealing.
Show students how to use the model text as a framework for their writing by displaying a copy of it and using different colours to highlight what can be reused and adapted.
For a variation, see the third homework suggestion in the *Planner* above.

1B.3 Wie spät ist es? Seite 44–45

Planner

Objectives
- Vocabulary: ask and say what time it is; ask and say when you have different subjects
- Grammar: *ich habe, du hast, er / sie hat, wir haben*
- Skills: use question words; use existing knowledge to work out new language

Resources
- Student Book, pages 44–45
- CD 1, tracks 54–57
- Foundation and Higher Workbooks, page 26
- Workbook audio: CD 3 and 4, track 43
- Copymaster 27 (ex. 2)
- Interactive OxBox, Unit 1B

Key language
Wie spät ist es? Es ist neun Uhr. Es ist halb neun. Es ist Viertel vor neun. Es ist Viertel nach neun. Es ist Mittag. Es ist Mitternacht.
Wann haben wir Deutsch? Um wie viel Uhr haben wir Englisch? Um wie viel Uhr beginnt Mathe? Wir haben um zehn Uhr Sport. Kunst beginnt um halb zwölf.

Framework references
R&W 2.4; IU 3.1; KAL 4.3, 4.5, 4.6; LLS 5.4

Starters
- Copymaster 27, ex. 2.
- Before beginning work on telling the time, revise numbers by counting forwards and backwards around the class. See also number games and counting games suggested in the *Planner* for spread 0.2.
- Using a clock face with movable hands (either a real one or a clock displayed on the interactive whiteboard or OHP), say some times in German and invite students to come out and set the clock hands to the corresponding time. Alternatively, set the times yourself and ask *Wie spät ist es?* Or students could do a similar activity in pairs, drawing simple clock faces for each other and taking turns to say the corresponding times.

Plenaries
- Invite a volunteer to set the time on your clock (see second starter), keeping it hidden from the class. He or she provides a clue, e.g. the time is between 9 a.m. and midday, or it's between midday and the end of afternoon school. Students take turns to guess the time. Whoever guesses correctly comes out and sets the clock to a new time, and so on. This activity is very effective in helping students to memorise the time phrases because they inevitably have to say lots of times before guessing the correct one.
- Student Book page 45, ex. 8 and / or *Challenge*.

Homework
- Students write out in full the times shown on the watches in ex. 2–3.
- Pairs work together to write a dialogue between two students at the beginning of the school day. Tell them to include: subjects, times, opinions, a reference to school equipment, and at least two different forms of the verb *haben*, e.g.
A: *Wie spät ist es?*
B: *Es ist Viertel vor neun.*
A: *Oh nein! Mathe beginnt um neun Uhr. Ich finde Mathe schwer … und ich habe keinen Taschenrechner!*
B: *Wann haben wir Sport? …*
Invite them to perform their dialogue to the class in a following lesson. To encourage the class to remain focused, ask them to note down the subjects, times, opinions, etc.

1B.3 Meine Schule

AT 1.2
AT 3.2
LLS 5.4

1 Hör zu und lies.
Students read and listen to three short exchanges between Nico and Ali. These provide a model for asking and saying the time and show use of *wir haben* (which is formally introduced on page 45).
Read through the *Wie spät ist es?* panel and compare German *halb neun* with English "half past eight". Ask students if they notice something familiar about *Viertel*: if they identify the word *vier*, they may be able to deduce "a fourth" and then "quarter".

CD 1, track 54 Seite 44, Übung 1

a – Wie spät ist es?
   – Viertel vor acht.
b – Es ist zehn Uhr.
   – Zehn Uhr? Oh nein – wir haben Mathe …
c – Es ist halb eins.
   – Super – wir haben Sport!

AT 1.1–2

2 Hör zu (1–6). Was passt zusammen?
Students listen to the times and choose a watch to correspond with each one.

Answers: **1** d; **2** b; **3** e; **4** c; **5** f; **6** a

CD 1, track 55 Seite 44, Übung 2

1 Es ist Viertel vor sechs.
2 Es ist halb elf.
3 Es ist Viertel nach zwölf.
4 Es ist sieben Uhr.
5 Es ist neun Uhr.
6 Es ist Viertel nach zwei.

AT 2.1–2

3 Wähle die richtige Uhrzeit.
Students take turns to say a time from the watches (a–f); their partner responds by pointing to the corresponding watch, e.g.
A: *Es ist Viertel vor sechs.*
B: points to watch d.

AT 1.2
AT 3.2
KAL 4.6

4 Hör zu und lies.
Students read and listen to the conversation between Nico and Ali about their school timetable. This dialogue introduces how to ask and say what time something happens using *wir haben* (*Um wie viel Uhr haben wir …? Wann haben wir …? Um …*).
Remind students of their list of question forms begun on spread 1B.1 (see the teaching notes for *Think* on page 64 of this book): they can now add *Um wie viel Uhr* to their list.

CD 1, track 56 Seite 45, Übung 4

– Um wie viel Uhr haben wir Informatik?
– Um Viertel vor neun.
– Und wann haben wir Erdkunde?
– Um elf.
– Und Geschichte – wann haben wir Geschichte?
– Um Viertel vor eins.
– Und um wie viel Uhr haben wir Französisch?
– Um halb zwei.

LLS 5.4

Think
Students already know that *ich habe* means "I have". They use this knowledge to work out the meaning of *wir haben*.

AT 3.2

5 Schreib die Uhrzeiten für Nico auf.
Referring to the dialogue in ex. 4, students note down the times of Nico's subjects.

Answers: Informatik: 8.45; Erdkunde: 11.00; Geschichte: 12.45; Französisch: 1.30

KAL 4.3, 4.5

6 Füll die Lücken aus.
After reading through the *Grammatik* information on *ich habe, du hast, er / sie hat* and *wir haben*, students copy and complete the sentences using the correct forms of the verb *haben*.

Answers: **a** haben; **b** habe; **c** hast; **d** hat

AT 1.2–3
IU 3.1

7 Hör zu. Richtig oder falsch?
Kathi is updating her school timetable. Students listen as she talks through the subjects and times. They work out whether sentences a–f are true or false. As an extra challenge, ask them to correct the false times.
Point out that Kathi's first subject begins at 8 a.m. Explain that the school day generally begins earlier in Germany than in the UK but may finish around lunchtime or early afternoon (although all-day schools are becoming more widespread).

Answers: **a** richtig; **b** falsch (8.45); **c** falsch (10.00); **d** richtig; **e** richtig; **f** falsch (1.30)

1B.4 Meine Schule

🎧 **CD 1, track 57** Seite 45, Übung 7

So, und jetzt der Stundenplan für morgen. Also: Wann haben wir Mathe? Um acht Uhr … Und wann haben wir Französisch? Um Viertel nach neun – nein, um Viertel vor neun … Und Deutsch – um wie viel Uhr haben wir Deutsch? Um zehn Uhr … So, und um wie viel Uhr haben wir Sport? Um halb elf – ach nein, um elf Uhr … Und wann haben wir Geschichte? Um Viertel nach zwölf … Und Religion – um wie viel Uhr haben wir Religion? Um halb zwei …

AT 2.2 **8** 👥 **Wann haben wir …?**
Referring to the subjects and times (a–e), students practise asking and saying what time they have the subjects, e.g.
A: *Wann haben wir Englisch?*
B: *Um ein Uhr.*

AT 4.2 **Challenge**
R&W 2.4 Students write sentences for a–e in ex. 8, explaining what time each subject begins. A model sentence is provided: *(Englisch) beginnt um (ein Uhr)*.

Answers:
a *Englisch beginnt um ein Uhr.* **b** *Erdkunde beginnt um halb zwölf.* **c** *Geschichte beginnt um Viertel nach acht.* **d** *Sport beginnt um Viertel vor elf.* **e** *Kunst beginnt um halb eins.*

1B.4 Mein Schultag   Seite 46–47

Planner

Objectives
- Vocabulary: say the days of the week; ask and say on what day you have different subjects
- Grammar: "verb second" word order
- Skills: work out meaning; identify language patterns

Resources
- Student Book, pages 46–47
- CD 1, tracks 58–60
- Foundation and Higher Workbooks, page 27
- Copymasters 27 (ex. 1), 28 (ex. 1–2), 29, 30 (ex. 4–5), 31
- Interactive OxBox, Unit 1B

Key language
Montag, Dienstag, Mittwoch, Donnerstag, Freitag, Samstag, Sonntag
Am Montag habe ich Musik.

Framework references
R&W 2.3, 2.4; IU 3.1; KAL 4.4; LLS 5.3, 5.4

Starters
- Copymaster 27, ex. 1,
- Student Book page 46, ex. 1 and the *Think* activity: students work out the days of the week and compare them with their English equivalents.
- Display all seven days of the week, out of sequence and with letters missing, e.g. Fr_ _t_ _, D_ _ns_ _g. Set a time limit for students to write them out in the correct sequence with the missing letters filled in.
- Call out a school subject; students respond by putting it into a sentence. Point out that they aren't restricted to language from this spread but can also draw on language from earlier in the unit, e.g.
Teacher: *Mathe!*
Student: *Am Montag habe ich Mathe* (or *Ich mag Mathe*, or *Mathe ist mein Lieblingsfach*, or *Wann haben wir Mathe?*, or *Mathe beginnt um elf Uhr*, etc.)

Plenaries
- Lie detectors. Working in pairs, students take turns to give their partner information about their school timetable, some of which must be true and some of which must be false. Their partner tries to detect what is a lie, e.g.
A: *Am Montag habe ich Spanisch.*
B: *Ja, richtig.*
A: *Okay, richtig. Am Dienstag habe ich Sport.*
B: *Richtig.*
A: *Falsch!*
Students win a point for each lie they detect, and a point for each lie they tell that goes undetected.
- Student Book page 47, ex. 7: *Gedächtnisspiel* in pairs.

Homework
- Students write out their own school timetable in German. They can refer to this when they do ex. 6.
- Student Book page 47, *Challenge*.

1B.4 Meine Schule

AT 3.1 / LLS 5.3, 5.4 — **1 Lies die Wörter. Wie heißen sie auf Englisch?**
Students work out the days of the week.

LLS 5.3, 5.4 — **Think**
Students deduce the meaning of *Tag* by comparing German *Montag*, *Dienstag*, etc. with English Mon*day*, Tues*day*, etc. Challenge them to suggest a literal English translation for the only day of the week that doesn't follow this *-tag* pattern (*Mittwoch* – midweek).

AT 1.1 — **2 Hör zu. Ist alles richtig?**
Students listen to check their answers to ex. 1.

🎧 CD 1, track 58 — Seite 46, Übung 2

Montag – Monday
Dienstag – Tuesday
Mittwoch – Wednesday
Donnerstag – Thursday
Freitag – Friday
Samstag – Saturday
Sonntag – Sunday

AT 1.2 / IU 3.1 — **3 Hör zu. Was passt zusammen?**
A teenager talks about his weekly school timetable. Students listen and choose a picture to correspond with each day of the week. Draw attention to sentence f (*Am Samstag …*) and point out that some schools in Germany do have lessons on Saturday mornings.

Answers: **a** 6; **b** 7; **c** 1; **d** 4; **e** 2; **f** 5; **g** 3

🎧 CD 1, track 59 — Seite 46, Übung 3

a Am Montag habe ich Musik.
b Am Dienstag habe ich Erdkunde.
c Am Mittwoch habe ich Sport.
d Am Donnerstag habe ich Kunst.
e Am Freitag habe ich Informatik.
f Am Samstag habe ich Biologie.
g Am Sonntag habe ich keine Schule!

KAL 4.4 — **Think**
Play the recording again and ask students what they notice about the position of the verb in the example sentences. Compare German *Am Montag habe ich Musik* with English "On Monday I have music".

AT 4.2 / KAL 4.4 — **4 Schreib neue Sätze.**
After reading through the *Grammatik* box on verb as second idea, students rewrite sentences a–f beginning with a time phrase.

Answers: **a** Am Freitag habe ich Sport. **b** Am Montag habe ich Englisch. **c** Am Mittwoch habe ich Kunst. **d** Am Donnerstag habe ich Französisch. **e** Am Samstag habe ich Naturwissenschaften. **f** Am Sonntag habe ich keine Schule.

AT 1.2 — **5 Hör zu. Finde die passenden Bilder.**
Students listen to six teenagers discussing their school timetable. They identify which two subjects each person has on each of the days mentioned.

Answers: **a** Katja: 2, 5; **b** Markus: 10, 6; **c** Vera: 3, 8; **d** Thorsten: 7, 12; **e** Anne: 11, 4; **f** Ralf: 1, 9

🎧 CD 1, track 60 — Seite 47, Übung 5

Vera: Katja, was hast du am Montag?
Katja: Am Montag habe ich Mathe und Musik – super!
Vera: Markus, was hast du am Dienstag?
Markus: Am Dienstag habe ich Englisch und Informatik – ja, Informatik.
Katja: Vera, was hast du am Mittwoch?
Vera: Am Mittwoch? Am Mittwoch habe ich Französisch und Sport.
Katja: Thorsten, was hast du am Donnerstag?
Thorsten: Am Donnerstag habe ich Kunst und Spanisch – langweilig!
Markus: Anne, was hast du am Freitag?
Anne: Am Freitag habe ich Geschichte und Deutsch – nein, Geschichte und Erdkunde.
Markus: Ralf, was hast du am Samstag?
Ralf: Also, am Samstag habe ich Religion und Naturwissenschaften.

AT 4.2 / R&W 2.4 / KAL 4.4 — **6 Was hast du wann? Schreib fünf Sätze.**
Students write five sentences about their own timetable, following the pattern *Am (Montag) habe ich (Deutsch)*. If students have already written out their timetable in German (see homework suggestions in the *Planner* above), they can refer to this when doing ex. 6.

AT 2.2 — **7 Gedächtnisspiel.**
Students play a memory game:
A: *Am Montag habe ich Mathe.*
B: *Am Montag habe ich Mathe und Kunst.*
A: *Am Montag habe ich Mathe, Kunst und …*

1B.5 Meine Schule

AT 4.2–3
R&W 2.3, 2.4
Challenge
Students expand their sentences from ex. 6 to include their opinion. Suggest that they also include some times, e.g. *Am Montag habe ich Deutsch. Fantastisch! Deutsch beginnt um zehn Uhr. Ich finde Deutsch sehr interessant!*

Afterwards, ask students to compare the texts they've written for ex. 6 and *Challenge*. Point out that the addition of adjectives and opinions adds interest to the text and gives it more impact.

1B.5 Ninas Videoblog
Seite 48–49

Planner

Objectives
- Vocabulary: talk about school subjects and times
- Grammar: "verb second" word order
- Skills: work out meaning from context; recognise the importance of high-frequency words

Video
- Video blog 1B

Resources
- Student Book, pages 48–49
- CD 1, tracks 61–62
- Foundation and Higher Workbooks, page 28
- Workbook audio: CD 3 and 4, track 44
- Interactive OxBox, Unit 1B

Key language
Am Montag habe ich Deutsch.
Um zehn Uhr haben wir Pause / Mittagspause.
Medienwissenschaften, Turnen, Kochen

Framework references
L&S 1.2; R&W 2.3, 2.4; KAL 4.2, 4.4; LLS 5.4, 5.7

Starters
- Before watching Nina's video blog, give students a few minutes to read through the multiple-choice answers in ex. 1 to make sure they understand the language. Three new words come up in e–f and on the video blog: *Medienwissenschaften*, *Turnen* and *Kochen*. Students may be able to work out *Kochen* (sounds like "cooking") and *Medienwissenschaften* (if they think about what *Medien* looks and sounds like), but they are unlikely to deduce *Turnen*. All three words are listed in the Unit 1B *Vokabular* list, so students can look them up. Ask them to work out the pronunciation of the words too, so that they know what to listen for. Encourage them to predict the answers to questions c, e and f, based on what they've seen of Nina so far.
- Teacher versus the class. For quick revision of times before listening to the ex. 2 recording, give students a minute to try to memorise the list of times in ex. 2, then ask them to close their books. Set a time limit and challenge the class to tell you all the times listed, in German and in English. They win a point for each correct time they say; you win a point for any times listed that they fail to say correctly within the time limit.

Plenaries
- After checking students' answers to ex. 1, challenge them to write a full sentence for each of a–f. (*Es ist Dienstag. Es ist sieben Uhr. Mein Lieblingsfach ist Italienisch. Italienisch beginnt um Viertel vor neun. Ich mag Medienwissenschaften und Turnen. Ich mag Latein und Kochen nicht.*)
- In pairs, students sort the school day described in ex. 2 into chronological order, using their answers to the ex. 2 recording. They take turns to say a sentence each, e.g.
A: *Um acht Uhr haben wir Mathe.*
B: *Um Viertel vor neun haben wir Chemie.*
A: *Um halb zehn …*
- Student Book page 49, ex. 4.

Homework
- Students write their own video blog about school subjects. Refer them to the text they wrote for *Challenge* on spread 1B.4. They may be able to include some times (as in Nina's blog) but bear in mind that they have so far only been taught how to say "on the hour", "quarter past", "quarter to" and "half past", so if their timetable has lessons beginning at other times ("ten past", "twenty-five to", etc.) they won't yet know how to say these. If the appropriate technology is available, students could record their video blogs and play them back to the class.
- Students write five questions to test their partner's knowledge of Unit 1B. Encourage them to include questions about vocabulary, grammar, culture (differences between school routine in Germany and the UK) or information about the main characters from the video, and to compile a separate answer sheet. Students exchange their questions with their partner in the next lesson. Alternatively, collect in everyone's questions and use them in a class quiz.

1B.5 Meine Schule

1 Sieh dir Ninas Videoblog an. Wähle die richtige Antwort.

See the *Planner* above for a starter activity to help students prepare for Nina's video blog and work out new language (*Turnen*, *Kochen* and *Medienwissenschaften*) in the multiple-choice options. After doing the starter, students watch the video and choose the correct option (1 or 2) in answer to each question.

Answers: **a** 1; **b** 2; **c** 2; **d** 2; **e** 2; **f** 1

Video blog 1B
CD 1, track 61   Seite 48, Übung 1

Es ist Dienstag und es ist sieben Uhr. Um acht haben wir Latein. Ich mag Latein nicht – Latein ist schwer. Um Viertel vor neun habe ich mein Lieblingsfach: Italienisch! Italienisch ist sehr interessant. Um Viertel vor elf haben wir Medienwissenschaften – super! Der Lehrer ist sehr gut. Um halb zwölf haben wir Turnen. Ich mag Turnen – Turnen ist prima. Um Viertel vor eins haben wir Kochen. Ich finde Kochen langweilig!
Und du? Welche Fächer hast du heute? Und was ist dein Lieblingsfach?

Think

Students are prompted to consider the difference between *es ist* zehn Uhr (*it is* ten o'clock) and *um* zehn Uhr (*at* ten o'clock). They should remember *um* + times from spread 1B.3; but if not, they should be able to use context to work it out.
Point out that although it is important to know topic words (like *Geschichte*, *Latein*, etc.), it is equally important to know the meaning of high-frequency words like *um* and *es ist* because they do affect meaning. Explain that these little words can be used in any context so they are likely to come up more frequently than topic-specific words.

2 Hör zu (1–9). Was passt zusammen?

Students listen to a boy talking about his school timetable. They match each of his statements (1–9) to a time and a subject (a–i).

Answers: **1** 8:00 d; **2** 8:45 i; **3** 9:30 e; **4** 10:00 g; **5** 10:45 c; **6** 11:30 a; **7** 12:15 h; **8** 13:00 b; **9** 13:45 f

CD 1, track 62   Seite 49, Übung 2

1 Um acht Uhr haben wir Mathe.
2 Um Viertel vor neun haben wir Chemie.
3 Um halb zehn haben wir Pause.
4 Um zehn Uhr haben wir Latein.
5 Um Viertel vor elf haben wir Kunst.
6 Um halb zwölf haben wir Italienisch.
7 Um Viertel nach zwölf haben wir Mittagspause.
8 Um ein Uhr haben wir Sport.
9 Um Viertel vor zwei haben wir Musik.

3 Was haben wir?

Before students begin this activity, point out the reminder of "verb second" word order in the *Grammatik* box. Students then ask and answer questions about the school timetable shown, e.g.
A: *Was haben wir um halb zehn?*
B: *Um halb zehn haben wir Pause.*

4 Schreib neue Sätze.

Students rewrite each sentence beginning with a time phrase.

Answers: **a** Um zehn Uhr haben wir Sport. **b** Um halb zwölf haben wir Musik. **c** Um ein Uhr haben wir Italienisch. **d** Um halb elf haben wir Kunst. **e** Um zwölf Uhr haben wir Pause.

Challenge

Supported by the language grid, students write sentences as in ex. 4 to describe their school timetable for one day. Remind them to use adjectives and opinions for interest and emotional effect, otherwise their text will lack impact because it will just be a list of subjects and days of the week. See also the first homework suggestion in the *Planner* above.

73

1B.6 Meine Schule

1B.6 Sprachlabor
Seite 50–51

Planner

Objectives
- Grammar: *der / die / das*; *wir + haben*; "verb second" word order
- Skills: work out the meaning of unknown words; pronounce the ö sound

Resources
- Student Book, pages 50–51
- CD 1, track 63
- Foundation and Higher Workbooks, pages 29–30
- Copymasters 33, 34
- Interactive OxBox, Unit 1B

Framework references
R&W 2.2; KAL 4.1, 4.3, 4.4, 4.5; LLS 5.3, 5.4, 5.5

Der, die, das

KAL 4.3 **1 Choose the correct articles.**

Answers: **a** der; **b** der; **c** das; **d** die; **e** der; **f** die

KAL 4.3 / LLS 5.5 **2 Find the articles for these words (*der / die / das*) in a dictionary.**

Answers: **a** die; **b** der; **c** die; **d** der; **e** das; **f** die

Wir + haben

KAL 4.3, 4.5 **3 Translate the sentences into German.**

Answers: **a** Du hast Französisch. **b** Sie hat Englisch. **c** Wir haben Geschichte. **d** Ich habe Musik. **e** Er hat Mathe. **f** Wir haben Erdkunde.

Word order

KAL 4.4 **4 Write new sentences.**

Answers: **a** Am Montag haben wir Sport. **b** Am Freitag haben wir Informatik. **c** Am Donnerstag haben wir Spanisch. **d** Am Mittwoch haben wir Englisch. **e** Am Samstag haben wir Kunst. **f** Am Dienstag haben wir Biologie.

Guessing the meaning of unknown words

R&W 2.2 / LLS 5.3, 5.4 This section presents various reading strategies to help students cope with unfamiliar language: identify words that look similar to English words; deduce meaning from context; use the component parts of a compound word to work out the meaning of the whole word; use visuals and headings as clues.

5 What English words do the underlined ones resemble?

Answers: **a** rucksack; **b** Danish; **c** telephone

6 What do the underlined words mean?

Answers: **a** big; **b** free; **c** brightly coloured, multicoloured

7 Can you work out what each whole word means?
Point out the colour-coding: green for the neuter part of the compound noun, pink for the feminine part. Explain that a compound noun always takes the gender of its final element, e.g. *Schulkind* and *Musikzimmer* are neuter, *Englischlehrerin* is feminine.

Answers: **a** schoolchild; **b** music room; **c** English teacher (female)

Pronunciation of the ö sound

KAL 4.1 **8 Listen and note how many ö sounds you can hear. (1–9)**

🎧 **CD 1, track 63**   Seite 51, Übung 8

– ö … ö … ö
1 Österreich
2 Zoo
3 Ordner
4 Löwe
5 Französisch
6 schon
7 schön
8 doof
9 Schildkröte

1B.7 Meine Schule

1B.7 Extra Star — Seite 52

Planner

Objectives
- Vocabulary: know the words for school subjects, equipment and times
- Grammar: "verb second" word order
- Skills: practise common spellings; use visuals as clues to work out meaning

Resources
- Student Book, page 52
- Copymaster 35

AT 3.1 **1 Find eight school subjects.**
Students solve the word snake.

Answers: Deutsch, Mathe, Informatik, Geschichte, Kunst, Englisch, Erdkunde, Französisch

AT 4.1 **2 Fill in the gaps.**
Students fill in the missing letters to find five items of school equipment.

Answers: a ein Heft; b ein Lineal; c ein Bleistift; d ein Füller; e ein Buch

AT 3.2 **3 Match each time (a–f) with a picture (1–6).**

Answers: a 5; b 6; c 2; d 3; e 4; f 1

AT 4.2 **4 Unscramble the word order in these sentences.**
Students rewrite the sentences using "verb second" word order.

Answers: a Am Montag habe ich Spanisch. b Am Freitag habe ich Sport. c Am Dienstag habe ich Kunst. d Am Samstag habe ich Geschichte. e Am Donnerstag habe ich Religion. f Am Mittwoch habe ich Informatik.

1B.7 Extra Plus — Seite 53

Planner

Objectives
- Vocabulary: talk about school subjects and timetables; give opinions
- Grammar: "verb second" word order
- Skills: adapt a text

Resources
- Student Book, page 53
- Copymaster 36

AT 4.1 **1 Schreib die Schulfächer auf.**
Students write the school subject represented by each picture.

Answers: a Deutsch; b Mathe; c Englisch; d Geschichte; e Naturwissenschaften; f Erdkunde

AT 4.2 **2 Schreib die richtige Zeit auf.**
Students write the time shown on each watch.

Answers: a Es ist zehn Uhr. b Es ist Viertel nach zwölf. c Es ist halb zehn. d Es ist Viertel vor elf. e Es ist zwei Uhr.

AT 3.3 **3 Lies. Welches Bild passt?**
Students read about a girl's timetable and her opinion of school subjects. They work out which set of pictures (a or b) corresponds with the text.

Answer: b

AT 4.3 **4 Schreib Sätze für das andere Bild.**
Students write a text to describe the other set of pictures (set a). Suggest that they adapt the paragraph in ex. 3, but that they expand and vary it where possible, e.g. by adding more opinions and using different word order.

Example answer: Am Montag habe ich Deutsch, Mathe und Kunst. Um acht Uhr habe ich Deutsch und um Viertel nach neun habe ich Mathe. Ich mag Deutsch. Deutsch ist mein Lieblingsfach. Ich mag Mathe nicht. Ich finde Mathe schwer. Um halb elf habe ich Kunst. Ich mag Kunst. Kunst ist prima und der Lehrer ist nett. Und um zehn Uhr habe ich Erdkunde. Ich mag Erdkunde nicht. Ich finde Erdkunde langweilig.

1B.8 Meine Schule

1B.8 Testseite

Seite 54

Planner

Resources
- Student Book, page 54
- CD 1, track 64
- Foundation and Higher workbooks, page 31
- Copymasters 25, 26
- Assessment, Unit 1B

AT 1.2–3

1 Listen (a–f) and match the pictures to the words. Listen again and choose ✓ or ✗ for each.
Students hear six statements about school subjects and times. On the first listening, they identify which subject corresponds with each day of the week. On the second listening, they indicate whether the opinion of each subject is positive or negative. As an extra challenge, ask students to note the opinion adjectives.

Answers: **a** 6 ✗; **b** 2 ✓; **c** 1 ✓; **d** 5 ✗; **e** 3 ✓; **f** 4 ✓

🎧 **CD 1, track 64**   Seite 54, Übung 1

a Am Montag haben wir Erdkunde. Erdkunde ist langweilig.
b Am Dienstag haben wir Spanisch. Ich finde Spanisch super.
c Am Mittwoch haben wir Mathe. Ich mag Mathe!
d Am Donnerstag haben wir Englisch. Englisch ist nicht gut.
e Am Freitag haben wir Geschichte. Ich finde Geschichte interessant.
f Am Samstag haben wir Deutsch. Deutsch ist prima!

AT 2.2

2 Say the following times.

Answers: **1** Es ist acht Uhr. **2** Es ist halb elf. **3** Es ist ein Uhr. **4** Es ist Viertel nach elf. **5** Es ist halb eins. **6** Es ist Viertel vor zehn.

AT 3.3

3 Read Andi's message and write down the answers in English.

Answers: **a** biology, German, art, RE and French; **b** biology 8.45, German 9.30, art 10.45, RE 11.30, French 1.00; **c** biology is his favourite subject, he finds German boring, he likes art / it's great, he finds RE very interesting, he finds French difficult and the teacher isn't nice

AT 4.2–3

4 Answer these questions for yourself.
Students answer questions about school, including: favourite subject, what they think of English and maths, what subject they have today at 9.30, one subject they have on Tuesdays, two things they have in their school bag.

1B.8 Meine Schule

1B Lesen
Seite 154

> **Planner**
>
> **Resources**
> - Student Book, page 154
>
> **Framework references**
> R&W 2.1, 2.2; IU 3.1, 3.2

Lieblingsfächer in Deutschland

AT 3.1 **1 Look at the survey results above. Are these sentences true or false?**
Students look at the statistics about favourite school subjects in Germany. They work out whether the statements in English are true or false.

Answers: **a** *false;* **b** *true;* **c** *true;* **d** *false*

AT 3.2–3 **2 Match speech bubbles a–d to the school bags 1–4.**
Students read texts a–d about favourite subjects. They find an appropriate school bag for each person.

Answers: **a** *2;* **b** *4;* **c** *3;* **d** *1*

Follow-up
- Refer students to the class survey they did on spread 1B.2 (ex. 8) and ask them to sort the results by gender. Which subjects are preferred by boys and which by girls? How does this compare with the German results?
- Students draw (or use photos of) their own school bag or ideal school bag and write a few sentences about their favourite subject, as in ex. 2.
- Students choose a favourite musician, sports personality, actor or other celebrity and imagine what their favourite subject might have been when they were at school. They draw a school bag for them and write a few sentences (as in ex. 2) explaining what their favourite subject is.
- If you have a partner school in a German-speaking country, this is a good opportunity to compare school routine, e.g. which subjects are studied in each school, typical weekly timetable, amount of homework, clothes worn to school, after-school clubs, etc.

1B Meine Schule

Foundation Workbook

1B.1 Mein Klassenzimmer (Seite 24)

AT 3.1–2 **1 Fill the gaps with a question word or article from the box below.**

Answers: **a** Wer, die; **b** Was, die; **c** Was, der; **d** Wer, der; **e** Wer, der; **f** Was, der

AT 1.1–2 **2 What do these people have? Put a tick or a cross.**

Answers: **a** pencil ✓, ruler ✗; **b** ink pen ✓, exercise book ✗; **c** textbook ✓, calculator ✗; **d** school bag ✓, file ✗

CD 3, track 41 — Seite 24, Übung 2

a Ich habe einen Bleistift, aber kein Lineal.
b Ich habe einen Füller, aber kein Heft.
c Ich habe ein Buch, aber keinen Taschenrechner.
d Ich habe eine Schultasche, aber keinen Ordner.

1B.2 Schulfächer (Seite 25)

AT 4.1 **1 Fill in the crossword with school subjects.**

Answers: <u>Waagerecht</u>: **1** Spanisch; **5** Mathe; **6** Biologie; **10** Musik; **11** Chemie; **12** Erdkunde; <u>Senkrecht</u>: **1** Sport; **2** Informatik; **3** Latein; **4** Deutsch; **7** Geschichte; **8** Kunst; **9** Physik

AT 1.2 **2 Listen and decide what these people think of the subjects. Answer in English.**

Answers: **a** super, stupid; **b** great, interesting; **c** super, stupid; **d** boring, great

CD 3, track 42 — Seite 25, Übung 2

a Spanisch ist super, aber Französisch ist doof.
b Informatik ist prima und Mathe ist interessant.
c Kunst ist super, aber Erdkunde ist doof.
d Englisch ist langweilig, aber Sport ist prima.

1B.3 Wie spät ist es? (Seite 26)

AT 3.1 **1 Draw lines to link the times to the clocks.**

Answers: 12.15 Viertel nach zwölf; 15.45 Viertel vor vier; 06.00 sechs Uhr; 09.15 Viertel nach neun; 11.45 Viertel vor zwölf; 16.15 Viertel nach vier; 00.00 Mitternacht; 08.45 Viertel vor neun

AT 1.2 **2 Listen and fill in the gaps in the timetable to show when each lesson starts.**

Answers: **1** 8.15 art; **2** 9.00 maths; **3** 9.45 English; **4** 11.15 French; **5** 12.30 ICT; **6** 14.15 sport

CD 3, track 43 — Seite 26, Übung 2

– Wann haben wir Kunst?
– Um Viertel nach acht.
– Wann haben wir Mathe?
– Um neun Uhr.
– Wann haben wir Englisch?
– Um Viertel vor zehn.
– Um wie viel Uhr haben wir Französisch?
– Um Viertel nach elf.
– Um wie viel Uhr haben wir Informatik?
– Um halb eins.
– Um wie viel Uhr haben wir Sport?
– Um Viertel nach zwei.

1B.4 Mein Schultag (Seite 27)

AT 3.1 **1 Find the German words for the days of the week in this grid (across, down or diagonally).**

Answers:

		S	A	M	S	T	A	G		
D			I		G					
O			T	A						
N			T							
N		N	W					G		
E		N	M	O	N	T	A	G	A	
R	O		C				T			
S			H		I					
T			D	I	E	N	S	T	A	G
A				R						
G			F							

AT 4.2 **2 Unjumble these sentences to say what subjects these people have on which day.**

Answers: (the subjects in each sentence can be in any order) **a** Am Donnerstag habe ich Musik und Mathe. **b** Am Montag habe ich Erdkunde und Spanisch. **c** Am Freitag habe ich Kunst und Biologie. **d** Am Dienstag habe ich Latein und Englisch. **e** Am Mittwoch habe ich Informatik und Deutsch.

1B.5 Ninas Videoblog (Seite 28)

AT 4.1 **1 Fill in this timetable in German for Monday, Tuesday and Wednesday. There may be some double lessons.**

Answers: see ex. 2

AT 1.2 **2 Now listen and fill in the lessons for Thursday and Friday.**

1B Meine Schule

Answers:

	Montag	Dienstag	Mittwoch	Donnerstag	Freitag
08.45	Religion	Mathe	Italienisch	Informatik	Musik
10.00	Geschichte	Mathe	Italienisch	Deutsch	Mathe
10.45	Kunst	Erdkunde	Chemie	Deutsch	Latein
11.30	Biologie	Deutsch	Französisch	Geschichte	Religion
12.15	Spanisch	Informatik	Englisch	Physik	Sport
13.00	Sport	Französisch	Englisch	Geschichte	Sport

CD 3, track 44 Seite 28, Übung 2

- Am Donnerstag um Viertel vor neun haben wir Informatik.
- Am Freitag um zehn Uhr habe ich Mathe.
- Am Donnerstag um halb zwölf habe ich Geschichte.
- Am Freitag um Viertel nach zwölf haben wir Sport.
- Am Donnerstag um zehn Uhr habe ich Deutsch.
- Am Donnerstag um ein Uhr haben wir Geschichte.
- Am Freitag um Viertel vor neun habe ich Musik.
- Am Donnerstag um Viertel nach zwölf haben wir Physik.
- Am Freitag um Viertel vor elf haben wir Latein.
- Am Freitag um halb zwölf habe ich Religion.

1B.6A Sprachlabor (Seite 29)

1 Write in the correct word for 'the' for these words. The gender is given in brackets.

Answers: der Stuhl, der Lehrer, das Heft, der Direktor, der Schreibtisch, die Lehrerin, die Schülerin, die Bibliothek, das Klassenzimmer, die Tafel, der Schüler, der Schulhof

2 Use the correct form of *haben* in these sentences.

Answers: **a** habe; **b** hat; **c** haben; **d** hast; **e** haben; **f** habe

3 Write sentences based on the clues. Use the *wir* form.

Answers: **a** Am Dienstag haben wir Mathe. **b** Am Montag haben wir Informatik. **c** Am Freitag haben wir Kunst. **d** Am Mittwoch haben wir Musik. **e** Am Donnerstag haben wir Deutsch.

1B.6B Think (Seite 30)

1 Use the clues to help you find the words. Write the words in English and German.

Answers: **a** calculator – Taschenrechner; **b** file – Ordner; **c** desk – Schreibtisch; **d** fountain pen – Füller; **e** geography – Erdkunde; **f** chair – Stuhl; **g** midnight – Mitternacht; **h** Wednesday – Mittwoch; **i** ICT – Informatik; **j** ruler – Lineal

2 Circle any word that you can immediately recognise because it is so similar to an English word. If there are any borderline cases, discuss them with others in the class.

Answers: <u>Obvious</u>: Englisch, fantastisch, interessant, Latein, super, Spanisch, Sport, Mathe, Musik; <u>Borderline</u>: Stuhl

3 These are all words you have come across in this unit. Can you remember how to pronounce them? Say them out loud.

Students practise the *o* sound.

1B Meine Schule

Higher Workbook

1B.1 Mein Klassenzimmer (Seite 24)

AT 4.1–2 · 1 Fill the gaps with a question word, an article and a noun from the box.

Answers: **a** *Wer, die Schülerin;* **b** *Was, die Tafel;* **c** *Was, der Schreibtisch;* **d** *Wer, der Lehrer;* **e** *Wer, der Schüler;* **f** *Was, der Stuhl*

AT 1.1–2 · 2 What do these people have? Put a tick or a cross.

Answers: **a** *pencil ✓, ruler ✗;* **b** *ink pen ✓, exercise book ✗;* **c** *textbook ✓, calculator ✗;* **d** *school bag ✓, file ✗*

CD 4, track 41 Seite 24, Übung 2

a Ich habe einen Bleistift, aber kein Lineal.
b Ich habe einen Füller, aber kein Heft.
c Ich habe ein Buch, aber keinen Taschenrechner.
d Ich habe eine Schultasche, aber keinen Ordner.

AT 4.2 · 3 Now write out what they say. Listen again to check.

Answers: see ex. 2 transcript

1B.2 Schulfächer (Seite 25)

AT 4.1 · 1 Solve the clues, then fill in the crossword with school subjects in German.

Answers: <u>Waagerecht</u>: **1** *Spanisch;* **5** *Mathe;* **6** *Biologie;* **10** *Musik;* **11** *Chemie;* **12** *Erdkunde;* <u>Senkrecht</u>: **1** *Sport;* **2** *Informatik;* **3** *Latein;* **4** *Deutsch;* **7** *Geschichte;* **8** *Kunst;* **9** *Physik*

AT 1.2 · 2 Listen and decide what the subjects are and what the people think of them. Answer in English.

Answers: **a** *Spanish is super, French is stupid;* **b** *ICT is great, maths is interesting;* **c** *art is super, geography is stupid;* **d** *English is boring, sport is great*

CD 4, track 42 Seite 25, Übung 2

a Spanisch ist super, aber Französisch ist doof.
b Informatik ist prima und Mathe ist interessant.
c Kunst ist super, aber Erdkunde ist doof.
d Englisch ist langweilig, aber Sport ist prima.

1B.3 Wie spät ist es? (Seite 26)

AT 1.2 · 1 Listen and fill in the gaps in the timetable to show when each lesson starts.

Answers: **1** *8.15 art;* **2** *9.00 maths;* **3** *9.45 English;* **4** *11.15 French;* **5** *12.30 ICT;* **6** *14.15 sport*

CD 4, track 43 Seite 26, Übung 1

– Wann haben wir Kunst?
– Um Viertel nach acht.
– Wann haben wir Mathe?
– Um neun Uhr.
– Wann haben wir Englisch?
– Um Viertel vor zehn.
– Um wie viel Uhr haben wir Französisch?
– Um Viertel nach elf.
– Um wie viel Uhr haben wir Informatik?
– Um halb eins.
– Um wie viel Uhr haben wir Sport?
– Um Viertel nach zwei.

AT 4.2 · 2 Write in the times next to the clocks.

Answers: 12.15 Viertel nach zwölf; 15.45 Viertel vor vier; 06.00 sechs Uhr; 09.15 Viertel nach neun; 11.45 Viertel vor zwölf; 16.15 Viertel nach vier; 00.00 Mitternacht; 08.45 Viertel vor neun

1B.4 Mein Schultag (Seite 27)

AT 3.1 · 1 Find the German words for the days of the week in this grid (across, down or diagonally).

Answers: Montag, Dienstag, Mittwoch, Donnerstag, Freitag, Samstag, Sonntag (See wordsearch grid above for Foundation Workbook 1B.4, ex. 1.)

AT 4.2 · 2 Unjumble these sentences to say what subjects these people have on which day. Then translate each sentence into English.

Answers: (the subjects in each sentence can be in any order) **a** *Am Donnerstag habe ich Musik und Mathe. (On Thursday I have music and maths.)* **b** *Am Montag habe ich Erdkunde und Spanisch. (On Monday I have geography and Spanish.)* **c** *Am Freitag habe ich Kunst und Biologie. (On Friday I have art and biology.)* **d** *Am Dienstag habe ich Latein und Englisch. (On Tuesday I have Latin and English.)* **e** *Am Mittwoch habe ich Informatik und Deutsch. (On Wednesday I have ICT and German.)*

1B.5 Ninas Videoblog (Seite 28)

AT 1.2 · 1 Listen and fill in the lessons for Thursday and Friday. There may be some double lessons.

Answers: see ex. 2

1B Meine Schule

CD 4, track 44 — Seite 28, Übung 1

- Am Donnerstag um Viertel vor neun haben wir Informatik.
- Am Freitag um zehn Uhr habe ich Mathe.
- Am Donnerstag um halb zwölf habe ich Geschichte.
- Am Freitag um Viertel nach zwölf haben wir Sport. Das ist eine Doppelstunde.
- Am Donnerstag um zehn Uhr habe ich Deutsch. Das ist auch eine Doppelstunde.
- Am Donnerstag um ein Uhr haben wir Geschichte.
- Am Freitag um Viertel vor neun habe ich Musik.
- Am Donnerstag um Viertel nach zwölf haben wir Physik.
- Am Freitag um Viertel vor elf haben wir Latein.
- Am Freitag um halb zwölf habe ich Religion.

AT 3.2 Now fill in the timetable in German for Monday, Tuesday and Wednesday using the information below. There may be some double lessons.

Answers:

	Montag	Dienstag	Mittwoch	Donnerstag	Freitag
08.45	Religion	Mathe	Italienisch	Informatik	Musik
10.00	Geschichte	Mathe	Italienisch	Deutsch	Mathe
10.45	Kunst	Erdkunde	Chemie	Deutsch	Latein
11.30	Biologie	Deutsch	Französisch	Geschichte	Religion
12.15	Spanisch	Informatik	Englisch	Physik	Sport
13.00	Sport	Französisch	Englisch	Geschichte	Sport

AT 4.2 3 Choose five subjects and write down your opinions, using *Ich finde …* and words like *prima*, *langweilig* etc.

Answers: students' own answers

1B.6A Sprachlabor (Seite 29)

1 Write in the correct word for 'the' for these words. If you don't know the gender, or can't work it out, look it up.

Answers: der Stuhl, der Lehrer, das Heft, der Direktor, der Schreibtisch, die Lehrerin, die Schülerin, die Bibliothek, das Klassenzimmer, die Tafel, der Schüler, der Schulhof

2 Insert the person and the correct form of *haben* into these sentences.

Answers: **a** habe ich; **b** hat er; **c** haben wir; **d** hast du; **e** haben wir; **f** habe ich

3 Write sentences based on the clues. Write each sentence three times, using the *ich* form, the *er* form and the *wir* form.

Answers: **a** Am Dienstag habe ich (hat er, haben wir) Mathe. **b** Am Montag habe ich (hat er, haben wir) Informatik. **c** Am Freitag habe ich (hat er, haben wir) Kunst. **d** Am Mittwoch habe ich (hat er, haben wir) Musik.

1B.6B Think (Seite 30)

1 Use the clues to help you find the words. Write the words in English and German.

Answers: **a** calculator – Taschenrechner; **b** file – Ordner; **c** desk – Schreibtisch; **d** fountain pen – Füller; **e** geography – Erdkunde; **f** chair – Stuhl; **g** midnight – Mitternacht; **h** Wednesday – Mittwoch; **i** ICT – Informatik; **j** ruler – Lineal

2 Circle any word that you can immediately recognise because it is so similar to an English word. If there are any borderline cases, discuss them with others in the class.

Answers: <u>Obvious</u>: Englisch, fantastisch, interessant, Latein, super, Spanisch, Sport, Mathe, Musik; <u>Borderline</u>: Stuhl

3 Translate these words into German, write them down and then say them out loud.
Students practise pronunciation of the *o* sound.

Answers: doof, Ordner, Montag, Sport, Sonntag, Nashorn, Religion, Wolf

81

2A Freizeit und Hobbys

Unit 2A Freizeit und Hobbys — Unit overview grid

Page reference	Objectives	Grammar	Skills and pronunciation	Key language	Framework	AT level
Pages 56–57 **2A.1 Ich spiele gern Fußball**	Say what sports and musical instruments you like and don't like playing	*Gern* and *nicht gern* Present tense of a regular verb (*spielen*)	Pronounce words which look alike in English and German	*Spielst du gern …? Ich spiele gern/nicht gern … Basketball, am Computer, Federball, Flöte, Fußball, Geige, Gitarre, Klavier, Schlagzeug, Tennis, Volleyball.*	R&W 2.1, 2.4 L&S 1.1, 1.2 KAL 4.1, 4.3, 4.5, 4.6 LLS 5.1, 5.3, 5.5	1.2, 2.2, 3.2–3, 4.2–3
Pages 58–59 **2A.2 Das mache ich am liebsten**	Say what you like and prefer doing, and what your favourite hobbies are	*Gern, lieber, am liebsten* Second and third person singular of *fahren, lesen* and *sehen* (present tense)	Focus on intonation as an aid to understanding	*Was machst du gern/lieber/am liebsten? Ich fahre gern Skateboard/Rad. Ich chatte gern im Internet. Ich gehe gern ins Kino/einkaufen. Ich lese gern. Ich sehe gern fern. Ich höre gern Musik. Ich besuche gern meine Freunde. Ich spiele gern Rugby. Ich chatte lieber im Internet. Ich fahre am liebsten Skateboard.*	L&S 1.1, 1.2, 1.3, 1.4 R&W 2.1, 2.4 KAL 4.1, 4.3, 4.5 LLS 5.4, 5.5	1.2–4, 2.2–3, 3.2–3, 4.2–3
Pages 60–61 **2A.3 Ich liebe Computerspiele**	Give opinions of different types of computer games	Extended sentences using *denn* How to say "them" (*sie*)	Use familiar language to work out the meaning of new words	*das Abenteuerspiel, das Lernspiel, das Musikspiel, das Quizspiel, das Sportspiel, das Tanzspiel cool, klasse, lustig, nützlich, schrecklich, spannend Wie findest du Quizspiele? Magst du Lernspiele? Ich finde sie gut/nicht gut/sehr gut. Ich mag sie (nicht), denn ich finde sie langweilig/denn sie sind lustig.*	L&S 1.1, 1.2, 1.4 R&W 2.1, 2.2, 2.4 KAL 4.2, 4.4 LLS 5.2, 5.3, 5.4, 5.5	1.1, 1.3, 2.2–3, 3.1–3, 4.1–3

2A Freizeit und Hobbys

Page reference	Objectives	Grammar	Skills and pronunciation	Key language	Framework	AT level
Pages 62–63 **2A.4 Wie oft machst du das?**	Say how often you do something	Word order with time expressions	Adapt previously learned language to create new expressions	am Montag/Dienstag, etc. am Morgen, am Nachmittag, am Abend, am Wochenende, einmal/zweimal/dreimal in der Woche, jeden Tag/Monat, jede Woche, jedes Jahr Ich spiele einmal in der Woche Gitarre/am Computer. Ich fahre jeden Tag Skateboard/Rad. Ich schwimme am Morgen. Ich tanze am Montag. Ich sehe am Abend fern. Ich gehe am Wochenende ins Kino/Café.	L&S 1.1, 1.2 R&W 2.4 KAL 4.2, 4.4 LLS 5.3, 5.4	1.2, 1.4, 2.2, 3.2, 4.2–3
Pages 64–65 **2A.5 Am Wochenende**	Talk about leisure activities	Expressions of time and frequency Second and third person singular of *fahren, lesen* and *sehen*	Pronounce *a* and *ä* (*ich fahre, du fährst, er/sie fährt*)	Ich mag … (nicht), denn … anstrengend, (nicht) gut, klasse, langweilig, schlecht, spannend, toll Ich spiele (gern/nicht gern) Basketball/Fußball/Tennis. Ich fahre (gern/nicht gern) Rad/Skateboard/Ski. Ich schwimme/tanze (gern/nicht gern). Ich sehe mir (gern/nicht gern) Volleyball/Rugby im Fernsehen an.	L&S 1.4 R&W 2.4 KAL 4.1, 4.3, 4.5 LLS 5.1, 5.5	2.2–3, 3.3, 4.2–4

2A Freizeit und Hobbys

Unit 2A: Week-by-week overview
(Three-year KS3 Route: assuming six weeks' work or approximately 10–12.5 hours)
(Two-year KS3 Route: assuming four weeks' work or approximately 6.5–8.5 hours)

About Unit 2A, *Freizeit und Hobbys*: In this unit, students talk about sports, musical instruments and other hobbies: they express likes, dislikes, preferences and opinions, and say how often they do particular activities. Work on sentence structure continues: students build extended sentences using *denn* and other linking words, and use correct word order with time expressions and with *gern/nicht gern/lieber/am liebsten*. They learn the full present tense conjugation of a regular verb (*spielen*) and find out about some verbs that undergo a vowel change in the second and third person singular of the present tense (*fahren, lesen, sehen*).

Learning strategies include: how to keep a record of new language to facilitate learning; tips on working out meaning when listening (intonation and body language); and adapting previously learned language to generate new language. Students also learn how to pronounce words that look similar in German and English.

Three-Year KS3 Route

Week	Resources	Objectives
1	2A.1 Ich spiele gern Fußball 2A.6 Sprachlabor ex. 1–2 and 7–8	Say what sports and musical instruments you like and don't like playing *Gern/nicht gern*; the present tense of a regular verb (*spielen*) Pronounce words which look alike in English and German
2	2A.2 Das mache ich am liebsten 2A.6 Sprachlabor ex. 3 and 4	Say what you like and prefer doing, and what your favourite hobbies are *Gern, lieber, am liebsten*; the second and third person singular of *fahren, lesen* and *sehen* (present tense) Focus on intonation as an aid to understanding
3	2A.3 Ich liebe Computerspiele 2A.6 Sprachlabor ex. 5–6	Give opinions of different types of computer games Build extended sentences using *denn*; use *sie* (them) Use familiar language to work out the meaning of new words
4	2A.4 Wie oft machst du das?	Say how often you do something Word order with time expressions Adapt previously learned language to create new expressions

Two-Year KS3 Route

Week	Resources	Objectives
1	2A.1 Ich spiele gern Fußball (*Omit Challenge*) 2A.6 Sprachlabor ex. 1–2	Say what sports and musical instruments you like and don't like playing *Gern/nicht gern*; the present tense of a regular verb (*spielen*) Pronounce words which look alike in English and German
2	2A.2 Das mache ich am liebsten 2A.6 Sprachlabor ex. 3 and 4	Say what you like and prefer doing, and what your favourite hobbies are *Gern, lieber, am liebsten*; the second and third person singular of *fahren, lesen* and *sehen* (present tense) Focus on intonation as an aid to understanding
3	2A.3 Ich liebe Computerspiele (*Omit ex. 7*) 2A.6 Sprachlabor ex. 5–6	Give opinions of different types of computer games Build extended sentences using *denn*; use *sie* (them) Use familiar language to work out the meaning of new words
4	2A.4 Wie oft machst du das? (*Omit ex. 3*) 2A.8 Vokabular 2A.8 Testseite	Say how often you do something Word order with time expressions Adapt previously learned language to create new expressions Key vocabulary and learning checklist Assessment in all four skills

2A Freizeit und Hobbys

	Three-Year KS3 Route			Two-Year KS3 Route	
Week	Resources	Objectives	Week	Resources	Objectives
5	2A.5 Am Wochenende	Talk about leisure activities Expressions of time and frequency; the second and third person singular of *fahren, lesen* and *sehen* (present tense) Pronounce *a* and *ä* correctly (*ich fahre, du fährst, er/sie fährt*)			
6	2A.7 Extra (Star/Plus) 2A.8 Vokabular 2A.8 Testseite 2A Lesen	Reinforcement and extension of the language of the unit Key vocabulary and learning checklist Assessment in all four skills Further reading to explore the language of the unit and cultural themes			

2A.1 Freizeit und Hobbys

2A.1 Ich spiele gern Fußball
Seite 56–57

Planner

Objectives
- Vocabulary: say what sports and musical instruments you like and don't like playing
- Grammar: *gern / nicht gern*; the present tense of a regular verb (*spielen*)
- Skills: pronounce words which look alike in English and German

Video
- Video clip 2A

Resources
- Student Book, pages 56–57
- CD 1, track 65
- Foundation and Higher Workbooks, page 32
- Workbook audio: CD 3 and 4, track 45
- Interactive OxBox, Unit 2A

Key language
Spielst du gern …?
Ich spiele gern / nicht gern … Basketball, am Computer, Federball, Flöte, Fußball, Geige, Gitarre, Klavier, Schlagzeug, Tennis, Volleyball

Framework references
R&W 2.1, 2.4; L&S 1.1, 1.2; KAL 4.1, 4.3, 4.5, 4.6; LLS 5.1, 5.3, 5.5

Starters
- Before beginning work on page 56, display the nouns from ex. 1–2 in three groups: sports in one group (*Fußball, Basketball, Tennis, Federball*), musical instruments in another group (*Flöte, Gitarre, Schlagzeug, Klavier, Geige*), and *am Computer* on its own. Jumble up the corresponding English words and display them alongside. Students work in pairs to: (1) match the German to the English; and (2) work out how to pronounce the words. They check their answers and pronunciation by listening to the ex. 1 recording.
- In pairs, groups or as a whole class, students draw or mime the activities from page 56 for their classmates to guess, e.g.
  A: draws a heart and guitar, or mimes playing the guitar while looking happy.
  B: *Ich spiele gern Gitarre!*

Plenaries
- For a variation on ex. 3, ask each student to secretly note down their favourite five activities from page 56; their partner asks questions to find out what they are. Who works out their partner's preferences in the fewest guesses?
  Point out that students must answer in full sentences, saying *Ich spiele gern* if it's something on their list and *Ich spiele nicht gern* if it isn't on their list, e.g.
  A: *Spielst du gern Federball?*
  B: *Ja, ich spiele gern Federball.* (or *Nein, ich spiele nicht gern Federball.*)
- Dice game in pairs to practise the conjugation of *spielen*. Display the full set of verb endings with numbers beside them, corresponding to the dots on the dice: 1 = *ich spiele*, 2 = *du spielst*, 3 = *er / sie / es spielt*, 4 = *wir spielen*, 5 = *ihr spielt*, 6 = *sie / Sie spielen*. Students take turns to roll the dice and say the corresponding part of the verb. The aim is to be the first person to say all parts of the verb.
  As students play, start erasing or concealing parts of the verb, so that they have to rely increasingly on memory. Some students may be able to play the game entirely from memory. Increase the challenge by asking them to say a full sentence instead of just the subject + verb, e.g. *Er spielt nicht gern Tennis.*

Homework
- Students choose their favourite sports personalities and musicians and write two sentences for each one: *Ich spiele gern …* (+ the sport or instrument that he / she is famous for playing), and *Ich spiele nicht gern …* (which students will probably need to invent), e.g. Andy Murray: *Ich spiele gern Tennis. Ich spiele nicht gern Geige.*
- Student Book page 57, ex. 6 and / or *Challenge*.

Video clip 2A: Ali der Große!
Synopsis:
The four teenagers are out together. Kathi and Nico are listening to music on Kathi's iPhone, sharing the same set of earphones: they seem only to have eyes for each other. Nina and Ali are starting to get bored with being around them, so they make plans to go to the cinema. However, Ali is so busy with his hobbies that it's impossible to find a day when they are both free. They decide to go straight away, leaving the two lovebirds to their own devices.

Play the video through a couple of times and ask questions to check that students understand the gist of it. Suggested focus:

2A.1 Freizeit und Hobbys

- What are Kathi and Nico talking about? (music)
- What is the building that the four teenagers stop outside? (a cinema)
- Which two film posters do we see? (Robin Hood, Prince of Persia)
- Which actor does Nina compare Ralf to? (Russell Crowe)
- What time does Ali say it is at the end of the clip? (*halb vier* – half past three)
- Who goes to see the film? (Nina and Ali)
- Challenge students to identify in the clip as many hobbies as they can: music, going to the cinema, tennis, guitar, skateboard, theatre, football, swimming, basketball, reading, singing in a band.
- Once students have been introduced to the vocabulary in ex. 1–2, play the clip again and ask them to raise their hand whenever one of the activities is mentioned.

Video clip 2A

Kathi: Oh, ich liebe dieses Lied! Es ist mein Lieblingslied … Ich singe gern … aber ich höre lieber Musik … Am liebsten treffe ich mich mit meinen Freunden … oder mit meinem Freund … Wahnsinn – wir mögen immer dieselben Sachen …

Ali: Dieser Film ist super!
Nina: Welcher?
Ali: Dieser hier mit Russell Crowe.
Nina: Oh, ja … ich finde, Ralf sieht aus wie Russell Crowe.
Ali: … Er ist so nett, so intelligent, so schön …
Nina: Hör auf!
Nina: Gut, dann … Gehen wir ins Kino?
Ali: Wir? Also, du und ich?
Nina: Ja!
Ali: Und … Ralf? Der süße, intelligente, schöne Ralf?
Nina: Der ist doch der Star, oder?
Nina: Gut, dann … gehen wir am Montag?
Ali: Nein, das geht nicht. Am Montag spiele ich Tennis.
Nina: Echt? Ralf spielt auch Tennis.
Nina: Und am Dienstag?
Ali: Nee, am Dienstag habe ich Gitarrenunterricht.
Nina: Kein Problem … Ralf spielt kein Instrument … Gut, dann Mittwoch?
Ali: Sorry, am Mittwoch kaufe ich mit meinem Vater ein neues Skateboard. Und bevor du was sagst … Ralf fährt auch Skateboard …
Nina: Ich weiß … aber am Donnerstag geht nicht. Da habe ich Theaterklub. Also muss es wohl Freitag sein.

Ali: Fußballtraining. Hey, sorry!
Nina: So viele Hobbys, Ali! Hast du noch andere Hobbys?
Ali: Ich schwimme, ich spiele gern Basketball, und natürlich lese ich auch sehr gern.
Nina: Ich lese auch gern …
Ali: Und Musik – ich singe in 'ner Band …
Nina: Du singst?
Ali: Hey Nina, warum gehen wir nicht jetzt ins Kino? Es ist halb vier. Und wir haben doch Zeit, oder?
Nina: Super Idee! … Und Kathi und Nico?
Ali / Nina: Nee.

Sprachpunkt
Ich singe gern.
Ich höre lieber Musik.
Am Montag spiele ich Tennis.
Am Dienstag habe ich Gitarrenunterricht.

AT 1.2 / KAL 4.6 — 1 Hör zu und wiederhole. (1–10)

Students listen while looking at the pictures. Pause the recording after each sentence and encourage students to repeat while focusing on the corresponding picture.
Check that they understand what the hearts represent: football + heart symbol = I like playing football, guitar + heart crossed through = I don't like playing guitar. Read through the *Grammatik* box on *gern* and *nicht gern*.

CD 1, track 65 — Seite 56, Übung 1

1 Ich spiele gern Fußball.
2 Ich spiele gern Flöte.
3 Ich spiele nicht gern Gitarre.
4 Ich spiele gern am Computer.
5 Ich spiele nicht gern Basketball.
6 Ich spiele gern Schlagzeug.
7 Ich spiele nicht gern Klavier.
8 Ich spiele nicht gern Tennis.
9 Ich spiele gern Geige.
10 Ich spiele nicht gern Federball.

KAL 4.1 / LLS 5.3 — Think

Play the ex. 1 recording again and focus on the difference between the German and English pronunciation of some of the words (*Gitarre, Computer, Basketball, Tennis*). Then look at the printed versions of the words in ex. 2 and compare the German and English spellings.

2A.2 Freizeit und Hobbys

AT 3.2 | **2 Lies die Sätze. Was passt zusammen?**
Students match sentences a–h to pictures 1–10.

Answers: **a** 4; **b** 7; **c** 1; **d** 9; **e** 2; **f** 3; **g** 10, 6; **h** 8, 5

AT 2.2 | **3 Macht Dialoge.**
Students ask each other whether they like doing the ten activities from ex. 1, using the model question-and-answer sequence provided.

AT 3.3 / R&W 2.1 | **4 Lies den Text. Finde die passenden Bilder.**
This text about a family's leisure activities shows the verb *spielen* in the first, second and third person singular and the third person plural. Students identify pictures to represent the different people's hobbies.

Students could work on this text in teams in a "human photocopier" activity. Make several copies of the text and display it at four or five stations around the room. Divide the class into teams. A student from each team goes to one of the texts, reads it and tries to memorise the information. They return to their team and complete as much of the activity as they can. A second person from each team then goes out to the text and returns with some more information, then a third person, and so on until they have completed the activity.

Answers: **Ulrike:** 3, 6; **Achim:** 4, 5, 7; **Diane:** 2; **Eltern:** 1

KAL 4.3, 4.5 / LLS 5.1 | **5 Füll die Lücken aus.**
Students read through the *Grammatik* box, which shows the present tense conjugation of *spielen*. They then complete the English gap-fill explanation.

Answers: All forms of the verb "spielen" have the same stem. The stem of regular verbs is formed by taking the infinitive form (spielen) and removing the -en ending (spiel<u>en</u>). The following endings are then added to the stem: ich: <u>-e</u>; du: <u>-st</u>; er / sie / es: <u>-t</u>. The <u>wir</u>, <u>sie</u> and <u>Sie</u> forms are the same. They end in <u>-en</u>. The <u>ihr</u> form ends in <u>-t</u>.

AT 4.2 / KAL 4.3, 4.5 | **6 Schreib Sätze mit *spielen*.**
Students write a sentence for each of a–f, using the correct form of *spielen* and replacing each picture with the corresponding sport or musical instrument. Encourage them to add *gern* or *nicht gern*, as in the example answer.

Answers: **a** Ich spiele (gern / nicht gern) Gitarre. **b** Du spielst (gern / nicht gern) Basketball. **c** Er spielt (gern / nicht gern) Tennis. **d** Wir spielen (gern / nicht gern) Fußball. **e** Ihr spielt (gern /nicht gern) Klavier. **f** Sie spielen (gern / nicht gern) am Computer.

AT 4.3 / R&W 2.4 / LLS 5.5 | **Challenge**
Students write five sentences about what they and their friends and family like and don't like doing, using *spielen* and *gern / nicht gern*. They are encouraged to use a dictionary to research words for other sports and musical instruments.

2A.2 Das mache ich am liebsten
Seite 58–59

Planner

Objectives
- Vocabulary: say what you like and prefer doing, and what your favourite hobbies are
- Grammar: *gern, lieber, am liebsten*; the second and third person singular of *fahren, lesen* and *sehen* (present tense)
- Skills: focus on intonation as an aid to understanding

Video
- Video blog 2A

Resources
- Student Book, pages 58–59
- CD 1, tracks 66–67
- Foundation and Higher Workbooks, page 33
- Workbook audio: CD 3 and 4, track 46
- Copymasters 39, 40 (ex. 1–2)
- Interactive OxBox, Unit 2A

Key language
Was machst du gern / lieber / am liebsten?
Ich fahre gern Skateboard. Ich fahre gern Rad. Ich chatte gern im Internet. Ich gehe gern ins Kino. Ich gehe gern einkaufen. Ich lese gern. Ich sehe gern fern. Ich höre gern Musik. Ich besuche gern meine Freunde. Ich spiele gern Rugby.
Ich chatte lieber im Internet. Ich fahre am liebsten Skateboard.

2A.2 Freizeit und Hobbys

Framework references
L&S 1.1, 1.2, 1.3, 1.4; R&W 2.1, 2.4; KAL 4.1, 4.3, 4.5; LLS 5.4, 5.5

Starters
- Copymaster 39
- Student Book page 58, ex. 1: students match the captions to the pictures and use their knowledge of German sound–spelling patterns to work out how to pronounce them.
- Display the activities from page 58 as mismatched sentence halves, e.g.

ich chatte lieber	Rad
ich fahre gern	ins Kino
ich gehe gern	fern
ich sehe am liebsten	im Internet
… etc.	… etc.

Set a time limit for students to match them up and write them out in German and English. To increase the challenge, use heart symbols in place of the words *gern*, *lieber* and *am liebsten*, e.g. *ich chatte* ♥♥, *ich fahre* ♥, so that students have to fill these in as well as matching the sentence halves.

Plenaries
- Teacher versus the class. Choose three activities from page 58 and write three corresponding sentences using *gern*, *lieber* and *am liebsten*, keeping them hidden from the class, e.g. *Ich höre gern Musik. Ich fahre lieber Rad. Ich gehe am liebsten ins Kino.* The class try to guess what the sentences are, e.g.
Student A: *Ich sehe gern fern?*
Teacher: *Nein!*
Student B: *Ich gehe gern ins Kino?*
Teacher: *Äh, ja … und nein.*
Student C: *Ich gehe am liebsten ins Kino?*
Teacher: *Ja!*
Student D: *Ich …*
Set a time limit: if the class are able to work out all three sentences within the time limit, they win; if not, the teacher wins. This game can also be played in pairs or groups.
- Memory game in pairs. Student A begins by saying he / she likes doing an activity, using *gern*; B repeats A's sentence and adds another activity, using *lieber*; A then finishes off by repeating the two previous activities and adding a third, using *am liebsten*. Student B then begins another sequence of three, e.g.
A: *Ich sehe gern fern.*
B: *Ich sehe gern fern, aber ich lese lieber.*
A: *Ich sehe gern fern, aber ich lese lieber. Ich chatte am liebsten im Internet.*
B: *Ich fahre gern Rad.*
A: *Ich fahre gern Rad, aber ich … lieber …*
Encourage them to vary the persons of the verb, e.g. by doing a sequence using *ich* then a sequence using *er* or *sie*.

Homework
- Student Book page 59, ex. 4.
- Student Book page 59, *Challenge*.
- Students write their own video blog (similar to Ali's) about their hobbies and interests. As support, provide the transcript of Ali's blog (see teaching notes for ex. 3 and the *Follow-up* to ex. 3 below). If the appropriate technology is available, students could record their video blogs and play them back to the class.

AT 1.2
AT 3.2
KAL 4.1
LLS 5.4

1 Was passt zusammen? Hör zu. Ist alles richtig?
Students match the captions (1–9) to the pictures (a–i) and use their knowledge of German sound–spelling patterns to work out how to pronounce them. Make sure they understand the effect that *gern* has on each sentence: *Ich fahre Skateboard* – I go skateboarding, *Ich fahre gern Skateboard* – I like going skateboarding.
Students then listen to the recording to check their answers and pronunciation.

🎧 CD 1, track 66   Seite 58, Übung 1

a Ich fahre gern Skateboard.
b Ich chatte gern im Internet.
c Ich gehe gern ins Kino.
d Ich lese gern.
e Ich sehe gern fern.
f Ich gehe gern einkaufen.
g Ich höre gern Musik.
h Ich fahre gern Rad.
i Ich besuche gern meine Freunde.

Answers: **a** 5; **b** 2; **c** 4; **d** 6; **e** 3; **f** 7; **g** 9; **h** 8; **i** 1

2A.2 Freizeit und Hobbys

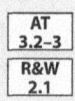

2 Welches Hobby ist das?
Before beginning this activity, point out the support box on *gern*, *lieber* and *am liebsten* and elicit their meanings. Students then read the texts and indicate which activities (from ex. 1) each person likes doing, prefers doing and what their favourite activity is.

Answers: **Richard:** likes h, prefers b, favourite activity is a; **Alenka:** likes g, prefers d, favourite activity is e; **Hannes:** likes f, prefers i, favourite activity is c

Think
Before playing Ali's video blog, read through the listening tip: it is often possible to work out how someone feels about something by focusing on their intonation and tone of voice. Point out that if you can actually see the person too (e.g. face to face or on a video), it helps even more because you can see their facial expressions, body language and any other visual information.

3 Sieh dir Alis Videoblog an. Füll die Tabelle aus.
Students watch Ali's video blog and fill in the grid to show what he likes doing and prefers doing, and what his favourite activities are. Although some of the language here is new to students (*Zeitung, lange Bücher*), the visuals on the video provide support.
Play the video again and challenge students to note any additional details they hear. Alternatively, display a copy of the transcript and ask students to identify key language: see Follow-up below.

Answers: **gern:** reading newspapers, skateboarding; **lieber:** listening to music, reading books, swimming; **am liebsten:** playing basketball

Video blog 2A
CD 1, track 67   Seite 59, Übung 3

Hallo! Ich bin's, Ali. Ich komme aus Berlin, wie ihr wisst, und ich habe viele Hobbys, denn ich bin sehr aktiv und ziemlich intelligent. Also, was mache ich gern?
Ich lese gern, aber ich höre lieber Musik, denn ich bin sehr musikalisch: ich finde Rockmusik klasse!
Ich lese gern Zeitung, aber ich lese lieber lange Bücher – sie sind toll!
Ich fahre gern Skateboard – das macht Spaß! – aber ich schwimme lieber. Am liebsten spiele ich Basketball. Das finde ich toll!
Und du? Was machst du gern, und was machst du am liebsten?

Also, ich muss jetzt los – ich spiele heute Abend auf einem Konzert mit meiner Band. Bis später! Tschüs!

Follow-up
Display a transcript of Ali's video blog and ask students to identify some key words and phrases, e.g.
- the German for "I swim" (*ich schwimme*)
- three nouns on the theme of music (apart from the word *Musik*) that look the same or almost the same as English words (*Rockmusik, Konzert, Band*)
- the German for "newspaper" and "long books" (*Zeitung, lange Bücher*)
- three adjectives that Ali uses to describe himself (*aktiv, intelligent, musikalisch*)
- two adjectives that he uses to describe his hobbies (*klasse, toll*)
- the German for "very" (*sehr*) and "fairly / quite" (*ziemlich*) – these were introduced in Unit 1A.

4 Schreib Sätze für die Bilder.
Students write a caption for each picture, using *gern*, *lieber* and *am liebsten*.
Point out the example answer (*Sie spielt gern Fußball*) and make sure students realise they need to use the *er* and *sie* forms of the verb here, not the *ich* form. Refer them to spread 2A.1 for present tense endings of regular verbs, and point out the *Grammatik* box on verbs that undergo a vowel change in the *du* and *er / sie* forms (*fahren, sehen, lesen*).

Answers: **a** Sie spielt gern Fußball. **b** Er liest gern. **c** Sie geht gern ins Kino. **d** Er spielt lieber Gitarre. **e** Sie sieht lieber fern. **f** Sie fährt lieber Skateboard. **g** Er spielt am liebsten Rugby. **h** Sie spielt am liebsten am Computer. **i** Er fährt am liebsten Rad.

5 Macht eine Umfrage.
Students interview six of their classmates about their preferred leisure activities, using the model questions provided. Suggest that they prepare for this by drawing out a grid to note down the answers (similar to Ali's grid in ex. 3, but with the six people's names listed down the left-hand column).

Challenge
Students write a few sentences about what they and other people like doing, what they prefer doing and what their favourite activity is. Suggest that they include some of the people they interviewed in ex. 5.
Make sure they realise they'll need to use the *ich* and *er / sie* forms of the verb here, and refer them to the *Grammatik* box again.

2A.3 Freizeit und Hobbys

2A.3 Ich liebe Computerspiele
Seite 60–61

Planner

Objectives
- Vocabulary: give opinions of different types of computer games
- Grammar: extended sentences using *denn*; *sie* (them)
- Skills: use familiar language to work out the meaning of new words

Resources
- Student Book, pages 60–61
- CD 1, tracks 68–69
- Foundation and Higher Workbooks, page 34
- Workbook audio: CD 3 and 4, track 47
- Interactive OxBox, Unit 2A

Key language
das Abenteuerspiel, das Lernspiel, das Musikspiel, das Quizspiel, das Sportspiel, das Tanzspiel
cool, klasse, lustig, nützlich, schrecklich, spannend
Wie findest du Quizspiele? Magst du Lernspiele?
Ich finde sie gut / nicht gut / sehr gut. Ich mag sie (nicht), denn ich finde sie langweilig / denn sie sind lustig.

Framework references
L&S 1.1, 1.2, 1.4; R&W 2.1, 2.2, 2.4; KAL 4.2, 4.4; LLS 5.2, 5.3, 5.4, 5.5

Starters
- Student Book page 60, ex. 1.
- Display the names of some current computer games. Try to include all the types of game listed on page 60. Set a time limit for students to copy out the list, say what type of game each one is and add an opinion, e.g. *Guitar Hero: Das ist ein Musikspiel. Ich finde Musikspiele cool.*
- Students complete each other's puzzles: see first homework suggestion.

Plenaries
- Before beginning this activity, you may wish to build up a list of positive and negative adjectives on the board for students to refer to (see ex. 4 and the *Follow-up* to ex. 4). Students then play word tennis in pairs: A has first "serve" and says he / she likes or doesn't like a type of computer game; B returns A's serve by making an appropriate comment, e.g.
A: *Ich mag Quizspiele.*
B: *Sie sind interessant.*
A: *Ich mag Abenteuerspiele nicht.*
B: *Sie sind doof.*
Make sure they swap over so that B has a turn at serving. If you are doing this activity towards the end of work on page 61, ask students to build longer sentences using *denn*:
A: *Ich mag Quizspiele, …*
B: *… denn sie sind interessant / denn ich finde sie interessant.*
- Students choose a few computer games that might be appropriate for their favourite sports personalities, musicians, TV stars, etc. They write sentences (omitting the people's names) on behalf of the people, e.g. *Ich heiße … Ich mag Sportspiele, denn ich finde sie spannend*. They write a separate list of the people's names, out of sequence. Students swap with their partner and match the names to the sentences.

Homework
- Students prepare a puzzle to test their partner on the types of computer game and opinion adjectives, e.g. a wordsearch, crossword, word snake, anagrams. Alternatively, ask them to find pictures of actual games (e.g. adverts torn from magazines, etc.) for their partner to label in German and give their opinion of, e.g. FIFA – *Das ist ein __ spiel. Ich finde __ spiele __.*
Prompt them to prepare an answer sheet. They swap puzzles with their partner in a following lesson.
- Student Book page 61, *Challenge*.

AT 3.1 | **LLS 5.3, 5.4**
1 Was ist das?
Students match the types of computer game to the corresponding pictures. Afterwards, talk about what clues helped them to do this, e.g. cognates, process of elimination.

AT 1.1
2 Hör zu (a–f). Ist alles richtig?
Students listen to check their answers to ex. 1.

Answers: **a** *das Quizspiel*; **b** *das Sportspiel*; **c** *das Musikspiel*; **d** *das Abenteuerspiel*; **e** *das Lernspiel*; **f** *das Tanzspiel*

2A.3 Freizeit und Hobbys

CD 1, track 68 — Seite 60, Übung 2

a Das ist ein Quizspiel.
b Das ist ein Sportspiel.
c Das ist ein Musikspiel.
d Das ist ein Abenteuerspiel.
e Das ist ein Lernspiel.
f Das ist ein Tanzspiel!

R&W 2.2 / LLS 5.4 — Think

This learning tip looks at German compound nouns. It points out that if you know the meaning of the component parts of a word, it can help you to work out the meaning of the whole word or other related words, e.g. if *Tanzspiel* (*Tanz* + *Spiel*) is a "dance game", the verb *tanzen* must mean "to dance".

AT 3.2–3 / R&W 2.1 — 3 Lies und beantworte die Fragen.

These texts introduce some new adjectives: six teenagers say what they think of computer games. Students identify the different opinions.

Answers: **a** Birte; **b** Mareike; **c** Werner; **d** Meltem; **e** Barbara; **f** Rainer

LLS 5.2, 5.5 — 4 Schreib eine Liste.

Students list the opinion words from ex. 3 in German and English. Encourage them to use a dictionary or the Glossary to look up any words they can't work out and to double-check meanings.
Talk about ways to keep a record of new language, e.g. listing it alphabetically, sorting adjectives into positive and negative, grouping words according to context. Point out that it is important to keep clear and organised reference lists of new language because it makes it easier to learn it. See the skills section on spread 2A.6 (*Sprachlabor* ex. 5–6).

Answers: schrecklich – awful; spannend – exciting; lustig – funny; cool – cool; nützlich – useful; klasse – great

LLS 5.5 — Follow-up

Students work in pairs to add other positive and negative adjectives to their lists (ex. 4), e.g. *langweilig, interessant, doof, furchtbar*. Point out that the adjectives they learned on spread 1B.2 in the context of school subjects could also be used to describe computer games.

AT 1.3 / L&S 1.1, 1.2 — 5 Hör zu (1–6). Welches Spiel ist das?

Students hear six people saying what they think of different types of computer game. On the first listening, they note down the type of game mentioned by each person. On the second listening, they add a tick or cross to show whether the person likes or dislikes the game. For an extra challenge, ask students to note the opinion adjectives and any additional comments. Draw attention to the word *Leichtathletikspiele* in 3 and challenge students to work out what *Leichtathletik* is (athletics).

Answers: **1** quiz games ✓ (super); **2** dance games ✗ (awful); **3** sports games ✓ (cool – likes football / athletics); **4** music games ✓ (funny – likes singing); **5** adventure games ✓ (exciting); **6** learning games ✗ (useful but boring)

CD 1, track 69 — Seite 61, Übung 5

1 Ich finde Quizspiele super.
2 Ich mag Tanzspiele nicht, denn ich finde Tanzen schrecklich.
3 Ich finde Sportspiele cool. Ich mag zum Beispiel Fußball – oder Leichtathletikspiele.
4 Musikspiele wie SingStar finde ich lustig, denn ich singe gern.
5 Abenteuerspiele wie Machinarium sind spannend!
6 Lernspiele sind nützlich, aber ich mag sie nicht, denn ich finde sie langweilig.

AT 4.1–2 / KAL 4.2, 4.4 — 6 Schreib die Wörter richtig auf.

Students copy out a–f and solve the anagrams. These sentences provide a model for expressing and justifying opinions, and show how to build a more complex sentence using *denn*.
Challenge students to recall any other linking words they know (e.g. *und, aber*).
Elicit the meaning of *sie* (they) in sentences a, d and f, and compare with *Ich finde sie langweilig / gut*, etc. (I find them boring / good, etc.) in the two language boxes. Ask students to supply a third meaning of *sie* (she).
Point out that using *sie* (them) can help to add interest and variety to spoken and written work because it avoids repetition.
Compare the following two short exchanges:
Wie findest du Quizspiele? – Ich mag Quizspiele, denn ich finde Quizspiele lustig.
Wie findest du Quizspiele? – Ich mag sie, denn ich finde sie lustig.
Point out that the first example sounds very repetitive because *Quizspiele* is used three times; the second example avoids this repetition through use of *sie*.

2A.4 Freizeit und Hobbys

Answers: a Ich mag Sportspiele, denn sie sind spannend. **b** Ich finde Lernspiele gut. **c** Ich finde Quizspiele super. **d** Ich mag Musikspiele nicht, denn sie sind schrecklich. **e** Ich finde Abenteuerspiele lustig. **f** Ich mag Tanzspiele sehr gern, denn sie sind klasse.

AT 2.2–3
L&S 1.4

7 Wie findest du Computerspiele?
Students exchange opinions of different types of computer game. Encourage them to justify their opinions in longer sentences using *denn*, and to avoid repetition through use of *sie* (them).

AT 4.3
R&W 2.4

Challenge
Students write five sentences to express their opinions of computer games. Encourage them to justify their opinions in longer sentences using *denn*, and to use *sie* (them) to avoid repetition.

2A.4 Wie oft machst du das?   Seite 62–63

Planner

Objectives
- Vocabulary: say how often you do something
- Grammar: word order with time expressions
- Skills: adapt previously learned language to create new expressions

Video
- Video clip 2A

Resources
- Student Book, pages 62–63
- CD 1, tracks 70–72
- Foundation and Higher Workbooks, page 35
- Workbook audio: CD 3 and 4, track 48
- Copymasters 40 (ex. 3), 41, 42, 43
- Interactive OxBox, Unit 2A

Key language
am Montag / Dienstag, etc.
am Morgen, am Nachmittag, am Abend, am Wochenende, einmal / zweimal / dreimal in der Woche, jeden Tag / Monat, jede Woche, jedes Jahr
Ich spiele einmal in der Woche Gitarre / am Computer. Ich fahre jeden Tag Skateboard / Rad. Ich schwimme am Morgen. Ich tanze am Montag. Ich sehe am Abend fern. Ich gehe am Wochenende ins Kino / Café.

Framework references
L&S 1.1, 1.2; R&W 2.4; KAL 4.2, 4.4; LLS 5.3, 5.4

Starters
- In pairs, students race against the clock to recall the days of the week. Who can remember all seven days in order and spell them correctly? Alternatively, display the days of the week in jumbled order with their vowels missing or as anagrams, and challenge students to write them out correctly in sequence.
- Ask students to close their books. Write a gap-fill sentence (activity plus time expression, from pages 62–63) on the board, showing only the initial letter of each word, e.g. I _ _ / s _ _ _ _ _ / j _ _ _ _ / T _ _ / G _ _ _ _ _ _ (= *Ich spiele jeden Tag Gitarre*). Challenge students to identify the complete sentence or individual words. Fill in any words or letters they identify, or add extra letters as clues. If the class work out the sentence within a time limit, they win a point; if not, the point goes to the teacher. Repeat with other sentences. This game could also be played in pairs.

Plenaries
- Students play a competitive dice game in pairs to practise the language from ex. 1–2. Number the photos in ex. 1 as 1–6 to correspond with the dots on the dice, e.g. 1 = *ich spiele Gitarre*, 2 = *ich schwimme*, etc. Do the same with the time expressions in ex. 2, e.g. 1 = *am Montag*, 2 = *am Wochenende*, 3 = *am Nachmittag*, etc. Students then take turns to roll the dice twice: the first number corresponds to an activity, the second corresponds to a time expression, e.g.
A: (rolls a two and a three) *Ich schwimme am Nachmittag*.
The first person to say all six activities and time expressions is the winner.
- Student Book page 63, ex. 6.

Homework
- Student Book page 62, ex. 4.
- Student Book page 63, *Challenge*.
- Students write a few sentences about the typical lifestyle of a very fit, active person (e.g. *Ich heiße Axel Aktiv! Ich bin sehr sportlich. Ich schwimme jeden Tag und ich spiele dreimal in der Woche Tennis …*) and a very lazy person (e.g. *Ich heiße Frieda Faul! Ich bin nicht sportlich. Ich spiele jeden Tag am Computer – am Nachmittag und am Abend …*).

93

2A.4 Freizeit und Hobbys

AT 1.2
AT 3.2

1 Hör zu (1–6). Was passt zusammen?
Students listen and match the recorded statements to the pictures and captions.

Answers: **1** c; **2** a; **3** f; **4** b; **5** d; **6** e

🎧 **CD 1, track 70**   Seite 62, Übung 1

1 Ich sehe am Abend fern.
2 Ich spiele einmal in der Woche Gitarre.
3 Ich gehe am Nachmittag ins Café.
4 Ich schwimme am Montag.
5 Ich spiele jeden Tag am Computer.
6 Ich gehe am Wochenende ins Kino.

AT 3.2
KAL 4.2, 4.4
LLS 5.3, 5.4

2 Wie sagt man …?
Students identify the six time expressions in the captions for ex. 1. Talk about the clues that help with this, e.g. they know that *Tag* is "day" so *jeden Tag* must be "every day"; they know that *Mittag* is "noon", so *Nachmittag* could be "afternoon"; *ein* is "one" and *Woche* looks a bit like "week" so *einmal in der Woche* must be "once a week".
Look at the position of each time expression in the ex. 1 captions: subject + verb + time expression (+ the rest of the sentence). Elicit the English translation of each German sentence and compare word order in English and German.

Answers: **a** am Montag; **b** am Wochenende; **c** am Nachmittag; **d** einmal in der Woche; **e** am Abend; **f** jeden Tag

AT 1.2

3 Hör zu und füll die Lücken aus.
Students listen to the recording to find the missing time expression for each statement a–f.

Answers: **a** jeden Tag; **b** einmal in der Woche; **c** am Mittwoch; **d** am Wochenende; **e** am Nachmittag; **f** am Abend

🎧 **CD 1, track 71**   Seite 62, Übung 3

a Ich spiele jeden Tag Fußball.
b Ich schwimme einmal in der Woche.
c Er geht am Mittwoch ins Kino.
d Sie fährt am Wochenende Skateboard.
e Wir hören am Nachmittag Musik.
f Sie sehen am Abend fern.

R&W 2.4
KAL 4.2

Think
This learning tip shows students how to extend their vocabulary by adapting familiar language, e.g. if *am Donnerstag* is "on Thursday", then "on Friday" must be *am Freitag*; if *einmal / zweimal in der Woche* means "once / twice a week", "three times a week" must be *dreimal in der Woche*.

AT 3.2

4 Lies die Wörterschlange.
Students follow up on the learning tip by identifying six new time expressions in the word snake. They list them with their English translations.

Answers: jedes Jahr – every year; am Morgen – in the morning; jeden Monat – every month; am Donnerstag – on Thursday; jede Woche – every week; zweimal in der Woche – twice a week

AT 2.2

5 A sagt einen Buchstaben und eine Zahl. B sagt die passenden Sätze.
Students take turns to give each other the letter (a–f) of a leisure activity and the number (1–6) of a time expression; their partner builds a sentence, e.g.
A: *b und drei.*
B: *Ich schwimme jeden Tag.*

AT 4.2–3
R&W 2.4
KAL 4.2, 4.4

6 Schreib Sätze.
Students write six sentences based on the pictures and symbols in ex. 5. They use each activity and each time expression at least once.

🎥 **7 Sieh dir das Video an. Beantworte die Fragen.**

AT 1.4
L&S 1.1, 1.2

Play video clip 2A again, focusing on the conversation between Ali and Nina. Students answer questions about their hobbies and interests. For question 2, ask them to consider whether Ali and Nina really do have this hobby in common – what makes them think this?

Answers: **1** Monday: he's playing tennis; Tuesday: guitar lesson; Wednesday: he's buying a new skateboard with his dad; Friday: football training; **2** reading (it's unlikely that they have this hobby in common, because we see from the video that Ali enjoys serious books whereas Nina likes glossy magazines)

2A.5 Freizeit und Hobbys

Video clip 2A
CD 1, track 72　　　　　　　Seite 63, Übung 7

Ali:	Dieser Film ist super!
Nina:	Welcher?
Ali:	Dieser hier mit Russell Crowe.
Nina:	Oh, ja … ich finde, Ralf sieht aus wie Russell Crowe.
Ali:	… Er ist so nett, so intelligent, so schön …
Nina:	Hör auf!
Nina:	Gut, dann … Gehen wir ins Kino?
Ali:	Wir? Also, du und ich?
Nina:	Ja!
Ali:	Und … Ralf? Der süße, intelligente, schöne Ralf?
Nina:	Der ist doch der Star, oder?
Nina:	Gut, dann … gehen wir am Montag?
Ali:	Nein, das geht nicht. Am Montag spiele ich Tennis.
Nina:	Echt? Ralf spielt auch Tennis.
Nina:	Und am Dienstag?
Ali:	Nee, am Dienstag habe ich Gitarrenunterricht.
Nina:	Kein Problem … Ralf spielt kein Instrument … Gut, dann Mittwoch?
Ali:	Sorry, am Mittwoch kaufe ich mit meinem Vater ein neues Skateboard. Und bevor du was sagst … Ralf fährt auch Skateboard …
Nina:	Ich weiß … aber am Donnerstag geht nicht. Da habe ich Theaterklub. Also muss es wohl Freitag sein.
Ali:	Fußballtraining. Hey, sorry!
Nina:	So viele Hobbys, Ali! Hast du noch andere Hobbys?
Ali:	Ich schwimme, ich spiele gern Basketball, und natürlich lese ich auch sehr gern.
Nina:	Ich lese auch gern …
Ali:	Und Musik – ich singe in 'ner Band …
Nina:	Du singst?
Ali:	Hey Nina, warum gehen wir nicht jetzt ins Kino? Es ist halb vier. Und wir haben doch Zeit, oder?
Nina:	Super Idee! … Und Kathi und Nico?
Ali / Nina:	Nee.

Follow-up
Play the clip again and challenge students to identify the other hobbies mentioned by Ali (swimming, basketball, music / he sings in a band) and what Nina is doing on Thursday (drama club).

AT 4.3 | R&W 2.4 — Challenge
Students imagine they've been invited out to the cinema but don't want to go. They write five excuses, saying what they're doing on each day and how often they usually do each activity.

2A.5 Am Wochenende　　　　　　　Seite 64–65

Planner

Objectives
- Vocabulary: talk about leisure activities
- Grammar: expressions of time and frequency; the second and third person singular of *fahren*, *lesen* and *sehen* (present tense)
- Skills: pronounce *a* and *ä* correctly (*ich fahre, du fährst, er / sie fährt*)

Resources
- Student Book, pages 64–65
- Foundation and Higher Workbooks, page 36
- Copymaster 44
- Interactive OxBox, Unit 2A

Key language
Ich mag … (nicht), denn …
anstrengend, (nicht) gut, klasse, langweilig, schlecht, spannend, toll
Ich spiele (gern / nicht gern) Basketball / Fußball / Tennis.
Ich fahre (gern / nicht gern) Rad / Skateboard / Ski.
Ich schwimme / tanze (gern / nicht gern).
Ich sehe mir (gern / nicht gern) Volleyball / Rugby im Fernsehen an.

Framework references
L&S 1.4; R&W 2.4; KAL 4.1, 4.3, 4.5; LLS 5.1, 5.5

Starters
- Before beginning work on the *Chatpartner* text, tell students to keep their books closed and to think about Nina, Kathi, Nico and Ali from the video clips. Display the eleven leisure activities that are mentioned in the text: *einkaufen, in Cafés gehen, Fußball, Radfahren, Sudoku, Fernsehen, Skateboard, Musik hören, Mathe, Bücher lesen, Freunde besuchen*. Challenge students to match the activities to the teenagers, based on what they know of their personalities: there are three activities per person, and one activity (*Radfahren*) is used twice. Students then open their books and check their predictions against the text.
- Allow students a few minutes with a bilingual dictionary to research the German words for any sports they are interested in that haven't come up yet. They may need these for the class survey (ex. 4) and

95

2A.5 Freizeit und Hobbys

group discussion (ex. 5). Invite them to share the new vocabulary with the class. Write it on the board and encourage everyone to make a note of it.

Plenaries
- Ask students to close their books, then read out details about the four teenagers from the *Chatpartner* text, some of them true and others false. Challenge students to identify the errors. They win a point for each error they spot, and an extra point if they can correct it; the teacher wins a point for each error the class fail to spot:
  Teacher: *Ali geht am liebsten in Cafés.*
  Student A: *Nein, Nina geht am liebsten in Cafés.* (= 2 points)
  Teacher: *Nico spielt jeden Tag Fußball.*
  Student B: *Nein, er spielt Fußball am Wochenende.* (= 2 points)
  Alternatively, students could do this in pairs.
- Students play a memory game in pairs using the sports from this spread, e.g.
  A: *Er spielt Fußball.*
  B: *Er spielt Fußball und er fährt Ski.*
  A: *Er spielt Fußball, er fährt Ski und …*
  For a more challenging version, encourage them to vary the persons of the verb. For an easier alternative, students could use the structure *Ich finde (+ Sport) toll*, so that the only element they need to change is the name of the sport.

Homework
- Students choose their favourite two teenagers (Kathi, Nina, Nico or Ali) and translate their profiles into English. Able students could translate all four profiles.
- Students imagine they have found a compatible *Chatpartner* for one of the four teenagers. They write a profile about the partner, e.g. *Sam ist ein Chatpartner für Ali. Er ist sehr intelligent und er mag Mathe und Naturwissenschaften. Sam spielt gern am Computer – er spielt am liebsten Lernspiele …*
- Student Book page 65, *Challenge*.

---

1 Lies den Text.
Refer students to the *Grammatik* box on irregular verbs and ask them to identify examples in the four teenagers' internet profiles.

Answers: **Kathi:** fährt; **Nina:** sieht; **Nico:** fährt; **Ali:** liest

Think
This pronunciation tip focuses on the vowel sounds in *fahre* and *fährt / fährst*. Point out that although the difference between *a* and *ä* is very subtle in writing, the two sounds are completely different.

2 Lies den Text oben noch einmal. Füll die Lücken aus.
Students fill in the missing present tense verbs, referring to the *Grammatik* box and the internet profiles (*Chatpartner*) for support.

Answers: **a** fährt; **b** hört; **c** sieht; **d** fährt; **e** liest

3 Sieh dir Sabines Kalender an. Schreib Sätze.
Students look at Sabine's illustrated diary and write a sentence for each day to explain what she does, using the *sie* (she) form of the verb throughout. They make up their own choice of activity for Sunday. This is an opportunity for them to research something different, e.g. *Sie ist am Sonntag müde! Sie faulenzt und sieht fern!*

Answers: *Sabine spielt am Montag Fußball. Sie fährt am Dienstag Skateboard. Sie spielt am Mittwoch Volleyball. Sie schwimmt am Donnerstag. Sie spielt am Freitag Tennis. Sie tanzt am Samstag.* (Students' own choice for Sunday.)

4 Macht eine Umfrage in der Klasse.
Students carry out a class survey to find out the sports preferences of their classmates. The suggested questions are: *Welchen Sport magst du und warum? Welchen Sport magst du nicht und warum? Welchen Sport machst du? Welchen Sport siehst du dir im Fernsehen an?* Tell students to draw out a survey sheet like the grid shown on page 65 – this will help them to record the responses clearly.

5 Vergleicht eure Antworten.
Students work in small groups comparing their own answers to the survey questions (ex. 2) and asking each other how often they do the activities, e.g.
A: *Ich spiele Fußball. Spielst du Fußball?*
B: *Ja, wie oft machst du das?*
A: *Ich mache das jeden Tag! Und du?*
B: *Ich mache das am Wochenende.*
C: *Ich spiele nicht gern Fußball. Und du?*
D: *Ich …*

Challenge
Students write an internet profile describing their hobbies, using the third person singular as in ex. 1. Encourage them to build longer sentences using linking words (*und*, *aber*) and to express and justify their opinions using *denn*.

2A.6 Freizeit und Hobbys

2A.6 Sprachlabor

Seite 66–67

Planner

Objectives
- Grammar: regular and irregular verbs in the present tense; word order
- Skills: how to keep a record of new language; pronounce German words that look like English words

Resources
- Student Book, pages 66–67
- CD 1, tracks 73–74
- Foundation and Higher Workbooks, pages 37–38
- Copymasters 45, 46
- Interactive OxBox, Unit 2A

Framework references
KAL 4.1, 4.3, 4.4, 4.5; LLS 5.1, 5.2, 5.3, 5.5, 5.8

Regular and irregular endings for verbs

1 Match the German and the English.
Students match the German subject pronouns to their English equivalents.

Answers: *ich* – I; *du* – you (singular); *er / sie / es* – he / she / it; *wir* – we; *ihr* – you (plural); *sie* – they; *Sie* – you (formal)

2 Choose the correct form of the verb *spielen*. [KAL 4.3, 4.5] [LLS 5.1]

Answers: **a** spiele; **b** spielt; **c** spielen; **d** spielst; **e** spielt; **f** spielt

3 Fill in the missing letters in these verb forms.

Answers: **a** sieht; **b** liest; **c** fahre; **d** fährt; **e** lesen; **f** siehst

Word order

4 Read the captions for pictures a and b. Put the words in the right order. [KAL 4.4]

Answers: **a** Er spielt am liebsten Schlagzeug. **b** Sie fahren gern Skateboard. Er fährt lieber Rad.

Keeping a record of new language

[LLS 5.2, 5.5, 5.8] These tips suggest some ways to keep a record of new language to make it easier to learn it. For example, students are encouraged to group words according to whether they are positive or negative, which should make it easier to remember their meanings. Another tip suggests associating different activities with particular adjectives, e.g. if students find tennis and football exciting, they list them all together: *spannend – Tennis, Fußball*. Discuss other types of language that students have met so far in the course and ask them to suggest ways of categorising it, e.g. family members could be grouped as masculine and feminine; school subjects could be grouped with all languages together, all science and maths subjects together, all practical subjects together, etc.
Talk about other types of reference list, e.g. alphabetical lists. Look at the *Vokabular* lists in the Student Book, which are organised by topic and theme: do students think this is an effective way to list new language?

5 Put these words into positive or negative columns.
Students sort the adjectives and other words according to whether they are positive or negative.

Answers: **positive:** toll, gern, mag, spannend, lustig; **negative:** nicht gut, langweilig, schlecht, nicht gern, mag nicht, furchtbar

6 Find other adjectives from this unit and add them to your list.
Students expand their lists (ex. 4) by adding other adjectives and opinions.

Pronouncing words which look like English words

[KAL 4.1] [LLS 5.1, 5.3] Students are reminded that although many English and German words look very similar, they are pronounced differently.

7 Listen to these words and note the difference between the English and German pronunciation.
Each word is spoken twice, with first the English pronunciation and then the German.

97

2A.7 Freizeit und Hobbys

🎧 CD 1, track 73   Seite 67, Übung 7

a	Basketball	f	Handball
b	Sofa	g	Magazin
c	Auto	h	Station
d	Musik	i	Butter
e	Radio	j	Marmelade

8 First try to pronounce the following words. Then listen to check.

🎧 CD 1, track 74   Seite 67, Übung 8

a	Flöte	f	Jacke
b	Gitarre	g	Englisch
c	Supermarkt	h	Banane
d	Lampe	i	CD-Spieler
e	Mathematik	j	Joghurt

2A.7 Extra Star   Seite 68

Planner

Objectives
- Vocabulary: practise words for hobbies, likes and dislikes
- Grammar: *gern, lieber, am liebsten*
- Skills: read for gist and detail

Resources
- Student Book, page 68
- Copymaster 47

AT 4.1   **1 Fill in the missing letters.**

Students copy and complete a list of sports and musical instruments.

Answers: **a** *Fußball;* **b** *Geige;* **c** *Volleyball;* **d** *Gitarre;* **e** *Klavier*

AT 3.1–2   **2 Match the sentences with the pictures.**

Students choose a picture to represent each statement about sports and musical instruments. Here, they show that they understand the topic words (i.e. names of sports and musical instruments); in ex. 3, they move on to identifying the detail (likes and dislikes).

Answers: **a** *2;* **b** *5;* **c** *4;* **d** *1;* **e** *6;* **f** *3*

AT 3.1–2   **3 Mark each sentence in activity 2 with + or – to show whether it is positive or negative.**

Answers: **a** *+;* **b** *–;* **c** *–;* **d** *+;* **e** *–;* **f** *–*

AT 3.2   **4 Match the sentence halves.**

Answers: **a** *4;* **b** *1;* **c** *5;* **d** *2;* **e** *3*

AT 4.2   **5 Write a sentence for each picture, using the jumbled-up phrases in the box.**

Answers: **a** *Ich chatte gern mit Freunden.* **b** *Ich gehe gern einkaufen.* **c** *Ich spiele lieber Gitarre.* **d** *Ich lese lieber.* **e** *Ich fahre am liebsten Skateboard.* **f** *Ich spiele am liebsten Fußball.*

2A.8 Freizeit und Hobbys

2A.7 Extra Plus Seite 69

> **Planner**
>
> **Objectives**
> - Vocabulary: talk about hobbies; express and justify opinions
> - Grammar: use *denn*; use correct word order with time expressions
> - Skills: build longer sentences
>
> **Resources**
> - Student Book, page 69
> - Copymaster 48

AT 4.3

1 Schreib Sätze für die Bilder.

Students write a sentence about sports and hobbies in response to each set of pictures and symbols. They use *denn* to justify the opinions.

Answers: **a** *Ich spiele gern Fußball, aber ich spiele lieber Rugby, denn es ist toll.* **b** *Ich spiele nicht gern Volleyball, denn es ist langweilig.* **c** *Ich fahre gern Skateboard, denn es ist super, aber ich spiele nicht gern Flöte, denn es ist schwierig.* **d** *Ich schwimme nicht gern, denn es ist anstrengend, aber ich spiele gern Fußball, denn es ist klasse.* **e** *Ich sehe gern fern, denn es ist gut, aber ich gehe am liebsten ins Kino, denn es ist interessant.* **f** *Ich lese gern, denn es ist interessant, aber ich besuche am liebsten meine Freunde, denn es ist toll.*

AT 3.3–4

2 Lies den Text. Richtig oder falsch?

Students read Svenja's text about hobbies and decide whether each statement is true or false. Ask them to correct the false statements.

Answers: **a** R; **b** F (she likes cycling); **c** R; **d** R; **e** F (she goes with her brother); **f** F (her friends like computer games but she doesn't)

AT 4.3–4

3 Wie oft machst du das? Wie findest du es, und warum?

Students choose six activities pictured on pages 68–69 (or use their own choice of activities). They write a short text for each, saying how often they do it and expressing their opinion using *denn*, e.g. *Ich fahre zweimal in der Woche Skateboard. Ich finde das toll, denn ich bin sehr sportlich.*

2A.8 Testseite Seite 70

> **Planner**
>
> **Resources**
> - Student Book, page 70
> - CD 1, track 75
> - Foundation and Higher Workbooks, page 39
> - Copymasters 37, 38
> - Assessment, Unit 2A

AT 1.3

1 Listen to Samira. Copy and complete the grid with the information you hear.

Students note down details of each person's leisure activities.

Answers: **Samira:** plays volleyball, at the weekend, super; **brother:** listens to music (on the internet), every day, great; **mother:** reads (books), in the evening, interesting; **father:** watches movies, goes to cinema once a week, fun

2A Freizeit und Hobbys

CD 1, track 75 — Seite 70, Übung 1

Ich heiße Samira. Ich spiele sehr gern Volleyball. Ich bin in einer Mannschaft und ich spiele am Wochenende. Ich finde das super.
Mein Bruder liebt Musik. Er hört Musik im Internet. Er macht das jeden Tag, denn er findet das klasse.
Meine Mutter liest gern Bücher. Sie liest am Abend. Meine Mutter findet Lesen interessant.
Mein Vater sieht sehr gern Filme. Er geht einmal in der Woche ins Kino, denn er findet das lustig.

AT 3.4 **2 Read Bernhard's email and answer the questions below in English.**

Answers: **a** goes cycling; **b** he likes it / it's great; **c** he doesn't like it / finds it boring; **d** skateboarding; **e** goes skiing; **f** five times a week; **g** it's good

AT 2.3 **3 Discuss your hobbies with a partner.**

Students interview each other about their hobbies: what they do, when, their opinion, what they don't like doing. Questions and basic prompts are provided.

Encourage them to expand their answers to say what they prefer doing (*lieber*) and what their favourite activities are (*am liebsten*), and to give reasons for their likes and dislikes using *denn*.

AT 4.3 **4 Look at the picture and imagine you are Mark. Write a few sentences saying what you do in your spare time.**

Encourage students to invent details and opinions, and to build longer sentences using *denn*. If this activity is too challenging for your students, support them by providing a gap-fill text or a few prompts.

Example answer: Ich spiele gern Gitarre, denn es ist lustig und ich bin sehr musikalisch. Ich spiele zweimal in der Woche Gitarre, am Montag und am Mittwoch. Aber ich fahre am liebsten Skateboard, denn es ist total klasse! Ich fahre jeden Tag Skateboard!

2A Lesen
Seite 155

Planner

Resources
- Student Book, page 155

Framework references
R&W 2.1, 2.2; LLS 5.4

Im Internet!

1 Read the texts for Carsten, Katharina and Heiko. Can you guess what a and b mean?
Students read three teenagers' comments on an internet forum. They work out the meaning of two key phrases.

Answers: **a** social networks; **b** I download music

AT 3.3–4 **2 Read the texts and answer the questions.**
Students identify how each teenager uses the internet.

Answers: **a** Carsten and Heiko; **b** Katharina and Heiko; **c** Carsten and Heiko; **d** Katharina; **e** Carsten; **f** Heiko

AT 3.4 **3 Read the text on the right and answer the questions in English.**
Students read the text about German singer Lena Meyer-Landrut and answer questions in English.

Answers: **a** a city; **b** ballet; **c** singing; **d** she's had a number one hit in Europe; **e** English; **f** they are her favourite singers; **g** she downloads music and chats with her friends; **h** because she often goes to other countries and towns to sing, so it's practical to be able to talk to her friends on Facebook

Follow-up
- Students choose the forum message that most closely describes their own use of the internet and translate it into English.
- Students identify in the messages any words, phrases and sentences that apply to themselves. They use them to write their own paragraph about their own internet habits.
- Students look up the singers Lena Meyer-Landrut, Adele and Jack Johnson on the internet. They find out a few facts about their favourite to share with their partner (or with the class) in a following lesson.

2A Freizeit und Hobbys

Foundation Workbook

2A.1 Ich spiele gern Fußball (Seite 32)

AT 1.2 **1** Listen to these people saying what hobbies they have. Work out who is who and write the names.

Answers: **a** *Sophie;* **b** *Carsten;* **c** *Lukas;* **d** *Heino;* **e** *Tim;* **f** *Marie;* **g** *Dennis;* **h** *Jessica;* **i** *Rebecca;* **j** *Arzu*

> 🎧 **CD 3, track 45**   Seite 32, Übung 1
>
> – Ich heiße Heino. Ich spiele am Computer.
> – Ich heiße Jessica. Ich spiele Gitarre.
> – Ich heiße Lukas. Ich spiele Tennis.
> – Ich heiße Arzu. Ich spiele Klavier.
> – Ich heiße Dennis. Ich spiele Basketball.
> – Ich heiße Sophie. Ich spiele Fußball.
> – Ich heiße Tim. Ich spiele Schlagzeug.
> – Ich heiße Marie. Ich spiele Geige.
> – Ich heiße Carsten. Ich spiele Flöte.
> – Ich heiße Rebecca. Ich spiele Federball.

AT 3.3 **2** Read this paragraph. Choose five correct sentences from the list below and tick them.

Answers: the correct sentences are: a, c, d, e, g

3 Draw lines to link the words.

Answers: ich spiele, du spielst, er spielt, wir spielen, ihr spielt, sie spielen

2A.2 Das mache ich am liebsten (Seite 33)

AT 3.2 **1** Insert numbers to show the correct word order in these jumbled sentences.

Answers: **a** *2, 1, 4, 3 (Ich gehe gern einkaufen);* **b** *1, 5, 3, 2, 4 (Ich chatte gern im Internet);* **c** *2, 1, 4, 3 (Ich höre gern Musik);* **d** *4, 3, 2, 1 (Ich fahre gern Rad);* **e** *2, 1, 4, 3 (Ich sehe gern fern);* **f** *3, 2, 1 (Ich lese gern)*

AT 1.2–3 **2** Put ticks by each picture to show what Ali likes (✓), prefers (✓✓) and likes best (✓✓✓).
Answers: **a** *✓✓✓;* **b** *✓✓✓;* **c** *✓✓;* **d** *✓;* **e** *✓;* **f** *✓*

> 🎧 **CD 3, track 46**   Seite 33, Übung 2
>
> Hallo! Ich bin Ali aus Berlin.
> Ich bin musikalisch und sportlich. Ich höre gern Musik.
> Ich spiele am liebsten Gitarre.
> Ich lese gern Zeitung, aber ich lese lieber Bücher.
> Ich fahre gern Skateboard.
> Am liebsten spiele ich Basketball.

3 Choose the correct verb form.

Answers: **a** *fahre;* **b** *spielt;* **c** *hört;* **d** *lese;* **e** *geht;* **f** *spielst*

2A.3 Ich liebe Computerspiele (Seite 34)

AT 3.1 **1** Complete this advert for a *ZOOM* computer game. Write in the correct words.

Answers: Lernst du Deutsch? Das ZOOM-Spiel ist <u>cool</u>! Es ist <u>lustig</u> und <u>spannend</u>. Das ZOOM-Spiel ist nicht <u>langweilig</u>. Findest du Deutsch <u>schrecklich</u>? Nicht mit ZOOM. Es ist <u>super</u> und auch <u>nützlich</u>.

AT 1.2 **2** What do these people think of each type of game? Write the answer in English.

Answers: **a** *terrible;* **b** *funny;* **c** *useful;* **d** *cool;* **e** *exciting;* **f** *super*

> 🎧 **CD 3, track 47**   Seite 34, Übung 2
>
> **a** Ich finde Quizspiele schrecklich.
> **b** Ich finde Musikspiele lustig.
> **c** Ich finde Lernspiele nützlich.
> **d** Ich finde Tanzspiele cool.
> **e** Ich finde Abenteuerspiele spannend.
> **f** Ich finde Sportspiele super.

AT 3.2 **3** Unjumble the second half of each sentence.

Answers: **a** *Ich mag Sportspiele, denn sie sind super.* **b** *Ich mag Lernspiele nicht, denn sie sind langweilig.* **c** *Ich mag Musikspiele, denn sie sind lustig.* **d** *Ich mag Abenteuerspiele nicht, denn sie sind schrecklich.*

2A.4 Wie oft machst du das? (Seite 35)

AT 3.1 **1** Find the correct expression for each picture and write the correct letter in each box.

Answers: **1** *b;* **2** *e;* **3** *d;* **4** *c;* **5** *a*

AT 1.2 **2** Listen and draw lines to link the activity with when it is done.

Answers: **a** *every day;* **b** *in the afternoon;* **c** *three times a week;* **d** *on Thursday;* **e** *at the weekend;* **f** *in the evening*

> 🎧 **CD 3, track 48**   Seite 35, Übung 2
>
> **a** Ich fahre jeden Tag Rad.
> **b** Ich spiele am Nachmittag Gitarre.
> **c** Ich tanze dreimal in der Woche.
> **d** Ich schwimme am Donnerstag.
> **e** Ich spiele am Wochenende Golf.
> **f** Ich sehe am Abend fern.

2A Freizeit und Hobbys

AT 3.2
AT 4.1
3 Fill in the gaps to show how often you do these things. It doesn't have to be true!

Answers: students' own answers

2A.5 Am Wochenende (Seite 36)

AT 4.1–2
1 Unscramble the hobby and write in *gern* or *nicht gern*.

Answers: **a** *Ich spiele gern Schlagzeug.* **b** *Ich spiele nicht gern Fußball.* **c** *Ich spiele gern Volleyball.* **d** *Ich spiele gern Federball.* **e** *Ich spiele nicht gern Gitarre.*

AT 3.2
2 Put in the correct verb.

Answers: **a** *chatte;* **b** *gehe;* **c** *finde;* **d** *lese;* **e** *schwimme;* **f** *fahre*

AT 3.2
3 Write in *gern*, *lieber* or *am liebsten*.

Answers: **a** *lieber;* **b** *am liebsten;* **c** *gern;* **d** *lieber;* **e** *am liebsten*

2A.6A Sprachlabor (Seite 37)

1 Interpret the pictures and decide on the person (*ich*, *du* etc.) and the verb form (*spiele* etc.).

Answers: **a** *Ich spiele Fußball.* **b** *Sie spielen Tennis.* **c** *Spielst du Gitarre?* **d** *Spielt ihr am Computer?* **e** *Wir spielen Schach.* **f** *Er spielt Klavier.*

2 Draw lines to link the 'person' and the correct verb form.

Answers: ich fahre, du fährst, er / sie / es fährt, wir fahren, ihr fahrt, sie / Sie fahren; ich lese, du liest, er / sie / es liest, wir lesen, ihr lest, sie / Sie lesen

2A.6B Think (Seite 38)

1 Write P (positive) or N (negative) by these words and expressions.

Answers: <u>Positive</u>: *gut, super, gern, lustig, prima;* <u>Negative</u>: *langweilig, nicht gern, schlecht, furchtbar, nicht so gut*

2 Put together the syllables to make the German words for sports and musical instruments. Insert them in the grid and identify the shaded word. Each word has been started for you.

Answers: **a** *Rugby;* **b** *Tennis;* **c** *Klavier;* **d** *Gitarre;* **e** *Schwimmen.* The shaded word is: <u>Geige</u>. It means: <u>violin</u>.

3 Say these words out loud. In that list, can you spot two singular nouns and two plural nouns?

Answers: <u>singular nouns</u>: *Schlange, Gitarre;* <u>plural nouns</u>: *Hunde, Freunde*

2A Freizeit und Hobbys

Higher Workbook

2A.1 Ich spiele gern Fußball (Seite 32)

AT 1.2 / AT 4.2 **1** Listen to these people saying what hobbies they have. Work out who is who and write sentences.

Answers: **a** Sophie spielt Fußball. **b** Carsten spielt Flöte. **c** Lukas spielt Tennis. **d** Heino spielt am Computer. **e** Tim spielt Schlagzeug. **f** Marie spielt Geige. **g** Dennis spielt Basketball. **h** Jessica spielt Gitarre. **i** Rebecca spielt Federball. **j** Arzu spielt Klavier.

> 🎧 **CD 4, track 45** — Seite 32, Übung 1
>
> – Ich heiße Heino. Ich spiele am Computer.
> – Ich heiße Jessica. Ich spiele Gitarre.
> – Ich heiße Lukas. Ich spiele Tennis.
> – Ich heiße Arzu. Ich spiele Klavier.
> – Ich heiße Dennis. Ich spiele Basketball.
> – Ich heiße Sophie. Ich spiele Fußball.
> – Ich heiße Tim. Ich spiele Schlagzeug.
> – Ich heiße Marie. Ich spiele Geige.
> – Ich heiße Carsten. Ich spiele Flöte.
> – Ich heiße Rebecca. Ich spiele Federball.

AT 3.3 **2** Read this paragraph. Tick the sentences that are *richtig* (true) and put a cross by the ones that are *falsch* (false).

Answers: **a** ✓; **b** X; **c** ✓; **d** ✓; **e** ✓; **f** X; **g** ✓; **h** X

2A.2 Das mache ich am liebsten (Seite 33)

AT 4.2 **1** Unjumble these sentences and write them out correctly.

Answers: **a** Ich gehe gern einkaufen. **b** Ich chatte gern im Internet. **c** Ich höre gern Musik. **d** Ich fahre gern Rad. **e** Ich sehe gern fern. **f** Ich lese gern.

AT 1.3 **2** Put ticks by each picture to show what Ali likes (✓), prefers (✓✓) and likes best (✓✓✓).
Answers: **a** ✓✓✓; **b** ✓✓✓; **c** ✓✓; **d** ✓; **e** ✓; **f** ✓

> 🎧 **CD 4, track 46** — Seite 33, Übung 2
>
> Hallo! Hier spricht Ali aus Berlin.
> Also, ich bin musikalisch und auch sportlich. Ich höre gern Musik, aber ich spiele am liebsten Gitarre.
> Ich lese gern Zeitung, aber ich lese lieber Bücher.
> Ich fahre gern Skateboard, aber am liebsten spiele ich Basketball.

3 Choose the correct verb form.
Answers: **a** fahre; **b** spielt; **c** hört; **d** lese; **e** geht; **f** spielst

2A.3 Ich liebe Computerspiele (Seite 34)

AT 3.1 **1** Complete this advert for a *ZOOM* computer game. Write in the correct words.

Answers: Lernst du Deutsch? Das ZOOM-Spiel ist <u>cool</u>! Es ist <u>lustig</u> und <u>spannend</u>. Das ZOOM-Spiel ist nicht <u>langweilig</u>. Findest du Deutsch <u>schrecklich</u>? Nicht mit ZOOM. Es ist <u>super</u> und auch <u>nützlich</u>.

AT 1.2–3 **2** What does this person think of each type of game? Write the answer in German.

Answers: **a** schrecklich; **b** lustig; **c** nützlich; **d** cool; **e** spannend; **f** super

> 🎧 **CD 4, track 47** — Seite 34, Übung 2
>
> Ich finde das Quizspiel schrecklich, aber ich finde das Musikspiel lustig.
> Das Lernspiel ist nützlich und ich finde das Tanzspiel cool.
> Ich finde das Abenteuerspiel spannend und ich finde das Sportspiel super.

AT 4.2 **3** Translate the second half of each sentence into German, using *denn*.

Answers: **a** Ich mag Sportspiele, denn sie sind super. **b** Ich mag Lernspiele nicht, denn sie sind langweilig. **c** Ich mag Musikspiele, denn sie sind lustig. **d** Ich mag Abenteuerspiele nicht, denn sie sind schrecklich.

2A.4 Wie oft machst du das? (Seite 35)

AT 3.1 **1** Find the correct expression for each picture and write the expression below each one.

Answers: **a** am Montag; **b** am Nachmittag; **c** jeden Tag; **d** am Wochenende; **e** am Abend

AT 1.2 **2** Listen and write in below each picture, in English, when it is done.

Answers: **a** every day; **b** in the afternoon; **c** three times a week; **d** on Thursday; **e** at the weekend; **f** in the evening

> 🎧 **CD 4, track 48** — Seite 35, Übung 2
>
> **a** Ich fahre jeden Tag Rad.
> **b** Ich spiele am Nachmittag Gitarre.
> **c** Ich tanze dreimal in der Woche.
> **d** Ich schwimme am Donnerstag.
> **e** Ich spiele am Wochenende Golf.
> **f** Ich sehe am Abend fern.

2A Freizeit und Hobbys

AT 4.2-3 **3** Write four sentences saying what you do and how often. They don't have to be true!

Answers: students' own answers

2A.5 Am Wochenende (Seite 36)

AT 3.1 **1** Draw lines to match the German and English expressions.

Answers: am Wochenende – at the weekend; am Mittwoch – on Wednesday; jede Woche – every week; am Abend – in the evening; zweimal in der Woche – twice a week; jeden Tag – every day

AT 4.2-3 **2** Write six sentences about yourself, using the time expressions above and vocabulary about activities you have learned in this unit.

Answers: students' own answers

AT 3.3-4 **3** Read the paragraph and note down: two things Claas is positive about and why; two things he is negative about and why.

Answers: positive: computer games – exciting, playing ice hockey with brother – it's tough but cool; negative: shopping – expensive, watching TV – boring

2A.6A Sprachlabor (Seite 37)

1 Interpret the pictures and write sentences describing them.

Answers: a Ich spiele Fußball. b Sie spielen Tennis. c Spielst du Gitarre? d Spielt ihr am Computer? e Wir spielen Schach. f Er spielt Klavier.

2 Fill in the gaps.

Answers: ich fahre, du fährst, er / sie / es fährt, wir fahren, ihr fahrt, sie / Sie fahren; ich lese, du liest, er / sie / es liest, wir lesen, ihr lest, sie / Sie lesen

2A.6B Think (Seite 38)

1 Write P (positive) or N (negative) by these words and expressions.

Answers: Positive: gut, super, gern, lustig, prima; Negative: langweilig, nicht gern, schlecht, furchtbar, nicht so gut

2 Put together the syllables to make the German words for sports and musical instruments. Insert them in the grid and identify the shaded word. Each word has been started for you.

Answers: a Rugby; b Tennis; c Klavier; d Gitarre; e Schwimmen. The shaded word is: Geige. It means: violin.

3 Translate these words into German and say them out loud. They all have an -e on the end. In that list, can you spot two singular nouns and two plural nouns?

Answers: Schlange, (ich) fahre, (ich) spiele, (ich) sehe, Hunde, Freunde, (ich) gehe, Gitarre; singular nouns: Schlange, Gitarre; plural nouns: Hunde, Freunde

2B Wo wohnst du?

Unit 2B Wo wohnst du? Unit overview grid

Page reference	Objectives	Grammar	Skills and pronunciation	Key language	Framework	AT level
Pages 72–73 **2B.1 Meine Region**	Say where you live and whether you like it; say what the weather is like in your region	*Es ist* + adjectives	Pronounce the *ch* sound	Woher kommst du? Wo wohnst du? Ich komme aus (Deutschland). Ich wohne in (Köln). Wo ist das? Das ist im Norden/Süden/Osten/Westen. Das ist im Nordosten/Nordwesten/Südosten/Südwesten. Gefällt es dir? Ja, es gefällt mir gut. Nein, es gefällt mir nicht. Wie ist das Wetter? Es ist sonnig, kalt, heiß, neblig, windig, wolkig, schön, warm. Es regnet. Es schneit. Es gewittert. Es friert.	L&S 1.1, 1.2 R&W 2.4, 2.5 KAL 4.1 LLS 5.2, 5.3, 5.4, 5.6	1.2, 2.2, 3.2, 4.2–3
Pages 74–75 **2B.2 Hier wohne ich**	Describe what type of house and neighbourhood you live in	*Ich wohne in* + *einem/einer/einem …* Present tense of *wohnen*	Adapt familiar language to generate new language; work out new language from the component parts of compound words	Wo wohnst du? Ich wohne in der Stadt, in einem Dorf, in einer Wohnsiedlung, auf dem Land, am Stadtrand. Ich wohne in einer Wohnung. Ich wohne in einem Einfamilienhaus, Doppelhaus, Reihenhaus, Bungalow. Ich wohne (nicht) gern …, denn … Das finde ich grün, interessant, langweilig, laut, schön, toll. manchmal	L&S 1.1 R&W 2.2, 2.4 KAL 4.2, 4.3, 4.5 LLS 5.1, 5.4	1.1, 1.3, 2.2–3, 3.1–3, 4.2–3
Pages 76–77 **2B.3 Mein Haus**	Describe the rooms in your house or flat and where they are	Learn numbers up to 100	Use existing knowledge to work out language rules	Numbers up to 100 Das ist … der Balkon, der Garten, der Keller, die Dusche, die Garage, die Küche, das Badezimmer, das Esszimmer, das Schlafzimmer, das Wohnzimmer Wie ist (die Küche)? cool, groß, kalt, klein, laut, praktisch, schön, super im Erdgeschoss, im ersten/zweiten Stock	L&S 1.1, 1.2 R&W 2.2, 2.4, 2.5 LLS 5.1, 5.4, 5.7	1.1, 1.3, 2.1–3, 3.1–2, 4.3

105

2B Wo wohnst du?

Page reference	Objectives	Grammar	Skills and pronunciation	Key language	Framework	AT level
Pages 78–79 **2B.4 Mein Zimmer**	Say what is in your room and where things are	Es gibt + einen/eine/ein ... Prepositions + dative (der/die/das become dem/der/dem)	Understand the importance of learning the gender of new nouns	Es gibt/In meinem Zimmer gibt es ... einen Computer, einen Fernseher, einen Kleiderschrank, einen Schreibtisch, einen Stuhl, eine Lampe, eine Stereoanlage, ein Bett, ein Poster, ein Regal, ein Sofa auf, hinter, in, neben, unter, vor, zwischen	L&S 1.1, 1.4 R&W 2.4 KAL 4.3, 4.4 LLS 5.1, 5.4, 5.8	1.2–3, 2.2, 3.3, 4.2–3
Pages 80–81 **2B.5 Kathis Videoblog**	Describe your house and your dream house	Recycle the key grammar points of the unit	Read for sense and extract information from texts	mein Traumhaus, meine Traumwohnung in den Bergen, am Meer, in der Stadt, auf dem Land	L&S 1.1, 1.2, 1.5 R&W 2.1, 2.2, 2.5 LLS 5.7	1.4, 2.3–4, 3.3–4, 4.2–4

Unit 2B: Week-by-week overview
(Three-year KS3 Route: assuming six weeks' work or approximately 10–12.5 hours)
(Two-year KS3 Route: assuming four weeks' work or approximately 6.5–8.5 hours)

About Unit 2B, Wo wohnst du?: In this unit, students exchange information about where they live: they describe the weather, say what type of neighbourhood and house they live in, and give detailed descriptions of their home and own room. They also learn numbers up to 100 (in the context of house numbers). The *Lesen* page provides an opportunity to find out some facts and figures about German-speaking countries and learn about life in an area of Germany. Students develop their knowledge of the German case system: they use the nominative case (*das ist + der/die/das*), *es gibt* + accusative (*In meinem Zimmer gibt es einen/eine/ein ...*) and a range of prepositions followed by the dative (*in/hinter/auf*, etc. + *dem/der/dem*). They review present tense endings of regular verbs (*wohnen*), learn new ways to express likes, dislikes and opinions, and continue to use linking words to build extended sentences. Learning strategies are given emphasis throughout. The pronunciation focus is *ch*.

	Three-Year KS3 Route			Two-Year KS3 Route	
Week	**Resources**	**Objectives**	**Week**	**Resources**	**Objectives**
1	2B.1 Meine Region 2B.6 Sprachlabor ex. 5 and 6	Say where you live and whether you like it; say what the weather is like in your region Es ist + adjectives Pronounce the ch sound	1	2B.1 Meine Region (Omit Challenge) 2B.6 Sprachlabor ex. 5 and 6	Say where you live and whether you like it; say what the weather is like in your region Es ist + adjectives Pronounce the ch sound
2	2B.2 Hier wohne ich 2B.6 Sprachlabor ex. 1	Describe what type of house and neighbourhood you live in Ich wohne in einem/einer/einem ...; present tense of wohnen Adapt familiar language to generate new language; work out new language from the component parts of compound words	2	2B.2 Hier wohne ich (Omit ex. 9) 2B.6 Sprachlabor ex. 1	Describe what type of house and neighbourhood you live in Ich wohne in einem/einer/einem ...; present tense of wohnen Adapt familiar language to generate new language; work out new language from the component parts of compound words

2B Wo wohnst du?

	Three-Year KS3 Route			Two-Year KS3 Route	
Week	Resources	Objectives	Week	Resources	Objectives
3	2B.3 Mein Haus	Describe the rooms in your house or flat and where they are Learn numbers up to 100 Use existing knowledge to work out language rules	3	2B.3 Mein Haus (*Omit ex. 5 and 8*)	Describe the rooms in your house or flat and where they are Learn numbers up to 100 Use existing knowledge to work out language rules
4	2B.4 Mein Zimmer 2B.6 Sprachlabor ex. 2–4	Say what is in your room and where things are *Es gibt einen/eine/ein …*; prepositions followed by the dative (*der/die/das* become *dem/der/dem*) Understand the importance of learning the gender of new nouns	4	2B.4 Mein Zimmer (*Omit ex. 3 and 8–9*) 2B.6 Sprachlabor ex. 2–4 2B.8 Vokabular 2B.8 Testseite	Say what is in your room and where things are *Es gibt einen/eine/ein …*; prepositions followed by the dative (*der/die/das* become *dem/der/dem*) Understand the importance of learning the gender of new nouns Key vocabulary and learning checklist Assessment in all four skills
5	2B.5 Kathis Videoblog	Describe your house and your dream home Recycle the key grammar points of the unit Read for sense and extract information from texts			
6	2B.7 Extra (Star/Plus) 2B.8 Vokabular 2B.8 Testseite 2B Lesen	Reinforcement and extension of the language of the unit Key vocabulary and learning checklist Assessment in all four skills Further reading to explore the language of the unit and cultural themes			

2B.1 Wo wohnst du?

2B.1 Meine Region
Seite 72–73

Planner

Objectives
- Vocabulary: say where you live and whether you like it; say what the weather is like in your region
- Grammar: *es ist* + adjectives
- Skills: pronounce the *ch* sound

Video
- Video clip 2B

Resources
- Student Book, pages 72–73
- CD 2, tracks 2–3
- Foundation and Higher Workbooks, page 40
- Workbook audio: CD 3 and 4, track 49
- Copymasters 51 (ex. 2–3), 53 (ex. 1), 54 (ex. 2)
- Interactive OxBox, Unit 2B

Key language
Woher kommst du? Wo wohnst du?
Ich komme aus (Deutschland). Ich wohne in (Köln).
Wo ist das? Das ist im Norden / Süden / Osten / Westen.
Das ist im Nordosten / Nordwesten / Südosten / Südwesten.
Gefällt es dir? Ja, es gefällt mir gut. Nein, es gefällt mir nicht.
Wie ist das Wetter? Es ist sonnig / kalt / heiß / neblig / windig / wolkig / schön / warm.
Es regnet / schneit / gewittert / friert.

Framework references
L&S 1.1, 1.2; R&W 2.4, 2.5; KAL 4.1; LLS 5.2, 5.3, 5.4, 5.6

Starters
- Copymaster 51, ex. 2–3.
- Students look at the map and texts on page 72. Challenge them to identify the German for:
  - Germany, Austria, Switzerland, Munich, Cologne, Vienna, Geneva
  - in the north, in the south, in the west, in the east
  - I live in, I come from (they should remember these from spread 0.4)
  - I like it, I don't like it (to give them a clue, point out that once they've identified everything else, there are only two sentences left to choose from).
- Student Book page 73, ex. 4: students match the weather phrases to the pictures.

Plenaries
- Ask students to note down three key words for each person (from the map and texts on page 72), e.g. *Lukas: Deutschland, Köln, Westen*. For Markus and Suse, they could add a tick or cross to indicate whether they like or dislike where they live. Write the interview questions on the board: *Woher kommst du? Wo wohnst du? Gefällt es dir?* Students then try to reconstruct the four interviews, referring only to their notes and the interview questions written on the board.
- Student Book page 73, ex. 7: memory game using the weather phrases.

Homework
- Student Book page 72, ex. 3.
- Student Book page 73, ex. 8 and / or *Challenge*.
- Students apply the strategies from spread 2B.6 (*Sprachlabor* Techniques for learning new words) to try to learn the weather phrases.

Video clip 2B: Nina in Gefahr!

Synopsis:
Nina and Kathi are going away for the weekend to stay with Nina's Uncle Robert in Dresden. Outside the railway station, Nina realises she must have left her maths test in her room at home – she got a very bad mark in the test so doesn't want her mother to find it! She phones Ali and asks him to go to her home and hide the test before her mother sees it. The scene switches to Nina's room, where Ali is searching for the test. Nina gives him instructions over the phone but the test is nowhere to be found. Back at home after the weekend, Nina searches for the test herself, but in vain. She phones her mother, expecting the worst … then suddenly finds the test in her bag. It has been there all weekend!

Play the video through a couple of times and ask questions to check that students understand the gist of it. Suggested focus:

- From the images we see at the start (trains, departure times, travellers with luggage, Kathi and Nina carrying rucksacks), ask students to guess what is happening (the girls are setting off on a train journey). Challenge them to spot where exactly they are going (Dresden) and who they'll be visiting (Nina's Uncle Robert).
- Pause the clip at the train departures board. Ask students how many languages they see (German, English, French) and then what the German and French words for "departure" are (*Abfahrt, départ*). Use the platform numbers and town names as an opportunity to revise numbers and spellings.
- Invite students to guess what Nina's problem is (outside the railway station at the start of the clip). They'll be able to tell from the way she rifles through her bag that she's left something behind,

2B.1 Wo wohnst du?

but can they explain the problem in more detail? Challenge them to identify the item she's lost and the school subject involved (maths test) and her mark in the test (five).

- Whose photo does Ali find under Nina's bed? Challenge students to recall how Nina usually describes him. (Nico's brother Ralf – *so wundervoll, so schön, so intelligent, so sportlich …*)

Video clip 2B

(*Kathi and Nina at the railway station*)
Kathi: Nico und ich, wir mögen genau dieselben Sachen … er mag Mathe und ich auch … er hasst Sport … genau wie ich … Er hört gern dieselbe Musik wie ich …
Nina: Ja, ja. Also. Das ist der Hauptbahnhof. Und wir fahren jetzt mit dem Zug zu Onkel Robert nach Dresden.
Kathi: Okay, super!
Nina: Ich habe irgendwas vergessen … Mist, wo ist er?
Kathi: Wer denn?
Nina: Mein Mathe-Test. Ich habe eine fünf – total furchtbar!
Kathi: Eine fünf? … Nicht gut!
Nina: Er liegt bestimmt auf meinem Bett. Und … dann geht meine Mama in mein Zimmer – oh nein!
Kathi: Auch nicht gut!
Nina: Ich muss sofort nach Hause.
Kathi: Nein, nein. Keine Panik. Ähh … ruf doch einfach Ali an.
Nina: Okay.

(*Ali is in Nina's room looking for the test*)
Ali: Okay, ich bin in deinem Zimmer.
Nina: Der Mathe-Test ist auf dem Bett.
Ali: Auf dem Bett… nein – da ist nichts.
Nina: Was? Ist er unter dem Bett?
Ali: Äh … nein, da ist auch … nichts.
Nina: Dann hinter dem Schreibtisch.
Ali: Hinter dem Schreibtisch … nein.
Nina: Ich weiß – vor dem Stuhl.
Ali: Vor dem Stuhl – nein, da ist auch nichts.
Nina: Oh nein … ich weiß es: zwischen dem Bett und dem Kleiderschrank!
Ali: Zwischen dem Bett und dem Kleiderschrank – nein, da ist nichts.
Nina: Oder vielleicht neben der Lampe?
Ali: Neben der Lampe … nein, auch nicht!
Nina: Oh nein – was mache ich bloß? Sie hat den Test schon! Sie weiß alles! Ich bin erledigt!
Ali: Ist er vielleicht woanders? In der Küche? Im Wohnzimmer?
Nina: Nein, es ist hoffnungslos! Geh einfach.
Ali: Sicher?

Nina: Ja. Danke, Ali.
Ali: (*leaves Nina's room and says goodbye to Nina's mother*) Ich habe das Buch, Frau Neumann. Vielen Dank noch mal.

(*Two days later, Nina arrives back home*)
Nina: (*reads a message from her mother*) „Bin auf der Arbeit. Bitte ruf sofort an." Ruf sofort an. Oh Mist … sie weiß es!
Nina: (*talks to Kathi on the phone*) Kathi, ich finde den Mathe-Test nicht. Nirgends! … Nicht in der Küche … nicht im Wohnzimmer … und nicht im Flur … Kathi, ich rufe dich später noch mal an, okay?
Nina: (*phones her mother*) Hallo, Mama, ich bin's … Ja, ich bin zu Hause … Ja, das Wetter war schön … (*finds test in her bag*) … Ja, war ein sehr sehr schönes Wochenende. Sehr schön. Tschüs! (*puts phone down*) Ja!

Sprachpunkt
Der Mathe-Test ist auf dem Bett.
Zwischen dem Bett und dem Kleiderschrank.
Neben der Lampe.
In der Küche? Im Wohnzimmer?

AT 1.2
AT 3.2

1 Hör zu (1–4). Wer spricht?

See the *Planner* above for a starter activity based on the map. Students then listen while looking at the map, photos and captions. They note down the people's names in the order they hear them. Students should remember *Ich komme aus …* and *Ich wohne in …* from spread 0.4. Ask a few questions about the texts to check for comprehension.

Answers: Lukas, Anne, Markus, Suse

CD 2, track 2   Seite 72, Übung 1

1 – Woher kommst du, Lukas? Wo wohnst du?
   – Also, ich komme aus Deutschland, und ich wohne in Köln. Das ist im Westen.
2 – Und du, Anne? Woher kommst du? Und wo wohnst du?
   – Ich komme aus Österreich. Ich wohne in Wien. Das ist im Osten.
3 – Markus, woher kommst du? Und wo wohnst du?
   – Ich? Ich komme aus Deutschland, und ich wohne in München. Das ist im Süden.
   – Gefällt es dir in München?
   – Ja, es gefällt mir gut.
4 – Woher kommst du, Suse? Wo wohnst du?
   – Ich komme aus der Schweiz. Ich wohne in Zürich. Das ist im Norden.
   – Gefällt es dir in Zürich?
   – Nein, es gefällt mir nicht.

2B.1 Wo wohnst du?

LLS 5.6

Follow-up
Play the recording again and encourage students to read aloud the teenagers' answers. The boys could answer on behalf of Lukas and Markus, and the girls on behalf of Anne and Suse. Point out the tip on pronouncing *ch* and insist on correct pronunciation of *Österreich*, *München* and *Zürich*.
To exploit the texts and the recording further, give students a few moments to try to memorise where each person is from and where they live, then ask them to close their books. Play the recording, but pause it before the name of each country, town and region and challenge students to supply the missing words.
Able students could progress to reconstructing the interviews from key words: see first plenary suggestion in the *Planner* above.

AT 2.2

2 Ratespiel! Wo wohnst du?
Students play a game based on the map. They take turns to say which country and region they live in; their partner searches on the map and identifies the town, e.g.
A: *Ich komme aus Deutschland. Ich wohne im Norden.*
B: *Du wohnst in Bremen!*

AT 4.2–3
R&W 2.4

3 Wo wohnst du? Schreib Sätze.
Students write a speech bubble for themselves, explaining where they come from, where they live and whether they like it. Alternatively, they write a speech bubble on behalf of their favourite celebrity.

AT 3.2
KAL 4.1
LLS 5.3, 5.4

4 Was passt zusammen?
Students match the weather phrases to the corresponding pictures. Afterwards, discuss what clues helped them to do this, e.g. similarity to English words, process of elimination. Encourage them to try sounding out the words – they can check their pronunciation in ex. 5.

Answers: **a** 2; **b** 8; **c** 4; **d** 12; **e** 7; **f** 3; **g** 10; **h** 6; **i** 1; **j** 9; **k** 5; **l** 11

AT 1.2

5 Hör zu (1–12). Ist alles richtig?
Students listen to check their answers to ex. 4 and their pronunciation of the weather phrases.

CD 2, track 3   Seite 73, Übung 5

1	Es regnet.	7	Es ist windig.
2	Es ist sonnig.	8	Es ist kalt.
3	Es ist wolkig.	9	Es schneit.
4	Es ist heiß.	10	Es ist schön.
5	Es gewittert.	11	Es friert.
6	Es ist warm.	12	Es ist neblig.

AT 4.2

6 Schreib Sätze.
Referring to the weather symbols on the map of Germany, students write short sentences to describe the weather in different towns / regions.

Answers: **Hamburg:** *Es regnet.* **Im Westen:** *Es ist heiß.* **Berlin:** *Es ist sonnig.* **Dortmund:** *Es ist wolkig.* **Im Süden:** *Es schneit.* **Im Osten:** *Es ist windig.*

AT 2.2
LLS 5.2

7 Gedächtnisspiel!
Students play a memory game to practise the weather phrases, e.g.
A: *Es ist warm.*
B: *Es ist warm und windig.*
A: *Es ist warm, windig und …*
Can any pairs remember all twelve phrases? Discuss this type of activity as a memorisation technique: how effective do students find it? A lot of new language comes up in this unit (weather phrases, types of neighbourhood / house / flat, rooms and furniture, prepositions) so it is worth spending some time in advance focusing on how students are going to learn all these words. See spread 2B.6 (*Sprachlabor* Techniques for learning new words, ex. 5). Encourage students to try out different strategies throughout their work on this unit.

AT 4.2–3

8 Schreib Sätze.
Students write a description of today's weather, saying whether they like it or not.

AT 4.3
R&W 2.4, 2.5

Challenge
Students look at the map of Europe on page 14 of the Student Book, choose a country and imagine they live there. They write a blog saying which town and region they live in, describing the weather, and saying whether they like it or not.
Encourage them to produce an actual mock-up of a blog page, e.g. including a personal profile (as on the *Videoblog* pages in most units of the Student Book).

2B Wo wohnst du?

2B.2 Hier wohne ich

Seite 74–75

Planner

Objectives
- Vocabulary: describe what type of house and neighbourhood you live in
- Grammar: *ich wohne in einem / einer / einem …*; present tense of *wohnen*
- Skills: adapt familiar language to generate new language; work out new language from the component parts of compound words

Resources
- Student Book, pages 74–75
- CD 2, tracks 4–6
- Foundation and Higher Workbooks, page 41
- Workbook audio: CD 3 and 4, track 50
- Copymasters 52 (ex. 3), 54 (ex.3), 55
- Interactive OxBox, Unit 2B

Key language
Wo wohnst du? Ich wohne in der Stadt / in einem Dorf / in einer Wohnsiedlung / auf dem Land / am Stadtrand.
Ich wohne in einer Wohnung. Ich wohne in einem Einfamilienhaus / Doppelhaus / Reihenhaus / Bungalow.
Ich wohne (nicht) gern …, denn …
Das finde ich grün / interessant / langweilig / laut / schön / toll.
manchmal

Framework references
L&S 1.1; R&W 2.2, 2.4; KAL 4.2, 4.3, 4.5; LLS 5.1, 5.4

Starters
- Before students open their books at page 74, they work with a partner to come up with five different types of area where people live, e.g. town centre, village, suburbs, housing estate, mountains, countryside, by the sea. They make a list, then open their books and look at photos a–e: how many places from their list do they see? Who has the most matches? The photos should help students to deduce the meaning of the new phrases. Encourage them to have a go at reading the phrases aloud, using their knowledge of German pronunciation.
- Student Book page 75, ex. 5: challenge students to match the German words to the photos of different types of housing. Afterwards, talk about any clues they used: see also the *Follow-up* to ex. 6 in the teaching notes below.
- Before looking at the present tense of *wohnen* (page 75), ask students to close their books and to try to recall the present tense of *spielen* (from spread 2A.1). To support them, display the subject pronouns in a list with the stem of the verb (*ich spiel_, du spiel_, er / sie spiel_*, etc.) and the jumbled-up endings alongside; challenge students to copy out the list with the endings in the correct places.

Plenaries
- After working on ex. 3, students tell their partner how they feel about the five locations in ex. 1, e.g. *Ich wohne nicht gern in der Stadt, denn es ist laut. Ich finde das furchtbar.*
Alternatively, tell them they must always contradict each other, i.e. if A says something positive about a place, B says something negative, and vice versa, e.g.
A: *Ich wohne gern auf dem Land, denn es ist grün.*
B: *Ich wohne nicht gern auf dem Land! Ich finde das furchtbar, denn es ist langweilig.*
- Students play a game in pairs to consolidate the different types of houses and neighbourhoods. Student A calls out a number 1–5 (from photos 1–5 in ex. 5) and a letter a–e (from photos a–e in ex. 1). B says a corresponding sentence and adds whether they like where they live together with an opinion, e.g.
A: *Nummer drei und e.*
B: *Ich wohne in einem Doppelhaus auf dem Land. Ich wohne gern hier, denn es ist grün.*

Homework
- Student Book page 74, ex. 4.
- Student Book page 75, *Challenge*.

AT 1.2
AT 3.2

1 Hör zu und lies.
This activity introduces phrases to describe different neighbourhoods. See the *Planner* above for a starter activity before students open their books at page 74.
Students then listen while following the text. Encourage them to read aloud, imitating the pronunciation.

2B.2 Wo wohnst du?

CD 2, track 4 — Seite 74, Übung 1

a – Wo wohnst du, Jana?
– Ich wohne in der Stadt.
b – Wo wohnst du, Tobias?
– Ich wohne in einem Dorf.
c – Und du, Sandra? Wo wohnst du?
– Ich wohne am Stadtrand.
d – Ulf, wo wohnst du?
– Ich wohne in einer Wohnsiedlung.
e – Wo wohnst du, Katrin?
– Ich wohne auf dem Land.

AT 2.2

2 Wo wohnst du?
Students take turns to ask and answer the question *Wo wohnst du?*, pretending to be the people in ex. 1.

AT 3.1

3 Was passt zusammen?
Students match the German adjectives to their English equivalents.
Once they've done this, ask them to choose adjectives to describe what they think of the five locations in ex. 1, e.g. *in der Stadt: laut; auf dem Land: grün.* Encourage them to use adjectives they've learned in other contexts (e.g. *interessant, spannend, lustig*) as well as the ones listed here.

Answers: **a** 3; **b** 4; **c** 5; **d** 1; **e** 2

KAL 4.2

Think
This activity encourages students to adapt language they already know to generate new language – an important skill in language learning. They already know that *Ich spiele gern Tennis* means "I like playing tennis", so what would they add to *Ich wohne in der Stadt* to make it mean "I like living in the town"? (*Ich wohne gern in der Stadt*)

AT 3.3
AT 4.3
R&W 2.4

4 Lies Saschas Nachricht. Schreib eine Antwort.
Students use Sascha's text as a model for writing a similar paragraph about themselves, saying where they're from, where they live, whether they like living in their neighbourhood and why. To help them, display a copy of Sascha's text, using one colour for the basic framework that students can reuse (*Ich heiße … und ich komme aus … Ich wohne …*, etc.) and a different colour for the words and phrases that students can replace with their own (*Sascha, Österreich, auf dem Land*, etc.). Encourage students to use some of the adjectives they came up with in ex. 3.

AT 3.2

5 Was passt zusammen?
This activity introduces types of accommodation. Students choose a picture to represent where each person lives.

Answers: **Nina:** 4; **Ali:** 1; **Anna:** 3; **Maik:** 2; **Nico:** 5

AT 1.2

6 Hör zu. Ist alles richtig?
Students listen to check their answers to ex. 5.

CD 2, track 5 — Seite 75, Übung 6

Nina: Ich wohne in einer Wohnung. Das ist Foto vier.
Ali: Ich wohne in einem Reihenhaus. Das ist Foto eins.
Anna: Ich wohne in einem Doppelhaus. Das ist Foto drei.
Maik: Ich wohne in einem Bungalow. Das ist Foto zwei.
Nico: Ich wohne in einem Einfamilienhaus. Das ist Foto fünf.

R&W 2.2
LLS 5.4

Follow-up
Point out that it is sometimes possible to work out new language from the component parts of compound words.
Help students to deconstruct the nouns in ex. 5:
- *Doppelhaus* = literally "double house", i.e. a house that is split down the middle – in English we call it a semi-detached house
- *Einfamilienhaus* = literally "one-family house", i.e. a whole house (not divided into two) that is lived in by one family – in English we call it a detached house
- *Reihe* = "series" / "row", so *Reihenhäuser* are literally houses in rows – in English we call them terraced houses.

Point out that this sort of creative thinking is a useful technique for working out new language and an important skill in language learning.

KAL 4.3, 4.5
LLS 5.1

7 Füll die Lücken aus.
Referring to the *Grammatik* box on *ich wohne in + einem / einer*, students fill in the missing words in sentences a–f.
Remind them that they have come across this sort of thing before in German, i.e. the words for "the" and "a" sometimes change depending on the gender of the noun they relate to and what comes before them in the sentence, e.g. *Ich habe einen* + masculine nouns. Point out that this is why it is so important to learn the gender of nouns, because the gender determines what happens to words like "the" and "a".

Answers: **a** einem; **b** einem; **c** einer; **d** einem; **e** einem; **f** einer

2B.3 Wo wohnst du?

AT 1.2–3
L&S 1.1

8 Hör zu. Wo wohnen Jens, Maria, Jonas, Lene und Sven? Mach Notizen.

Students listen and note in German where each person lives. Tell them that for each person they may note two words only: the type of accommodation and the neighbourhood. Point out that it might help to abbreviate some of the words (e.g. *R-haus* instead of *Reihenhaus*, *E-f-haus* instead of *Einfamilienhaus*) but that they must make sure they can understand their notes afterwards because they may need them in ex. 9.

Answers: **Jens:** *Reihenhaus, Stadtrand;* **Maria:** *Doppelhaus, Stadt;* **Jonas:** *Wohnung, Wohnsiedlung;* **Lene:** *Einfamilienhaus, Land;* **Sven:** *Bungalow, Dorf*

🎧 **CD 2, track 6** Seite 75, Übung 8

- Wo wohnst du, Jens?
- Ich wohne in einem Reihenhaus am Stadtrand.
- Und du, Maria? Wo wohnst du?
- Ich? Ich wohne in einem Doppelhaus in der Stadt.
- Jonas, wo wohnst du?
- Also, ich wohne in einer Wohnung in einer Wohnsiedlung.
- Und wo wohnst du, Lene?
- Ich wohne in einem Einfamilienhaus auf dem Land.
- Sven, und du? Wo wohnst du?
- Tja, ich wohne in einem Bungalow in einem Dorf.

AT 4.2
R&W 2.4
KAL 4.3, 4.5

9 Schreib Sätze für Jens, Maria, Jonas, Lene und Sven.

Referring to their notes from ex. 8, students build a full sentence for each person to explain where they live. Refer them to the present tense conjugation of *wohnen* and remind them to use the *er / sie* form of the verb (instead of *ich*, which was used on the recording).

Afterwards, play the recording again so that students can check their answers.

Answers: see ex. 8 transcript

AT 2.2–3

10 👥 Wo wohnst du? Macht Dialoge.

Students exchange information about where they live. Encourage them to add opinions.

AT 4.3
R&W 2.4

Challenge

Students write a description of where they live. They are encouraged to give as many details as they can, e.g. country, region, what the weather is like, neighbourhood and type of house. Prompt them to include likes / dislikes and opinions, and to build longer sentences using linking words.

2B.3 Mein Haus Seite 76–77

Planner

Objectives
- Vocabulary: describe the rooms in your house or flat and say where they are
- Grammar: learn numbers up to 100
- Skills: use existing knowledge to work out language rules

Resources
- Student Book, pages 76–77
- CD 2, tracks 7–10
- Foundation and Higher Workbooks, page 42
- Workbook audio: CD 3 and 4, track 51
- Copymaster 52 (ex. 1, 2, 4)
- Interactive OxBox, Unit 2B

Key language
Numbers up to 100
Das ist … der Balkon, der Garten, der Keller, die Dusche, die Garage, die Küche, das Badezimmer, das Esszimmer, das Schlafzimmer, das Wohnzimmer

Wie ist (die Küche)?
cool, groß, kalt, klein, laut, praktisch, schön, super
im Erdgeschoss, im ersten / zweiten Stock

Framework references
L&S 1.1, 1.2; R&W 2.2, 2.4, 2.5; LLS 5.1, 5.4, 5.7

Starters
- Student Book page 76, ex. 1: this activity provides an opportunity to revise numbers up to 31 before higher numbers are introduced. See also the number games and counting games in the *Planner* for spread 0.2.
- Student Book page 77, ex. 6. Before playing the recording, challenge students to match the list of rooms in German to the numbered areas on the house plan. Some of the words are instantly recognisable because of their similarity to English, and learners of French may recognise *Dusche* as being similar to French *douche*. Students may also be able to make the link between *Wohn* (in *Wohnzimmer*) and the verb *wohnen*, and thereby deduce that *Wohn*zimmer is "<u>living</u> room".

2B.3 Wo wohnst du?

Plenaries
- Student Book page 76, ex. 5. Alternatively, students could play a guessing game based on ex. 5: they each write down a number (either from ex. 5 or from a different selection of numbers), keeping it hidden from their partner, then take turns to guess each other's number, e.g.
  A: *Wo wohnst du? Nummer einundneunzig?*
  B: *Nein!* (or *Ja!*)
  Who works out their partner's house number in the fewest guesses?
- Students play a dice game in pairs based on the house plan in ex. 6. The numbers on the dice correspond to the numbers on the plan (but since there are ten areas on the plan, students will need to throw the dice twice to get numbers 7–10). The aim is to be the first to "visit" all ten areas of the house and add a comment about each of them. For example:
  A: (throws a six) *Das ist der Keller. Der Keller ist kalt.*
  B: (throws a six and a three = nine) *Das ist das Badezimmer. Das Badezimmer ist schön.*

Homework
- Students apply the strategies suggested on spread 2B.6 (*Sprachlabor* Techniques for learning new words) to try to learn the new language from this spread.
- Student Book page 77, *Challenge*.

AT 1.1 / AT 2.1 **1 Hör zu – was kommt danach?**
This activity revises numbers 20–31 before higher numbers are introduced in ex. 2. There is a pause on the recording after each number to allow students to repeat it and say the next number in the sequence.

CD 2, track 7   Seite 76, Übung 1
zwanzig … einundzwanzig … zweiundzwanzig … dreiundzwanzig … vierundzwanzig … fünfundzwanzig … sechsundzwanzig … siebenundzwanzig … achtundzwanzig … neunundzwanzig … dreißig … einunddreißig

AT 1.1 / AT 3.1 **2 Hör zu und lies.**
This activity introduces numbers 40–100 (in tens). Students listen, read and repeat.

CD 2, track 8   Seite 76, Übung 2
vierzig, fünfzig, sechzig, siebzig, achtzig, neunzig, hundert

LLS 5.1 Think
Students are encouraged to use their knowledge of numbers 1–31 to work out how to say numbers 32–99.

AT 1.1 **3 Hör zu und finde die passenden Zahlen.**
Students listen and identify the numbers.

Answers: 57, 65, 32, 51, 62, 74, 93, 44, 87, 46, 39, 84

CD 2, track 9   Seite 76, Übung 3
siebenundfünfzig … fünfundsechzig … zweiunddreißig … einundfünfzig … zweiundsechzig … vierundsiebzig … dreiundneunzig … vierundvierzig … siebenundachtzig … sechsundvierzig … neununddreißig … vierundachtzig

AT 2.1 **4 Was kommt danach?**
Students take turns to say a number; their partner says the following number.

AT 2.1 **5 Wo wohnst du?**
Students practise numbers in the context of house numbers. Referring to the house plaques, students take turns to ask and say which number they live at, e.g.
A: *Wo wohnst du?*
B: *Nummer zweiundvierzig.*

AT 1.3 / L&S 1.1 / LLS 5.7 **6 Hör zu. Was passt zusammen?**
See the *Planner* above for a starter activity to help students prepare for listening: they match the list of rooms in German to the numbered areas on the house plan.
Students then listen as Nico shows Kathi around his house, and check whether they have identified the rooms correctly. Clues are provided by the sound effects.

Answers: **a** der Balkon – 8; **b** der Garten – 4; **c** der Keller – 6; **d** die Dusche – 10; **e** die Garage – 5; **f** die Küche – 1; **g** das Badezimmer – 9; **h** das Esszimmer – 2; **i** das Schlafzimmer – 7; **j** das Wohnzimmer – 3

2B.3 Wo wohnst du?

🎧 **CD 2, track 10**   Seite 77, Übung 6 und 7

- So, das ist unser Haus. Hier ist also das Erdgeschoss … Das ist die Küche …
- Oh, die Küche ist schön – Guten Tag, Frau …!
- Und das ist das Esszimmer. Es ist nicht groß.
- Aha.
- Und das ist das Wohnzimmer.
- Hallo Britta! … Das Wohnzimmer ist groß! Und das ist der Garten?
- Ja, das ist der Garten – klein, aber schön! … Und das ist die Garage. Es ist ziemlich laut in der Garage! Oh – hi Ulli!
- Und was ist das?
- Das ist der Keller.
- Uuuh – es ist kalt im Keller!
- So, jetzt sind wir im ersten Stock … Das ist mein Schlafzimmer …
- Dein Zimmer ist total cool! … Und das ist der Balkon – er ist super!
- So, und das ist das Badezimmer.
- Das Badezimmer ist sehr schön!
- Und das ist die Dusche!
- Ein Badezimmer und eine Dusche – sehr praktisch! … Und im zweiten Stock?
- Im zweiten Stock? Es gibt keinen zweiten Stock!
- Es gibt keinen zweiten Stock? Aber Nico, deine Familie ist so groß!
- Ja!

R&W 2.2 / LLS 5.4 **Follow-up**
Look more closely at the compound nouns in the list of rooms. First, challenge students to work out what the German for "room" is (*Zimmer*). They should be able to deduce this from *Wohnzimmer* (living room), *Esszimmer* (dining room), *Schlafzimmer* (bedroom) and *Badezimmer* (bathroom).
Students may already have recognised *Wohn* (in *Wohnzimmer*) as being related to the verb *wohnen* (to live). Point out that *Ess*, *Schlaf* and *Bade* are related to the verbs *essen*, *schlafen* and *baden*. Challenge students to work out the meanings of these verbs, e.g. if *Esszimmer* is a dining room (i.e. a room for dining or eating in), what do they think the verb *essen* means? Similarly, if *Schlafzimmer* is a bedroom (a room for sleeping in) and *Badezimmer* is a bathroom (a room for bathing in), what could the verbs *schlafen* and *baden* mean?

AT 1.3 / L&S 1.2 / LLS 5.7 **7 Hör noch einmal zu. Wie sind die Zimmer im Haus? Mach Notizen.**
Before doing ex. 7, point out the list of adjectives and invite students to match each one to a room in Nico's house (ex. 6), e.g. *kalt* might relate to the cellar or possibly the garage, *praktisch* is likely to relate to the kitchen, bathroom or shower.
Play the ex. 6 recording again so that students can check their predictions. Make sure they note the correct answers because they will need them in ex. 8.

Answers: die Küche – schön; das Esszimmer – nicht groß; das Wohnzimmer – groß; der Garten – klein, schön; die Garage – (ziemlich) laut; der Keller – kalt; Nicos Schlafzimmer – (total) cool; der Balkon – super; das Badezimmer – (sehr) schön; die Dusche – (sehr) praktisch

AT 2.2–3 **8 Was ist das? Wie ist das?**
Students take turns to ask each other what the rooms (on the house plan) are and what they are like (referring to their answers in ex. 7), e.g.
A: *Nummer 1 – was ist das?*
B: *Das ist die Küche.*
A: *Wie ist die Küche?*
B: *Die Küche ist schön.*

AT 3.2 **9 Lies den Dialog. Wo sind die Zimmer?**
Students read the conversation: Ali is describing his house to Kathi. Students identify where each room is: on the ground floor, the first floor or the second floor.

Answers: **im Erdgeschoss:** *die Küche;* **im 1. Stock:** *das Wohnzimmer, der Balkon, das Esszimmer, das Badezimmer;* **im 2. Stock:** *die Dusche, die Schlafzimmer (= bedrooms)*

AT 4.3 / R&W 2.4, 2.5 **Challenge**
Students draw out a house plan (representing their own or an imaginary house) and write a description of it, saying where the rooms are. Encourage them to add comments about the rooms, e.g. *Die Küche ist klein, aber sehr praktisch*. Suggest that they produce it in the style of an estate agent's property advertisement.

2B.4 Wo wohnst du?

2B.4 Mein Zimmer
Seite 78–79

Planner

Objectives
- Vocabulary: say what is in your room and where things are
- Grammar: *es gibt einen / eine / ein …*; prepositions followed by the dative (*der / die / das* become *dem / der / dem*)
- Skills: understand the importance of learning the gender of new nouns

Video
- Video clip 2B

Resources
- Student Book, pages 78–79
- CD 2, tracks 11–12
- Foundation and Higher Workbooks, page 43
- Workbook audio: CD 3 and 4, track 52
- Copymasters 51 (ex. 1), 53 (ex. 2–3), 54 (ex. 1)
- Interactive OxBox, Unit 2B

Key language
Es gibt / In meinem Zimmer gibt es … einen Computer, einen Fernseher, einen Kleiderschrank, einen Schreibtisch, einen Stuhl, eine Lampe, eine Stereoanlage, ein Bett, ein Poster, ein Regal, ein Sofa
auf, hinter, in, neben, unter, vor, zwischen

Framework references
L&S 1.1, 1.4; R&W 2.4; KAL 4.3, 4.4; LLS 5.1, 5.4, 5.8

Starters
- Copymaster 51, ex. 1.
- For a quick recap of key language from the unit so far and to prompt a review of learning strategies (see spread 2B.6: Techniques for learning new words), ask everyone to choose four words or phrases in English from the *Vokabular* list (page 87). They test how well their partner knows each phrase by challenging them to: say it in German, write it correctly, then put it into a sentence. (If you do this at the beginning of work on spread 2B.4, tell students to choose language from the first three spreads only.)
- Beat the clock. To begin a lesson before introducing prepositions, tell the class to keep their books closed and challenge them to remember all eleven items from Ali's bedroom (a–k on page 78) within a time limit:
Teacher: (sets a stopwatch) *Okay, los geht's …*
Student A: *Es gibt ein Bett.*
Teacher: *Richtig, ein Punkt!*
Student B: *Es gibt …*

Plenaries
- Students play a memory game in pairs:
A: *In meinem Zimmer gibt es ein Bett.*
B: *In meinem Zimmer gibt es ein Bett und einen Stuhl.*
A: *In meinem Zimmer gibt es ein Bett, einen Stuhl und …*
Can any pairs list all eleven furniture items from ex. 1?
- In pairs, students talk about the picture of Ali's bedroom, taking turns to name the items of furniture and say where they are. They give one piece of information at a time, e.g.
A: *In Alis Zimmer gibt es einen Stuhl.*
B: *Ja, der Stuhl ist vor …*
A: *Und es gibt einen Computer …*
To make this competitive, tell them that the person who has the last word is the winner. This encourages students to draw on prior learning to say as much as they can, e.g. by adding opinions, saying what colour things are, etc. When one of the pair can find nothing else to say about the picture, their partner wins the game.

Homework
- Student Book page 78, ex. 4.
- Student Book page 79, ex. 9 and / or *Challenge*.

AT 1.2
KAL 4.4
LLS 5.1, 5.4

1 Hör zu. Was passt zusammen?
Students listen to the bedroom description while looking at the picture. They match the list of words (a–k) to the furniture items in the picture, using a range of strategies to work out meaning: cognates, familiar language (they learned *Stuhl* and *Schreibtisch* in Unit 1B), links with words they already know (they may link *Fernseher* with *ich sehe fern*, which they learned in Unit 2A), process of elimination. You may wish to draw attention to word order (*In meinem Zimmer gibt es …*). Ask students where they have met this "verb second" word order before (Unit 1B: *Am Montag habe ich Mathe*, etc.).

Answers: **a** 2; **b** 9; **c** 11; **d** 1; **e** 4; **f** 3; **g** 8; **h** 5; **i** 10; **j** 7; **k** 6

🎧 **CD 2, track 11** Seite 78, Übung 1

Also, das ist mein Zimmer. In meinem Zimmer gibt es ein Bett. Es gibt auch einen Schreibtisch, und es gibt eine Lampe. In meinem Zimmer gibt es einen Kleiderschrank und ein Regal. Es gibt einen Fernseher und ein Poster. In meinem Zimmer gibt es ein Sofa und einen Stuhl. Und es gibt auch einen Computer.

2B.4 Wo wohnst du?

KAL 4.3
LLS 5.1

Think

Read through the information about *es gibt* + indefinite article. Students may remember (from Unit 1B) that *Schreibtisch* and *Stuhl* are masculine nouns, and they could check the genders of the other furniture items in the Glossary or a dictionary. Once they've done this, they'll see that, after *es gibt*, the word "a" changes to *einen* only with masculine nouns; with feminine and neuter nouns, it remains as *eine* and *ein* respectively. Ask students where they have come across this sort of thing before (*ich habe* + *einen / eine / ein* in Unit 1A).

Take this opportunity to emphasise how important it is to learn the gender of nouns. Point out that you need to know the gender to work out which form of the indefinite (or definite) article to use.

KAL 4.3

2 Füll die Lücken aus.

Students fill in the correct forms of the indefinite article: *einen*, *eine* or *ein*.

Answers: **a** *ein*; **b** *einen*; **c** *einen*; **d** *eine*; **e** *ein*; **f** *einen*

AT 2.2

3 Macht Sätze.

Students take turns to point to items of furniture in the picture. Their partner responds with a full sentence, e.g.
A: *Nummer 5!*
B: *In meinem Zimmer gibt es ein Bett.*

AT 4.2
R&W 2.4
KAL 4.4

4 Was gibt es in deinem Zimmer? Schreib sechs Sätze.

Students describe what is in their room. Encourage them to vary the word order, as in the ex. 1 recording: *In meinem Zimmer gibt es …* and *Es gibt …* If appropriate, encourage them to add comments, e.g. *Das finde ich toll, Es gefällt mir gut.*

AT 1.2–3
L&S 1.1

5 Sieh dir das Video an. Was ist die richtige Reihenfolge?

Play the middle section of video clip 2B, in which Ali is in Nina's room looking for the missing maths test. Students note the order in which the furniture items are mentioned. Ask them to identify the two rooms mentioned towards the end of the clip (kitchen, living room).

Answers: **1** *bed;* **2** *desk;* **3** *chair;* **4** *wardrobe;* **5** *lamp*

Video clip 2B
CD 2, track 12   Seite 78, Übung 5

Ali: Okay, ich bin in deinem Zimmer.
Nina: Der Mathe-Test ist auf dem Bett.
Ali: Auf dem Bett… nein – da ist nichts.
Nina: Was? Ist er unter dem Bett?
Ali: Äh … nein, da ist auch … nichts.
Nina: Dann hinter dem Schreibtisch.
Ali: Hinter dem Schreibtisch … nein.
Nina: Ich weiß – vor dem Stuhl.
Ali: Vor dem Stuhl – nein, da ist auch nichts.
Nina: Oh nein … ich weiß es: zwischen dem Bett und dem Kleiderschrank!
Ali: Zwischen dem Bett und dem Kleiderschrank – nein, da ist nichts.
Nina: Oder vielleicht neben der Lampe?
Ali: Neben der Lampe … nein, auch nicht!
Nina: Oh nein – was mache ich bloß? Sie hat den Test schon! Sie weiß alles! Ich bin erledigt!
Ali: Ist er vielleicht woanders? In der Küche? Im Wohnzimmer?
Nina: Nein, es ist hoffnungslos! Geh einfach.
Ali: Sicher?
Nina: Ja. Danke, Ali.

Follow-up

- The video clip can be used to introduce the prepositions. Play it again and pause after each one (*auf dem Bett*, *unter dem Bett*, etc.). Challenge students to work out what each preposition means from what they see on the video, e.g. pause after *auf dem Bett* and ask students where Ali is looking – <u>on</u> the bed.
Play the video again. Each time students hear a preposition, they repeat it and place their pen (or something else from their school bag) in the corresponding position, e.g. <u>on top of</u> their pencil case, <u>under</u> their pencil case, <u>behind</u> their pencil case, etc.

- Students play a game using a pen or other item from their school bags. They take turns to place the pen on top of a book, under a book, inside their pencil case, etc.; their partner responds as quickly as possible by saying the corresponding preposition, e.g. student A places the pen under a book, B responds immediately by saying *Unter!*; A moves the pen beside the book, B quickly says *Neben!* If B hesitates for too long, A wins; they swap over.

2B.5 Wo wohnst du?

KAL 4.3
LLS 5.1

6 Schreib die richtigen Wörter auf.
Read through the *Grammatik* information about prepositions followed by the dative. Point out (see the *Think* box) that *in + dem* usually becomes *im*. Emphasise again that it is very important to know the gender of nouns, because the gender determines the form of the definite or indefinite article.
Students then complete sentences a–f with the correct prepositions + *dem / der / dem*. The language box at top right lists all the prepositions in German and English.

Answers: **a** neben dem; **b** auf dem; **c** hinter der; **d** im; **e** unter dem; **f** unter dem

AT 4.2

7 Wo ist alles in Alis Zimmer? Schreib Sätze.
Students look at the picture of Ali's bedroom on page 78. They write sentences using prepositions to describe where the items are.

AT 2.2
L&S 1.4
KAL 4.3
LLS 5.1, 5.8

8 Ist alles richtig?
Students compare their answers for ex. 7. Encourage them to evaluate their partner's sentences, not only in terms of the prepositions but also to check whether the correct forms of the definite article have been used. Insist that they aim to do this activity entirely in German, e.g.
A: *Wo ist die Lampe? Was hast du?*
B: *Die Lampe ist auf der Schreibtisch.*
A: *Nein, nicht auf der Schreibtisch – auf dem Schreibtisch!*
B: *Ach ja, auf dem Schreibtisch …*

AT 3.3

9 Lies den Text. Wo sind die Möbel?
Students read the bedroom description and identify each item of furniture on the plan.

Answers: **1** bed; **2** lamp; **3** computer; **4** desk; **5** chair; **6** sofa; **7** wardrobe

AT 4.3
R&W 2.4

Challenge
Students write a description of a bedroom, saying where everything is and adding their opinions. This could be their own room, their ideal room or an invented description of a celebrity's room.
Encourage them to focus on accuracy, e.g. by making sure they use the correct form of the indefinite and definite articles (*es gibt + einen / eine / ein …*, prepositions + *dem / der …*).

2B.5 Kathis Videoblog
Seite 80–81

Planner

Objectives
- Vocabulary: describe your house and your dream house
- Grammar: recycle the key grammar points of the unit
- Skills: read for sense and extract information from texts

Video
- Video blog 2B

Resources
- Student Book, pages 80–81
- CD 2, tracks 13–14
- Foundation and Higher Workbooks, page 44
- Workbook audio: CD 3 and 4, track 53
- Copymaster 56
- Interactive OxBox, Unit 2B

Key language
mein Traumhaus, meine Traumwohnung
in den Bergen, am Meer, in der Stadt, auf dem Land

Framework references
L&S 1.1, 1.2, 1.5; R&W 2.1, 2.2, 2.5; LLS 5.7

Starters
- Before watching Kathi's video blog (ex. 1), allow students time to work with the questions, making sure that they understand all the language and trying to predict some of the answers. Point out that they can use the photo of Kathi's house as a clue, together with what they already know of Kathi. They check their predictions by watching the video.

2B.5 Wo wohnst du?

- Before students begin ex. 3, set a time limit and challenge them to find in the text: one country (*Amerika*); one city (*Los Angeles*); two weather conditions (*sonnig, heiß*); three rooms (*Kinozimmer, Musikzimmer, Keller*); five leisure activities (*ich schwimme, Filme / DVDs, ich spiele Gitarre, ich spiele Schlagzeug, ich singe*).

Plenaries
- Teacher versus the class. Make a few statements about Kathi's house, some of them true and some false. Challenge students to spot what is false. The class win a point for each error they spot and an extra point if they can correct it; you win a point for each error they fail to spot, e.g.
Teacher: *Kathi wohnt in Österreich.*
Class: *Falsch … Kathi wohnt in Berlin.* (= 2 points)
Depending on when you do this activity, you could also include information about Nina's ideal house (ex. 3).
- In pairs, students review the strategies that they've been using throughout this unit to learn new language: see spread 2B.6 (*Sprachlabor* Techniques for learning new words, ex. 5). What works best for them? Allow time for feedback and whole-class discussion.

Homework
- Students write and record a video blog about where they live: see *Follow-up* to ex. 2.
- Student Book page 81, *Challenge*.
- Students write five questions to test their partner's knowledge of Unit 2B. Encourage them to include questions about vocabulary and grammar, and to compile a separate answer sheet. Students exchange their questions with their partner in the next lesson. Alternatively, collect in everyone's questions and use them in a class quiz.

---

1 Sieh dir das Video an. Wähle die richtigen Antworten.

AT 1.4
L&S 1.1, 1.2
LLS 5.7

Students watch Kathi's video blog and choose option 1 or 2 in answer to each question. See the *Planner* above for a starter activity to help students prepare for watching the video.

Answers: **a** 1; **b** 2; **c** 1; **d** 2; **e** 1; **f** 2

Video blog 2B
CD 2, track 13
Seite 80, Übung 1

Ich wohne in Berlin, aber ich bin Österreicherin und ich komme aus Wien. Wir haben dort ein Haus am Stadtrand. Es ist sehr schön – und sehr groß: das Haus hat zehn Schlafzimmer, vier Badezimmer und zwei Wohnzimmer. Wir haben natürlich auch eine Küche – die ist auch sehr groß und modern. Der Garten ist auch sehr groß. Mein Bruder spielt dort Fußball, und ich spiele Tennis. Mein Zimmer ist im dritten Stock. Es hat zwei Balkons. In meinem Zimmer gibt es einen Kleiderschrank – der ist auch sehr groß! In meinem Zimmer gibt es auch zwei Sofas, drei Stühle, zwei Computer und einen Fernseher. Ich liebe mein Zimmer! Und wie ist dein Zimmer? Ist es auch sehr groß?

Follow-up
Play the video again and ask students to note the answers to the following questions:
1 How many bedrooms, bathrooms and living rooms are there in Kathi's house?
2 What is the kitchen like?
3 What is the garden like?
4 What sport does Kathi's brother play in the garden?
5 Describe Kathi's bedroom.

Answers: **1** ten bedrooms, four bathrooms, two living rooms; **2** very big and modern; **3** very big; **4** he plays football; **5** it has two balconies, two sofas, three chairs, two computers and a TV

2 Wo wohnst du? Macht Dialoge.

AT 2.3–4

Students take turns to interview each other about their own home. Encourage them to answer in as much detail as they can and to express their opinions.

Follow-up

AT 2.3–4
L&S 1.5

Students write and record a video blog about where they live. Encourage them to include something from each spread of Unit 2B: the region where they live, the weather, type of house and neighbourhood, description of house and own room, and plenty of opinions. Each video blog can then be played back to the class in a following lesson for peer evaluation.

3 Hör zu und lies. Richtig oder falsch?

AT 1.4
AT 3.4
R&W 2.1, 2.2

Students read and listen to Nina's description of her ideal house, and work out whether statements a–f are true or false. Ask them to correct the false statements.
Before students begin, point out that the photo provides a clue about Nina's ideal house, so this should help with some of the questions. Explain that they won't need to understand every word of the text in order to complete the task. Encourage students to attempt the questions by identifying key words and familiar language in the text, deducing unknown language and making sensible guesses.

Answers: **a** false (in the US / California); **b** false (there's a garden); **c** true; **d** true; **e** true; **f** true

119

2B.6 Wo wohnst du?

CD 2, track 14 — Seite 81, Übung 3

Mein Traumhaus ist ein Haus in Kalifornien. Das ist in Amerika. Das Haus ist in Los Angeles – es ist ein Haus am Meer. Das Haus ist total groß und es gibt einen Garten. Es gibt auch ein großes Schwimmbad im Garten – in Los Angeles ist es immer sonnig und heiß, und ich schwimme jeden Tag! Es gibt ein Kinozimmer im Erdgeschoss. Dort schaue ich mit meinen Freunden und Freundinnen Filme und DVDs. Es gibt auch ein Musikzimmer im Keller – ich spiele dort Gitarre und Schlagzeug, und ich singe.

AT 3.3 / AT 4.2 — **4 Füll die Lücken aus.**
Students fill in the missing words in a description of an ideal home, choosing from the words provided.

Answers: Mein Traumhaus ist <u>ein Bungalow</u> in Berlin. Das ist im <u>Osten</u> von Deutschland. Dort ist es manchmal <u>sonnig</u>, aber es <u>regnet</u> oft. Mein Traumhaus ist sehr <u>schön</u>. Es gibt vier <u>Schlafzimmer</u> und eine <u>Küche</u>. Es gibt auch einen <u>Garten</u>.

AT 4.3–4 / R&W 2.5 — **Challenge**
Students find a photo of their ideal home (or draw a picture), and write a description of it. Encourage them to write in as much detail as they can, following the list of prompts provided.

2B.6 Sprachlabor
Seite 82–83

Planner

Objectives
- Grammar: prepositions + dative; *es gibt* + *einen* / *eine* / *ein* …
- Skills: techniques for learning new words; pronounce the *ch* sound

Resources
- Student Book, pages 82–83
- CD 2, track 15
- Foundation and Higher Workbooks, pages 45–46
- Workbook audio: CD 3 and 4, track 54
- Copymasters 57, 58
- Interactive OxBox, Unit 2B

Framework references
KAL 4.1, 4.3; LLS 5.1, 5.2, 5.5, 5.8

Ich wohne in einem / einer / einem …

KAL 4.3 / LLS 5.1 — **1 Fill in the gaps with the correct articles.**

Answers: **a** einem; **b** einem; **c** einer; **d** einem; **e** einer

Es gibt + einen / eine / ein …

KAL 4.3 / LLS 5.1 — **2 Choose the correct article.**

Answers: **a** ein; **b** einen; **c** einen; **d** ein; **e** einen; **f** eine

KAL 4.3 / LLS 5.1 — **3 Complete the sentence with the furniture on the right.**

Answers: In meinem Zimmer gibt es ein Sofa, ein Bett, einen Stuhl, einen Schreibtisch, einen Computer und eine Lampe.

Prepositions + dative

KAL 4.3 / LLS 5.1 — **4 True or false? Write the false sentences correctly in German.**

Answers: **a** Falsch. Die Lampe ist auf dem Schreibtisch. **b** Richtig. **c** Falsch. Die Schultasche ist im Kleiderschrank. **d** Richtig. **e** Falsch. Der Stuhl ist vor dem Schreibtisch. **f** Falsch. Die Stereoanlage ist unter dem Schreibtisch.

120

2B.7 Wo wohnst du?

Techniques for learning new words

LLS 5.2, 5.5, 5.8

5 Discuss your order of techniques with a partner.

A range of strategies are suggested to help students learn new words. These include tips on how to keep a record of new language (colour-coding, grouping language into categories, etc.) as well as suggestions on how to go about learning it (copying out new words, saying them aloud).

Students rate the list of strategies 1–5 in order of what works best for them, then compare with a partner. Invite them to suggest any other strategies that they find useful, e.g. always learn the gender and plural when learning a new noun, work with a friend and test each other, write difficult words onto sticky notes and put them in key places around the house (e.g. on the fridge, on their bedroom door) so that they can't avoid seeing them, associate words with mimes or images, etc.

A "learning checklist" is also provided. Students are encouraged to refer to these four criteria to help them evaluate how well they know a new word: Do they understand it when listening and reading? Can they say it correctly? Can they spell it correctly? Can they use it in a sentence?

The *ch* sound

KAL 4.1

6 Listen carefully. How often do you hear *ch*?

🎧 **CD 2, track 15**   Seite 83, Übung 6

- ch … ch … ch
- Wellensittich
- Klasse
- Chemie
- Kaninchen
- Tasche
- frech
- Schule
- Frankreich

2B.7 Extra Star   Seite 84

Planner

Objectives
- Vocabulary: use higher numbers; describe the furniture in your room
- Grammar: prepositions
- Skills: develop accuracy in written work

Resources
- Student Book, page 84
- Copymaster 59

AT 3.1

1 Match up the numbers and words.

Answers: **a** 4; **b** 2; **c** 6; **d** 5; **e** 1; **f** 3

AT 4.1

2 Write down the jumbled-up words.
Students solve the anagrams of furniture items.

Answers: **a** ein Computer; **b** ein Schreibtisch; **c** ein Fernseher; **d** eine Lampe; **e** ein Poster; **f** ein Regal

AT 4.1–2

3 Fill in the gaps with the noun and its article.
Encourage students to focus on accuracy by using reference materials to check spellings and to make sure they are using the correct form of the indefinite article.

Answers: **a** einem Einfamilienhaus; **b** einer Wohnung; **c** einem Dorf; **d** einem Bungalow; **e** einer Wohnsiedlung; **f** einem Doppelhaus

AT 3.2

4 Choose the correct word.
Students choose the correct prepositions to complete the description of a bedroom picture.

Answers: **a** neben; **b** unter; **c** auf; **d** im; **e** vor; **f** hinter

2B.8 Wo wohnst du?

2B.7 Extra Plus
Seite 85

> **Planner**
>
> **Objectives**
> - Vocabulary: use higher numbers; describe the furniture in your room
> - Grammar: prepositions; *es gibt einen / eine / ein …*
> - Skills: develop accuracy in written work
>
> **Resources**
> - Student Book, page 85
> - Copymaster 60

AT 4.1   **1 Schreib die Zahlen auf.**
Students write the figures in words.

Answers: **a** *fünfundvierzig;* **b** *einundachtzig;* **c** *siebenundsiebzig;* **d** *zweiunddreißig;* **e** *sechsundneunzig;* **f** *fünfzig*

AT 4.1–2   **2 Schreib die richtigen Wörter für die Zimmer auf.**
Students label the pictures of rooms and other areas of a house. Encourage them to focus on accuracy and to use reference materials (e.g. their own notes or the Student Book) to check not only spellings but also genders.

Answers: **a** *das Schlafzimmer;* **b** *die Küche;* **c** *der Balkon;* **d** *das Badezimmer;* **e** *das Wohnzimmer;* **f** *die Dusche;* **g** *das Esszimmer*

AT 4.2   **3 Kathis Zimmer. Schreib die richtigen Wörter auf.**
Students complete the description of Kathi's room. As in ex. 2, insist that they aim for accuracy, not only in spellings of the nouns but also in the form of the definite article.

Answers: **a** *im Kleiderschrank;* **b** *auf dem Regal;* **c** *neben dem Bett;* **d** *vor dem Schreibtisch;* **e** *unter dem Bett;* **f** *zwischen dem;* **g** *hinter dem Fernseher*

AT 4.3   **4 In meinem Zimmer gibt es … Schreib sechs Sätze für Kathi.**
Students write six sentences to say what is in Kathi's bedroom. Again, as in ex. 2–3, insist on accuracy and attention to detail in spellings and grammar.

Example answer: In meinem Zimmer gibt es ein Bett. Es gibt eine Katze unter dem Bett. Es gibt auch einen Kleiderschrank, ein Sofa, einen Schreibtisch und zwei Stühle. Es gibt eine Lampe neben dem Bett. Es gibt eine Stereoanlage auf dem Regal. In meinem Zimmer gibt es auch eine Gitarre, einen Fernseher und zwei Computer.

2B.8 Testseite
Seite 86

> **Planner**
>
> **Resources**
> - Student Book, page 86
> - CD 2, track 16
> - Foundation and Higher Workbooks, page 47
> - Copymasters 49, 50
> - Assessment, Unit 2B

AT 1.2–3   **1 Listen (1–6). Choose two pictures for each weather description. Tick (✓) or cross (✗) each one to show what the weather is and isn't doing!**
Students identify weather phrases.

Answers: **1** c ✓, h ✗; **2** b ✗, j ✓; **3** i ✓, f ✗; **4** d ✗, g ✓; **5** k ✓, a ✗; **6** e ✓, l ✗

🎧 **CD 2, track 16**   Seite 86, Übung 1
1. Es regnet, aber es ist nicht kalt.
2. Es ist nicht wolkig, aber es ist heiß.
3. Es friert, aber es schneit nicht.
4. Es ist nicht windig, aber es ist neblig.
5. Es ist warm, aber es ist nicht sonnig.
6. Es gewittert … und es ist nicht schön!

2B Wo wohnst du?

AT 4.3 **2 Where is everything? Write a sentence for each room.**
Students look at the house picture and describe where the rooms are.

Answers: Das Wohnzimmer ist im Erdgeschoss. Das Esszimmer ist im Erdgeschoss. Die Küche ist im ersten Stock. Das Badezimmer ist im ersten Stock. Das Schlafzimmer ist im zweiten Stock. Die Toilette ist im zweiten Stock.

AT 3.3–4 **3 Read Svenja's message and note a–e.**
Answers: a Svenja lives in a detached house on the edge of town. b Her house is small and modern, with a garden. c Her room (on the first floor) is big and very beautiful, with a balcony. d In her room, there's a bed, a desk, a sofa, a shelf and a TV. e The bed is next to the sofa, and the TV is on the shelf.

AT 2.3–4 **4 Complete these sentences as part of a mini-presentation about yourself.**
Students give a presentation about where they live. A list of sentence starters is provided, focusing on town / region / neighbourhood / type of house, what the weather is like, description of bedroom, and opinions.

2B Lesen   Seite 156

Planner

Resources
- Student Book, page 156

Framework references
R&W 2.1, 2.2, 2.3; IU 3.1, 3.2

Deutschland!

AT 3.2 **1 Read the notes above. Are these sentences true or false?**
Students read the facts and figures about Germany and work out whether sentences a–d are true or false. Point out that they could probably make sensible guesses before reading the text, based on what they already know about Germany.

Answers: a false (in towns); b true; c false (Switzerland); d true

AT 3.4 **2 Read the text on the left and answer the questions in English.**
Students answer questions about life on the island of Hallig Hooge.

Answers: a an island in the North Sea off the north-west coast of Germany; b 80; c there are only four pupils; d it's always windy, in winter it's cold and sometimes snows, in autumn and spring it's very windy and often stormy, in summer it's sometimes hot and it sometimes rains; e there's a sports ground and a playground; f it's sometimes boring but they have TV and the internet

Follow-up
- Ask students to compare the different style of the two texts on this page: the fact file is basically a list of facts and figures, with eye-catching headings and visuals to make it look more interesting and attract our attention; the Hallig Hooge text is a piece of descriptive writing, using adjectives to paint a vivid picture of life on the island. Which text do students feel is more effective in terms of attracting and maintaining our interest? Ask students to suggest other ways to present written information about a place, e.g. poetry, tourist information.
- Ask students to look up Hallig Hooge and the other Hallig islands on the internet. If time permits, put together a display. Students could produce a fact file about the island, in the same style as the fact file about Germany. Alternatively, students could just find out a few things to share with the class in a following lesson. See Google Images for photos, and the official Hooge website (www.hooge.de) for maps, tourist information and a glimpse into island life.
- Students could research information for a fact file about the UK, for comparison with the German facts and figures.

2B Wo wohnst du?

Foundation Workbook

2B.1 Meine Region (Seite 40)

AT 1.2 **1 Listen and write the names of the cities in the right places.**

Answers: <u>centre top</u>: Kiel; <u>left-hand side, top to bottom</u>: Bremerhaven, Krefeld, Offenburg; <u>centre bottom</u>: Friedrichshafen; <u>right-hand side, top to bottom</u>: Prenzlau, Cottbus, Passau

> 🎧 **CD 3, track 49**   Seite 40, Übung 1
> - Ich wohne in Prenzlau. Das ist im Nordosten.
> - Ich wohne in Passau. Das ist im Südosten.
> - Ich wohne in Krefeld. Das ist im Westen.
> - Ich wohne in Friedrichshafen. Das ist im Süden.
> - Ich wohne in Offenburg. Das ist im Südwesten.
> - Ich wohne in Cottbus. Das ist im Osten.
> - Ich wohne in Kiel. Das ist im Norden.
> - Ich wohne in Bremerhaven. Das ist im Nordwesten.

AT 3.2 **2 What's the weather like in these places? Circle the right phrase.**

Answers: Im Norden: Es ist sonnig. Im Nordwesten: Es ist wolkig. Im Süden: Es ist kalt. Im Westen: Es ist windig. Im Osten: Es regnet. Im Südwesten: Es schneit.

2B.2 Hier wohne ich (Seite 41)

AT 1.2 **1 Listen to these people saying where they live. Write a, b, c or d next to the correct picture.**

Answers: Dorf d; Stadt c; Wohnsiedlung a; Land b

> 🎧 **CD 3, track 50**   Seite 41, Übung 1
> a Ich wohne in einer Wohnsiedlung. Es ist langweilig.
> b Ich wohne auf dem Land. Es ist schön.
> c Ich wohne in der Stadt. Es ist toll.
> d Ich wohne in einem Dorf. Es ist furchtbar.

AT 3.1 **2 Decide whether these adjectives are positive or negative and write them in the correct columns.**

Answers: <u>Positive</u>: toll, interessant, super, schön; <u>Negative</u>: furchtbar, laut, langweilig, nicht gut

AT 1.2 **3 Now listen again and circle *richtig* (true) or *falsch* (false).**
Play the ex. 1 recording again, focusing on the opinion adjectives.

Answers: **a** falsch; **b** richtig; **c** richtig; **d** falsch

AT 4.2 **4 Complete these two sentences, one saying where you live and one saying what you think of it.**

Answers: students' own answers

2B.3 Mein Haus (Seite 42)

AT 1.2 **1 Listen and write in the numbers.**

Answers: **a** 85; **b** 32; **c** 620; **d** 48; **e** 57; **f** 150; **g** 24; **h** 38

> 🎧 **CD 3, track 51**   Seite 42, Übung 1
> a Opa ist fünfundachtzig Jahre alt.
> b Das Telefon kostet zweiunddreißig Euro.
> c Meine Schule hat sechshundertzwanzig Schüler.
> d Ich habe achtundvierzig Bücher.
> e Mein Haus ist Nummer siebenundfünfzig.
> f Ich habe hundertfünfzig Bonbons.
> g Das ist der Bus Nummer vierundzwanzig.
> h Die Schuhe sind Größe achtunddreißig.

AT 4.1 **2 Solve the clues and fill in the crossword.**

Answers: <u>Waagerecht</u>: **2** Garage; **4** Esszimmer; **5** Balkon; **7** Dusche; **8** Keller; <u>Senkrecht</u>: **1** Badezimmer; **3** Garten; **6** Küche

2B.4 Mein Zimmer (Seite 43)

AT 4.1 **1 Unjumble the words and write them in.**

Answers: In meinem Zimmer habe ich eine <u>Lampe</u> und eine <u>Stereoanlage</u>. Ich habe natürlich auch ein <u>Bett</u>, einen <u>Kleiderschrank</u> und einen <u>Schreibtisch</u>. Aber ich habe keinen <u>Computer</u> und kein <u>Sofa</u>.

AT 1.2 **2 A different room is being described. Identify where the items are and circle the correct words.**

Answers: **a** on; **b** under; **c** behind; **d** next to; **e** between the lamp and the stereo

> 🎧 **CD 3, track 52**   Seite 43, Übung 2
> a Die Lampe ist auf dem Schreibtisch.
> b Die Katze ist unter dem Bett.
> c Der Fußball ist hinter dem Kleiderschrank.
> d Das Bett ist neben dem Sofa.
> e Der Computer ist zwischen der Lampe und der Stereoanlage.

2B Wo wohnst du?

AT 4.2 **3 Complete the sentences to describe what's in your own room. Make sure you use words that fit – check whether it should be *ein*, *eine* or *einen*.**

Answers: students' own answers

2B.5 Kathis Videoblog (Seite 44)

AT 1.1 **1 Listen to these numbers and write them down (just the figures, not the words).**

Answers: a 55; b 23; c 72; d 99; e 86; f 68; g 47; h 82

🎧 CD 3, track 53		Seite 44, Übung 1
a fünfundfünfzig		e sechsundachtzig
b dreiundzwanzig		f achtundsechzig
c zweiundsiebzig		g siebenundvierzig
d neunundneunzig		h zweiundachtzig

AT 3.2 **2 Complete these sentences describing where things are.**

Answers: Der Vogel sitzt auf dem Haus. Nils ist im Haus. Der Keller ist unter dem Haus. Die Garage ist neben dem Haus. Das Rad ist vor dem Haus.

2B.6A Sprachlabor (Seite 45)

1 Write in *der* or *dem*.

Answers: a dem; b dem; c dem; d der; e der; f der; g dem, der; h dem; i im; j der

2 Circle the correct word.

Answers: a eine; b einen; c eine; d ein; e ein; f einen; g eine

2B.6B Think (Seite 46)

1 Listen to the words. Put a tick if you hear the sound 'ch' and a cross if you don't.

Answers: a ✗; b ✓; c ✓; d ✗; e ✓; f ✗; g ✓; h ✓; i ✗; j ✗

🎧 CD 3, track 54		Seite 46, Übung 1
a Tisch		f Klasse
b acht		g nicht
c ich		h Schach
d Schule		i klassisch
e machen		j Schreibtisch

2 Listen again and jot down the words as you go. Then say them out loud. Finally, check that you have spelled them correctly.

Answers: see ex. 1 transcript

3 Look back to the previous page (*Sprachlabor*). There are at least three nouns you haven't seen before but you can immediately work out what they mean. What are they?

Answers: Supermarkt, Post, Kathedrale

4 Practise using the correct words for 'a' in this sentence.

Answers: In meiner Tasche habe ich eine Zeitschrift, ein Buch, einen Teddy, ein Handy, einen DVD-Spieler und eine Maus!

2B Wo wohnst du?

Higher Workbook

2B.1 Meine Region (Seite 40)

AT 1.2 **1** Listen and write the names of the cities in the right places.

Answers: centre top: Kiel; left-hand side, top to bottom: Bremerhaven, Krefeld, Offenburg; centre bottom: Friedrichshafen; right-hand side, top to bottom: Prenzlau, Cottbus, Passau

🎧 CD 4, track 49 — Seite 40, Übung 1

- Ich wohne in Prenzlau. Das ist im Nordosten.
- Ich wohne in Passau. Das ist im Südosten.
- Ich wohne in Krefeld. Das ist im Westen.
- Ich wohne in Friedrichshafen. Das ist im Süden.
- Ich wohne in Offenburg. Das ist im Südwesten.
- Ich wohne in Cottbus. Das ist im Osten.
- Ich wohne in Kiel. Das ist im Norden.
- Ich wohne in Bremerhaven. Das ist im Nordwesten.

AT 4.1 **2** What's the weather like in these places? Write in the weather phrase.

Answers: Im Norden: Es ist sonnig. Im Nordwesten: Es ist wolkig. Im Süden: Es ist kalt. Im Westen: Es ist windig. Im Osten: Es regnet. Im Südwesten: Es schneit.

2B.2 Hier wohne ich (Seite 41)

AT 1.2 **1** Listen to these people saying where they live. Write down, in English, where they live and what they think of it.

*Answers: **a** housing estate, boring; **b** in the countryside, beautiful / nice; **c** in town, great; **d** village, terrible*

🎧 CD 4, track 50 — Seite 41, Übung 1

a Ich wohne in einer Wohnsiedlung. Es ist langweilig.
b Ich wohne auf dem Land. Es ist schön.
c Ich wohne in der Stadt. Es ist toll.
d Ich wohne in einem Dorf. Es ist furchtbar.

AT 3.2–3 **2** Write down in English ...

*Answers: **a** in the countryside; **b** yes; **c** it's not boring at all, it's totally cool, it's green, she thinks that's great*

AT 4.2–3 **3** Like Anke, write a couple of lines about where you live and what you think of it.

Answers: students' own answers

2B.3 Mein Haus (Seite 42)

AT 1.2 **1** Listen and write in the numbers.

*Answers: **a** 85; **b** 32; **c** 620; **d** 48; **e** 57; **f** 150; **g** 24; **h** 38*

🎧 CD 4, track 51 — Seite 42, Übung 1

a Opa ist fünfundachtzig Jahre alt.
b Das Telefon kostet zweiunddreißig Euro.
c Meine Schule hat sechshundertzwanzig Schüler.
d Ich habe achtundvierzig Bücher.
e Mein Haus ist Nummer siebenundfünfzig.
f Ich habe hundertfünfzig Bonbons.
g Das ist der Bus Nummer vierundzwanzig.
h Die Schuhe sind Größe achtunddreißig.

AT 4.1 **2** Now write out how each number in Activity 1 is spelled.

*Answers: **a** fünfundachtzig; **b** zweiunddreißig; **c** sechshundertzwanzig; **d** achtundvierzig; **e** siebenundfünfzig; **f** hundertfünfzig; **g** vierundzwanzig; **h** achtunddreißig*

AT 4.1 **3** Solve the clues and fill in the crossword.

*Answers: Waagerecht: **2** Garage; **4** Esszimmer; **5** Balkon; **7** Dusche; **8** Keller; Senkrecht: **1** Badezimmer; **3** Garten; **6** Küche*

2B.4 Mein Zimmer (Seite 43)

AT 1.3 **1** Listen to Mirco describing his room. Fill in the answers in English, saying what is where.

*Answers: **a** on the desk; **b** in the wardrobe; **c** next to the computer; **d** on the chair; **e** next to the bed; **f** on the desk behind the computer*

🎧 CD 4, track 52 — Seite 43, Übung 1

Also, hier ist mein Zimmer. Es ist cool. Der Computer ist auf dem Schreibtisch und der Fernseher ist neben dem Computer. Ich habe einen Kleiderschrank. Die Kleider sind natürlich in dem Kleiderschrank! Meine Katze sitzt auf dem Stuhl. Der Stuhl ist neben dem Bett. Die Lampe steht auf dem Schreibtisch hinter dem Computer.

AT 1.3 **2** Listen again and draw a sketch of Mirco's room.

AT 4.3–4 **3** Using what you have learned on this spread, write a paragraph describing where the things in your bedroom are. Make sure you use the prepositions correctly.

Answers: students' own answers

2B Wo wohnst du?

2B.5 Kathis Videoblog (Seite 44)

AT 1.1
AT 4.1
1 Listen to these numbers. Write down the numbers and also how they are spelled.

Answers: *a* 55 fünfundfünfzig; *b* 23 dreiundzwanzig; *c* 72 zweiundsiebzig; *d* 99 neunundneunzig; *e* 86 sechsundachtzig; *f* 68 achtundsechzig; *g* 47 siebenundvierzig; *h* 82 zweiundachtzig

🎧 **CD 4, track 53**   Seite 44, Übung 1

a	fünfundfünfzig	e	sechsundachtzig
b	dreiundzwanzig	f	achtundsechzig
c	zweiundsiebzig	g	siebenundvierzig
d	neunundneunzig	h	zweiundachtzig

AT 3.2 **2 Complete these sentences describing where things are.**

Answers: Der Vogel sitzt <u>auf</u> dem Haus. Nils ist <u>im</u> Haus. Der Keller ist <u>unter</u> dem Haus. Die Garage ist <u>neben</u> dem Haus. Das Rad ist <u>vor</u> dem Haus.

AT 4.3 **3 Write a few sentences describing what is in your room. Try to use new words, looking them up in a dictionary or online.**

Answers: students' own answers

2B.6A Sprachlabor (Seite 45)

1 Translate these expressions into German, using *der* or *dem*.

Answers: *a* auf dem Tisch; *b* unter dem Stuhl; *c* neben dem Schrank; *d* in der Tasche; *e* vor der Schule; *f* hinter der Tür; *g* zwischen dem Haus und der Garage; *h* vor dem Supermarkt; *i* im Auto; *j* vor der Post

2 Write in *einen*, *eine* or *ein*.

Answers: *a* einen; *b* eine; *c* eine; *d* ein; *e* ein; *f* einen; *g* eine

2B.6B Think (Seite 46)

1 Listen to the words. Put a tick if you hear the sound 'ch' and a cross if you don't.

Answers: *a* ✗; *b* ✓; *c* ✓; *d* ✗; *e* ✓; *f* ✗; *g* ✓; *h* ✓; *i* ✗; *j* ✗

🎧 **CD 4, track 54**   Seite 46, Übung 1

a	Tisch	f	Klasse
b	acht	g	nicht
c	ich	h	Schach
d	Schule	i	klassisch
e	machen	j	Schreibtisch

2 Listen again and jot down the words as you go. Then say them out loud. Finally, check that you have spelled them correctly.

Answers: see ex. 1 transcript

3 Look back to the previous page (*Sprachlabor*). There are at least three nouns you haven't seen before but you can immediately work out what they mean. What are they?

Answers: Supermarkt, Post, Kathedrale

4 Practise using the correct words for 'a' in this sentence.

Answers: In meiner Tasche habe ich <u>eine</u> Zeitschrift, <u>ein</u> Buch, <u>einen</u> Teddy, ein Handy, <u>einen</u> DVD-Spieler und <u>eine</u> Maus!

5 You can now write substantial paragraphs using the models presented in the Student Book, and adapting them. Write a few lines describing your ideal home.

Answers: students' own answers

127

3A   Guten Appetit!

Unit 3A   Guten Appetit!   Unit overview grid

Page reference	Objectives	Grammar	Skills and pronunciation	Key language	Framework	AT level
Pages 88–89 **3A.1 Was isst du gern?**	Say what you like and don't like to eat and drink; talk about meals	"Verb second" word order	Use familiar language in a new context	*Was isst/trinkst du (gern/nicht gern)? Ich esse/trinke (gern/nicht gern) … Brot (mit Marmelade/ Butter), Cornflakes, Fisch, Hähnchen, Joghurt, Kartoffeln, Käse, Müsli, Nudeln, Reis, Salat, einen Apfel, eine Banane, ein Ei Cola, Kaffee, Milch, Orangensaft, Tee, Wasser zum Frühstück, zum Mittagessen, zum Abendessen Zum Frühstück esse/trinke ich … meistens, normalerweise*	L&S 1.1, 1.2, 1.3 R&W 2.1, 2.4 IU 3.1, 3.2 KAL 4.2, 4.4, 4.6 LLS 5.3, 5.7, 5.8	1.1–3, 2.2–3, 3.1–3, 4.1, 4.3–4
Pages 90–91 **3A.2 Ein Eis, bitte!**	Buy food in a café or snack bar	*Ich möchte* + noun	Use polite language	*der Imbiss, die Bäckerei, die Eisdiele, die Pizzeria Ich esse gern … Bio-Brot, Bratwurst, Brötchen, Cheeseburger, Currywurst, Hamburger, Pizza, Pommes frites mit/ohne Käse, Ketchup, Mayonnaise, Oliven, Pilzen, Schinken, Spinat, Thunfisch, Tomaten, Zwiebeln ein Stück Apfelkuchen, ein Stück Schwarzwälder Kirschtorte, ein Erdbeereis, ein Schokoladeneis, ein Vanilleeis mit/ohne Sahne Was darf es sein? Was möchtest du? Ja bitte? Ich möchte …, bitte. Ich nehme …, bitte. Hier, bitte. Bitte sehr. Sonst noch etwas? Ist das alles?*	L&S 1.3 R&W 2.5 KAL 4.1, 4.2 LLS 5.4, 5.6	1.1–3, 2.2–3, 3.3, 4.3–4

Guten Appetit! 3A

Page reference	Objectives	Grammar	Skills and pronunciation	Key language	Framework	AT level
Pages 92–93 **3A.3 500 Gramm Käse, bitte!**	Say what food you want to buy; learn numbers up to 1,000	*Ich möchte* + noun Singular and plural units of quantity	Identify language patterns	Numbers up to 1,000 *Ich möchte … 250 Gramm, ein (halbes) Kilo, ein (halbes) Pfund einen Becher Joghurt, einen Liter Milch, eine Packung Kaffee, eine Tüte Brötchen, eine Scheibe Schinken, eine Dose Cola, eine Flasche Wasser, ein Glas Marmelade, ein Stück Käse (zwei, drei, …) Becher, Liter, Packungen, Tüten, Scheiben, Dosen, Flaschen, Gläser, Stücke Was darf es sein? Sonst noch etwas? Nein, danke. Das ist alles.*	R&W 2.4 KAL 4.3 LLS 5.1, 5.4, 5.6	1.1–3, 2.1–3, 3.2–3, 4.1–4
Pages 94–95 **3A.4 Ich esse kein Fleisch**	Say what you like and dislike eating, and what you do and don't eat; talk about healthy eating	*Man soll* + infinitive *Ich esse* + *kein(e)(n) …*	Use a wider range of structures; build longer sentences	*Ich esse/trinke (nicht) gern … Ich esse/trinke (keinen Fisch/keine Schokolade/ kein Wasser/keine Chips). Chips, Cola, Fastfood, Fisch, Fleisch, Gemüse, Milch, Obst, Schokolade, Wasser Man soll (keine Chips) essen. Man soll jeden Tag (Obst) essen.*	L&S 1.1, 1.2 R&W 2.1, 2.4 KAL 4.2, 4.3, 4.4, 4.5, 4.6 LLS 5.1, 5.3	1.2–4, 2.3–4, 3.1–4, 4.2–4
Pages 96–97 **3A.5 Nicos Videoblog**	Order a meal in a restaurant	"Verb second" word order *Ich möchte* + noun	Use polite language; use different strategies to work out meaning	*Was darf es sein? Was möchtest du? Ich möchte … Als (Vorspeise/ Hauptgericht/Nachspeise) nehme ich … Und zu trinken?*	L&S 1.1, 1.2 R&W 2.2, 2.5 IU 3.1, 3.2 LLS 5.4, 5.5	1.3–4, 2.3–4, 4.4

3A Guten Appetit!

Unit 3A: Week-by-week overview
(Three-year KS3 Route: assuming six weeks' work or approximately 10–12.5 hours)
(Two-year KS3 Route: assuming four weeks' work or approximately 6.5–8.5 hours)

About Unit 3A, *Guten Appetit!*: In this unit, students work in the context of food and drink. They talk about likes and dislikes, mealtimes and healthy eating, and learn some transactional language for buying food and drink in a shop, café or restaurant. They also learn how to form numbers between 100 and 1,000. There are opportunities to find out about German food specialities and to compare eating habits in Germany and the UK.
Familiar language is recycled (*gern/nicht gern, keinen/keine/kein*) and students continue to develop their knowledge of German sentence structure: they are introduced to *man soll* + infinitive, revisit "verb second" word order and are encouraged to use linking words to build longer sentences. Students also begin to recognise and use features of polite language (*ich möchte, bitte sehr*, etc.). The pronunciation focus is the long and short *u* sound.

Three-Year KS3 Route

Week	Resources	Objectives
1	3A.1 Was isst du gern? 3A.6 Sprachlabor ex. 1–2	Say what you like and don't like to eat and drink; talk about meals "Verb second" word order Use familiar language in a new context
2	3A.2 Ein Eis, bitte! 3A.6 Sprachlabor ex. 7–8 *(if you wish to work on pronunciation at this point)*	Buy food in a café or snack bar *Ich möchte* + noun Use polite language
3	3A.3 500 Gramm Käse, bitte!	Say what food you want to buy; learn numbers up to 1,000 *Ich möchte* + noun Singular and plural units of quantity Identify language patterns
4	3A.4 Ich esse kein Fleisch 3A.6 Sprachlabor ex. 3–4 and 5–6	Say what you like and dislike eating, and what you do and don't eat; talk about healthy eating *Man soll* + infinitive; *ich esse kein(e)(n)* … Use a wider range of structures; build longer sentences

Two-Year KS3 Route

Week	Resources	Objectives
1	3A.1 Was isst du gern? *(Omit Challenge)* 3A.6 Sprachlabor ex. 1–2	Say what you like and don't like to eat and drink; talk about meals "Verb second" word order Use familiar language in a new context
2	3A.2 Ein Eis, bitte! *(Omit Challenge)* 3A.6 Sprachlabor ex. 7–8 *(if you wish to work on pronunciation at this point)*	Buy food in a café or snack bar *Ich möchte* + noun Use polite language
3	3A.3 500 Gramm Käse, bitte! *(Omit Challenge)*	Say what food you want to buy; learn numbers up to 1,000 *Ich möchte* + noun Singular and plural units of quantity Identify language patterns
4	3A.4 Ich esse kein Fleisch *(Omit ex. 8)* 3A.6 Sprachlabor ex. 3–4 and 5–6 3A.8 Vokabular 3A.8 Testseite	Say what you like and dislike eating, and what you do and don't eat; talk about healthy eating *Man soll* + infinitive; *ich esse kein(e)(n)* … Use a wider range of structures; build longer sentences Key vocabulary and learning checklist Assessment in all four skills

3A Guten Appetit!

	Three-Year KS3 Route			Two-Year KS3 Route	
Week	Resources	Objectives	Week	Resources	Objectives
5	3A.5 Nicos Videoblog	Order a meal in a restaurant "Verb second" word order; *ich möchte* + noun Use polite language; use different strategies to work out meaning			
6	3A.7 Extra (Star/Plus) 3A.8 Vokabular 3A.8 Testseite 3A Lesen	Reinforcement and extension of the language of the unit Key vocabulary and learning checklist Assessment in all four skills Further reading to explore the language of the unit and cultural themes			

3A.1 Guten Appetit!

3A.1 Was isst du gern?   Seite 88–89

Planner

Objectives
- Vocabulary: say what you like and don't like to eat and drink; talk about meals
- Grammar: "verb second" word order
- Skills: use familiar language in a new context

Video
- Video clip 3A

Resources
- Student Book, pages 88–89
- CD 2, tracks 17–19
- Foundation and Higher Workbooks, page 48
- Workbook audio: CD 3 and 4, track 55
- Copymaster 63 (ex. 1)
- Interactive OxBox, Unit 3A

Key language
Was isst / trinkst du (gern / nicht gern)?
Ich esse / trinke (gern / nicht gern) …
Brot (mit Marmelade / Butter), Cornflakes, Fisch, Hähnchen, Joghurt, Kartoffeln, Käse, Müsli, Nudeln, Reis, Salat, einen Apfel, eine Banane, ein Ei
Cola, Kaffee, Milch, Orangensaft, Tee, Wasser
zum Frühstück, zum Mittagessen, zum Abendessen
Zum Frühstück esse / trinke ich …
meistens, normalerweise

Framework references
L&S 1.1, 1.2, 1.3; R&W 2.1, 2.4; IU 3.1, 3.2; KAL 4.2, 4.4, 4.6; LLS 5.3, 5.7, 5.8

Starters
- Copymaster 63 ex. 1
- In pairs, students use their knowledge of German pronunciation to work out how to say the food and drink items in ex. 1. They then listen to the ex. 1 recording to check.
- Students play a memory game in pairs. Student A has a few moments to try to memorise the 15 food and drink items in ex. 1; he / she then closes the book and recites as many items as possible. B checks against the book and keeps a tally. They then swap over. Who remembers the most items?

To increase the challenge, ask them to say a full sentence for each item, e.g. *Ich esse gern Käse, Ich trinke nicht gern Milch*, etc.

Plenaries
- In pairs, each student secretly notes down four items of food and drink (from a–o in ex. 1). They put a tick beside two of them and a cross beside the other two, to represent what they like and don't like. They then take turns to work out each other's likes and dislikes by asking *Isst / Trinkst du gern …?* Insist that they answer in full sentences. Who works out their partner's likes and dislikes in the fewest guesses?
- Divide the class into teams and write a single food word on the board. Explain that you want the teams to build the longest sentence possible around this word, but that they can only add one phrase at a time. Point out that the word order may need to change as the sentence grows. The team who keep going for longest are the winners. For example:
Teacher: writes *Fisch* on the board.
Team A: *Ich esse gern Fisch.*
Team B: *Ich esse nicht gern Fisch.*
Team C: *Zum Abendessen esse ich nicht gern Fisch.*
Team D: *Zum Abendessen esse ich nicht gern Fisch, aber …*
Team A: *Zum Abendessen esse ich nicht gern Fisch, aber ich esse …*
Team B: *Zum Abendessen esse ich nicht gern Fisch, aber ich esse meistens Hähnchen.*
Team C: *Zum Abendessen esse ich nicht gern Fisch, aber ich esse meistens Hähnchen mit …*

Homework
- Students start making a mini-dictionary or database of food and drink vocabulary, which they can add to as they work through this unit. Remind them to include the gender and (if appropriate) plural of each word – they can use the Glossary or a dictionary to research these. Ask them to think about how to list the words, e.g. grouped by gender, or grouped by type of food (all fruit together, all meat and fish together, all drinks together, etc.). Point out that they will meet a lot of food and drink vocabulary in this unit so they should try to learn it as they go along.
- Student Book page 89, ex. 8 and / or *Challenge*.

3A.1 Guten Appetit!

Video clip 3A: Nur noch Essen!

Synopsis:
It's Nina's birthday, and Ali and Nico are in town to buy her a surprise birthday cake. They speak to her on the phone and arrange to meet at the pizzeria later, but they don't mention her birthday – Nina feels hurt and disappointed because she thinks they've forgotten. The boys go shopping for food and eventually buy a birthday cake.
Later, the four friends meet up at the pizzeria. They have difficulty agreeing on pizza toppings, and Nina still seems hurt because she thinks no one has remembered her birthday. Eventually, after the meal, Ali presents Nina with the cake and everyone sings "Happy birthday".

Play the video through a couple of times and ask questions to check that students understand the gist of it. Challenge them to work out the occasion: it's Nina's birthday (if they don't spot the references to *Geburtstag* at the beginning of the clip, they'll recognise the tune of "Happy birthday" at the end). Can they work out Nina's mood? (She thinks they've all forgotten her birthday so she feels hurt and disappointed.)
Ask students to note down the food and drink items they see or hear mentioned: although they don't know the vocabulary yet, they may recognise some cognates and they'll be able to work out other items from the visuals.

Video clip 3A

(Ali and Nico are in town; Nico receives a phone call from Nina)

Nico: Hallo?
Nina: Wo bist du?
Nico: Ich bin in der Stadt mit Ali.
Nina: Mit Ali?
Nico: Ja.
Nina: Allein mit Ali?
Nico: Ja.
Nina: Und wo ist denn Kathi?
Nico: Sie passt auf ihren Bruder auf.
Nina: Ja, ja ... Komm schon – das macht doch bestimmt das Au-pair-Mädchen! Wo ist sie?
Nico: Nein, nein, wirklich. Sie babysittet. Um, du ... ich muss gehen ... wir sehen uns heute Abend in der Pizzeria um sieben, okay?
Nina: Okay ... *(puts phone down and speaks to herself)* Oh, herzlichen Glückwunsch zum Geburtstag, Nina! Oh, danke Nico!

Ali: Kathi babysittet? Das glaubt sie doch nie!
Nico: Also, wo finden wir jetzt einen leckeren Geburtstagskuchen für sie?
Ali: Ah ... dafür haben wir noch Zeit ... zuerst gibt es was zu essen!

(at the snack bar)
Nico: Guten Tag.
Ali: Hallo.
Verkäufer: Ja, bitte?
Ali: Ich möchte eine Currywurst, bitte.
Verkäufer: Mit Pommes?
Ali: Ja, mit Pommes und mit Ketchup und Mayonnaise.
Verkäufer: Und du? Was darf es sein?
Nico: Ich nehme auch eine Currywurst – oder nein, ich nehme lieber einfach nur Pommes.
Verkäufer: Fünf vierzig, bitte.
Nico: Danke.
Verkäufer: Bitte.

(at the market stall)
Verkäufer: Guten Morgen! Was darf es sein?
Ali: Ich möchte Käse, bitte.
Verkäufer: Wie viel?
Ali: 250 Gramm, bitte.
Verkäufer: Außerdem?
Ali: Und ich möchte 300 Gramm Oliven und einen Liter Olivenöl.
Verkäufer: Sonst noch etwas?
Ali: Nein danke, das ist alles.
Verkäufer: Bitte schön. Schönen Tag noch!

(at the baker's)
Ali: Als Geburtstagskuchen, wie wäre es mit der Schwarzwälder Kirschtorte? Ein Klassiker! Oder ein Käsekuchen?
Nico: Also, die Schwarzwälder Kirschtorte sieht lecker aus! Das ist eine gute Idee!
Ali: Okay ... Ich möchte gern eine Schwarzwälder Kirschtorte.
Verkäuferin: Gerne.

(at the pizzeria)
Ali: Oh, ich habe Hunger!
Nico: Ich auch!
Nina: Wie wär's mit einer Pizza mit Thunfisch ...
Alle: Kein Fisch!
Nina: Dann Schinken. Und Oliven.
Ali: Kein Fleisch!
Nina: Dann nehmen wir Spinat und Oliven ...
Kathi: Ich esse keinen Spinat ...
Nina: Dann eben ... Pilze und Zwiebeln?
Kathi: Oh, bitte, keine Zwiebeln!
Nina: Okay, dann eben keine Zwiebeln ... ich hab's ... nehmen wir Tomaten und Käse – eine Pizza Margherita!
Alle: Ja!

133

3A.1 Guten Appetit!

Ali: Herzlichen Glückwunsch, Nina.
Nina: Danke, Ali!
Ali, Kathi, Nico: *(they sing)* Zum Geburtstag viel Glück …

Sprachpunkt
Was darf es sein?
Ich möchte 300 Gramm Oliven.
Sonst noch etwas?
Nein danke, das ist alles.

AT 1.1–2 / AT 3.1 / LLS 5.3
1 Hör zu. Was ist die richtige Reihenfolge?
Students look at the food pictures and captions. They listen as Nina makes a shopping list and note the items mentioned. Point out the false friend: *Nudeln* (pasta, not noodles).

Answers: i, f, a, k, n, h, j, e, l, g, d, m, b, c, o

🎧 **CD 2, track 17** Seite 88, Übung 1

Also, was brauchen wir? Brot … Milch … Salat … einen Apfel für die Schule … und Fisch … und Kartoffeln … Orangensaft … ein Ei für Mama … Nudeln … und Käse … Reis … Hähnchen … eine Banane für Mama … und Joghurt … und Cola!

AT 1.2–3 / KAL 4.6
2 Hör zu. Was essen Kathi und Nina gern oder nicht gern?
This activity recycles *gern* and *nicht gern*, which students have already met in other contexts (hobbies, talking about where they live). Kathi and Nina are in the supermarket discussing what they like to eat and drink. Students listen and note which food and drink items (from ex. 1) the girls like and don't like.

Answers: **Kathi:** ✓ m, h, l; ✗ a, f, n; **Nina:** ✓ g, o, i, c; ✗ d, j

🎧 **CD 2, track 18** Seite 88, Übung 2

Kathi: Salat! Iiih! Ich esse nicht gern Salat! Oh lecker – Hähnchen! Ich esse gern Hähnchen! Und du – was isst du gern?
Nina: Käse – ich esse gern Käse. Und ich trinke gern Cola! Und was trinkst du gern? Milch?
Kathi: Milch – nein, danke! Ich trinke nicht gern Milch! Aber Kartoffeln: ich esse gern Kartoffeln!
Nina: Und ich esse gern Brot! Aber ich esse nicht gern Reis – Reis ist langweilig.
Kathi: Bäh – Fisch! Ich esse nicht gern Fisch! Aber ich esse gern Nudeln!
Nina: Und ich trinke nicht gern Orangensaft. Aber ich esse gern Joghurt.

KAL 4.2, 4.6
Think
Students are prompted to think about previous contexts in which they've used *gern* and *nicht gern* (hobbies, talking about where they live). Set a time limit and challenge them, in pairs, to write as many sentences as they can, e.g. *Ich wohne (nicht) gern auf dem Land, Ich spiele (nicht) gern Tennis*.

AT 4.1
3 Und du – was isst / trinkst du gern oder nicht gern?
Students copy out the food and drink items from ex. 1 in two lists: those they like and those they don't like.

AT 2.2
4 👥 Macht Dialoge.
Students ask and answer the questions *Was isst du (nicht) gern?* and *Was trinkst du (nicht) gern?*

AT 1.2–3 / AT 3.2–3 / KAL 4.2, 4.4
5 Hör zu und lies.
Students listen while reading the descriptions of breakfast, lunch and evening meal. These texts recycle "verb second" word order (first taught in Unit 1B in the context of school timetables), and introduce two new frequency expressions: *meistens, normalerweise*. Challenge students to work out the meaning of *mit* (with).

🎧 **CD 2, track 19** Seite 89, Übung 5

Nina: Zum Frühstück esse ich Cornflakes oder Müsli mit Milch, oder Brot mit Marmelade. Ich trinke meistens Kaffee.
Nico: Zum Mittagessen esse ich Hähnchen mit Reis oder Kartoffeln. Ich esse auch eine Banane oder einen Apfel. Und ich trinke Wasser.
Ali: Zum Abendessen esse ich Brot mit Butter und Käse oder ein Ei mit Salat. Ich trinke normalerweise Tee.

AT 3.2–3 / R&W 2.1 / LLS 5.3
6 Finde die passenden Bilder für Nina, Nico und Ali.
Students read the ex. 5 texts again. They choose the corresponding pictures (1–11) to show what Nina, Nico and Ali have for breakfast, lunch and supper. Point out another false friend: *Marmelade* (jam, not marmalade).

Answers: **Nina:** 5, 2, 7, 11; **Nico:** 3, 8, 10; **Ali:** 1, 4, 6, 9

3A.1 Guten Appetit!

IU 3.1 — **Follow-up**

Compare Nico's lunch with Ali's evening meal (see ex. 5). Explain that, traditionally, lunch in Germany would be the main meal of the day, and the evening meal would be more like a snack, e.g. bread and cheese or cold meats. However, eating habits in Germany are now becoming more varied, to fit in with working practices, so that many people now have their main meal in the evening.

Point out that although Nina's breakfast looks similar to a typical UK breakfast, it is also common in Germany to have savoury foods for breakfast, e.g. bread with cheese and / or cold meats, or boiled eggs.

AT 2.2–3 / **KAL 4.4** — **7 Was isst oder trinkst du? Macht Dialoge.**

Students talk about what they eat and drink for different meals. Point out the *Grammatik* box: if they begin with *Zum Frühstück / Mittagessen / Abendessen …*, they must remember to put the verb in second position (as in the ex. 5 texts). Ask them where they have met "verb second" word order before, e.g. when talking about school timetables (*Am Montag habe ich Mathe*) or their bedroom (*In meinem Zimmer gibt es …*).

Encourage them to use the two new frequency expressions from ex. 5 (*normalerweise* and *meistens*) and to comment on likes and dislikes, e.g. *Zum Frühstück esse ich meistens Müsli oder Cornflakes. Ich esse gern Müsli …*

AT 4.3 / **R&W 2.4** / **LLS 5.7, 5.8** — **8 Schreib einen Speiseplan.**

Students write a day's menu for themselves, stating their food and drink choices for breakfast, lunch and evening meal. Encourage them to write in full sentences, e.g. *Zum Frühstück esse ich …*

For the purposes of this activity and *Challenge*, it is worth sharing with able students some of the criteria for working towards a higher level, e.g.

- express and justify likes, dislikes and opinions (*Zum Mittagessen trinke ich nicht gern Wasser, denn es ist langweilig*)
- build more complex sentences using linking words (*und, denn, aber, oder*)
- vary the word order (*Zum Frühstück esse ich …, Ich esse …*) and use a range of structures, including language recycled from other contexts (*Ich esse gern Cornflakes aber ich esse lieber Joghurt und ich esse am liebsten Müsli*)
- be more precise by using words like *sehr, ziemlich, gar nicht,* etc. (*Ich finde Cola ziemlich schlecht*)
- show evidence of applying their knowledge of grammar to adapt set phrases and use grammar reference materials to check for accuracy
- use dictionaries to research new language, e.g. if the food or drink they want to write about hasn't been taught on this spread.

AT 4.4 / **R&W 2.4** / **LLS 5.7, 5.8** — **Challenge**

Students write a description of their lunchtime or evening meal. Encourage them to give as much detail as they can, including opinions. Talk through the criteria for working towards a higher level (see notes for ex. 8).

3A.2 Guten Appetit!

3A.2 Ein Eis, bitte!
Seite 90–91

Planner

Objectives
- Vocabulary: buy food in a café or snack bar
- Grammar: *ich möchte* + noun
- Skills: use polite language

Video
- Video clip 3A

Resources
- Student Book, pages 90–91
- CD 2, tracks 20–22
- Foundation and Higher Workbooks, page 49
- Workbook audio: CD 3 and 4, track 56
- Copymaster 63 (ex. 2), 66 (ex. 1)
- Interactive OxBox, Unit 3A

Key language
der Imbiss, die Bäckerei, die Eisdiele, die Pizzeria
Ich esse gern …
Bio-Brot, Bratwurst, Brötchen, Cheeseburger, Currywurst, Hamburger, Pizza, Pommes frites
mit / ohne … Käse, Ketchup, Mayonnaise, Oliven, Pilzen, Schinken, Spinat, Thunfisch, Tomaten, Zwiebeln
ein Stück Apfelkuchen, ein Stück Schwarzwälder Kirschtorte, ein Erdbeereis, ein Schokoladeneis, ein Vanilleeis
mit / ohne Sahne
Was darf es sein? Was möchtest du? Ja bitte?
Ich möchte …, bitte. Ich nehme …, bitte.
Hier, bitte. Bitte sehr.
Sonst noch etwas? Ist das alles?

Framework references
L&S 1.3; R&W 2.5; KAL 4.1, 4.2; LLS 5.4, 5.6

Starters
- Copymaster 63, ex. 2.
- In pairs, students work out the meaning of the new food and drink vocabulary on page 90. They try to match up the menus (a–d) to the places to eat (1–4), then listen to the ex. 1 recording to check whether they were right.
- Word tennis. Student A names a food item (e.g. *Pizza, Eis, Brötchen / Bio-Brot, Wurst / Hamburger*); B completes it by adding an appropriate topping or accompaniment, then names another food item for A to complete, and so on:
  A: *Bratwurst …*
  B: *… mit Ketchup! Apfelkuchen …*
  A: *… mit Sahne! Pizza …*
  B: *… mit Pilzen! …*
  When one of them gives an inappropriate topping or accompaniment, or hesitates for too long, their partner wins.
- Before beginning work on ex. 4 and 5, challenge students to match the following English expressions to their German equivalents in the dialogues:
  Is that all? / And you? What would you like? / Yes, please? / I would like four bread rolls, please. / And a piece of Black Forest gateau, please. / Here you are. Anything else? / I'll take a curried sausage too.
  They should be able to match them up by identifying familiar words and by a process of elimination.

Plenaries
- For a variation on ex. 2, students take turns to name a place to eat; their partner responds by saying what they eat there, e.g.
  A: *Der Imbiss.*
  B: *Ich esse einen Cheeseburger mit Pommes frites und Ketchup.*
- Display a dialogue on the board, OHP or interactive whiteboard – either one of the dialogues from page 91, or something similar. Read it through with the whole class, then erase one or two words / phrases. Challenge pairs (or groups of three if there are three speakers involved) to read it again, supplying the missing words. Erase even more words / phrases, then challenge students to read it again. Continue until only a skeleton of the original text remains. Can any pairs or groups reconstruct the whole dialogue from memory?

Homework
- Student Book page 90, ex. 3.
- Student Book page 91, *Challenge*.
- Students add the new food vocabulary from this spread to the database or mini-dictionary they began during work on the previous spread: see homework suggestions in the *Planner* for spread 3A.1.

136

3A.2 Guten Appetit!

1 Hör zu. Was passt zusammen (1–4 und a–d)?
AT 1.1–2
LLS 5.4

This activity introduces more food vocabulary together with the words for different eating places. Nico and Ali read out the menus (a–d) from an ice cream parlour, a pizzeria, a bakery and a snack bar. Students choose a place (1–4) to go with each menu.

Answers: **a** 2; **b** 1; **c** 4; **d** 3

CD 2, track 20   Seite 90, Übung 1

a Schau mal – die Eisdiele: Mmmhh … Vanilleeis – Schokoladeneis – Erdbeereis – mit Sahne – ohne Sahne.
b Und hier – die Pizzeria: Pizza mit Tomaten, Käse, Zwiebeln und Schinken – oder mit Pilzen und Oliven – oder mit Spinat und Thunfisch.
c Da – die Bäckerei: Brötchen – und Bio-Brot – oder Brötchen mit Käse oder Schinken – Schwarzwälder Kirschtorte – Apfelkuchen.
d Hier – der Imbiss: Bratwurst – Currywurst – toll … und Hamburger – oder Cheeseburger – Pommes frites mit Ketchup oder Mayonnaise.

Think
KAL 4.2
LLS 5.4

Point out *mit* (with) and *ohne* (without) in the menus. Elicit the meaning of *mit*, which students met on spread 3A.1. Challenge them to work out the meaning of *ohne*.

2 Ratespiel: Wo isst du gern?
AT 2.2

Students take turns to choose something from a menu; their partner names the corresponding place, e.g.
A: *Ich esse Pizza mit Tomaten, Käse, Zwiebeln und Schinken.*
B: *Das ist die Pizzeria.*

3 Schreib Sätze.
AT 4.3

Students write sentences to describe what they like and don't like eating in the four different places, e.g. *Die Pizzeria: Ich esse gern … aber ich esse nicht gern ….*

Follow-up
KAL 4.1

At some point during work on this spread, you may wish to look at the pronunciation focus of this unit: long *u* and short *u* (see also 3A.6 *Sprachlabor*, ex. 7 and 8). Ask students to find on spreads 3A.1 and 3A.2 all the food and drink words containing the *u* sound and to sort them into two groups: short *u* (*Butter*) and long *u* (e.g. *Nudeln, Wurst*). Challenge them to add other non-food words to each list, e.g. short *u* – *Mutter, lustig, Kunst*; long *u* – *Bruder, Musik, Schule*.

4 Sieh dir das Video an und lies.
AT 1.3
AT 3.3
LLS 5.6

Play the section of the video in which Ali and Nico buy sausage and chips from a snack bar. Students read and listen.
This dialogue and ex. 5 provide a model for buying food and drink. Encourage students to read aloud from the book, imitating the pronunciation and intonation. See also ex. 6 for comprehension questions on the two dialogues.

Video clip 3A
CD 2, track 21   Seite 91, Übung 4

Nico: Guten Tag.
Ali: Hallo.
Verkäufer: Ja bitte?
Ali: Ich möchte eine Currywurst, bitte.
Verkäufer: Mit Pommes?
Ali: Ja, mit Pommes und mit Ketchup und Mayonnaise.
Verkäufer: Und du? Was darf es sein?
Nico: Ich nehme auch eine Currywurst – oder nein, ich nehme lieber einfach nur Pommes.
Verkäufer: Fünf vierzig, bitte.
Nico: Danke.
Verkäufer: Bitte.

5 Hör zu und lies.
AT 1.3
AT 3.3
LLS 5.6

Students read and listen as Kathi buys bread rolls and cakes in a bakery. Encourage them to read aloud from the book, imitating the pronunciation and intonation.

CD 2, track 22   Seite 91, Übung 5

Verkäufer: Was möchtest du?
Kathi: Ich möchte vier Brötchen, bitte.
Verkäufer: Hier, bitte. Sonst noch etwas?
Kathi: Ja, ich nehme ein Stück Apfelkuchen.
Verkäufer: Bitte sehr. Ist das alles?
Kathi: Und ein Stück Schwarzwälder Kirschtorte, bitte.

6 Füll die Lücken aus.
AT 3.3

Students read the ex. 4 and 5 dialogues again and complete gap-fill sentences a–d.

Answers: **a** curried sausage, ketchup, mayonnaise; **b** chips; **c** four bread rolls; **d** slice of apple tart, slice of Black Forest gateau

137

3A.2 Guten Appetit!

LLS 5.6 **Follow-up**

For further practice of the dialogues in ex. 4 and 5:
- Play the video for ex. 4, with the sound turned down. Three students take on the roles of Nico, Ali and the *Verkäufer*, reading aloud from the book. Repeat with other groups of three. Who gives the most convincing performance?
- Two students begin to read dialogue 5 along with the CD. After the first few words, turn down the volume; the pair continue reading from the book. Turn the volume back up again for the final few words – how close are the pair to the timing of the recording? The aim is to finish at exactly the same time. Invite other pairs to try.

See also the second plenary suggestion in the *Planner* above.

LLS 5.4 **7 Wie sagt man das auf Deutsch?**

Students identify (in ex. 4 and 5) different ways to say phrases a–c in German.

Answers: **a** *Ja bitte? Was darf es sein? Was möchtest du?* **b** *Ich möchte …, Ich nehme;* **c** *Sonst noch etwas? Ist das alles?*

L&S 1.3 **Think**

This activity focuses on register: students decide whether the dialogue in the *Think* box is as polite as those in ex. 4 and 5. They should be able to deduce from its abrupt nature and the absence of phrases like *Ich möchte …*, *danke* and *bitte* that it is less polite.

Ask students to identify all the polite phrases in ex. 4 and 5. Point out that in German as in English it is less polite if you just name the item you want (e.g. *Eine Currywurst*) instead of saying *Ich möchte / nehme … bitte*. Explain *bitte sehr*, which depending on the context can mean "You're welcome" / "Don't mention it" or "Here you are".
Ask students to suggest other situations in which they might use polite language, e.g. talking to a teacher, their friends' parents, a police officer, doctor or anyone in authority, asking a stranger for directions, buying tickets, etc.

AT 2.3 **AT 4.3** **R&W 2.5** **8 Macht Dialoge.**

Students make up their own dialogues to buy snacks.
Encourage them to add humour or invent tricky situations, e.g. a customer who is very indecisive, a very polite waiter / waitress or shop assistant to contrast with a rude customer (or vice versa), a customer who asks for strange combinations of food (e.g. *Schokoladeneis mit Mayonnaise*). Suggest that they assign moods or personalities to their characters, e.g. angry, shy, sad, behaving suspiciously.
Invite students to practise their dialogues in pairs and perform them to the class.

AT 4.4 **R&W 2.5** **Challenge**

Students write an amusing menu for a week, combining as many items of food and drink as they can. Remind them of the criteria for achieving a higher level: see teaching notes for spread 3A.1 ex. 8.

3A Guten Appetit!

3A.3 500 Gramm Käse, bitte!
Seite 92–93

Planner

Objectives
- Vocabulary: say what food you want to buy; learn numbers up to 1,000
- Grammar: *ich möchte* + noun; singular and plural units of quantity
- Skills: identify language patterns

Resources
- Student Book, pages 92–93
- CD 2, tracks 23–26
- Foundation and Higher Workbooks, page 50
- Workbook audio: CD 3 and 4, track 57
- Copymasters 63 (ex. 3), 64, 65 (ex. 1–2), 67
- Interactive OxBox, Unit 3A

Key language
Numbers up to 1,000
Ich möchte …
250 Gramm, ein (halbes) Kilo, ein (halbes) Pfund
einen Becher Joghurt, einen Liter Milch, eine Packung Kaffee, eine Tüte Brötchen, eine Scheibe Schinken, eine Dose Cola, eine Flasche Wasser, ein Glas Marmelade, ein Stück Käse
(zwei, drei, …) Becher, Liter, Packungen, Tüten, Scheiben, Dosen, Flaschen, Gläser, Stücke
Was darf es sein? Sonst noch etwas? Nein, danke. Das ist alles.

Framework references
R&W 2.4; KAL 4.3; LLS 5.1, 5.4, 5.6

Starters
- Copymaster 63, ex. 3.
- Before introducing higher numbers, revise numbers below 100 with a numbers game or counting game: see those suggested in the *Planner* for spread 0.2.
- Student Book page 93, ex. 5. Students match the words to the pictures before listening to check their answers.
- Display a jumbled selection of words for quantities, packaging and items of food and drink, e.g. *Ich möchte … Joghurt / Bananen / ein Stück / ein Glas / ein Kilo / Kaffee / Käse / eine Packung / einen Becher / Marmelade*, etc. Students race against the clock to make matching pairs.

Plenaries
- Students make up number puzzles or maths sums for each other, with the numbers written in words, e.g. *siebenhundert ÷ siebzig = __*.
- Students make up shopping dialogues in pairs. See *Follow-up* to ex. 4.
- Call out a quantity or an item of packaging in the singular; students give you the plural, e.g.
Teacher: *Eine Packung.*
Student: *Zwei Packungen.*
To increase the challenge, ask them to put it into a sentence, e.g. *Ich nehme zwei Packungen Kaffee, bitte.*

Homework
- Student Book page 93, *Challenge*.
- Students update their database or mini-dictionary (see homework suggestions in the *Planner* for spread 3A.1) with any new food vocabulary from this spread, plus the quantities and types of container / packaging.

LLS 5.1 Think
Students look at the list of numbers between 100 and 1,000 and try to identify the pattern.

AT 4.1–2 1 Füll die Lücken aus.
Students fill in the missing numbers.

Answers: 600 sechshundert, 700 siebenhundert, 800 achthundert, 900 neunhundert

AT 1.1 2 Hör zu. Ist alles richtig?
Students listen to check their answers to ex. 1.

🎧 CD 2, track 23 Seite 92, Übung 2
hundert … zweihundert … dreihundert … vierhundert … fünfhundertsechsundsiebzig … sechshundert … siebenhundert … achthundert … neunhundert … tausend

AT 2.1–2 3 👥 Was ist die richtige Antwort?
Before students begin, revise numbers in general via a starter activity: see *Planner* above. Students then challenge each other to work out sums a–e. Point out that they must read out the sums in German and supply the answers in German too, e.g.
A: *Fünfundachtzig plus fünfunddreißig.*
B: *Hundertzwanzig.*
They could continue this by setting additional sums for each other.

3A.3 Guten Appetit!

4 Sieh dir das Video an. Füll die Lücken aus.
AT 1.3
AT 3.3
LLS 5.6
Play the section of video clip 3A in which Ali buys food from a market stall. Students read the dialogue and fill in the missing words. The script can then be used for oral practice, with students reading aloud in pairs. Play the video again with the sound turned down and invite pairs to read the parts of Ali and the sales assistant.

Answers: see underlined words in transcript

Video clip 3A
CD 2, track 24 Seite 92, Übung 4

Verkäufer:	Guten Morgen! Was darf es sein?
Ali:	Ich möchte <u>Käse</u>, bitte.
Verkäufer:	Wie viel?
Ali:	250 <u>Gramm</u>, bitte.
Verkäufer:	Außerdem?
Ali:	Und ich möchte <u>300</u> Gramm Oliven und einen <u>Liter</u> Olivenöl.
Verkäufer:	Sonst noch etwas?
Ali:	Nein danke, das ist alles.
Verkäufer:	Bitte schön. Schönen Tag noch!

AT 2.3 **Follow-up**
Students make up their own shopping dialogues, modelled on ex. 4. Prepare for this activity by inviting suggestions for types of food that are generally bought in grams (e.g. *400 Gramm Tomaten, 300 Gramm Käse, 250 Gramm Schinken*) and encourage students to use these in their dialogues so that they practise the higher numbers. Build up a list on the board for students to choose from.

5 Was passt zusammen? Ist alles richtig? Hör zu.
AT 1.2
AT 3.2
LLS 5.4
Students match the quantities of food and drink (a–i) to the pictures (1–9). Elicit the meanings of the quantities and packaging.

Answers: 1 h; 2 d; 3 f; 4 a; 5 i; 6 g; 7 b; 8 e; 9 c

CD 2, track 25 Seite 93, Übung 5

Ich möchte eine Scheibe Schinken, eine Dose Cola, ein Glas Marmelade, einen Becher Joghurt, einen Liter Milch, ein Stück Käse, eine Packung Kaffee, eine Flasche Wasser und eine Tüte Brötchen.

AT 1.2–3
KAL 4.3
6 Hör zu. Füll die Lücken aus.
Students listen to the shopping dialogue and fill in the quantities of each item on the supermarket receipt. Before playing the recording, point out the plural forms of the packaging listed in the key language box.

Answers: see underlining in transcript

CD 2, track 26 Seite 93, Übung 6

– Guten Tag! Was darf's sein?
– Ich möchte <u>vier Becher Sahne</u> und <u>zwei Flaschen Orangensaft</u>. Ich möchte auch <u>drei Packungen Tee</u>, bitte.
– Bitte sehr. Ist das alles?
– Nein, ich möchte auch <u>zwei Liter Milch</u> und <u>acht Scheiben Wurst</u>. Und ich möchte <u>zwei Tüten Brötchen</u>. Ich möchte auch <u>drei Becher Joghurt</u> und <u>sechs Dosen Cola</u>.
– Hier, bitte. Sonst noch etwas?
– Ja, ich möchte auch <u>zwei Gläser Marmelade</u> und <u>drei Stücke Butterkuchen</u>.

AT 2.3 **7 Macht Einkaufsdialoge.**
Students make up shopping dialogues based on shopping lists 1 and 2.

AT 4.3–4
R&W 2.4
Challenge
Students imagine they are planning a menu for a party or a dinner. They write a shopping list including all the items they need, followed by a shopping dialogue in which they buy everything on their list.

140

3A Guten Appetit!

3A.4 Ich esse kein Fleisch
Seite 94–95

Planner

Objectives
- Vocabulary: say what you like and dislike eating, and what you do and don't eat; talk about healthy eating
- Grammar: *man soll* + infinitive; *ich esse* + *kein(e)(n)* …
- Skills: use a wider range of structures; build longer sentences

Resources
- Student Book, pages 94–95
- CD 2, tracks 27–28
- Foundation and Higher Workbooks, page 51
- Workbook audio: CD 3 and 4, track 58
- Copymasters 63 (ex. 4), 65 (ex. 3), 66 (ex. 2–3), 68
- Interactive OxBox, Unit 3A

Key language
Ich esse / trinke (nicht) gern …
Ich esse / trinke (keinen Fisch / keine Schokolade / kein Wasser / keine Chips).
Chips, Cola, Fastfood, Fisch, Fleisch, Gemüse, Milch, Obst, Schokolade, Wasser
Man soll (keine Chips) essen. Man soll jeden Tag (Obst) essen.

Framework references
L&S 1.1, 1.2; R&W 2.1, 2.4; KAL 4.2, 4.3, 4.4, 4.5, 4.6; LLS 5.1, 5.3

Starters
- Copymaster 63, ex. 4.
- Student Book page 94, ex. 1. Ask students to compare their answers with their partner: do they agree on what is healthy and unhealthy?
- Set students a sudoku-style puzzle. Display a three-by-three grid, with *ich esse keinen Fisch, ich trinke kein Wasser* and *ich esse keine Chips* filled in as shown in the following answer grid and the rest of the squares blank. Display these words alongside the grid: *Milch, Schinken, Eis, Reis, Wurst, Gemüse.*
Challenge students to copy out the grid and fill in the blank squares using *ich esse* (or *trinke*) *kein(e)(n)* + the words provided, so that each row and each column contains one each of *keinen, keine* and *kein.*

One solution is:

ich esse keinen Fisch	ich trinke keine Milch	Ich esse kein Gemüse
ich esse keine Wurst	**ich trinke kein Wasser**	Ich esse keinen Schinken
ich esse kein Eis	ich esse keinen Reis	**ich esse keine Chips**

Plenaries
- Students take turns to say a sentence about each of the ten items listed in ex. 1, using either *Ich esse / trinke gern …* or *Ich esse / trinke kein(e)(n) …* But they must always contradict each other: if student A says something healthy, B must say something unhealthy, and vice versa, e.g.
A: *Ich esse gern Fisch.*
B: *Bäh! Ich esse keinen Fisch.*
A: *Ich esse kein Gemüse.*
B: *Mmm, lecker! Ich esse gern Gemüse.*
Make sure they swap over so that B has a turn at making the choices.
- Students write dietary advice for Jan (ex. 2) using *Man soll …*, e.g. *Jan, man soll kein Fastfood essen und keinen Kaffee trinken. Man soll Fisch essen – das ist gut. Und man soll jeden Tag Wasser trinken …*
- Working in pairs, students test each other on language from the database or mini-dictionary that they've been adding to throughout this unit (see homework suggestions in the *Planner* for spread 3A.1). They give each other English words and challenge their partner to: say them in German, write them correctly (including gender and plural, if appropriate), then put each one into a sentence.

Homework
- Students choose from ex. 1 their favourite two items together with two items that they don't like or don't eat at all. They write a sentence for each item, using *denn* to explain their preferences.
- Student Book page 95, ex. 7–8 and / or *Challenge*.

141

3A.4 Guten Appetit!

AT 3.1
LLS 5.3

1 Ist das gut (✓) oder schlecht (X)?
Students decide whether the food and drink items are healthy or not. Point out a false friend (*Chips* are crisps, not chips) and elicit from students two other false friends they've met in this unit (*Nudeln* – pasta, *Marmelade* – jam). Talk about students' answers and point out that it is not always straightforward deciding whether some foods are healthy or unhealthy, e.g. meat may be healthy or unhealthy depending on your point of view, how much of it you eat, what type of meat you eat, how you cook it, etc.

Answers: 1 X; 2 ✓; 3 ✓; 4 X; 5 X; 6 ✓; 7 ✓ or X; 8 ✓; 9 X; 10 ✓

AT 1.3–4
AT 3.3–4
R&W 2.1
KAL 4.6

2 Hör zu und lies. Wer isst und trinkt gut (✓) und wer schlecht (X)?
Students read and listen to two teenagers talking about their diet. They work out whether each person eats healthily or not.
Check that students understand the difference between *Ich esse kein(e)(n) …* (I don't eat …) and *Ich esse nicht gern …* (I don't like eating …).

Answers: Jan X; Mona ✓

🎧 **CD 2, track 27**   Seite 94, Übung 2

Jan: Ich esse gern Fastfood, und ich trinke sehr gern Kaffee. Ich esse keinen Fisch, denn ich finde Fisch doof. Ich trinke kein Wasser. Ich esse jeden Tag Hamburger und Pommes oder Pizza. Und ich esse jeden Tag ein Eis oder Kuchen.

Mona: Ich esse gern Fisch – Fisch mit Reis oder Kartoffeln. Oder ich esse Nudeln mit Tomaten und Käse. Aber ich esse kein Fleisch, denn ich mag Fleisch nicht. Ich esse jeden Tag eine Banane und eine Orange. Und ich trinke jeden Tag Wasser.

Follow-up

KAL 4.2
- Point out that ex. 2 is a good example of why it is so important to understand high-frequency words and phrases such as *kein(e)(n), (nicht) gern, jeden Tag, ich mag (nicht)*, etc. If students only understand the topic words (i.e. food and drink vocabulary), it is difficult to work out whether the diets in ex. 2 are healthy or not.
To demonstrate this, prepare a text about eating habits but blank out everything apart from the food and drink items. Try to make it deliberately misleading, e.g. include lots of healthy foods so that the diet looks healthy (*… Obst … Gemüse … Wasser … Fisch … Salat*). Show it to students and challenge them to assess the healthiness of the diet, then reveal the full text with the blanks filled in: *Ich esse kein Obst, denn es ist langweilig. Ich esse auch kein Gemüse und ich trinke kein Wasser. Ich finde Fisch furchtbar, und ich esse nicht gern Salat.* Clearly this describes an unhealthy diet but it was impossible to tell from the food words alone.

KAL 4.2, 4.4
- Ask students to find four linking words in the ex. 2 texts (*und, denn, oder, aber*) and to write a sentence using each one. Encourage them to choose a different context for each sentence, e.g. family (*Meine Schwester ist faul und frech*), school (*Ich mag Erdkunde, denn es ist interessant*), hobbies (*Ich spiele am liebsten Tennis oder Federball*), etc. Challenge students to write a single long sentence (in any context) containing all four linking words, e.g. *Ich spiele gern Fußball oder Rugby, denn ich bin sehr sportlich, aber ich spiele nicht gern am Computer und ich sehe nicht gern fern.*

AT 2.3–4
KAL 4.3, 4.6
LLS 5.3

3 👥 Macht ein Interview.
Students interview each other about eating habits and opinions of food. Point out the *Grammatik* box on *keinen / keine / kein* and insist that they use the correct form.
Make sure students realise that *Gemüse* is a neuter singular noun, translated into English as plural "vegetables": *ich esse kein* (neuter, singular) *Gemüse* – I don't eat vegetables.

🎥 **Follow-up**

AT 1.3–4
L&S 1.1, 1.2

Play the final section of video clip 3A, set in the pizzeria: the four teenagers are trying to agree on what sort of pizza to order, but it's tricky because everyone has different preferences. Students note down: the toppings suggested by Nina; the problem with each suggestion; and finally what type of pizza they order.

Answers: tuna – no one eats fish; ham and olives – Ali doesn't want meat; spinach and olives – Kathi doesn't eat spinach; mushrooms and onions – Kathi and Nico don't want onions; they eventually order a pizza with tomato and cheese

3A.4 Guten Appetit!

Video clip 3A (excerpt)

Ali: Oh, ich habe Hunger!
Nico: Ich auch!
Nina: Wie wär's mit einer Pizza mit Thunfisch …
Alle: Kein Fisch!
Nina: Dann Schinken. Und Oliven.
Ali: Kein Fleisch!
Nina: Dann nehmen wir Spinat und Oliven …
Kathi: Ich esse keinen Spinat …
Nina: Dann eben … Pilze und Zwiebeln?
Kathi: Oh, bitte, keine Zwiebeln!
Nina: Okay, dann eben keine Zwiebeln … ich hab's … nehmen wir Tomaten und Käse – eine Pizza Margherita!
Alle: Ja!

CD 2, track 28 *Seite 95, Übung 5*

1 Man soll jeden Tag Fastfood essen. Das ist ein schlechter Tipp!
2 Man soll keine Cola trinken. Das ist ein guter Tipp!
3 Man soll jeden Tag Obst essen. Das ist ein guter Tipp!
4 Man soll kein Wasser trinken. Das ist ein schlechter Tipp!
5 Man soll kein Gemüse essen. Das ist ein schlechter Tipp!
6 Man soll jeden Tag Milch trinken. Das ein ist guter Tipp!
7 Man soll jeden Tag Kuchen essen. Das ist ein schlechter Tipp!
8 Man soll keinen Fisch essen. Das ist ein schlechter Tipp!
9 Man soll keine Chips essen. Das ist ein guter Tipp!
10 Man soll jeden Tag Kaffee trinken. Das ist ein schlechter Tipp!

AT 3.2 / KAL 4.4 / KAL 4.5 / LLS 5.1

4 Lies die Tipps. Sind sie gut oder schlecht?
Students read the diet tips and decide whether each one is healthy or unhealthy. Point out that, as in ex. 2, they need to take account of the high-frequency words (*jeden Tag, kein*) as well as the food words in order to work out whether the tips are healthy or not.
Ask students what they notice about the verbs in 1–10. They should spot that each sentence contains two verbs: *man soll*, and an infinitive at the end of the sentence.
Look at the *Grammatik* box and make sure students understand the difference in meaning between the present tense (*Man isst jeden Tag Obst* – You / We eat fruit every day) and the use of *sollen* (*Man soll jeden Tag Obst essen* – You / We should eat fruit every day).

Answers: **1** schlecht; **2** gut; **3** gut; **4** schlecht; **5** schlecht; **6** gut; **7** schlecht; **8** schlecht; **9** gut; **10** schlecht

AT 1.2

5 Hör zu (1–10). Ist alles richtig?
Students listen to check their answers to ex. 4.

AT 4.2

6 Schreib die Sätze richtig auf.
Students copy out the sentences using correct word order.

Answers: **a** Man soll keine Chips essen. **b** Man soll keine Cola trinken. **c** Man soll keine Hamburger essen. **d** Man soll keine Mayonnaise essen. **e** Man soll keinen Kaffee trinken. **f** Man soll keine Schokolade essen.

AT 4.2

7 Schreib Sätze mit *Man soll* …
Students write sentences giving advice on what to eat, based on the pictures.

Answers: **1** Man soll jeden Tag Salat essen. **2** Man soll jeden Tag Wasser trinken. **3** Man soll Spinat essen. **4** Man soll Orangensaft trinken. **5** Man soll Nudeln essen. **6** Man soll Reis essen.

AT 4.2

8 Was soll man nicht essen? Schreib vier Sätze.
Students write four sentences giving advice on what not to eat.

AT 4.3–4 / R&W 2.4

Challenge
Students choose three items of food and drink that they like and three that they don't like or don't eat at all. They explain why they do or don't like each item, using *denn*, and then consider whether their choices are good or bad. They go on to give dietary advice to themselves, using *Man soll* …
Remind students of the criteria for achieving a higher level (see teaching notes for spread 3A.1 ex. 8).

3A.5 Guten Appetit!

3A.5 Nicos Videoblog
Seite 96–97

Planner

Objectives
- Vocabulary: order a meal in a restaurant
- Grammar: "verb second" word order; *ich möchte* + noun
- Skills: use polite language; use different strategies to work out meaning

Video
- Video blog 3A

Resources
- Student Book, pages 96–97
- CD 2, tracks 29–30
- Foundation and Higher Workbooks, page 52
- Workbook audio: CD 3 and 4, track 59
- Interactive OxBox, Unit 3A

Key language
Was darf es sein? Was möchtest du? Ich möchte …
Als (Vorspeise / Hauptgericht / Nachspeise) nehme ich …
Und zu trinken?

Framework references
L&S 1.1, 1.2; R&W 2.2, 2.5; IU 3.1, 3.2; LLS 5.4, 5.5

Starters
- Before playing Nico's video blog, challenge students to try to guess what the missing items are in ex. 1 a–h, based on what they've seen of Nico in the video clips so far. They may also be able to remember some of Nico's food and drink preferences from earlier in the unit. Once they've had a go at filling in the blanks, watch the video so that they can check how many items they guessed correctly.
- Student Book page 97, *Think* activity.

Plenaries
- In pairs, students interview each other about their own eating habits using questions a–h in ex. 1.
- Restaurant tennis. In pairs, student A names a course (*Als Vorspeise / Hauptgericht / Nachspeise / Getränk …*); B responds by suggesting an appropriate dish, e.g.
  A: *Als Hauptgericht möchte ich …*
  B: *… Omelett mit Käse.*
- Student Book page 97, ex. 4.

Homework
- Students write a blog profile for themselves (similar to Nico's profile on page 96) and complete sentences a–h in ex. 1 with details of their own eating habits. If the appropriate technology is available, they could record their own video blog and play it back to the class.
- Student Book page 97, *Challenge*.

---

1 Sieh dir das Video an. Beantworte die Fragen für Nico.

AT 1.4
L&S 1.1, 1.2
IU 3.1, 3.2

Students watch Nico's video blog and complete his answers to questions a–h. Encourage them to note down as much as they can on the first listening, then play the recording again so that they can fill in any remaining details.

Point out Nico's alternative wording in response to c and d: he says *zu Mittag* (instead of *zum Mittagessen*) and *zum Abendbrot* (instead of *zum Abendessen*). Challenge students to work out the literal meaning of *Abendbrot* (evening bread). Students may also notice that Nico refers to *Hühnchen* rather than *Hähnchen*: point out that both are possible in this context.

Answers: **a** Fleisch; **b** Brot mit Wurst; **c** Hühnchen oder Bratwurst mit Kartoffeln oder Reis; **d** Brötchen mit Butter und Schinken; **e** Fastfood (Cheeseburger oder Pommes oder Pizza); **f** Fisch, Gemüse; **g** Cola, Kaffee; **h** Milch

---

Video blog 3A
CD 2, track 29
Seite 96, Übung 1

Ich esse gern Fleisch! Zum Frühstück esse ich Brot mit Wurst. Zu Mittag esse ich dann Hühnchen oder Bratwurst mit Kartoffeln oder Reis. Und zum Abendbrot esse ich dann gern Brötchen mit Butter und Schinken. Und am Wochenende esse ich gern Fastfood – zum Beispiel Cheeseburger oder Pizza oder Pommes.
Und was ich nicht gern esse? Ich esse nicht gern Fisch, denn Fisch mag ich nicht. Ich esse auch nicht gern Gemüse, denn Gemüse ist doof. Ich trinke aber gern Cola, denn Cola mag ich. Ich trinke auch oft Kaffee – morgens und abends. Ich trinke aber nicht gern Milch, denn Milch ist furchtbar.
Was isst und trinkst du gern? Magst du auch gern Fleisch?

Think

R&W 2.2
LLS 5.4, 5.5

Before listening to the ex. 2 recording, point out the *Think* box on page 97, which asks students to use the pictures to work out the meaning of any new

144

3A.6 Guten Appetit!

words on the menu. Students should also be able to use context to work out the meaning of *Vorspeisen*, *Hauptgerichte*, *Nachspeisen* and *Getränke* (because all the dishes listed under *Vorspeisen* are starters, all those under *Hauptgerichte* are main courses, etc.). Some items on the menu are cognates, and students will recognise others from earlier in the unit. They use the Glossary or a dictionary to look up anything they can't work out.

AT 1.3–4
L&S 1.1, 1.2

2 Hör zu und lies die Speisekarte, Seite 97. Was bestellen Kathi und ihr Vater sich?

Kathi and her father are ordering a meal in a restaurant. Students listen and identify which items from the menu they order.

Play the recording again and help students to identify any phrases that they could use in their own dialogues (in ex. 3–4 and *Challenge*), e.g. *tut mir Leid*, (*Schnitzel*) *haben wir heute nicht*, *ich weiß nicht*.

Answers: **Kathis Vater:** a, e, h, m; **Kathi:** b, f, g, j

🎧 **CD 2, track 30**   Seite 96, Übung 2

Kellnerin:	Guten Tag! Ja bitte – was darf's sein?
Vater:	Guten Tag! Also, als Vorspeise nehme ich die Zwiebelsuppe – nein, die Tomatensuppe … und als Hauptgericht möchte ich Schnitzel mit Kartoffeln und Bohnen.
Kellnerin:	Tut mir Leid, Schnitzel haben wir heute nicht.
Vater:	Dann nehme ich Kotelett mit Pommes frites, Erbsen und Karotten.
Kellnerin:	Gern. Und als Nachspeise?
Vater:	Hmm … ich weiß nicht.
Kellnerin:	Der Kirschkuchen ist sehr gut.
Vater:	Nein, ich mag keine Kirschen. Ich nehme die Zitronentorte, bitte.
Kellnerin:	Und zu trinken?
Vater:	Ein Glas Wein, bitte.
Kellnerin:	Rotwein oder Weißwein?
Vater:	Rotwein, bitte.
Kellnerin:	Gern. Und du? Was möchtest du?
Kathi:	Als Vorspeise nehme ich Melone … nein, ich nehme den Salatteller.
Kellnerin:	Den Salatteller – gern. Und als Hauptgericht?
Kathi:	Ich möchte Omelett, bitte.
Kellnerin:	Omelett – mit Pilzen oder Käse?
Kathi:	Mit Pilzen, bitte.
Kellnerin:	Und als Nachspeise?
Kathi:	Haben Sie Schokoladeneis?
Kellnerin:	Ja.
Kathi:	Gut, ich nehme Schokoladeneis mit Sahne.
Kellnerin:	Gern. Und zu trinken?
Kathi:	Ich möchte Limonade, bitte.

AT 2.3

3 👥 Ist alles richtig?

Students check their answers to ex. 2 by acting out the dialogues for Kathi and her father.

AT 2.3–4

4 👥 Macht weitere Dialoge.

Students make up other restaurant dialogues. You may wish them to create their own menu first (see *Challenge*).

AT 4.4
R&W 2.5

Challenge

Students create their own restaurant menu, researching new food and drink vocabulary in a dictionary. They write a dialogue based on their menu.

Encourage them to invent some sort of situation to add humour or interest to their dialogue, e.g. an indecisive customer, a rude waiter, the restaurant doesn't have anything that the customer asks for. Students could invent moods or personalities for their characters, e.g. angry, sad, shy, overenthusiastic. Invite them to practise their dialogues in pairs and perform them to the class.

3A.6 Sprachlabor   Seite 98–99

Planner

Objectives
- Grammar: "verb second" word order; *gern / nicht gern*; *ich esse keinen / keine / kein …*; *man soll* + infinitive
- Skills: use linking words to build longer sentences; pronounce the long and short *u* sound

Resources
- Student Book, pages 98–99
- CD 2, track 31
- Foundation and Higher Workbooks, pages 53–54
- Copymasters 69, 70
- Interactive OxBox, Unit 3A

Framework references
KAL 4.1, 4.2, 4.3, 4.4, 4.5, 4.6; LLS 5.8

3A.6 Guten Appetit!

Word order

KAL 4.4   **1 Write new sentences.**

Answers: **a** Zum Mittagessen esse ich Pommes frites. **b** Zum Frühstück trinke ich Milch. **c** Zum Abendessen esse ich Wurst. **d** Zum Mittagessen trinke ich Wasser. **e** Zum Abendessen esse ich Salat. **f** Zum Frühstück esse ich Cornflakes.

Gern / nicht gern

KAL 4.2, 4.6   **2 Write new sentences for the pictures.**

Answers: **a** Ich esse gern Kartoffeln. **b** Ich esse nicht gern Joghurt. **c** Ich esse gern Brot. **d** Ich esse nicht gern Fleisch. **e** Ich esse gern Hamburger. **f** Ich esse nicht gern Obst.

Keinen / keine / kein

KAL 4.3, 4.6   **3 Fill in the gaps using keinen / keine / kein.**

Answers: **a** keinen; **b** kein; **c** keine; **d** keinen; **e** kein; **f** keine

Man soll ...

KAL 4.4, 4.5   **4 Write new sentences with man soll ...**

Answers: **a** Man soll jeden Tag Wasser trinken. **b** Man soll keine Pommesfrites essen. **c** Man soll Gemüse essen. **d** Man soll keine Cola trinken. **e** Man soll jeden Tag Obst essen. **f** Man soll keinen Kaffee trinken.

Using linking words

KAL 4.2   **5 Match the German and the English linking words.**

Answers: und – and; aber – but; oder – or; denn – because

LLS 5.8   **Think**
Students discuss the importance of using linking words, e.g. they help you to build longer, more complex sentences, they help to add interest and variety to what you say and write.

KAL 4.4   **6 Link each pair of sentences with a different linking word to make sense.**

Answers: **a** Ich esse gern Pizza und ich trinke gern Cola. **b** Ich trinke Orangensaft oder (ich trinke) Wasser. **c** Ich esse nicht gern Salat, aber ich esse gern Obst. **d** Ich esse kein Gemüse, denn Gemüse ist furchtbar.

Long u sound – short u sound

KAL 4.1   **7 Listen carefully: long u or short u? (1–8)**

Answers: **long:** 2, 3, 5, 7, 8; **short:** 1, 4, 6

CD 2, track 31		Seite 99, Übung 7 und 8
1 Butter	5 Kuchen	
2 Wurst	6 und	
3 Nudeln	7 furchtbar	
4 hundert	8 Thunfisch	

8 Listen again and practise pronouncing each word correctly.
Play the ex. 7 recording again. Students listen and repeat.

146

3A.7 Guten Appetit!

3A.7 Extra Star Seite 100

Planner

Objectives
- Vocabulary: talk about food and drink
- Grammar: "verb second" word order; *gern / nicht gern* and *kein*

- Skills: develop accuracy in written work; identify gist and detail

Resources
- Student Book, page 100
- Copymaster 71

AT 4.1 **1 Write a shopping list for Nina.**
Students fill in the missing letters to complete the food words. Encourage them to aim for complete accuracy and to use the Glossary to check any spellings they're unsure of.

Answers: **a** *Nudeln;* **b** *Hähnchen;* **c** *Kartoffeln;* **d** *Butter;* **e** *Joghurt;* **f** *Wurst*

AT 3.2 **2 Match the quantities with the items.**
Students match the quantities and packaging to the food and drink.

Answers: **a** *2;* **b** *4;* **c** *5;* **d** *6;* **e** *1;* **f** *3*

AT 4.2 **3 Unscramble the word order in these sentences.**
Encourage students to focus on accurate spelling when copying out the words. Pairs could check each other's sentences looking for missing umlauts, missing capital letters and other spelling errors.

Answers: **a** *Zum Abendessen esse ich Brötchen.* **b** *Zum Frühstück esse ich Müsli.* **c** *Zum Mittagessen esse ich Hähnchen.* **d** *Zum Frühstück trinke ich Kaffee.* **e** *Zum Mittagessen trinke ich Wasser.* **f** *Zum Abendessen trinke ich Tee.*

AT 3.2 **4 Match the sentences with the pictures. Does each person like or dislike it?**
Students choose a picture to represent each sentence about food and drink. They indicate (with ✓ or ✗) whether the sentences express likes or dislikes.

Answers: **a** *5 ✗;* **b** *1 ✗;* **c** *3 ✓;* **d** *2 ✗;* **e** *4 ✗;* **f** *6 ✓*

3A.7 Extra Plus Seite 101

Planner

Objectives
- Vocabulary: talk about food and drink
- Grammar: "verb second" word order; *gern / nicht gern* and *keinen / keine / kein*

- Skills: develop accuracy in written work; identify detail in written texts

Resources
- Student Book, page 101
- Copymaster 72

AT 4.1–2 **1 Schreib die Wörter auf.**
Students label the items of food and drink.

Answers: **a** *Schinken;* **b** *Kartoffeln;* **c** *Salat;* **d** *ein Apfel;* **e** *Nudeln;* **f** *Orangensaft*

AT 4.2–3 **2 Was isst und trinkst du gern / nicht gern / nicht? Schreib Sätze.**
Students write sentences to represent the pictures, describing what they do and don't eat and drink. Encourage them to aim for accuracy in terms of spellings, genders and grammar (*keinen, keine, kein*), and to use reference materials to check anything they are unsure of.

Answers: **a** *Ich esse nicht gern Käse.* **b** *Ich trinke keinen Kaffee.* **c** *Ich esse gern Obst.* **d** *Ich esse nicht gern Fleisch.* **e** *Ich esse keine Pizza.* **f** *Ich trinke gern Cola.*

AT 4.3 **3 Und zum Frühstück / Mittagessen / Abendessen? Schreib Sätze.**
Students write a sentence to represent each set of pictures (a–c), explaining what they eat and drink at different mealtimes. As in ex. 2, encourage them to focus on accuracy in terms of spellings and grammar.

3A.8 Guten Appetit!

Answers: **a** *Zum Frühstück esse ich Cornflakes mit Milch und ich trinke Kaffee.* **b** *Zum Mittagessen esse ich Hähnchen mit Reis und ich trinke Wasser.* **c** *Zum Abendessen esse ich Brötchen mit Käse und ich trinke Orangensaft.*

AT 3.3–4
4 Richtig, falsch oder nicht im Text?
Students read the text about eating habits and decide whether statements a–h are true, false or not in the text. Ask them to correct the false statements.

This activity requires students to identify detail (likes, dislikes and opinions) and show an understanding of a wider range of language (e.g. know that *ich trinke gern Kaffee* means the same as *ich mag Kaffee*).

Answers: **a** *richtig;* **b** *nicht im Text;* **c** *richtig;* **d** *richtig;* **e** *falsch (sie findet Fisch furchtbar);* **f** *nicht im Text;* **g** *richtig;* **h** *falsch (zum Abendessen trinkt sie Tee)*

3A.8 Testseite
Seite 102

Planner

Resources
- Student Book, page 102
- CD 2, track 32
- Foundation and Higher Workbooks, page 55
- Copymasters 61, 62
- Assessment, Unit 3A

AT 1.3
1 Listen to Nico. True or false?
Students listen to Nico buying groceries and work out whether a–f are true or false. Ask them to correct the false statements.

Answers: **a** *true;* **b** *false (a kilo);* **c** *false (a slice of ham);* **d** *false (a bottle of water);* **e** *true;* **f** *true*

🎧 **CD 2, track 32** Seite 102, Übung 1

Verkäuferin:	Guten Tag! Was darf es sein?
Nico:	Ich möchte Käse, bitte.
Verkäuferin:	Gern. Wie viel?
Nico:	500 Gramm, bitte. Und ich möchte ein Kilo Kartoffeln.
Verkäuferin:	Hier, bitte. Sonst noch etwas?
Nico:	Ja, eine Scheibe Schinken und eine Flasche Wasser.
Verkäuferin:	Ist das alles?
Nico:	Nein, ich möchte auch vier Becher Joghurt und sechs Dosen Cola, bitte.
Verkäuferin:	Bitte sehr. Sonst noch etwas?
Nico:	Nein, danke, das ist alles.

AT 3.3
2 Read the sentences and match them to the pictures.

Answers: **a** *4, 5, 6, 10;* **b** *3, 7, 12;* **c** *1, 9, 8, 13, 14;* **d** *2, 15, 11*

AT 2.3
3 Order the items of food below for two of you.

Example answers: **a** *Ich möchte Currywurst mit Pommes frites und Ketchup, bitte. Ich nehme auch einen Cheeseburger mit Pommes frites und Mayonnaise. Und ich möchte eine Flasche Cola und eine Flasche Wasser, bitte.* **b** *Ich möchte sechs Brötchen, ein Stück Apfelkuchen und ein Schokoladeneis mit Sahne, bitte. Ich nehme auch einen Kaffee, bitte.*

AT 4.3–4
4 Write at least one sentence for each of a–f.
Students explain: which types of food they like, and why; which food they don't like, and why not; what they don't eat at all, and why not; what they have for breakfast, lunch and evening meal.
Remind them of the criteria for achieving a higher level: see teaching notes for spread 3A.1 ex. 8.

3A Guten Appetit!

3A Lesen
Seite 157

Planner

Resources
- Student Book, page 157

Framework references
R&W 2.1, 2.2; IU 3.1, 3.2

Lieblingsessen in Deutschland

AT 3.1 **1 Match each picture to one of the dishes above.**
Students look at the results of a survey about the Top Ten foods in Germany. They choose a picture to represent each dish.

Answers: **1** f; **2** c; **3** j; **4** h; **5** i; **6** b; **7** e; **8** a; **9** d; **10** g

AT 3.2 **2 Look at the Top Ten German dishes (1–10) above. Are these sentences true or false?**
Students answer questions about the survey results.

Answers: **a** true; **b** true; **c** false

AT 3.4 **3 Read Ali's text and answer the questions in English.**
Students read Ali's text about his uncle's doner kebab stall.

Answers: **a** doner kebabs; **b** a doner kebab stall; **c** Turkey; **d** slices of grilled meat with flat (unleavened) bread or pitta bread, salad, onions, yoghurt sauce and garlic; **e** 15,000 in Germany and 1,400 in Berlin; **f** twice a week

Follow-up

- Students carry out a survey to find the Top Ten dishes in the class (*Was ist dein Lieblingsessen? – Ich esse am liebsten …*). They compare with the German survey results.
- Students identify where some of the dishes in ex. 1 come from, e.g. *Lasagne, Pasta Bolognese und Pizza kommen aus Italien; Döner Kebabs kommen aus der Türkei; Wiener Schnitzel kommen aus Wien / Österreich*. Which of these dishes are popular in the UK?
- Talk about international food stereotypes, e.g. Germany is often associated with sauerkraut, sausages and beer, France with snails and frogs' legs, England with roast beef, and fish and chips, Scotland with haggis.
- Ask students to find out something about German food and eating habits, e.g. the tradition of *Kaffee und Kuchen*, types of German bread, cheese, sausage, cakes / pastries, and other German dishes. The following websites may be of interest:
  - Young Germany (www.young-germany.de) – click on links to "Life in Germany" then "Food"
  - UK-German Connection (www.ukgermanconnection.org) – go to "the-voyage" section of the website, then "Lifestyle" and "Food"
  - the Goethe Institut's "Meet The Germans" (www.goethe.de/ins/gb/lp/prj/mtg/enindex.htm).
- Find some German café or restaurant menus online and ask students to identify the dishes.

3A Guten Appetit!

Foundation Workbook

3A.1 Was isst du gern? (Seite 48)

AT 3.1 **1 Draw lines to link the words to the items in the fridge.**

Answers: Salat – lettuce; Hähnchen – chicken; Cola – cola; Orangensaft – orange juice; Fisch – fish; Käse – cheese; Joghurt – yoghurt; Milch – milk; Wasser – water

AT 1.2–3 **2 Put a tick or cross to show what these people like and dislike.**

Answers: *a* <u>Nils</u>: muesli ✗, chicken ✓, pasta ✓, cola ✓, milk ✗; *b* <u>Susanne</u>: tea ✓, coffee ✗, chicken ✗, lettuce ✓, bread ✓, cheese ✓

🎧 **CD 3, track 55** Seite 48, Übung 2

a – Na, Nils, was isst und trinkst du gern?
 – Na ja, ich esse gern Hähnchen und Nudeln und ich trinke gern Cola. Was ich nicht gern esse? Müsli – igitt! Und ich trinke auch nicht gern Milch.
b – Und du, Susanne?
 – Also, ich esse gern Salat, Käse und Brot, aber ich esse nicht gern Hähnchen. Was ich nicht gern trinke, ist Kaffee. Das mag ich nicht. Aber Tee trinke ich gern.

---

3 Circle the correct word order. Remember, the verb always comes second.

Answers: *a* esse ich; *b* esse ich; *c* trinke ich

3A.2 Ein Eis, bitte! (Seite 49)

AT 3.1 **1 Draw lines to show where you would buy these items.**

Answers: <u>Pizzeria</u>: pizza with ham, pizza with olives; <u>Eisdiele</u>: ice cream in bowl, ice cream in cone; <u>Imbiss</u>: sausage, chips; <u>Bäckerei</u>: bread, cake

AT 1.2 **2 Listen and work out where these people are.**

Answers: *a* Imbiss; *b* Bäckerei; *c* Eisdiele; *d* Pizzeria; *e* Bäckerei; *f* Imbiss; *g* Pizzeria; *h* Eisdiele

---

🎧 **CD 3, track 56** Seite 49, Übung 2

a Ich möchte eine Currywurst mit Pommes.
b Ich möchte ein Käsebrötchen.
c Ich möchte ein Erdbeereis mit Sahne.
d Ich möchte eine Pizza mit Schinken.
e Ich möchte ein Stück Apfelkuchen.
f Ich möchte einen Hamburger.
g Ich möchte eine Pizza mit Oliven.
h Ich möchte ein Schokoladeneis ohne Sahne.

AT 1.2 **3 Listen again and write down, in English, what the people are ordering.**

Answers: *a* curried sausage with chips; *b* cheese roll; *c* strawberry ice cream with cream; *d* pizza with ham; *e* apple cake; *f* hamburger; *g* pizza with olives; *h* chocolate ice cream without cream

3A.3 500 Gramm Käse, bitte! (Seite 50)

AT 1.2 **1 Listen to some large numbers. In the boxes next to the numbers here, write the order you hear them in. The first one is done for you.**

Answers: see order of numbers in transcript below

🎧 **CD 3, track 57** Seite 50, Übung 1

a tausend
b achthundertvierundzwanzig
c sechshunderteinundneunzig
d zweihundertdreißig
e dreihundertzwanzig
f siebenhunderteinundvierzig
g hundertachtzig
h vierhundertfünfzig
i neunhundert
j fünfhundertsechsundsechzig

AT 3.2 **2 Circle the appropriate words.**

Answers: *a* einen Becher; *b* eine Packung; *c* eine Flasche; *d* eine Tüte; *e* einen Liter; *f* eine Flasche

AT 4.1–2 **3 Make a shopping list with these items.**

Answers: eine Dose Cola, eine Flasche Wasser, einen Becher Joghurt, 500 Gramm Schinken, sechs Bananen, einen Liter Milch

3A.4 Ich esse kein Fleisch (Seite 51)

1 Herr Gierig and Frau Gierig have completely opposite tastes. Complete the sentences using *keinen*, *keine* or *kein*.

Answers: <u>Frau Gierig</u>: Ich esse keine Bonbons. Ich esse keine Schokolade. Ich esse keine Pommes. Ich esse kein Fleisch. Ich esse keinen Apfelkuchen. Ich trinke keine Cola.

AT 1.2–3 **2 Listen to these people and write, in English, what they don't eat and why.**

Answers: *a* fish, doesn't like it; *b* sweets, they are stupid; *c* potatoes, they are boring; *d* water, cola is better; *e* fruit, it is awful

3A Guten Appetit!

🎧 **CD 3, track 58**   Seite 51, Übung 2

a Ich esse keinen Fisch, denn ich mag Fisch nicht.
b Ich esse keine Bonbons, denn ich finde Bonbons doof.
c Ich esse keine Kartoffeln, denn Kartoffeln sind langweilig.
d Ich trinke kein Wasser, denn Cola ist besser.
e Ich esse kein Obst, denn ich finde Obst furchtbar.

AT 4.2   **3** Look at Activity 1 again. Give Herr Gierig some good health advice, using *Man soll …* Go through all the things he eats and drinks.

Answers: Man soll keine Bonbons essen. Man soll keine Schokolade essen. Man soll keine Pommes essen. Man soll kein Fleisch essen. Man soll keinen Apfelkuchen essen. Man soll keine Cola trinken.

3A.5 Nicos Videoblog   (Seite 52)

AT 3.2   **1** Draw lines to the items. Each item needs two lines, one for its name and one for the amount.

Answers: eine Dose Suppe (soup), sechs Scheiben Schinken (ham), eine Flasche Mineralwasser (water), ein Becher Joghurt (yoghurt), eine Packung Chips (crisps), ein Glas Erdbeermarmelade (strawberry jam), 2 Kilo Kartoffeln (potatoes)

AT 4.2   **2** Write sentences to show these people's opinions of food.

Answers: a Ich esse gern Bratwurst. b Ich esse keine Pommes/ Ich esse nicht gern Pommes. c Ich esse gern Müsli. d Ich esse keinen Fisch/Ich esse nicht gern Fisch. e Ich esse gern Schokolade. f Ich esse kein Fleisch/Ich esse nicht gern Fleisch.

AT 1.3   **3** Listen to the interview and fill in the gaps in the text in English.

Answers: Lukas likes <u>muesli</u> for breakfast because <u>it's good</u>. He doesn't like <u>toast</u>, because <u>it's boring</u>. He drinks <u>orange juice</u> or <u>tea</u>, but not <u>milk</u>. He eats <u>hamburger</u> and <u>chips</u> at lunchtime but his sister doesn't approve. She says <u>chips aren't good</u>. In the evening, Lukas eats <u>bread</u> or <u>cake</u> but not <u>ham</u> or <u>cheese</u>.

🎧 **CD 3, track 59**   Seite 52, Übung 3

– Hallo Lukas. Heute geht's ums Essen und Trinken. Also, was isst du gern?
– Zum Frühstück esse ich Müsli, denn Müsli ist gut. Toast mag ich nicht, denn Toast ist langweilig. Ich trinke keine Milch; ich trinke lieber Orangensaft oder Tee.
– Und zum Mittagessen?

– Zum Mittagessen gehe ich gern zum Imbiss. Da esse ich gern Hamburger mit Pommes. Aber meine Schwester Anja sagt, Pommes sind nicht gut.
– Und was isst du zum Abendessen?
– Ich esse Brot oder Kuchen, aber keinen Schinken. Schinken und Käse mag ich nicht.

3A.6A Sprachlabor   (Seite 53)

1 Unjumble these sentences and write the words out in the correct order. Always start with the meal. Remember, the verb is always the second piece of information.

Answers: a Zum Frühstück esse ich Cornflakes. b Zum Abendessen esse ich Brot. c Zum Frühstück trinke ich Kaffee. d Zum Mittagessen esse ich Salat. e Zum Abendessen trinke ich Wasser. f Zum Mittagessen trinke ich Orangensaft.

2 Tell these people off for their bad habits. Use *man soll* and *keinen*, *keine* or *kein*.

Answers: a Man soll keine Bratwurst essen. b Man soll keine Computerspiele spielen. c Man soll keinen Whisky trinken. d Man soll kein Motorrad fahren. e Man soll keine Schokolade essen. f Man soll kein Bier trinken.

3 Choose whether the linking words in these sentences mean 'and', 'or', 'but' or 'because'.

Answers: a because; b and; c but; d or; e or; f and; g but; h because

3A.6B Think   (Seite 54)

1 What words should link these sentences?

Answers: a oder; b und; c aber; d aber; e denn; f denn; g und; h oder

2 Say these words out loud and put them into the correct column.

Answers: <u>short 'u'</u>: Hund, Mutter, zum, Butter, Erdkunde, Kunst, Bus; <u>long 'u'</u>: Nudeln, Schule, du, Joghurt, Musik, Bruder, Stuhl

3 Put these words into the correct column.

Answers: <u>Polite</u>: Ich möchte ein Eis, bitte! Ja, bitte. Nein, danke. Ein Eis, bitte. Bitte schön. Danke schön. <u>Not so polite</u>: Ein Eis! Nein. Ja. Ja? Hier!

151

3A Guten Appetit!

Higher Workbook

3A.1 Was isst du gern? (Seite 48)

AT 4.1 **1** Write in the German words for the items.

Answers: **a** Hähnchen; **b** Fisch; **c** Milch; **d** Wasser; **e** Käse; **f** Joghurt; **g** Orangensaft; **h** Cola; **i** Salat

AT 1.2–3 **2** Listen to these people saying what they do and don't like to eat and drink. Write in the items in English.

Answers: **a** <u>Nils</u>: likes chicken, pasta and cola; doesn't like muesli or milk; **b** <u>Susanne</u>: likes lettuce/salad, cheese, bread and tea; doesn't like chicken or coffee

---

🎧 **CD 4, track 55**   Seite 48, Übung 2

a – Na, Nils, was isst und trinkst du gern?
   – Na ja, ich esse gern Hähnchen und Nudeln und ich trinke gern Cola. Was ich nicht gern esse? Müsli – igitt! Und ich trinke auch nicht gern Milch.
b – Und du, Susanne?
   – Also, ich esse gern Salat, Käse und Brot, aber ich esse nicht gern Hähnchen. Was ich nicht gern trinke, ist Kaffee. Das mag ich nicht. Aber Tee trinke ich gern.

AT 4.2 **3** Write out these sentences in the correct order. Remember, the verb always comes second.

Answers: **a** Zum Frühstück esse ich Cornflakes. **b** Zum Mittagessen esse ich eine Banane. **c** Zum Abendessen trinke ich Wasser.

3A.2 Ein Eis, bitte! (Seite 49)

AT 3.1 **1** Draw lines to show where you would buy these items.

Answers: <u>Pizzeria</u>: pizza with ham, pizza with olives, <u>Eisdiele</u>: ice cream in bowl, ice cream in cone, <u>Imbiss</u>: sausage, chips, <u>Bäckerei</u>: bread, cake

AT 1.2 **2** Listen and work out where these people are.

Answers: **a** Imbiss; **b** Bäckerei; **c** Eisdiele; **d** Pizzeria; **e** Bäckerei; **f** Imbiss; **g** Pizzeria; **h** Eisdiele

---

🎧 **CD 4, track 56**   Seite 49, Übung 2

a Ich möchte eine Currywurst mit Pommes.
b Ich möchte ein Käsebrötchen.
c Ich möchte ein Erdbeereis mit Sahne.
d Ich möchte eine Pizza mit Schinken.
e Ich möchte ein Stück Apfelkuchen.
f Ich möchte einen Hamburger.
g Ich möchte eine Pizza mit Oliven.
h Ich möchte ein Schokoladeneis ohne Sahne.

AT 1.2 **3** Listen again and write down, in English, what the people are ordering.

Answers: **a** curried sausage with chips; **b** cheese roll; **c** strawberry ice cream with cream; **d** pizza with ham; **e** apple cake; **f** hamburger; **g** pizza with olives; **h** chocolate ice cream without cream

AT 4.2 **4** Write down four orders for things you'd like to eat. Don't forget to be polite!

Answers: students' own answers

3A.3 500 Gramm Käse, bitte! (Seite 50)

AT 1.2 **AT 4.1** **1** Listen to some large numbers. Write the numbers out in the order you hear them, first just the number, then the German word for it.

Answers: See transcript for numbers in words. Figures are: **a** 1,000; **b** 824; **c** 691; **d** 230; **e** 320; **f** 741; **g** 180; **h** 450; **i** 900; **j** 566

🎧 **CD 4, track 57**   Seite 50, Übung 1

a tausend
b achthundertvierundzwanzig
c sechshunderteinundneunzig
d zweihundertdreißig
e dreihundertzwanzig
f siebenhunderteinundvierzig
g hundertachtzig
h vierhundertfünfzig
i neunhundert
j fünfhundertsechsundsechzig

AT 3.2 **2** Write in the appropriate amounts.

Answers: **a** einen Becher; **b** eine Packung; **c** eine Flasche; **d** eine Tüte; **e** einen Liter; **f** eine Flasche

AT 4.2 **3** Make a shopping list with these items. Don't forget to include the amounts.

Answers: eine Dose Cola, eine Flasche Wasser, einen Becher Joghurt, 500 Gramm Schinken, sechs Bananen, einen Liter Milch

3A.4 Ich esse kein Fleisch (Seite 51)

1 Herr Gierig and Frau Gierig have completely opposite tastes. Complete the sentences using *keinen, keine* or *kein*.

Answers: <u>Frau Gierig</u>: Ich esse keine Bonbons. Ich esse keine Schokolade. Ich esse keine Pommes. Ich esse kein Fleisch. Ich esse keinen Apfelkuchen. Ich trinke keine Cola.

3A Guten Appetit!

AT 1.2–3 **2 Listen to these people and write, in English, what they don't eat and why.**

Answers: **a** fish, doesn't like it; **b** sweets, they are stupid; **c** potatoes, they are boring; **d** water, cola is better; **e** fruit, it is awful

🎧 **CD 4, track 58**   Seite 51, Übung 2

a Ich esse keinen Fisch, denn ich mag Fisch nicht.
b Ich esse keine Bonbons, denn ich finde Bonbons doof.
c Ich esse keine Kartoffeln, denn Kartoffeln sind langweilig.
d Ich trinke kein Wasser, denn Cola ist besser.
e Ich esse kein Obst, denn ich finde Obst furchtbar.

AT 4.2 **3 Look at Activity 1 again. Give Herr Gierig some good health advice, using *Man soll* … and *keinen/keine/kein*. Go through all the things he eats and drinks.**

Answers: Man soll keine Bonbons essen. Man soll keine Schokolade essen. Man soll keine Pommes essen. Man soll kein Fleisch essen. Man soll keinen Apfelkuchen essen. Man soll keine Cola trinken.

AT 4.2–3 **4 Now also say in each case what Herr Gierig should be eating and drinking. Choose healthy items from this unit.**

Answers: students' own answers

3A.5 Nicos Videoblog   (Seite 52)

AT 3.2 **1 Work out the items and amounts. Complete the shopping list in German.**

Answers: eine Dose Suppe, sechs Scheiben Schinken, eine Flasche Mineralwasser, ein Becher Joghurt, eine Packung Chips, ein Glas Erdbeermarmelade, 2 Kilo Kartoffeln

AT 4.2 **2 Write sentences to show these people's opinions of food.**

Answers: **a** Ich esse gern Bratwurst. **b** Ich esse keine Pommes/Ich esse nicht gern Pommes. **c** Ich esse gern Müsli. **d** Ich esse keinen Fisch/Ich esse nicht gern Fisch. **e** Ich esse gern Schokolade. **f** Ich esse kein Fleisch/Ich esse nicht gern Fleisch.

AT 1.3–4 **3 Listen to the interview. Make notes and write a few sentences in English about Lukas' eating and drinking habits.**

Answers: Lukas likes muesli for breakfast because it's good. He doesn't like toast, because it's boring. He drinks orange juice or tea, but not milk. He eats hamburger and chips at lunchtime but his sister doesn't approve. She says chips aren't good. In the evening, Lukas eats bread or cake but not ham or cheese.

🎧 **CD 4, track 59**   Seite 52, Übung 3

– Hallo Lukas. Heute geht's ums Essen und Trinken. Also, was isst du gern?
– Zum Frühstück esse ich Müsli, denn Müsli ist gut. Toast mag ich nicht, denn Toast ist langweilig. Ich trinke keine Milch; ich trinke lieber Orangensaft oder Tee.
– Und zum Mittagessen?
– Zum Mittagessen gehe ich gern zum Imbiss. Da esse ich gern Hamburger mit Pommes. Aber meine Schwester Anja sagt, Pommes sind nicht gut.
– Und was isst du zum Abendessen?
– Ich esse Brot oder Kuchen, aber keinen Schinken. Schinken und Käse mag ich nicht.

AT 2.3–4 **4 Listen again and note down the interviewer's three questions. Then ask a partner those questions. In your conversation, include: three meals, reasons, linking words.**

3A.6A Sprachlabor   (Seite 53)

1 Unjumble these sentences and write the words out in the correct order. Always start with the meal.

Answers: **a** Zum Frühstück esse ich Cornflakes. **b** Zum Abendessen esse ich Brot. **c** Zum Frühstück trinke ich Kaffee. **d** Zum Mittagessen esse ich Salat. **e** Zum Abendessen trinke ich Wasser. **f** Zum Mittagessen trinke ich Orangensaft.

2 Tell these people off for their bad habits. Use *man soll* and *keinen, keine* or *kein*.

Answers: **a** Man soll keine Bratwurst essen. **b** Man soll keine Computerspiele spielen. **c** Man soll keinen Whisky trinken. **d** Man soll kein Motorrad fahren. **e** Man soll keine Schokolade essen. **f** Man soll kein Bier trinken.

3 Translate these sentences into English.

Answers: **a** I don't eat fish because I think fish is horrible. **b** I play hockey and I also play tennis. **c** I like eating salad/lettuce but I don't like eating meat. **d** Shall we play on the computer or go for a meal/go to eat? **e** Grandfather is going to France or Sweden. **f** Sonja likes physics and chemistry. **g** Olaf likes chemistry but not physics. **h** We like learning German because it's fun.

3A.6B Think   (Seite 54)

1 What words should link these sentences?

2 Say these words out loud and put them into the correct column.

3 Put these words into the correct column.

Answers for ex. 1, 2 and 3: see answers for Foundation Workbook 3A.6B.

153

3B Mein Zuhause

Unit 3B Mein Zuhause — Unit overview grid

Page reference	Objectives	Grammar	Skills and pronunciation	Key language	Framework	AT level
Pages 104–105 **3B.1 Berlin, Berlin!**	Say what there is and isn't in a town; express opinions of places in a town	*Es gibt* + *ein(e)(n)/ kein(e)(n)* …	Evaluate and improve written work	*Es gibt* … *einen Bahnhof, einen Fernsehturm, einen Park, einen Supermarkt, einen Zoo, eine Kirche, eine Post, eine Skateboard-Bahn, eine U-Bahn-Station, ein Jugendzentrum, ein Kaufhaus, ein Kino, ein Museum, ein Schloss, ein Schwimmbad, ein Stadion in meinem Dorf, in meiner Gegend/Stadt Ich finde (mein Dorf/meine Gegend/meine Stadt) gut, interessant, langweilig, nicht gut, schrecklich, schlecht, toll.*	L&S 1.1, 1.2 KAL 4.3, 4.4, 4.6 LLS 5.2, 5.5, 5.7, 5.8	1.1–4, 2.2, 3.1, 3.4 4.2–4
Pages 106–107 **3B.2 Was kann man machen?**	Say what you can do in a place	*Ich kann/ Du kannst/ Man kann* + infinitive *Ich will/Du willst/Man will* + infinitive	Identify language patterns; adapt language to generate new language	*Man kann hier* … *schwimmen, Pizza essen, Kaffee trinken, Mountainbike fahren, ins Kino gehen, Fußball spielen, Freunde treffen, tanzen. Willst du Tennis spielen? Ich will in den Park gehen.*	R&W 2.3, 2.4, 2.5 KAL 4.4, 4.5, 4.6 LLS 5.1, 5.7, 5.8	1.1–2, 1.4, 2.2–4, 3.1–2, 3.4, 4.2–4
Pages 108–109 **3B.3 Wo ist das Kino?**	Ask for and give directions to places in a town	The imperative: *du* and *Sie* forms	Cope with unfamiliar language when listening	*Wo ist …? Geh/Gehen Sie … links, rechts, geradeaus. Nimm/Nehmen Sie … die (erste/zweite/dritte) Straße (links/rechts). Es ist auf der (linken/ rechten) Seite. über die Ampel, über die Kreuzung, über die Brücke*	L&S 1.1, 1.2, 1.3, 1.5 R&W 2.4, 2.5 KAL 4.5 LLS 5.4, 5.7, 5.8	1.2–4, 2.2–4, 3.2, 4.2–4

Mein Zuhause 3B

Page reference	Objectives	Grammar	Skills and pronunciation	Key language	Framework	AT level
Pages 110–111 **3B.4 Im Zoo**	Buy tickets and presents	*Ich möchte/nehme + ein(e)(n) …* Subject–verb inversion in questions	Work out language patterns; use polite language	*Kann ich Ihnen helfen? Ich möchte (eine Karte/zwei Karten) für (einen Erwachsene/zwei Erwachsene/ein Kind/zwei Kinder), bitte. Was kostet das? Das kostet … Euro. Ich suche ein Geschenk für … Ich (möchte/nehme) einen/eine/ein … der Lolli, der Schlüsselanhänger, das Notizbuch, die Plastikschlange, die Schachtel Schokolade, die Schneekugel*	L&S 1.1 IU 3.1 KAL 4.3, 4.6 LLS 5.6	1.1–4, 2.2–3, 3.1–3, 4.3–4
Pages 112–113 **3B.5 Besuchen Sie Zoomsdorf!**	Understand tourist information; explain what there is to see and do in a place, and suggest activities	The imperative: *du* and *Sie* forms *Man kann* + infinitive	Identify formality of language (*du* and *Sie*)	*Komm/Kommen Sie nach (Berlin, Hamburg)! Iss/Essen Sie (Berliner Spezialitäten, frischen Fisch)! Besuch/Besuchen Sie (den Zoo, die Galerien)! Fahr/Fahren Sie (mit dem Boot auf der Spree, mit dem Rad im Park)! Wohin kann man gehen? Wo/Was kann man (einkaufen, essen, trinken, machen)?*	L&S 1.1, 1.2, 1.3, 1.5 R&W 2.1, 2.2, 2.3, 2.4, 2.5 IU 3.2 KAL 4.5 LLS 5.7, 5.8	1.3–4, 2.2–4, 3.2, 3.4, 4.3–4

155

3B Mein Zuhause

Unit 3B: Week-by-week overview
(Three-year KS3 Route: assuming six weeks' work or approximately 10–12.5 hours)
(Two-year KS3 Route: assuming four weeks' work or approximately 6.5–8.5 hours)

About Unit 3B, *Mein Zuhause:* In this unit, students give detailed information about towns and other places: they say what buildings and facilities there are/aren't and what you can see and do in a place, suggest activities and express their opinion; they ask for and give directions, and buy tickets and souvenirs. They also find out about key tourist attractions and monuments in Berlin and other German towns.

Work on modal verbs continues: after meeting *man soll* + infinitive in Unit 3A, students now learn to use *können* and *wollen* + infinitive; *ich möchte* + noun is revisited. Students are introduced to the imperative (including when to use *du* and *Sie*), learn to ask questions by reversing the order of subject and verb (*Willst du …?* etc.) and recycle previously learned language (e.g. *es gibt* + *ein(e)(n)/kein(e)(n) …*, opinion adjectives). There are tips on how to evaluate and improve written work and on coping with unfamiliar language when listening. The pronunciation focus is *v* and *w*.

	Three-Year KS3 Route			**Two-Year KS3 Route**	
Week	**Resources**	**Objectives**	**Week**	**Resources**	**Objectives**
1	3B.1 Berlin, Berlin!	Say what there is and isn't in a town Express opinions of places in a town *Es gibt* + *ein(e)(n)/kein(e)(n) …* Evaluate and improve written work	1	3B.1 Berlin, Berlin!	Say what there is and isn't in a town Express opinions of places in a town *Es gibt* + *ein(e)(n)/kein(e)(n) …* Evaluate and improve written work
2	3B.2 Was kann man machen? 3B.6 Sprachlabor ex. 1–2 *(and 6–7 if you wish to work on pronunciation at this point)*	Say what you can do in a place *Ich kann/Du kannst/Man kann* + infinitive; *Ich will/Du willst/Man will* + infinitive Identify language patterns; adapt language to generate new language	2	3B.2 Was kann man machen? *(Omit ex. 7)* 3B.6 Sprachlabor ex. 1–2 *(and 6–7 if you wish to work on pronunciation at this point)*	Say what you can do in a place *Ich kann/Du kannst/Man kann* + infinitive; *Ich will/Du willst/Man will* + infinitive Identify language patterns; adapt language to generate new language
3	3B.3 Wo ist das Kino? 3B.6 Sprachlabor ex. 3	Ask for and give directions to places in a town The imperative: *du* and *Sie* forms Cope with unfamiliar language when listening	3	3B.3 Wo ist das Kino? *(Omit ex. 3)* 3B.6 Sprachlabor ex. 3	Ask for and give directions to places in a town The imperative: *du* and *Sie* forms Cope with unfamiliar language when listening
4	3B.4 Im Zoo 3B.6 Sprachlabor ex. 4–5	Buy tickets and presents *Ich möchte/nehme* + *ein(e)(n) …* Subject–verb inversion in questions Work out language patterns Use polite language	4	3B.4 Im Zoo *(Omit ex. 3 and 5)* 3B.6 Sprachlabor ex. 4–5 3B.8 Vokabular 3B.8 Testseite	Buy tickets and presents *Ich möchte/nehme* + *ein(e)(n) …* Subject–verb inversion in questions Work out language patterns Use polite language Key vocabulary and learning checklist Assessment in all four skills

3B Mein Zuhause

	Three-Year KS3 Route			Two-Year KS3 Route	
Week	Resources	Objectives	Week	Resources	Objectives
5	3B.5 Besuchen Sie Zoomsdorf!	Understand tourist information Explain what there is to see and do in a place, and suggest activities The imperative: *du* and *Sie* forms *Man kann* + infinitive Identify formality of language (*du* and *Sie*)			
6	3B.7 Extra (Star/Plus) 3B.8 Vokabular 3B.8 Testseite 3B Lesen	Reinforcement and extension of the language of the unit Key vocabulary and learning checklist Assessment in all four skills Further reading to explore the language of the unit and cultural themes			

3B.1 Mein Zuhause

3B.1 Berlin, Berlin!   Seite 104–105

Planner

Objectives
- Vocabulary: say what there is and isn't in a town; express opinions of places in a town
- Grammar: *es gibt + ein(e)(n) / kein(e)(n) …*
- Skills: evaluate and improve written work

Video
- Video clip 3B

Resources
- Student Book, pages 104–105
- CD 2, tracks 33–35
- Foundation and Higher Workbooks, page 56
- Workbook audio: CD 3 and 4, track 60
- Copymasters 75 (ex. 1), 76 (ex. 2–3), 77 (ex. 3)
- Interactive OxBox, Unit 3B

Key language
Es gibt …
einen Bahnhof, einen Fernsehturm, einen Park, einen Supermarkt, einen Zoo
eine Kirche, eine Post, eine Skateboard-Bahn, eine U-Bahn-Station
ein Jugendzentrum, ein Kaufhaus, ein Kino, ein Museum, ein Schloss, ein Schwimmbad, ein Stadion
in meinem Dorf, in meiner Gegend / Stadt
Ich finde (mein Dorf / meine Gegend / meine Stadt) gut, interessant, langweilig, nicht gut, schrecklich, schlecht, toll.

Framework references
L&S 1.1, 1.2; KAL 4.3, 4.4, 4.6; LLS 5.2, 5.5, 5.7, 5.8

Starters
- Copymaster 75, ex. 1.
- Before playing the ex. 1 recording, give students a few minutes to look at the captions and pictures (a–p) to make sure they understand what all the places are. Ask them to think about what helps them to work out the meanings, e.g. similarity to English words, using the visuals as clues. Encourage them to practise saying the words, then play the ex. 1 recording so that they can check their pronunciation.
- When students have learned the places in town (a–p) for homework, begin a lesson by asking them each to choose five places and test their partner on them. Explain that three points are available per place: one point if they can say it correctly (no point if their pronunciation sounds English!), another point if they can write / spell it accurately and give its gender, and a third if they can put it into a sentence.

Plenaries
- Student Book page 104, ex. 4.
- Students take turns to say what there is (and isn't) in an imaginary town and express appropriate comments about each place, e.g.
A: *Es gibt ein Schloss …*
B: *Das ist interessant! Aber es gibt keinen Park …*
A: *Ich finde das furchtbar. Es gibt einen Supermarkt …*
B: *… aber der Supermarkt ist langweilig! Es gibt …*
This helps them prepare for *Challenge*. Suggest that they start compiling a bank of all the adjectives they've learned in the course so far plus any new ones they learn.

Homework
- Challenge students to learn the places in town (a–p in ex. 1), including genders. In a following lesson, they work in pairs testing each other: see second starter activity.
- Student Book page 105, *Challenge*.

Video clip 3B: Eine Verabredung mit Nico!
Synopsis:
Nico is about to go on his first official date with Kathi, so Ali gives him advice on where to go and how to behave. Kathi and Nico go to the zoo, but they keep being interrupted by acquaintances asking them for directions … and when they bump into Kathi's friend Bernd, Nico is clearly jealous! Afterwards, in a café, Nico feels Kathi is rather quiet. She tells him her news: her family may have to go back to Vienna because of her father's job … Nico is devastated.

Play the video through a couple of times and ask questions to check that students understand the gist of it. Talk about some of the places in Berlin mentioned by Ali and Nico. Students may recognise *Fernsehturm* from Unit 0. Challenge them to work out what *Tierpark* is: if they remember (from Unit 1A) that *Tier* is an animal, they may be able to guess that *Tier + Park* is a zoo. Point out that *Ku'damm* is short for *Kurfürstendamm*, a famous street in Berlin. Focus on the exchanges between the characters:
- What do students think Nico and Frau Winter are talking about? Students should be able to deduce from Nico's body language that he is giving her directions.

3B.1 Mein Zuhause

- Can they explain Nico's reaction to Bernd? It's clear from Nico's facial expressions that he isn't pleased to have bumped into Bernd, and the way he brusquely steers Kathi away shows that he's jealous.
- Can students explain Kathi's and Nico's mood at the end of the clip? What do they think is happening? Students should be able to tell that the mood is gloomy, although they may not understand why – they may guess (incorrectly) that Kathi is ending their relationship. Suggest that students focus on a few key words in Kathi's last couple of lines that may help to explain: *Vater*, *Job*, *der Job ist in Wien* – i.e. Kathi's father may have to move to Vienna because of his job, and if this happens Kathi will have to leave Berlin.

Video clip 3B

(Ali advises Nico on where to go with Kathi)

Ali: Sag einfach zu allem ja. Und lach, wenn sie einen Witz erzählt. Und rede bloß nicht über *Star Wars*! Glaub mir, das funktioniert nie!
Nico: Okay. Und wo können wir hingehen?
Ali: Es gibt viel zu tun … Du kannst ins Museum gehen oder zum Fernsehturm … sehr romantisch. Der Ku'damm ist auch sehr interessant … oder … du kannst mit Kathi in den Tierpark gehen.
Nico: In den Tierpark? Mit Kathi?!
Ali: Ja, klar! Also, ich muss jetzt los. Viel Spaß!

(Nico and Kathi decide where to go)

Nico: Also, willst du ins Museum gehen? … Oder wir können auf den Fernsehturm gehen. … Der Ku'damm ist auch sehr interessant. … Oder willst du in den Tierpark gehen?
Kathi: Super Idee! Ich liebe Tiere.

(on the way to the zoo)

Nico: Guten Tag, Frau Winter. Wie geht es Ihnen?
Frau W: Hallo, Nico. Danke, gut … Deine Freundin?
Nico: Äh … nein.
Frau W: Gut, dass ich dich hier treffe! Ich kenne diese Gegend nicht so gut. Kannst du mir helfen?
Nico: Natürlich, Frau Winter.
Frau W: Wo ist hier das neue große Kaufhaus?
Nico: Ah, das Kaufparadies.
Frau W: Genau.
Nico: Ja, dann gehen Sie hier geradeaus … die zweite Straße rechts, die dritte Straße dann links … dann über die Ampel rüber. Dann auf der rechten Seite ist dann das Kaufhaus.
Frau W: Wie? Was? Also geradeaus und links …
Nico: Fast. Also … Sie gehen jetzt hier geradeaus … dann gehen Sie die zweite Straße nach rechts und die dritte dann nach links … dann gehen Sie über die Ampel rüber. Und auf der rechten Seite ist dann das Kaufhaus. Also hier.

Frau W: Ach ja …ganz einfach. Danke. Tschüs ihr zwei.
Nico: Schönen Tag noch, Frau Winter.
Kathi: Auf Wiedersehen.

(at the zoo)

Kathi: Schau dir mal die Lamas an! Die sind total süß.
Nico: Sie sind dumm. Und sie spucken.
Kathi: Sie spucken?
Nico: Ja.
Kathi: Warum?
Nico: Keine Ahnung.

Bernd: Hallo Kathi!
Kathi: Hallo Bernd. Schön dich zu sehen! Was machst du hier?
Bernd: Ich gehe zum Boarden. Weißt du vielleicht wo die nächste Skateboard-Bahn hier ist?
Kathi: Hmmm … also, geh die zweite Straße links und dann über die Kreuzung. Die Skateboard-Bahn ist auf der linken Seite.
Bernd: Also … zweite Straße links … dann über die Kreuzung … und dann auf der linken Seite. Und, Kathi, hast du vielleicht mal Lust ins Kino zu gehen, oder so was?
Nico: Entschuldige … wir haben jetzt keine Zeit mehr.
Kathi: Okay, tschüs, Bernd! Bis dann!

(at a café)

Nico: Du bist heute nicht sehr gesprächig.
Kathi: Bin ich nicht?
Nico: Was ist los?
Kathi: Nichts!
Nico: Hmm … das hört sich nicht wie „nichts" an.
Kathi: Ja, mein Vater soll vielleicht wieder den Job wechseln.
Nico: Na und? Das ist doch nicht so schlimm.
Kathi: Es ist schlimm – der Job ist in Wien. Wir können vielleicht nicht hier bleiben …
Nico: Oh! Verstehe!

Sprachpunkt

Willst du ins Museum gehen?
Wo ist hier das neue große Kaufhaus?
Geh die zweite Straße links und dann über die Kreuzung.
Gehen Sie hier geradeaus.

AT 1.1 / AT 3.1   **1 Hör zu (1–16). Was passt zusammen?**
Students listen and match each place mentioned to a picture and caption.
Point out the two different words for "zoo": *der Tierpark* (in video clip 3B) and *der Zoo* (in ex. 1).

Answers: **1** i; **2** k; **3** o; **4** a; **5** f; **6** p; **7** b; **8** e; **9** n; **10** j; **11** d; **12** l; **13** h; **14** c; **15** g; **16** m

3B.1 Mein Zuhause

CD 2, track 33 — Seite 104, Übung 1

1. Es gibt eine Skateboard-Bahn.
2. Es gibt ein Schwimmbad.
3. Es gibt ein Museum.
4. Es gibt einen Supermarkt.
5. Es gibt eine Post.
6. Es gibt ein Kino.
7. Es gibt einen Zoo.
8. Es gibt einen Fernsehturm.
9. Es gibt ein Jugendzentrum.
10. Es gibt ein Schloss.
11. Es gibt einen Park.
12. Es gibt ein Stadion.
13. Es gibt eine U-Bahn-Station.
14. Es gibt einen Bahnhof.
15. Es gibt eine Kirche.
16. Es gibt ein Kaufhaus.

AT 2.2 / KAL 4.3, 4.4 / KAL 4.6 / LLS 5.2

2 Gedächtnisspiel.
Before students begin this activity, point out the *Grammatik* box on *Es gibt (k)einen / (k)eine / (k)ein …* Ask them where they have met this structure before (in Unit 2B, when talking about items in their bedroom).
Students then play a memory game, listing as many places in town as they can, e.g.
A: *In meiner Stadt gibt es einen Park.*
B: *In meiner Stadt gibt es einen Park und eine Kirche.*
C: *In meiner Stadt gibt es einen Park, eine Kirche und …*
Challenge students to change the word order (*Es gibt in meiner Stadt einen Park …*).
Talk about this type of activity in terms of its effectiveness as a memorisation technique. Do students find it helps them to learn new language if they chant it aloud? Invite them to share learning strategies.

AT 1.2 / KAL 4.3, 4.6

3 Hör zu (1–6). Was gibt es (✓)? Was gibt es nicht (✗)?
Before playing the recording, elicit from students which two key structures they will need to distinguish between in this activity: *es gibt + einen / eine / ein …* and *es gibt + keinen / keine / kein …*.
Students listen and identify which places (from a–p in ex. 1) there are and aren't.

Answers: **1** c ✓, f ✗; **2** a ✓, b ✗; **3** l ✗, g ✓; **4** d ✓, n ✗; **5** i ✗, k ✓; **6** p ✗, o ✓

CD 2, track 34 — Seite 104, Übung 3

1. Es gibt einen Bahnhof, aber es gibt keine Post.
2. Es gibt einen Supermarkt, aber es gibt keinen Zoo.
3. Es gibt kein Stadion, aber es gibt eine Kirche.
4. Es gibt hier einen Park, aber es gibt hier kein Jugendzentrum.
5. Es gibt hier keine Skateboard-Bahn, aber es gibt ein Schwimmbad.
6. Es gibt kein Kino, aber es gibt hier ein Museum.

AT 4.2

4 Schreib Sätze für diese Bilder. Was gibt es? Was gibt es nicht?
Students write a sentence for each pair of pictures, saying what there is and isn't.

Answers: **a** Es gibt ein Stadion, aber es gibt keinen Zoo. **b** Es gibt einen Fernsehturm, aber es gibt kein Kaufhaus. **c** Es gibt ein Schwimmbad, aber es gibt kein Kino. **d** Es gibt einen Bahnhof, aber es gibt keine U-Bahn-Station. **e** Es gibt eine Kirche, aber es gibt keinen Park. **f** Es gibt ein Jugendzentrum, aber es gibt kein Schloss.

AT 3.4

5 Lies. Richtig (R) oder falsch (F)?
Students read an email from Kathi to her cousin, describing some of the things to see and do in Berlin. They work out whether statements a–f are true or false. Ask them to correct the false statements.

Answers: **a** false (there's lots for teenagers to do); **b** false (she thinks it's great because she loves animals); **c** true; **d** true; **e** false (she doesn't go often because she isn't very sporty); **f** false (there isn't one)

AT 1.3–4 / L&S 1.1, 1.2

6 Hör zu. Was sagt Ali?
Ali's friend is coming to visit Berlin. Ali talks to him on the phone, telling him what there is to see and do. Students listen and note the five places he mentions and what he says about them.
Tackle this activity in stages: on the first listening, students note the places mentioned; they then listen again and note as many extra details as they can.

Answers: **1** park – (very) big; **2** lots of cinemas – great films (German and English films, not French films); **3** TV Tower – fantastic; **4** swimming pool – (very) modern; **5** youth club – boring

3B.1 Mein Zuhause

CD 2, track 35 — Seite 105, Übung 6

Hallo? … Ah hallo Mehmet! Wie geht's? … Du möchtest nach Berlin kommen? Tolle Idee! Ja, komm! Hier ist es super. … Was es zu tun gibt? Also, es gibt hier einen Park – ja, einen Park – den Grunewald. Er ist sehr groß. … Ja … viele Kinos. Im Kino sind tolle Filme zu sehen. … Französische Filme? Nein – deutsche und englische. Und es gibt auch einen Fernsehturm. Der ist fantastisch. … Ein Schwimmbad haben wir auch. Es ist sehr modern. … Was? Ein Jugendzentrum? Ja, ein Jugendzentrum gibt es auch, aber es ist so langweilig. … Also, wann kommst du? …

AT 4.3–4
LLS 5.5, 5.7

Challenge

Students write a description of where they live, saying what there is (and isn't) in the area and expressing their opinions. They are encouraged to draw on all the adjectives they've learned so far to help them say what they think. (Refer them in particular to Units 1B, 2A and 2B for a reminder of adjectives. See also the second plenary in the *Planner* above, which should help them to prepare for this activity.)

LLS 5.8

Think

This skills box gives advice on how to evaluate and improve written work. Ask students if they can think of anything else to add to this list, e.g. use linking words to build longer sentences, add extra details and be more precise by using words like *sehr*, *ziemlich*, *gar nicht*, etc., use grammar reference materials to check endings, verb forms, etc. See also the teaching notes for Student Book 3A.1 ex. 8.

Encourage students to apply these tips to what they have written for *Challenge*. If appropriate, once students have completed *Challenge*, they could swap with a partner and evaluate each other's work: can they suggest any ways to improve their partner's text?

161

3B.2 Mein Zuhause

3B.2 Was kann man machen?

Seite 106–107

Planner

Objectives
- Vocabulary: say what you can do in a place
- Grammar: *ich kann / du kannst / man kann* + infinitive; *ich will / du willst / man will* + infinitive
- Skills: identify language patterns; adapt language to generate new language

Video
- Video clip 3B

Resources
- Student Book, pages 106–107
- CD 2, tracks 36–37
- Foundation and Higher Workbooks, page 57
- Workbook audio: CD 3 and 4, track 61
- Interactive OxBox, Unit 3B

Key language
Man kann hier schwimmen / Pizza essen / Kaffee trinken / Mountainbike fahren / ins Kino gehen / Fußball spielen / Freunde treffen / tanzen.
Willst du Tennis spielen? Ich will in den Park gehen.

Framework references
R&W 2.3, 2.4, 2.5; KAL 4.4, 4.5, 4.6; LLS 5.1, 5.7, 5.8

Starters
- Student Book page 106, ex. 1.
- Display a few sentences using the structure *Man kann* + infinitive, but with the words in jumbled order, e.g.
  Kaffee / kann / trinken / man / hier
  kann / hier / man / schwimmen
  Mountainbike / man / hier / fahren / kann

Display alongside a list of the places where you can do these activities, e.g. *Schwimmbad, Park, Café*. Set a time limit for students to copy out the sentences using correct word order and match each one to its corresponding place, e.g. the solution to the examples above would be:
Es gibt ein Café. Man kann hier Kaffee trinken.
Es gibt ein Schwimmbad. Man kann hier schwimmen.
Es gibt einen Park. Man kann hier Mountainbike fahren..

Plenaries
- Working in pairs, one student starts reading out each key phrase from ex. 1; their partner tries to complete each sentence with the correct infinitive, without looking in the book, e.g.
  A: *Man kann hier ins Kino …*
  B: *… gehen!*
  A: *Man kann hier Kaffee …*
  B: *… trinken!*
  Make sure they swap over so that A has a turn at completing the sentences.
- In pairs, students play a dice game practising the *ich*, *du* and *man* forms of *können* and *wollen*. The parts of the verbs are numbered 1–6 to correspond with the dots on the dice: 1 = *ich kann*, 2 = *du kannst*, 3 = *man kann*, 4 = *ich will*, 5 = *du willst*, 6 = *man will*. Students take turns to roll the dice and use the corresponding verb form in a sentence, which can be either a statement or a question, e.g. student A rolls a 5: *Willst du Pizza essen?*
  The first person to say all six verb forms is the winner.

Homework
- Student Book page 106, ex. 3.
- Student Book page 107, *Challenge*.

AT 3.1–2
KAL 4.4, 4.5
LLS 5.1

1 Lies die Sätze. Wähle das richtige Wort.
Students choose an infinitive to complete each sentence. They should be able to work these out by identifying familiar language and by a process of elimination.
Elicit from them where they've seen this sort of structure before, i.e. *Man* + verb + infinitive at the end of the sentence (*Man soll … essen / trinken* on spread 3A.4).

Answers: **a** schwimmen; **b** essen; **c** trinken; **d** fahren; **e** gehen; **f** spielen; **g** treffen; **h** tanzen

AT 1.1–2
AT 3.1–2

2 Hör zu (a–h). Ist alles richtig?
Students listen to check their answers to ex. 1.

🎧 **CD 2, track 36**   Seite 106, Übung 2

a Man kann hier schwimmen.
b Man kann hier Pizza essen.
c Man kann hier Kaffee trinken.
d Man kann hier Mountainbike fahren.
e Man kann hier ins Kino gehen.
f Man kann hier Fußball spielen.
g Man kann hier Freunde treffen.
h Man kann hier tanzen.

3B.2 Mein Zuhause

KAL 4.4, 4.5
LLS 5.1

Think
Referring to the completed sentences in ex. 1, students work out the rule for how to say what you can do (*Man kann ...*). They then adapt it to say "I can ...".

Answers: To say that one <u>can</u> do something, you use <u>man kann</u> + a second verb. The second verb ends in <u>-en</u> and is at the <u>end</u> of the sentence. (I can swim = Ich kann schwimmen)

AT 4.2

3 Schreib Sätze. Was kann man hier machen?
Students write sentences to describe what you can do at each of places a–f.

Answers: **a** Man kann hier Skateboard fahren. **b** Man kann hier tanzen. **c** Man kann hier schwimmen. **d** Man kann hier Pizza essen. **e** Man kann hier Fußball spielen. **f** Man kann hier Kaffee trinken.

AT 2.2

4 Kann man das machen?
Students take turns to ask each other which activities (a–h in ex. 1) they can and can't do, e.g.
A: (points to picture e) *Kann man hier schwimmen?*
B: *Nein, man kann hier nicht schwimmen! Das ist ein Kino!*

AT 3.4

5 Lies die Nachricht von Tatjana und wähle die richtigen Antworten.
Students read Tatjana's description of what there is to do in Munich. They choose the correct option to complete each sentence a–f.

Answers: **a** 2; **b** 3; **c** 2; **d** 3; **e** 1; **f** 3

R&W 2.3

Follow-up
Ask students to identify the following words and phrases in the text: Strange, isn't it? (*Komisch, oder?*); unfortunately (*leider*); what a shame! (*schade!*). Focus on *Komisch, oder?* and elicit from students the usual meaning of *oder* (or). Explain that when used as in Tatjana's text it means "isn't it?", "aren't they?", "won't you?", "don't you agree?", etc. Point out that expressions like this and *schade!* (at the end of the text) are colloquialisms that belong to a more informal style of writing, e.g. you might use them in an email to a friend but you wouldn't use them in a formal job application. Encourage students to begin making a reference list of words like this to add authenticity to their own speaking and writing.

AT 4.2
KAL 4.4, 4.5
KAL 4.6

6 Schreib die Fragen auf.
Students write questions to represent the pictures.

Answers: **a** Willst du ins Kino gehen? **b** Willst du Tennis spielen? **c** Willst du Pizza essen? **d** Willst du Skateboard fahren? **e** Willst du Mountainbike (or *Rad*) fahren?

Follow-up
The pronunciation focus of this unit is *v* and *w*: see ex. 6–7 on the *Sprachlabor* spread, 3B.6. Although you can work on the pronunciation activities at any appropriate point in the unit, you may wish to link them in with the *w* sound in *w*ollen: ich *w*ill, du *w*illst, man *w*ill.

AT 1.4

7 Sieh dir das Video an. Beantworte die Fragen.
Play the first section of the video: Ali advises Nico on where to take Kathi on their date, then Nico suggests the different ideas to Kathi. Students note down Nico's suggestions and Kathi's reaction to the final one.
As a follow-up, play the video again and ask students to spot different forms of *können* and *wollen*: see underlining in transcript.
Point out that *Ku'damm* is short for *Kurfürstendamm*, a famous street in Berlin.

Answers: **a** museum, TV Tower, Ku'damm (street in Berlin), zoo; **b** great idea because she loves animals

Video clip 3B
CD 2, track 37   Seite 107, Übung 7

(Ali advises Nico on where to go with Kathi)
Ali: Sag einfach zu allem ja. Und lach, wenn sie einen Witz erzählt. Und rede bloß nicht über *Star Wars*! Glaub mir, das funktioniert nie!
Nico: Okay. Und wo <u>können wir</u> hingehen?
Ali: Es gibt viel zu tun ... <u>Du kannst</u> ins Museum gehen oder zum Fernsehturm ... sehr romantisch. Der Ku'damm ist auch sehr interessant ... oder ... <u>du kannst</u> mit Kathi in den Tierpark gehen.
Nico: In den Tierpark? Mit Kathi?!
Ali: Ja, klar! Also, ich muss jetzt los. Viel Spaß!

(Nico and Kathi decide where to go)
Nico: Also, <u>willst du</u> ins Museum gehen? ... Oder <u>wir können</u> auf den Fernsehturm gehen. ... Der Ku'damm ist auch sehr interessant. ... Oder <u>willst du</u> in den Tierpark gehen?
Kathi: Super Idee! Ich liebe Tiere.

163

3B.3 Mein Zuhause

AT 2.3-4

Follow-up

In pairs, students make up a dialogue in which a girl or boy invites someone out to lots of different places, but the person says no to everything (with an appropriate excuse) until eventually agreeing to the final suggestion, e.g.
A: *Willst du Pizza essen?*
B: *Nein, ich finde Pizza furchtbar.*
A: *Willst du Fußball spielen?*
B: *Nein, denn ich bin nicht sportlich! …*
and so on, until finally:
A: *Kannst du am Samstag …?*
B: *Ja, am Samstag kann ich … Toll!*
If students have begun to compile a bank of adjectives (see second plenary in the *Planner* for spread 3B.1), it will help them to come up with excuses.

AT 4.3-4
R&W 2.4, 2.5
LLS 5.7, 5.8

Challenge

Students imagine they are creating a poster (or brochure) for their local tourist board, telling German-speaking visitors what there is to see and do in the area. They are encouraged to recycle language from Unit 2A, and will also need to research new language specific to your local area.
Point out the advice on achieving level 4, and refer students to the *Think* box at the end of spread 3B.1 for tips on evaluating and improving written work. If they need help structuring their work, suggest that they sketch out a mind map or spider diagram to help them group the information into paragraphs and sequence the paragraphs.

3B.3 Wo ist das Kino? Seite 108–109

Planner

Objectives
- Vocabulary: ask for and give directions to places in a town
- Grammar: use the *du* and *Sie* forms of the imperative
- Skills: cope with unfamiliar language when listening

Video
- Video clip 3B

Resources
- Student Book, pages 108–109
- CD 2, tracks 38–40
- Foundation and Higher Workbooks, page 58
- Workbook audio: CD 3 and 4, track 62
- Copymasters 75 (ex. 2), 76 (ex. 1), 77 (ex. 2), 78 (ex. 2), 79 (ex. 4–5)
- Interactive OxBox, Unit 3B

Key language
Wo ist …?
Geh / Gehen Sie … links / rechts / geradeaus.
Nimm / Nehmen Sie … die (erste / zweite / dritte) Straße (links / rechts).
Es ist auf der (linken / rechten) Seite.
über die Ampel, über die Kreuzung, über die Brücke

Framework references
L&S 1.1, 1.2, 1.3, 1.5; R&W 2.4, 2.5; KAL 4.5; LLS 5.4, 5.7, 5.8

Starters
- Copymaster 75, ex. 2.
- Before students begin ex. 1, ask them to identify (in a–k) the German for the following English words: first, second, third, left, right, go, take, street, side, straight ahead. Challenge them to translate a–k into English, using the symbols to help them.
- Agree on a gesture to represent each direction, e.g. *Geh links* = point to the left, *Geh geradeaus* = point straight ahead. You can then play *Simon sagt* (Simon says):
Teacher: *Simon sagt: Geh rechts!*
Class: all point to the right.
Teacher: *Nimm die dritte Straße links!*
Class: do nothing because you haven't said *Simon sagt*.
Confident students could take over your role, or students could play the game themselves in groups or pairs.

Plenaries
- Speed duel, practising directions in the *du* and *Sie* form. Two students stand up. Call out a direction in English, followed by the name of a person, e.g. the names may be teachers from your school or well-known public figures (to represent the *Sie* form) or students in your class (to represent the *du* form), or any TV or cartoon characters as long as it is clear whether to address them as *Sie* or *du*. The two students compete to translate the direction into German:
Teacher: *Go right, Mr Brown.*
Student: *Gehen Sie rechts, Herr Brown!*
Teacher: *Go straight ahead, Bart.*
Student: *Geh geradeaus, Bart!*
Whoever gives you the correct answer first remains standing; the other student sits down and is replaced by another challenger.

3B.3 Mein Zuhause

- Mystery tour: in pairs, students take turns to give each other directions to places on the map (page 108). The partner follows the directions and identifies the destination, e.g.
A: *Nimm die zweite Straße rechts. Es ist auf der linken Seite.*
B: *Das ist f – die Kirche!*
Instead of using the map on page 108, try to obtain some simple street maps of places in your local area so that students can describe a longer, more complicated route.

Homework
- Student Book page 109, ex. 3.
- Students draw a simple map, decide on a secret location for some buried treasure, and write a set of directions leading to the treasure. In the next lesson, their partner follows the directions to locate the treasure.
- Student Book page 109, *Challenge*.

AT 1.2 / AT 3.2 / KAL 4.5 / LLS 5.4

1 Hör zu (1–11). Was passt zusammen?
Students listen and match the directions to the symbols and captions. (See *Planner* above for a starter activity before playing the recording.)

Answers: **1** b; **2** g; **3** e; **4** c; **5** f; **6** k; **7** i; **8** a; **9** j; **10** h; **11** d

CD 2, track 38 — Seite 108, Übung 1
1 Geh rechts.
2 Nimm die erste Straße rechts.
3 Nimm die zweite Straße links.
4 Geh geradeaus.
5 Nimm die dritte Straße links.
6 Es ist auf der rechten Seite.
7 Nimm die dritte Straße rechts.
8 Geh links.
9 Es ist auf der linken Seite.
10 Nimm die zweite Straße rechts.
11 Nimm die erste Straße links.

AT 1.2–3 / L&S 1.1, 1.3 / KAL 4.5

2 Hör zu (1–7). Wohin gehen sie?
Before listening, read through the *Grammatik* box on the *du* and *Sie* forms of the imperative. Point out that both forms will be used on the recording.
Students then listen and identify where each person wants to go. On the first listening, they note the name of the place; on the second listening, they follow the directions and work out which letter on the map (a–g) represents each place. Picture prompts representing places in town are shown beside ex. 2.
To exploit the *du* and *Sie* forms of the imperative, play the recording again, pausing after each person asks for directions. Students focus on who is asking the question (an adult or a teenager / child?) and work out which form of the imperative will be used in the response, e.g. in number 1, the person asking for directions is an adult female, so the *Sie* form will be used in the response.

Answers: **1** Supermarkt c; **2** Kirche f; **3** Schwimmbad a; **4** Schloss d; **5** Stadion e; **6** Bahnhof g; **7** Zoo b

CD 2, track 39 — Seite 108, Übung 2
1 Woman: Wo ist der Supermarkt, bitte?
  Boy: Nehmen Sie die dritte Straße links. Der Supermarkt ist auf der rechten Seite.
2 Girl: Wo ist die Kirche, bitte?
  Man: Nimm die zweite Straße rechts. Die Kirche ist auf der linken Seite.
3 Boy: Wo ist das Schwimmbad, bitte?
  Woman: Nimm die erste Straße links. Das Schwimmbad ist auf der linken Seite.
4 Man: Wo ist das Schloss, bitte?
  Girl: Gehen Sie geradeaus.
5 Woman: Wo ist das Stadion, bitte?
  Boy: Nehmen Sie die dritte Straße rechts. Das Stadion ist auf der rechten Seite.
6 Girl: Wo ist der Bahnhof, bitte?
  Man: Nimm die erste Straße rechts. Der Bahnhof ist auf der linken Seite.
7 Woman: Wo ist der Zoo, bitte?
  Boy: Nehmen Sie die zweite Straße links. Der Zoo ist auf der rechten Seite.

AT 4.2–3

3 Wo ist das Schwimmbad? Schreib Sätze für a–c in Übung 2.
Referring to the map on page 108 and their answers to ex. 2, students write directions to places a–c. Encourage them to use both the *du* form and the *Sie* form.

Answers: **a** Nimm die erste Straße links. Das Schwimmbad ist auf der linken Seite. **b** Nimm die zweite Straße links. Der Zoo ist auf der rechten Seite. **c** Nehmen Sie die dritte Straße links. Der Supermarkt ist auf der rechten Seite.

3B.3 Mein Zuhause

4 Wo ist das Schloss, bitte? Macht Dialoge für d–g in Übung 2.
Students ask for and give directions to places d–g on the map.

5 Sieh dir das Video an. Beantworte die Fragen.
Before playing the video for ex. 5, read through the *Think* box, which provides some tips to help with listening. Remind students of other listening strategies, e.g. in ex. 5 they can predict (by reading the questions) that they are going to hear places in town and directions, so they can prepare for listening by thinking of all the places in town and directions they know in German. This provides a focus for listening and makes it easier to maintain concentration.

Point out that listening activities are often accompanied by visuals, which provide clues as to what might come up. Look at the three symbols and captions above the *Think* box (*über die Ampel, über die Kreuzung, über die Brücke*) and elicit their meanings.

Play the section of video clip 3B in which Nico and Kathi give directions to Frau Winter and Kathi's friend Bernd. Students answer the questions in English. Encourage them to note down as much information as they can on the first listening, then play the video as many times as necessary to enable them to fill in any details they've missed.

As a follow-up, play the video again and ask students to spot the difference between Nico's directions to Frau Winter and Kathi's directions to Bernd (Nico uses *Sie* when speaking to Frau Winter, Kathi uses *du* to speak to Bernd). Focus on formality of language, e.g. when Nico and Kathi speak to Frau Winter they tend to be quite polite (*Guten Tag, Wie geht es Ihnen?, Auf Wiedersehen*) whereas with Bernd the language is more informal (*Hallo, Schön dich zu sehen, Tschüs*).

Answers: **a** department store; **b** go straight on, take the second street on the right then the third street on the left, then cross over the traffic lights and the department store is on the right-hand side; **c** skatepark; **d** take the second street on the left, go over the crossroads and the skatepark is on the left-hand side

Video clip 3B
CD 2, track 40   Seite 109, Übung 5

Nico: Guten Tag, Frau Winter. Wie geht es Ihnen?
Frau W: Hallo, Nico. Danke, gut … Deine Freundin?
Nico: Äh … nein.
Frau W: Gut, dass ich dich hier treffe! Ich kenne diese Gegend nicht so gut. Kannst du mir helfen?

Nico: Natürlich, Frau Winter.
Frau W: Wo ist hier das neue große Kaufhaus?
Nico: Ah, das Kaufparadies.
Frau W: Genau.
Nico: Ja, dann gehen Sie hier geradeaus … die zweite Straße rechts, die dritte Straße dann links … dann über die Ampel rüber. Dann auf der rechten Seite ist dann das Kaufhaus.
Frau W: Wie? Was? Also geradeaus und dann links …
Nico: Fast. Also … Sie gehen jetzt hier geradeaus … dann gehen Sie die zweite Straße nach rechts und die dritte dann nach links … dann gehen Sie über die Ampel rüber. Und auf der rechten Seite ist dann das Kaufhaus. Also hier.
Frau W: Ach ja … ganz einfach. Danke. Tschüs ihr zwei.
Nico: Schönen Tag noch, Frau Winter.
Kathi: Auf Wiedersehen.
…
Bernd: Hallo Kathi!
Kathi: Hallo Bernd. Schön dich zu sehen! Was machst du hier?
Bernd: Ich gehe zum Boarden. Weißt du vielleicht wo die nächste Skateboard-Bahn hier ist?
Kathi: Hmmm … also, geh die zweite Straße links und dann über die Kreuzung. Die Skateboard-Bahn ist auf der linken Seite.
Bernd: Also … zweite Straße links … dann über die Kreuzung … und dann auf der linken Seite. Und, Kathi, hast du vielleicht mal Lust ins Kino zu gehen, oder so was?
Nico: Entschuldige … wir haben jetzt keine Zeit mehr.
Kathi: Okay, tschüs, Bernd! Bis dann!

Challenge
Using the map on page 108 (or maps of your local town or area, if you prefer), students write a tour of the town. They are encouraged to give an opinion about each place they mention. Refer them to the *Think* box at the end of spread 3B.1 for tips on evaluating and improving written work.

Students could record their text in the style of an audio tour. If they choose to do this, encourage them to use a few colloquialisms to add interest and authenticity, e.g. *Magst du Fußball? Also, nimm die zweite Straße rechts … und hier ist das Stadion! Man kann hier Manchester United sehen – fantastisch, oder? … Viel Spaß!*

3B.4 Mein Zuhause

3B.4 Im Zoo

Seite 110–111

Planner

Objectives
- Vocabulary: buy tickets and presents
- Grammar: *ich möchte / nehme + einen / eine / ein …*; subject–verb inversion in questions
- Skills: work out language patterns; use polite language

Resources
- Student Book, pages 110–111
- CD 2, tracks 41–43
- Foundation and Higher Workbooks, page 59
- Workbook audio: CD 3 and 4, track 63
- Copymasters 77 (ex. 1), 78 (ex. 3–4), 79 (ex. 1–3), 80
- Interactive OxBox, Unit 3B

Key language
Kann ich Ihnen helfen?
Ich möchte (eine Karte / zwei Karten) für (einen Erwachsenen / zwei Erwachsene / ein Kind / zwei Kinder), bitte.
Was kostet das? Das kostet … Euro.
Ich suche ein Geschenk für …
Ich (möchte / nehme) einen / eine / ein …
der Lolli, der Schlüsselanhänger, das Notizbuch, die Plastikschlange, die Schachtel Schokolade, die Schneekugel

Framework references
L&S 1.1; IU 3.1; KAL 4.3, 4.6; LLS 5.6

Starters
- Prices come up on this spread, so you may wish to begin with some number games or counting games: see suggestions in the *Planner* for spread 0.2.
- Before playing the ex. 4 recording, challenge students to work out how to say "I would like" + items a–f: *Ich möchte + einen / eine / ein …* This involves changing *der*, *die* and *das* (in a–f) to the accusative form of the indefinite article. Students then listen to the recording to check whether their sentences are correct.

Plenaries
- Student Book page 110, ex. 2.
- In pairs, students use their answers from ex. 3 to reconstruct a few of the ex. 3 dialogues. Play the recording again so that they can check their own versions against the originals.
- In pairs, students use the dialogues in ex. 6 as a model for making up their own dialogues about buying souvenirs. They could stick to the items in ex. 4 or use dictionaries to look up other items that might typically be bought as souvenirs. Before they begin, help them to come up with some questions (e.g. *Mag er / sie …? Trinkt er / sie …? Spielt er / sie …? Liest er / sie …?*) and reasons why something might or might not be suitable (*denn er / sie mag … nicht, denn er / sie findet … furchtbar / toll*, etc., *denn er / sie ist nicht sportlich / musikalisch*, etc.). This should give them ideas for the *Challenge* activity.

Homework
- Give students a few questions about German euro coins and challenge them to research the answers on the internet, e.g. What symbols of Germany appear on German euro coins? (the Brandenburg Gate, the federal eagle, an oak twig); What is the lettering around the edge of German euro coins? (the first few words of Germany's national anthem: *Einigkeit und Recht und Freiheit* – unity and justice and freedom); What is the current exchange rate between the euro and the pound?
Try to bring some German euro coins into class for students to look at when you go through the answers.
- Students write out one of the dialogues from ex. 2. Alternatively, they could write out one or more of the ex. 3 dialogues, reconstructed from their answers to ex. 3. (See also second plenary.)
- Student Book page 111, *Challenge*.

AT 1.2–3
AT 3.2–3

1 Hör zu und lies. Beantworte die Fragen.
A family are buying tickets for the zoo. Students read and listen to the cartoon strip, and answer the questions in English.

Answers: **a** three; **b** two adults and a child; **c** How much does it cost?; **d** Here you are (Remind students that depending on the context it can also mean "You're welcome" or "Don't mention it"); **e** Thank you. Have fun! / Enjoy yourselves!

CD 2, track 41 Seite 110, Übung 1

Verkäuferin: Guten Tag. Kann ich Ihnen helfen?
Adult male: Ich möchte drei Karten, bitte.
Verkäuferin: Für Erwachsene oder Kinder?
Adult male: Zwei Erwachsene und ein Kind. Was kostet das?
Verkäuferin: Das kostet 32 Euro.
Adult male: Bitte schön, 32 Euro.
Verkäuferin: Danke. Viel Spaß!

167

3B.4 Mein Zuhause

LLS 5.6 **Follow-up**
Display the ex. 1 dialogue on the board, OHP or interactive whiteboard. Students read it aloud. Blank out a few words or phrases and ask them to read it again, filling in the missing items. Repeat this several times, blanking out more words / phrases each time, until eventually students are reciting most or all of it from memory.

AT 2.2–3 **2 Macht Dialoge.**
Students make up dialogues to buy tickets for 1–3, following the model in ex. 1.

Answers: **1** vier Karten / für zwei Erwachsene und zwei Kinder / 40 Euro; **2** zwei Karten / für einen Erwachsenen und ein Kind / 20 Euro; **3** fünf Karten / für zwei Erwachsene und drei Kinder / 48 Euro

AT 1.3–4 **3 Hör zu. Füll die Tabelle aus.**
L&S 1.1 Students listen and note down details of the tickets that each person wants to buy. Dialogues a–c follow roughly the same pattern of the dialogue in ex. 1, but d–e are slightly different so students may find them more challenging.

Answers: **a** 3 tickets, 2 adults and a child, €19; **b** 4 tickets, 1 adult and 3 children, €25; **c** 2 tickets, 2 children, €12; **d** 3 tickets, 1 adult and 2 children, €16; **e** 5 tickets, 3 adults and 2 children, €28

CD 2, track 42 *Seite 111, Übung 3*

a – Guten Tag. Kann ich Ihnen helfen?
– Ich möchte bitte drei Karten.
– Für Erwachsene oder Kinder?
– Für zwei Erwachsene und ein Kind. Was kostet das?
– Das kostet neunzehn Euro.
b – Guten Tag. Kann ich Ihnen helfen?
– Ich möchte bitte vier Karten.
– Für Erwachsene oder Kinder?
– Für einen Erwachsenen und drei Kinder. Was kostet das?
– Das kostet fünfundzwanzig Euro.
c – Hallo. Kann ich dir helfen?
– Ja, bitte. Ich möchte zwei Karten.
– Für Erwachsene oder Kinder?
– Für zwei Kinder, bitte. Was kostet das?
– Das kostet zwölf Euro.
d – Guten Tag. Kann ich Ihnen helfen?
– Guten Tag. Wir möchten bitte drei Karten für einen Erwachsenen und zwei Kinder.
– Also, ein Erwachsener und zwei Kinder. Das kostet dann sechzehn Euro, bitte.
– Bitte schön, sechzehn Euro.
– Danke. Auf Wiedersehen.
e – Guten Morgen. Kann ich Ihnen helfen?
– Hallo. Ich möchte bitte drei Karten für Erwachsene.
– Drei Erwachsene? Das kostet achtzehn Euro.
– Haben sie auch Kinderkarten?
– Ja, klar.
– Ich möchte auch zwei Karten für Kinder.
– OK. Also, fünf Karten – drei Erwachsene, zwei Kinder. Das kostet dann achtundzwanzig Euro.

IU 3.1 **Follow-up**
Draw attention to the prices that come up on this page, and ask students if they know what the German currency was before the euro. See also first homework suggestion in the *Planner* above.

AT 1.1 **4 Hör zu (1–6). Was passt zusammen?**
AT 3.1 This activity introduces the vocabulary for some typical souvenirs. Before playing the recording, see the *Planner* above for a starter activity. Students then listen and match sentences 1–6 to the souvenirs a–f.

Answers: **1** c; **2** e; **3** b; **4** d; **5** f; **6** a

CD 2, track 43 *Seite 111, Übung 4*

1 Ich möchte einen Lolli, bitte.
2 Ich möchte ein Notizbuch.
3 Ich nehme eine Schneekugel, bitte.
4 Ich möchte eine Plastikschlange.
5 Ich nehme eine Schachtel Schokolade.
6 Ich möchte einen Schlüsselanhänger, bitte.

AT 2.2 **5 Was möchtest du?**
KAL 4.3 Students take turns to ask and say which souvenirs they would like, e.g.
A: *Was möchtest du?* (pointing to picture c)
B: *Ich möchte* (or *nehme*) *einen Lolli, bitte.*
Point out the reminder about *einen / eine /* ein and insist that they use the correct forms.

AT 3.3 **6 Lies die Dialoge und finde die Sätze im Text.**
Students read the two short dialogues about buying presents. They search the text for the German translations of English expressions a–e.

Answers: **a** Ich suche ein Geschenk. **b** Schreibt sie gern? **c** Möchte sie …? **d** Isst er gern …? **e** Ich nehme …

168

3B.5 Mein Zuhause

KAL 4.6 Think
Students use key phrases in the dialogues to work out the rule about asking questions in German *(When you ask a question in German you move the verb to the beginning of the sentence).* Take this opportunity to revise other ways of asking questions, e.g. using question words *(Wie? Was? Wann? Wie viel? Wo?* etc.).

AT 4.3–4 Challenge
Students write two dialogues: one buying tickets, and the other discussing a present for a person of their choice. They are encouraged to give reasons why a present might or might not be suitable: *Das ist (k)eine gute Idee, denn …*

3B.5 Besuchen Sie Zoomsdorf!   Seite 112–113

Planner

Objectives
- Vocabulary: understand tourist information; explain what there is to see and do in a place, and suggest activities
- Grammar: use the *du* and *Sie* forms of the imperative; *man kann* + infinitive
- Skills: identify formality of language (*du* and *Sie*)

Video
- Video blog 3B

Resources
- CD 2, tracks 44–45
- Student Book, pages 112–113
- Foundation and Higher Workbooks, page 60
- Workbook audio: CD 3 and 4, track 64
- Interactive OxBox, Unit 3B

Key language
Komm / Kommen Sie nach (Berlin / Hamburg)! Iss / Essen Sie (Berliner Spezialitäten / frischen Fisch)! Besuch / Besuchen Sie (den Zoo / die Galerien)! Fahr / Fahren Sie (mit dem Boot auf der Spree / mit dem Rad im Park)! Wohin kann man gehen? Wo / Was kann man (einkaufen / essen / trinken / machen)?

Framework references
L&S 1.1, 1.2, 1.3, 1.5; R&W 2.1, 2.2, 2.3, 2.4, 2.5; IU 3.2; KAL 4.5; LLS 5.7, 5.8

Starters
- Student Book page 112, ex. 1.
- Use students' posters (ex. 4) as a talking point at the start of a lesson, e.g. ask *Was gibt es hier? Was kann man hier besuchen? / sehen? / machen? / essen?*
- Call out key sentence starters from the unit (e.g. *Gehen Sie …, Willst du …?, Man kann …, Ich möchte …, Besuch …*). Challenge students to complete each one with any appropriate phrase, e.g.
Teacher: *Gehen Sie …*
Student: *… links* (or *ins Kino* or *über die Ampel*, etc.).
Teacher: *Ich möchte …*
Student: *… zwei Karten, bitte* (or *einen Lolli, bitte* or *ins Kino gehen*).

Plenaries
- Challenge students to come up with as many alternative endings as they can for the sentence starters *Iss / Essen Sie, Besuch / Besuchen Sie* and *Fahr / Fahren Sie* in ex. 1, e.g. *Essen Sie (Schokolade, Pizza, Eis), Besuchen Sie (das Schloss, das Museum, die Skateboard-Bahn), Fahren Sie (Skateboard, Ski, Mountainbike).* If appropriate, include other imperatives, e.g. *Kauf / Kaufen Sie, Spiel / Spielen Sie, Geh / Gehen Sie.* Allow time for the class to share their ideas: this will help them to prepare for ex. 4 and the *Challenge* activity.
- Call out tourist attractions or activities in Berlin, Hamburg and Munich. (Refer to ex. 1, 5 and 6, or to any of the information about Berlin that has come up in the course so far.) With books closed, students try to remember which city they are associated with. They respond with *Komm* (or *Kommen Sie*) *nach* + the name of the city, e.g.
Teacher: *Das Oktoberfest!*
Class: *Komm nach München!*
Teacher: *Essen Sie frischen Fisch!*
Class: *Kommen Sie nach Hamburg!*

Homework
- Student Book page 112, ex. 4.
- Student Book page 113, *Challenge*.
- Students write five questions to test their partner's knowledge of Unit 3B (vocabulary, grammar and culture) and compile a separate answer sheet. They exchange their questions with their partner in the next lesson. Alternatively, collect in everyone's questions and use them in a class quiz.

3B.5 Mein Zuhause

1 Was passt zusammen? Schreib Sätze.
This activity revisits the imperative in the context of tourist activities. Students match sentence halves.

Answers: **a** Komm nach Berlin! Iss Berliner Spezialitäten! Besuch den Zoo! Fahr mit dem Boot auf der Spree! **b** Kommen Sie nach Hamburg! Besuchen Sie die Galerien! Fahren Sie mit dem Rad im Park! Essen Sie frischen Fisch!

Think
Students identify which jigsaw is aimed at adults and which at young people. They should spot that the Hamburg advert uses the *Sie* form of the imperative so must be aimed at adults, whereas the Berlin one uses the *du* form so is intended for young people.

2 Hör zu. Was ist die richtige Reihenfolge für die Bilder?
Students listen to an advert for the imaginary tourist destination of Zoomsdorf. They identify places a–g on the Zoomsdorf poster in the order they are mentioned.
To help them prepare for listening, ask them to try to predict any key words or phrases they might hear in connection with each picture, e.g. picture f: *Restaurant, essen*; picture d: *Rad fahren, Park*; picture b: *Boot*.
Play the recording again and ask students to note down additional details about the places mentioned, e.g. comments and opinions.

Answers: e, d, c, f, g, b, a

CD 2, track 44 Seite 112, Übung 2

Kommen Sie nach Zoomsdorf – hier gibt es Attraktionen für Jung und Alt!
Lieben Sie Tiere? Besuchen Sie den Zoo. Er ist immer interessant.
Sind sie sportlich? Dann fahren Sie im Park Rad oder schwimmen Sie in unserem fantastischen neuen Schwimmbad.
Und am Abend? Haben Sie Hunger? Essen Sie italienische, französische und deutsche Spezialitäten.
Lieben Sie Kultur? Besuchen Sie das historische Museum. Es ist sehr interessant.
Lieben Sie Natur? Machen sie eine Bootsfahrt auf dem Fluss.
Oder möchten Sie sich entspannen? Lesen Sie ein gutes Buch.
Hmmm … wie entspannend ist es in Zoomsdorf!

Follow-up
Ask students to consider features of the language in ex. 2 that make it successful as an advertisement (they may have done some work on this in English lessons). For example, the use of rhetorical questions and the imperative is a technique often used in advertisements for persuasive effect. This style of writing (or speaking) has more impact than a straightforward list of Zoomsdorf's attractions. Remind students that they know another way (in addition to the imperative) to tell people what to do, which they learned in Unit 3A in the context of healthy eating: *Man soll … essen / trinken*. Point out that *Man soll* could be used in the context of tourist information too, e.g. *Man soll / Du sollst eine Bootsfahrt machen*. Compare the two structures: *man soll* is often used to give advice or suggestions, whereas the imperative is used to give direct instructions. How effective do students think *Man soll* would be if used here instead of the imperative?

3 Was kann man in Zoomsdorf besuchen?
Students take turns to recommend activities for each other, referring to the pictures on the Zoomsdorf poster. Their partner names the corresponding picture, e.g.
A: *Besuch den Zoo!*
B: *Das ist Bild e.*

4 Mach ein Poster für deinen Wohnort.
Students adapt the sentences from ex. 1 to make a tourist leaflet about their own home town or area. See first plenary suggested in the *Planner* above for an activity to help them prepare for this.

5 Sieh dir Ninas Videoblog an. Beantworte die Fragen auf Englisch.
Students watch Nina's video blog about Berlin and answer questions in English.
Ask if they can tell who Nina is addressing here – a friend, because she uses the *du* form throughout. Point out the informal *Halli hallo* (Hi) at the beginning.

Answers: **a** TV Tower; **b** visit a museum; **c** the zoo; **d** she can go shopping and meet her friends (they all live here)

Video blog 3B
CD 2, track 45 Seite 113, Übung 5

Halli hallo. Wie geht's? Du möchtest Berlin besuchen? Prima. Hier gibt es sehr viel zu tun. Wo fange ich an? Als Erstes geh zum Fernsehturm … Der ist spitze. Von da aus siehst du ganz Berlin. Dann geh zum Brandenburger Tor. Wenn es regnet, besuche ein Museum … Wenn es sonnig ist, geh in den Zoo … Dort gibt es Giraffen, Elefanten – alle möglichen Tierarten. Es gibt auch tolle Geschäfte und Kaufhäuser. Ich mag Berlin, denn ich kann hier einkaufen … und natürlich kann ich mich mit meinen Freunden treffen … Sie wohnen alle hier.
Und wie ist deine Stadt? Was gibt es dort zu tun?

3B.6 Mein Zuhause

Follow-up
Play the video blog again and challenge students to note all the places mentioned and what Nina says about them.

Answers: TV Tower – it's great, you can see the whole of Berlin from there; the Brandenburg Gate; museum; zoo – you can see giraffes, elephants and all sorts of animals; great shops and department stores

AT 3.4
R&W 2.1, 2.2, 2.3
IU 3.2

6 Lies den Text. Beantworte die Fragen.
Students read the magazine-style feature about Munich and answer questions in English. Talk about what makes it successful as an advertisement, e.g. descriptive language, rhetorical questions, the imperative.

Answers: a in the centre; b shops, department store, restaurants; c international and German specialities; d go on the Ferris wheel and meet friends from all over the world; e walk through the park (Englischer Garten) in the snow

AT 2.2–3
7 Stell Fragen.
Students take turns to ask and answer questions about what you can do in Munich. Key questions are provided.

AT 2.3–4
AT 4.3–4
L&S 1.3, 1.5
R&W 2.3, 2.4, 2.5
LLS 5.7, 5.8

Challenge
Students imagine they are inviting someone to their home area. They prepare a presentation, suggesting things to see and do, and either record it (like Nina's video blog) or produce a written text.
Remind students to use a range of structures, e.g. rhetorical questions and the imperative (*Magst du Geschichte? – Besuchen Sie das Schloss!*), *Es gibt + ein(e)(n) …*, *Man kann* + infinitive, comments and opinions, as in the Munich text (ex. 6). Point out that they can use the underlined phrases in the Munich text as a framework. Refer them to the *Think* box at the end of spread 3B.1 for tips on evaluating and improving their work.

3B.6 Sprachlabor

Seite 114–115

Planner

Objectives
- Grammar: *können* and *wollen* (all forms); word order with modal verbs; the imperative (*du* and *Sie*)
- Skills: ask questions; pronounce *v* and *w*

Resources
- Student Book, pages 114–115
- CD 2, tracks 46–48
- Foundation and Higher Workbooks, pages 61–62
- Workbook audio: CD 3 and 4, track 65
- Copymasters 81, 82
- Interactive OxBox, Unit 3B

Framework references
KAL 4.1, 4.4, 4.5, 4.6; LLS 5.1

Können, wollen

KAL 4.4, 4.5
1 Put the words into the correct order.
As a follow-up, ask students to translate the sentences into English.

Answers: a Ich will in den Zoo gehen. b Ich kann meine Großeltern besuchen. c Er will das Fußballspiel sehen. d Wir können im Restaurant essen. e Sie kann das Stadion nicht finden. f Sie können mit der U-Bahn fahren.

2 Make sentences using the correct forms of *können* and *wollen*.
Ask students to translate the sentences into English.

Answers: a Er kann schwimmen. b Du willst (im Restaurant) essen. c Man kann das Museum besuchen. d Wir wollen ins Kino gehen. e Sie können Rad (or Mountainbike) fahren.

The imperative

KAL 4.5
3 Change the following statements into instructions.

Answers: a Geh die zweite Straße rechts! b Gehen Sie die erste Straße links! c Nimm die dritte Straße rechts! d Nehmen Sie die dritte Straße links! e Trink Orangensaft! f Essen Sie Obst! g Hör Musik! h Gehen Sie über die Kreuzung!

3B.7 Mein Zuhause

Follow-up
Read out a list of imperatives (including both *du* and *Sie* forms) and ask students to identify which are formal and which are informal, e.g. **1** *Geh geradeaus!* **2** *Gehen Sie rechts!* **3** *Geh links!* **4** *Iss den Apfel!* **5** *Trinken Sie ein Glas Wasser!* **6** *Mach deine Hausaufgaben!* **7** *Kommen Sie hier!*

Answers: 1, 3, 4 and 6 are informal

Asking questions

KAL 4.4, 4.6 This section focuses on asking questions using subject–verb inversion. Remind students that they can also ask questions by using question words, e.g. *Wie? Was? Wann? Wie viel? Wo?* etc.

4 Turn each statement into a question.

Answers: **a** *Gehst du ins Kino?* **b** *Macht er Hausaufgaben?* **c** *Fahren wir Rad?* **d** *Sehen sie (or Sie) fern?* **e** *Tanzt sie gern?* **f** *Essen sie (or Sie) gern Schokolade?*

LLS 5.1 **5 Listen (a–d). Is it a statement or a question?**
Students focus on intonation to help them distinguish between statements and questions.

Answers: a and d are questions

🎧 **CD 2, track 46** Seite 115, Übung 5

a Spielt er Fußball?
b Du trinkst ein Glas Limonade.
c Wir gehen ins Kino.
d Fahren sie alle Rad?

Pronunciation of *v* and *w*

KAL 4.1 **6 First try to pronounce these words. Then listen and repeat.**

🎧 **CD 2, track 47** Seite 115, Übung 6

a	wollen	f	Wein
b	wohnen	g	Wort
c	Erwachsene	h	vier
d	schwimmen	i	viel
e	Wien	j	voll

7 Listen. Do you hear *v* or *w*?

Answers: **a** w; **b** w; **c** v; **d** v; **e** w; **f** w; **g** v; **h** w

🎧 **CD 2, track 48** Seite 115, Übung 7

a	schwarz	e	Kiwi
b	Wilhelm	f	wie
c	verstehen	g	vor
d	Kurve	h	Krawatte

3B.7 Extra Star Seite 116

Planner

Objectives
- Vocabulary: recognise the names for places in a town and say what you can do there; give directions
- Grammar: *es gibt + (k)ein(e)(n) …; man kann +* infinitive; the imperative

- Skills: read for gist and detail

Resources
- Student Book, page 116
- Copymaster 83

AT 3.2 **1 Look at the picture. Are the sentences true or false?**
Students identify places in a town.

Answers: **a** true; **b** true; **c** false; **d** true; **e** false; **f** true

AT 3.2 **AT 4.2** **2 Fill the gaps with the words from the box on the right.**
Students choose the correct infinitive to complete each sentence.

Answers: **a** *essen*; **b** *fahren*; **c** *trinken*; **d** *gehen*; **e** *tanzen*

3B.8 Mein Zuhause

AT 3.3 **3 Read Britta's email and answer the questions.**

Answers: **a** it's great; **b** park, swimming pool, museum; **c** swimming pool; **d** it's big, she can meet her friends there; **e** there's no youth club; **f** to the park

AT 4.1–2 **4 Write down which directions you would give.**
Students fill in the missing letters to complete the directions.

Answers: **a** Gehen Sie links. **b** Geh rechts. **c** Geh geradeaus. **d** Nimm die zweite Straße links.

3B.7 Extra Plus   Seite 117

Planner

Objectives
- Vocabulary: say what places there are (and aren't) in a town and what you can do there
- Grammar: *es gibt + (k)ein(e)(n)…; man kann* + infinitive
- Skills: cope with unfamiliar language

Resources
- Student Book, page 117
- Copymaster 84

AT 3.4 **1 Was gibt es zu tun?**
The texts describe what there is for young people to see and do in two German cities: Rüdesheim and Germering. Students note in English the activities that you can do in each place.
Some of the key words here may be unfamiliar to students, e.g. *Schlittschuh, wandern*. Encourage them to try working out their meanings without resorting to a dictionary (e.g. *wandern* looks a bit like the English word "wandering" so students might deduce that it means "walking"). They can then use a dictionary afterwards to check anything they were unable to work out.

Answers: **a** mountain biking, walking; **b** swimming, ice skating (also shopping and visiting museums and galleries in nearby Munich)

AT 3.4 **2 Lies den Text noch einmal. Wer ist das?**
Students read the texts again and identify which person each question relates to.

Answers: **a** Evi; **b** Evi; **c** Axel; **d** Evi; **e** Axel; **f** Evi

AT 4.3–4 **3 Willkommen in Mittelstadt! Was gibt es hier (nicht)? Was kann man (nicht) machen? Schreib Sätze.**

Students look at the poster advertising Mittelstadt. They write a description saying what there is (and isn't) to see and do there. Encourage them to add in details and comments / opinions instead of just listing what there is and isn't, e.g. *In Mittelstadt gibt es ein Schwimmbad. Im Sommer und im Winter kann man hier schwimmen. Das ist total klasse!*

3B.8 Testseite   Seite 118

Planner

Resources
- Student Book, page 118
- CD 2, track 49
- Foundation and Higher Workbooks, page 63
- Copymasters 73, 74
- Assessment, Unit 3B

AT 3.4 **1 Read the email and choose the correct answer.**
Students answer questions about things to see and do in Saarbrücken.

Answers: **a** 2; **b** 3; **c** 1; **d** 2; **e** 3; **f** 1

AT 1.2–3 **2 Listen (1–6). Which places are mentioned? What do people think about them (positive ✓ or negative ✗)?**
To increase the challenge of this activity, ask students to note down as much extra detail as they can.

173

3B Mein Zuhause

Answers: **1** zoo ✓; **2** supermarket ✗ (boring); **3** stadium ✓ (it's in the east of the town, watches football matches there); **4** cinema ✗ (it's modern and big but tickets are expensive); **5** railway station ✗ (boring); **6** castle ✓

🎧 **CD 2, track 49**   Seite 118, Übung 2

1. Es gibt einen Zoo. Er ist total gut.
2. Es gibt einen Supermarkt, aber ich finde den Supermarkt und Einkaufen langweilig.
3. Es gibt im Osten der Stadt ein Stadion, und ich sehe mir dort Fußballspiele an. Das ist klasse.
4. Es gibt ein modernes großes Kino, aber ich finde es nicht gut, denn die Karten kosten zu viel.
5. Es gibt in der Stadt einen Bahnhof, aber der ist langweilig.
6. Hier gibt es ein Schloss. Das Schloss finde ich wirklich toll.

AT 2.2–3   **3** 👥 **Make dialogues.**

Students ask for and give directions to places in town and say what they think of each place. They follow the symbols and prompts provided.

AT 4.3–4   **4 Write a report on your own town using the bullet points.**

Students describe their own town or area, saying what there is to see and do, what you can and can't do there, and expressing their opinions. Remind them of the tips for improving their writing: see *Think* box at the end of spread 3B.1.

3B Lesen   Seite 158

Planner

Resources
- Student Book, page 158

Framework references
R&W 2.1, 2.2; IU 3.1, 3.2

Eine Reise durch Berlin

R&W 2.1, 2.2 / IU 3.1, 3.2 This page provides information about some of the main places of interest in Berlin, including some history about the former East and West Berlin.

AT 3.4   **1 Find the correct photo for each paragraph above.**

Students read the information about Berlin and identify the places mentioned.

Answers: **a** 2; **b** 5; **c** 4; **d** 3; **e** 1

2 Find the German words for a–g in the texts above.
Students locate key words and phrases in the Berlin text.

Answers: **a** Hauptstadt; **b** Einwohner; **c** ein beliebter Treffpunkt; **d** ein Museum über die Geschichte; **e** ein großer Wald; **f** ist sehr berühmt; **g** ein nationales Symbol

Follow-up
- Students choose their favourite place(s) in Berlin and translate the corresponding paragraph(s) into English.
- Students look online for some of the places in Berlin that have been mentioned in Unit 3B. A good place to start might be Google Images or the Berlin Tourism Board (www.visitberlin.de). Some places have their own websites: the Berlin Zoo (www.zoo-berlin.de), KaDeWe (www.kadewe.de), the TV Tower (www.tv-turm.de). The Café Kranzler (mentioned in paragraph d of the Berlin text) has its own site (www.cafekranzler.de), where students can view menus and a photo gallery.
- Students choose another major city in Germany, Austria or Switzerland, and find out some facts and figures about it, something about its history and the key tourist attractions. They could produce a class display or give a presentation.

3B Mein Zuhause

Foundation Workbook

3B.1 Berlin, Berlin! (Seite 56)

AT4.1 **1 Solve the clues and fill in the crossword.**

Answers: <u>Waagerecht</u>: **1** Supermarkt; **4** Post; **6** Schwimmbad; **8** Stadion; **9** Kirche; **10** Zoo; <u>Senkrecht</u>: **1** Schloss; **2** Park; **3** Kino; **5** Bahnhof; **7** Museum

AT 1.2–3 **2 Put numbers in the boxes to show the order in which you hear the places mentioned. Anything not mentioned, leave blank.**

Answers: **1** post office; **2** railway station; **3** department store; **4** stadium; **5** youth club; **6** cinema; **7** skatepark; **8** park; **9** museum

> 🎧 **CD 3, track 60**   Seite 56, Übung 2
>
> Ich wohne in einer kleinen Stadt, aber es gibt genug zu tun. Hier in Neustadt gibt es eine Post und einen Bahnhof. Es gibt auch ein Kaufhaus, aber kein Stadion, denn die Stadt ist zu klein. Hier ist es nicht so toll für junge Leute, weil wir kein Jugendzentrum haben. Es gibt aber ein Kino und eine Skateboard-Bahn. Es gibt auch einen Park – das finde ich sehr gut – und ein Museum – das finde ich nicht so interessant.

AT 1.3 **3 Listen again. Note, in English, which places don't exist in this town.**

Answers: no stadium, no youth club

4 Choose the correct word for 'a'.

Answers: **a** einen; **b** ein; **c** eine; **d** einen; **e** ein; **f** einen

3B.2 Was kann man machen? (Seite 57)

AT 3.2 **1 Where can you do these things? Write in the right number.**

Answers: **a** 3; **b** 4; **c** 7; **d** 1; **e** 2; **f** 8; **g** 5; **h** 6

AT 1.3 **2 Listen to Claudia describing Schwerin. Circle *falsch* (false) or *richtig* (true).**

Answers: **a** falsch; **b** richtig; **c** falsch; **d** richtig; **e** falsch; **f** falsch; **g** richtig; **h** falsch

> 🎧 **CD 3, track 61**   Seite 57, Übung 2
>
> Hier in Schwerin ist es toll. Es gibt einen großen Park und auch ein altes Schloss. Man kann im Park Rad fahren und Tischtennis spielen. Fußball kann man nicht spielen; das ist verboten. Es gibt ein Kino in der Stadt und auch Restaurants. Hier kann man gut essen. Schwerin ist im Osten.

AT 4.1 **3 Complete the sentences.**

Answers: **a** ein Restaurant, essen; **b** einen Park, Fußball spielen; **c** ein Kino, einen Film sehen; **d** eine Schule, Englisch lernen; **e** einen Zoo, Löwen sehen

3B.3 Wo ist das Kino? (Seite 58)

AT 3.2 **1 Draw lines to link the directions to the pictures.**

Answers: **1** b; **2** h; **3** c; **4** e; **5** g; **6** d; **7** f; **8** a

AT 1.2 **2 Use the pictures in Activity 1 again. Listen and write in the numbers for the instructions given.**

Answers: **a** 5; **b** 8; **c** 4; **d** 7; **e** 3; **f** 2; **g** 1; **h** 6

> 🎧 **CD 3, track 62**   Seite 58, Übung 2
>
> **a** Nimm die zweite Straße links.
> **b** Geh rechts.
> **c** Es ist auf der rechten Seite.
> **d** Nimm die erste Straße rechts.
> **e** Geh geradeaus.
> **f** Nimm die dritte Straße rechts.
> **g** Geh links.
> **h** Es ist auf der linken Seite.

AT3.2 **3 Write in the names of the places.**

Answers: **a** first left: Bahnhof; **b** second right: Kaufhaus; **c** straight on: Schwimmbad; **d** first right: Post; **e** second left: Schloss

3B.4 Im Zoo (Seite 59)

AT 3.1 **1 Draw lines to link the words to the pictures.**

Answers: **a** zwei Erwachsene und ein Kind; **b** drei Erwachsene; **c** zwei Karten; **d** drei Karten; **e** vier Kinder; **f** zwei Kinder

AT 1.1 **2 What do these people want? Write the answers in English.**

Answers: **a** a book; **b** a mobile phone; **c** a fried sausage; **d** a strawberry ice cream; **e** a key ring; **f** a present

> 🎧 **CD 3, track 63**   Seite 59, Übung 2
>
> **a** Ich möchte ein Buch.
> **b** Ich möchte ein Handy.
> **c** Ich möchte eine Bratwurst.
> **d** Ich möchte ein Erdbeereis.
> **e** Ich möchte einen Schlüsselanhänger.
> **f** Ich möchte ein Geschenk.

3B Mein Zuhause

AT 4.2   **3** Unjumble these questions so the words are in the right order.

Answers: **a** Möchtest du ein Buch? **b** Möchtest du ein Handy? **c** Möchtest du eine Bratwurst? **d** Möchtest du ein Erdbeereis? **e** Möchtest du einen Schlüsselanhänger? **f** Möchtest du ein Geschenk?

3B.5 Besuchen Sie Zoomsdorf! (Seite 60)

AT 3.2   **1** Put a tick or cross by these sentences to show whether they are true or not.

Answers: **a** ✗; **b** ✓; **c** ✗; **d** ✓; **e** ✗; **f** ✓; **g** ✗

AT 1.3   **2** Listen to Ergül talking about Delmenhorst, the town where he lives. Answer the questions with 'Yes' or 'No'.

Answers: **a** no; **b** yes; **c** yes; **d** yes; **e** no; **f** yes

> 🎧 **CD 3, track 64**   Seite 60, Übung 2
>
> Hallo! Ich wohne in Delmenhorst. Das ist eine kleine Stadt in Norddeutschland. Es gibt ein Schwimmbad. Man kann dort gut schwimmen. Es gibt auch einen Park. Am Wochenende kann ich mit meinen Freunden in den Park gehen und Skateboard fahren. Es gibt in Delmenhorst ein Kino, aber kein Stadion. Man kann aber zum Weser-Stadion in Bremen fahren.

AT 4.2   **3** Write the instructions next to each picture.

Answers: **a** Nehmen Sie die dritte Straße links. **b** Gehen Sie geradeaus. **c** Gehen Sie rechts. **d** Gehen Sie links. **e** Nehmen Sie die zweite Straße links. **f** Nehmen Sie die erste Straße rechts.

3B.6A Sprachlabor (Seite 61)

1 Circle the correct word.

Answers: **a** kann; **b** will; **c** können; **d** kann; **e** Willst; **f** wollen

2 Choose words from below to fill the gaps in these instructions.

Answers: **a** Gehen Sie; **b** Iss; **c** Nimm; **d** Fahren Sie; **e** Kommen Sie; **f** Kauf

3 Now write down the letters of the instructions in Activity 2 which are: a) given to an adult; b) given to a child or friend.

Answers: **a** Gehen Sie, Fahren Sie, Kommen Sie (a, d, e); **b** Iss, Nimm, Kauf (b, c, f)

4 Say these words out loud. Some you know, some you will have to work out. Then listen to the recording to check you got them right.

> 🎧 **CD 3, track 65**   Seite 61, Übung 4
>
> Achterbahn … will … wild … voll … sprechen … schwimmen … wohne … wollen … besuchen … möchte … Schloss … Weimar … vielleicht … bevor

3B.6B Think (Seite 62)

1 Read the advert and write, beside each sentence: 'Invitation', 'You can' or 'There is'.

Answers: **a** Invitation; **b** Invitation; **c** Invitation; **d** Invitation; **e** Invitation; **f** There is; **g** There is; **h** You can; **i** You can

2 Read the advert again. Write an advert for a different place. Use the sentences in the advert and change the details to those below.

Answers: Kommen Sie nach Worpswede! Besuchen Sie die Galerien! Fahren Sie Bimmelbahn! Essen Sie Aal! Kaufen Sie Postkarten. Es gibt alte Häuser. Man kann Pferdekutsche fahren. Man kann Künstler sehen.

3 What kind of place is: a) the Heide-Park Soltau? b) Worpswede?

Answers: **a** a theme park/amusement park; **b** a town for artists/cultural town

4 What do you think a *Künstler* is? Your knowledge of school subjects will help.

Answer: an artist

3B Mein Zuhause

Higher Workbook

3B.1 Berlin, Berlin! (Seite 56)

[AT4.1] 1 Solve the clues and fill in the crossword.

Answers: <u>Waagerecht</u>: **1** Supermarkt; **4** Post; **6** Schwimmbad; **8** Stadion; **9** Kirche; **10** Zoo; <u>Senkrecht</u>: **1** Schloss; **2** Park; **3** Kino; **5** Bahnhof; **7** Museum

[AT 1.2–3] 2 Put numbers in the boxes to show the order in which you hear the places mentioned. Anything not mentioned, leave blank.

Answers: **1** post office; **2** railway station; **3** department store; **4** stadium; **5** youth club; **6** cinema; **7** skatepark; **8** park; **9** museum

> **CD 4, track 60**   Seite 56, Übung 2
>
> Ich wohne in einer kleinen Stadt, aber es gibt genug zu tun. Hier in Neustadt gibt es eine Post und einen Bahnhof. Es gibt auch ein Kaufhaus, aber kein Stadion, denn die Stadt ist zu klein. Hier ist es nicht so toll für junge Leute, weil wir kein Jugendzentrum haben. Es gibt aber ein Kino und eine Skateboard-Bahn. Es gibt auch einen Park – das finde ich sehr gut – und ein Museum – das finde ich nicht so interessant.

[AT 1.3] 3 Listen again and note down, in English, at least three opinions expressed by the speaker.

Answers: *It isn't so great for young people here because we don't have a youth club. There's also a park – that's very good. There's a museum – that's not so interesting*

4 Write in *einen*, *eine* or *ein*.

Answers: **a** einen; **b** ein; **c** eine; **d** einen; **e** ein; **f** einen

3B.2 Was kann man machen? (Seite 57)

[AT 3.2] 1 Identify the places and write in the word.

Answers: **a** Jugendzentrum; **b** Café; **c** Disco; **d** Pizzeria; **e** Stadion; **f** Kino; **g** Schwimmbad; **h** Skateboard-Bahn

[AT 1.3] 2 Listen to Claudia describing Schwerin. Answer the questions in English.

Answers: **a** it's great; **b** a large park and an old castle; **c** go cycling and play table tennis; **d** play football; **e** one; **f** yes; **g** in the east

> **CD 4, track 61**   Seite 57, Übung 2
>
> Hier in Schwerin ist es toll. Es gibt einen großen Park und auch ein altes Schloss. Man kann im Park Rad fahren und Tischtennis spielen. Fußball kann man nicht spielen; das ist verboten. Es gibt ein Kino in der Stadt und auch Restaurants. Hier kann man gut essen. Schwerin ist im Osten.

[AT 4.2–3] 3 Write sentences to fit the pictures.

Answers: **a** *Es gibt ein Restaurant. Man kann hier essen.* **b** *Es gibt einen Park. Man kann hier Fußball spielen.* **c** *Es gibt ein Kino. Man kann hier einen Film sehen.* **d** *Es gibt eine Schule. Man kann hier Englisch lernen.* **e** *Es gibt einen Zoo. Man kann hier Löwen sehen.*

3B.3 Wo ist das Kino? (Seite 58)

[AT 4.2] 1 Write the correct phrases below the pictures.

Answers: **a** *geradeaus;* **b** *die zweite Straße links;* **c** *die dritte Straße rechts;* **d** *rechts;* **e** *die erste Straße rechts;* **f** *links;* **g** *auf der linken Seite;* **h** *auf der rechten Seite*

[AT 1.2–3] 2 Use the pictures in Activity 1 again. Listen and write in the letters for the instructions given (2 letters each time).

Answers: **a** a, b; **b** d, f; **c** a, h; **d** e, b; **e** a, c; **f** e, b; **g** f, d; **h** f, g

> **CD 4, track 62**   Seite 58, Übung 2
>
> **a** Geh geradeaus und nimm die zweite Straße links.
> **b** Geh rechts und dann links.
> **c** Geh geradeaus und es ist auf der rechten Seite.
> **d** Nimm die erste Straße rechts. Und dann die zweite Straße links.
> **e** Geh geradeaus und nimm die dritte Straße rechts.
> **f** Nimm die erste Straße rechts und die zweite Straße links.
> **g** Geh links und dann rechts.
> **h** Geh links und es ist auf der linken Seite.

[AT 4.2–3] 3 Write out the questions and answers.

Answers: **a** *Wo ist der Bahnhof? Nehmen Sie die erste Straße links.* **b** *Wo ist das Schloss? Nehmen Sie die zweite Straße links.* **c** *Wo ist das Schwimmbad? Gehen Sie geradeaus.* **d** *Wo ist das Kaufhaus. Nehmen Sie die zweite Straße rechts.* **e** *Wo ist die Post? Nehmen Sie die erste Straße rechts.*

3B Mein Zuhause

3B.4 Im Zoo (Seite 59)

1 Add the right captions to the pictures.

Answers: *a* zwei Erwachsene und ein Kind; *b* drei Erwachsene; *c* zwei Karten; *d* drei Karten; *e* vier Kinder; *f* zwei Kinder

2 What do these people want? Write the answers in English.

Answers: *a* a book; *b* a mobile phone; *c* a fried sausage; *d* a strawberry ice cream; *e* a key ring; *f* a present

---

CD 4, track 63 — Seite 59, Übung 2

a Ich möchte ein Buch.
b Ich möchte ein Handy.
c Ich möchte eine Bratwurst.
d Ich möchte ein Erdbeereis.
e Ich möchte einen Schlüsselanhänger.
f Ich möchte ein Geschenk.

---

3 Listen to Activity 2 again and turn the statements into questions.

Answers: *a* Möchtest du ein Buch? *b* Möchtest du ein Handy? *c* Möchtest du eine Bratwurst? *d* Möchtest du ein Erdbeereis? *e* Möchtest du einen Schlüsselanhänger? *f* Möchtest du ein Geschenk?

3B.5 Besuchen Sie Zoomsdorf! (Seite 60)

1 Write sentences saying what things do and don't exist in this village. Mention: a department store, a supermarket, a church, a castle, a skateboard track, a train station and a TV tower.

Answers: *a* Es gibt kein Kaufhaus. *b* Es gibt keinen Supermarkt. *c* Es gibt eine Kirche. *d* Es gibt ein Schloss. *e* Es gibt keine Skateboard-Bahn. *f* Es gibt einen Bahnhof. *g* Es gibt keinen Fernsehturm.

2 Listen to Ergül talking about Delmenhorst, the town where he lives. Answer the questions in English.

Answers: *a* in North Germany; *b* there's a good swimming pool in Delmenhorst; *c* he can go skateboarding in the park with his friends; *d* yes; *e* he can go to the Weser Stadium in Bremen

---

CD 4, track 64 — Seite 60, Übung 2

Hallo! Ich wohne in Delmenhorst. Das ist eine kleine Stadt in Norddeutschland. Es gibt ein Schwimmbad. Man kann dort gut schwimmen. Es gibt auch einen Park. Am Wochenende kann ich mit meinen Freunden in den Park gehen und Skateboard fahren. Es gibt in Delmenhorst ein Kino, aber kein Stadion. Man kann aber zum Weser-Stadion in Bremen fahren.

---

3 Write the instructions next to each picture.

Answers: *a* Nehmen Sie die dritte Straße links. *b* Gehen Sie geradeaus. *c* Gehen Sie rechts. *d* Gehen Sie links. *e* Nehmen Sie die zweite Straße links. *f* Nehmen Sie die erste Straße rechts.

3B.6A Sprachlabor (Seite 61)

1 Insert the correct form of *können* or *wollen*.

Answers: *a* kann; *b* will; *c* können; *d* kann; *e* Willst; *f* wollen

2 Fill in the gaps in these instructions.

Answers: *a* Gehen Sie; *b* Iss; *c* Nimm; *d* Fahren Sie; *e* Kommen Sie; *f* Kauf

3 Say these words out loud. Some you know, some you will have to work out. Then listen to the recording to check you got them right.

CD 4, track 65 — Seite 61, Übung 3

Achterbahn … will … wild … voll … sprechen … schwimmen … wohne … wollen … besuchen … möchte … Schloss … Weimar … vielleicht … bevor

---

3B.6B Think (Seite 62)

1 Insert the correct sentence beginnings from the box below.

Answers: *a* Kommen Sie; *b* Besuchen Sie; *c* Fahren Sie; *d* Essen Sie; *e* Kaufen Sie; *f* Es gibt; *g* Es gibt; *h* Man kann; *i* Man kann

2 How many sentences in the advert: a) invite you to do something? b) tell you what there is? c) tell you what you can do?

Answers: *a* five (a–e); *b* two (f, g); *c* two (h, i)

3 Read the advert again. Write an advert for a different place. Use the sentences in the advert and change the details to those below.

Answers: Kommen Sie nach Worpswede! Besuchen Sie die Galerien! Fahren Sie Bimmelbahn! Essen Sie Aal! Kaufen Sie Postkarten! Es gibt alte Häuser. Man kann Pferdekutsche fahren. Man kann Künstler sehen.

4 Adapt the advert again to make an advert for your own town. Unsure of any vocabulary? Look it up in the dictionary!

Answers: students' own answers

4A Modestadt Berlin!

Unit 4A Modestadt Berlin!   Unit overview grid

Page reference	Objectives	Grammar	Skills and pronunciation	Key language	Framework	AT level
Pages 120–121 **4A.1 Die Jeans ist cool!**	Talk about clothes and say what you think of them	Singular noun + *ist*, plural noun + *sind*	Recycle previously learned language to express opinions; identify cognates and false friends	*der Kapuzenpullover, der Mantel, der Pullover, der Rock, die Bluse, die Hose, die Jacke, die Jeans, die Lederjacke, das Hemd, das Kleid, das T-Shirt, die Ballerinas, die Shorts, die Sportschuhe, die Stiefel Wie findest du …? Wie gefällt dir …? Gefällt dir …? Ich mag … (nicht). … gefällt mir (nicht). Ich finde … hässlich, cool, schick, schön, alt, neu, modisch, altmodisch, bequem, unbequem, teuer, billig, lässig sehr, total, ziemlich*	L&S 1.1, 1.2, 1.3, 1.4 R&W 2.4, 2.5 KAL 4.2, 4.3, 4.4, 4.5 LLS 5.1, 5.3, 5.5	1.1, 2.2–3, 3.1–3, 4.3–4
Pages 122–123 **4A.2 Coole Outfits**	Say what you usually wear and what you would like to wear	The accusative case (*ich trage einen/eine/ein* + adjective + noun) Present tense of *tragen* *Ich möchte* + infinitive	Identify language patterns; apply knowledge of grammar (the accusative) in a new context	*Ich trage einen gelben Rock/eine blaue Bluse/ein grünes Top/schwarze Schuhe. Ich möchte eine schicke Jeans tragen/kaufen/haben. Ich möchte einkaufen gehen. Ich möchte modisch/cool/schick/lässig sein. bunt normalerweise*	R&W 2.4, 2.5 KAL 4.3, 4.4, 4.5 LLS 5.1, 5.8	1.4–5, 2.3, 3.3–4, 4.3–5
Pages 124–125 **4A.3 Wir gehen einkaufen!**	Go shopping for clothes Give opinions of clothes	The accusative case (*der* becomes *den*) Object pronouns (*ihn, sie, es*)	Identify language patterns	*Wie findest du (den karierten Rock/die blaue Hose/das gestreifte Hemd)? Ich finde ihn/sie/es … (+ opinion adjectives). (zu) teuer, (zu) groß, (zu) klein, (zu) altmodisch Wie gefällt dir …? Wie ist …? … gefällt mir (nicht). Ich mag ihn/sie/es (nicht). Es steht dir nicht. Es geht. Wie kann ich dir helfen? Ich möchte … anprobieren, bitte. Natürlich. Die Kabine ist um die Ecke/hier links/hier rechts. Ich kaufe ihn/sie/es nicht, danke. Ich möchte ihn/sie/es (nicht) kaufen.*	L&S 1.1, 1.4 KAL 4.2, 4.3 LLS 5.1, 5.6	1.4–5, 2.3–5, 3.3–4, 4.4–5

179

4A Modestadt Berlin!

Page reference	Objectives	Grammar	Skills and pronunciation	Key language	Framework	AT level
Pages 126–127 **4A.4 Die Hose ist zu klein!**	Talk about problems with clothes and say what clothes you're going to buy	The future tense (*werden* + infinitive) The comparative (e.g. *kleiner als*)	Prepare for and evaluate language tasks	*Mein neuer Rock ist zu groß. Meine neue Hose ist zu klein. Mein Outfit ist zu alt. Deshalb werde ich einkaufen gehen. Ich werde ihn/sie/es umtauschen. Ich werde ihn/sie/es eine Größe größer/kleiner kaufen. Ich werde ein neues Outfit kaufen. Ich möchte gut aussehen. Die Bluse ist (viel) besser als das T-Shirt.*	R&W 2.4, 2.5 KAL 4.3, 4.4, 4.5 LLS 5.1, 5.3, 5.7, 5.8	1.4–5, 2.4, 3.4–5, 4.3–5
Pages 128–129 **4A.5 Das trage ich!**	Talk about designer clothing and school uniform	First, second and third person singular of some common verbs (*tragen*, *kaufen*) *Ich möchte* + infinitive	Adapt and build texts	*Was trägst du gern? Ich trage … Wo kaufst du ein? Ich kaufe meine Kleidung bei … Trägst du eine Schuluniform? Was trägst du in der Schule? In der Schule trage ich … Wie findest du die Schuluniform? Was möchtest du tragen? Ich möchte … tragen. die Krawatte, die Schuluniform, die Straßenkleidung*	L&S 1.1, 1.2, 1.4, 1.5 R&W 2.4, 2.5 IU 3.1, 3.2 LLS 5.7, 5.8	1.4, 2.3–5, 3.4–5, 4.4–5

Unit 4A: Week-by-week overview
(Three-year KS3 Route: assuming six weeks' work or approximately 10–12.5 hours)
(Two-year KS3 Route: assuming four weeks' work or approximately 6.5–8.5 hours)

About Unit 4A, *Modestadt Berlin!*: In this unit, students work in the context of clothes and fashion: they describe and compare clothes and express opinions about them, talk about what they usually wear, what they would like to wear and what they're going to buy, and go shopping for clothes. They discuss school uniform, and there are opportunities to find out about German fashion designers.

Students make progress with verbs: they use *ich möchte* + infinitive to refer to what they would like to do in the future, and learn the future tense (*werden* + infinitive). Work on the case system continues: students are introduced to object pronouns (*ihn*, *sie*, *es*) and adjective endings in the accusative case. They also learn to use the comparative form of adjectives.

There is a strong focus on accuracy and attention to detail in productive work: students receive tips on checking and improving their written work, and learn how to evaluate language tasks in terms of what needs to be done to achieve a particular level. They cope with increasingly challenging texts, using a range of strategies to help with understanding. The pronunciation focus is *isch*, *ich* and *ig*.

Three-Year KS3 Route

Week	Resources	Objectives
1	**4A.1 Die Jeans ist cool!** **4A.6 Sprachlabor ex. 5–6** *(if you wish to work on pronunciation at this point)*	Talk about clothes and say what you think of them Singular noun + *ist*, plural noun + *sind* Recycle previously learned language to express opinions; identify cognates and false friends

Two-Year KS3 Route

Week	Resources	Objectives
1	**4A.1 Die Jeans ist cool!** *(Omit ex. 4)* **4A.6 Sprachlabor ex. 5–6** *(if you wish to work on pronunciation at this point)*	Talk about clothes and say what you think of them Singular noun + *ist*, plural noun + *sind* Recycle previously learned language to express opinions; identify cognates and false friends

4A Modestadt Berlin!

	Three-Year KS3 Route			Two-Year KS3 Route	
Week	Resources	Objectives	Week	Resources	Objectives
2	4A.2 Coole Outfits	Say what you usually wear and what you would like to wear The accusative case (*ich trage* + *einen/eine/ein* + adjective + noun); present tense of *tragen*; *ich möchte* + infinitive Identify language patterns; apply knowledge of grammar (the accusative) in a new context	2	4A.2 Coole Outfits	Say what you usually wear and what you would like to wear The accusative case (*ich trage* + *einen/eine/ein* + adjective + noun); present tense of *tragen*; *ich möchte* + infinitive Identify language patterns; apply knowledge of grammar (the accusative) in a new context
3	4A.3 Wir gehen einkaufen! 4A.6 Sprachlabor ex. 1–2	Go shopping for clothes; give opinions of clothes The accusative case (*der* becomes *den*) Object pronouns (*ihn*, *sie*, *es*) Identify language patterns	3	4A.3 Wir gehen einkaufen! (Omit Challenge) 4A.6 Sprachlabor ex. 1–2	Go shopping for clothes; give opinions of clothes The accusative case (*der* becomes *den*) Object pronouns (*ihn*, *sie*, *es*) Identify language patterns
4	4A.4 Die Hose ist zu klein! 4A.6 Sprachlabor ex. 3 and 4	Talk about problems with clothes and say what clothes you are going to buy The future tense (*werden* + infinitive) The comparative (e.g. *kleiner als*) Prepare for and evaluate language tasks	4	4A.4 Die Hose ist zu klein! (Omit ex. 4) 4A.6 Sprachlabor ex. 3 and 4 4A.8 Vokabular 4A.8 Testseite	Talk about problems with clothes and say what clothes you are going to buy The future tense (*werden* + infinitive) The comparative (e.g. *kleiner als*) Prepare for and evaluate language tasks Key vocabulary and learning checklist Assessment in all four skills
5	4A.5 Das trage ich!	Talk about designer clothing and school uniform First, second and third person singular of some common verbs (*tragen*, *kaufen*) *Ich möchte* + infinitive Adapt and build texts			
6	4A.7 Extra (Star/Plus) 4A.8 Vokabular 4A.8 Testseite 4A Lesen	Reinforcement and extension of the language of the unit Key vocabulary and learning checklist Assessment in all four skills Further reading to explore the language of the unit and cultural themes			

4A Modestadt Berlin!

4A.1 Die Jeans ist cool!

Seite 120–121

Planner

Objectives
- Vocabulary: talk about clothes and say what you think of them
- Grammar: singular noun + *ist*, plural noun + *sind*
- Skills: recycle previously learned language to express opinions; identify cognates and false friends

Video
- Video clip 4A

Resources
- Student Book, pages 120–121
- CD 2, track 50
- Foundation and Higher Workbooks, page 64
- Workbook audio: CD 3 and 4, track 66
- Copymasters 87 (ex. 1–2), 88 (ex. 1), 91 (ex. 1)
- Interactive OxBox, Unit 4A

Key language
der Kapuzenpullover, der Mantel, der Pullover, der Rock
die Bluse, die Hose, die Jacke, die Jeans, die Lederjacke
das Hemd, das Kleid, das T-Shirt
die Ballerinas, die Shorts, die Sportschuhe, die Stiefel
Wie findest du …? Wie gefällt dir …? Gefällt dir …?
Ich mag … (nicht). … gefällt mir (nicht). Ich finde …
hässlich, cool, schick, schön, alt, neu, modisch, altmodisch,
bequem, unbequem, teuer, billig, lässig
sehr, total, ziemlich

Framework references
L&S 1.1, 1.2, 1.3, 1.4; R&W 2.4, 2.5; KAL 4.2, 4.3, 4.4, 4.5; LLS 5.1, 5.3, 5.5

Starters
- Copymaster 87, ex. 1–2.
- Student Book page 120, *Think*.
- Revise colours by eliciting the colours of items a–l on page 120. For a quick competitive starter, set a time limit and challenge students (in pairs) to list in German all the colours they can see in a–l. When the time is up, go through the colours: who has the most?
- When students have learned the clothes vocabulary a–l for homework, begin a lesson by asking them each to choose five clothes words to test their partner on. Explain that three points are available per item: one point if they can say it correctly (no point if their pronunciation sounds English!), another point if they can write / spell it accurately and give its gender, and a third if they can put it into a sentence (e.g. by giving an opinion of it or saying what colour it is).

Plenaries
- At the end of your first lesson on clothes, students test each other in pairs to see how many of clothing items a–l they can remember: one partner checks against the book while the other recites as many as possible (including colours, if you wish), then they swap over. Who remembers the most? Follow this up by asking them to learn the clothes vocabulary (including spellings and genders) for homework: see first homework suggestion below.
- Working in pairs, each student notes down the letters of their four favourite clothing items on page 120 (a–l), keeping them hidden from their partner. They try to guess each other's favourites, e.g.
  A: *Magst du die Jeans?*
  B: *Nein! Die Jeans ist total hässlich.*
  A: *Magst du …?*
  Encourage them to give reasons for their opinions and to speak with appropriate tone of voice and facial expression. The winner is the person who works out their partner's favourites in the fewest guesses.

Homework
- Challenge students to learn the clothing vocabulary (a–l), including spellings and genders. In a following lesson, they work in pairs testing each other: see third starter activity.
- Student Book page 121, *Challenge*.

Video clip 4A: Ein Imagewechsel für Ali!
Synopsis:
L&S 1.1, 1.2

Ali confesses to Kathi that he wants to change his image (to impress Nina), so Kathi suggests going shopping with him. They go first to a market, but Kathi isn't keen on the clothes there. Then she takes him to a designer shop where they have a lot more success.

Later, they meet Nico and Nina outside the cinema. Ali is wearing his new shirt and Nina looks impressed – is she beginning to see him in a new light?

Play the video through a couple of times and ask questions to check that students understand the gist of it. When they are familiar with the clothing vocabulary (from ex. 1) and adjectives (ex. 2), ask them to identify any that come up in the clip. Draw attention to the word *Turnschuhe* in Ali's first couple of lines: *Sportschuhe* is the word introduced in ex. 1, but students may remember *Turnen* from Unit 1B.

4A.1 Modestadt Berlin!

Talk about the colours of the clothes we see on the video.

🎥 Video clip 4A

Ali: Ich bin mir nicht sicher, was ich will … es ist nur … ich habe das Gefühl … ich trage immer das Gleiche. Blaue Jeans, weiße Turnschuhe, weißes T-Shirt und diese Jacke. Jeden Tag!
Kathi: Ich mag diese Jacke! Sie ist echt cool.
Ali: Ja, du magst sie vielleicht … aber Ni…
Kathi: Verstehe … hör mal … du kennst dich mit vielem aus, aber in Sachen Kleidung bin ich die Expertin!

(at the market)
Ali: Wie findest du das karierte Hemd? Ich finde es schick.
Kathi: Ich mag es nicht. Ich denke, es steht dir nicht.
Ali: Und das gestreifte T-Shirt? Wie findest du es?
Kathi: Ich finde es hässlich.
Ali: Wie findest du den grauen Pullover? Ich mag ihn.
Kathi: Ja … Du kannst ihn ja mal anprobieren. Ich passe auf deine Jacke auf.
Ali: Schau mal! Der Pullover ist sehr bequem. Ich mag ihn.
Kathi: *(doubtful)* Ja, es geht …
Ali: Und gar nicht teuer!
Kathi: Bequem, aber nicht cool!
Ali: Nicos Bruder, Ralf, sieht immer cool aus …
Kathi: Ja, er ist echt cool. Viel cooler als Nico …
Kathi: Ich denke, wir werden hier nichts finden. Ich zeige dir mal einen richtigen Laden.

(in a designer boutique)
Kathi: Also, welches gefällt dir besser? Das weiße T-Shirt oder das blaue?
Ali: Äh … das blaue ist netter, finde ich.
Kathi: Möchtest du dieses Hemd anprobieren?
Ali: Ralf trägt nur T-Shirts … äh … ich meine … T-Shirts sind cooler …
Kathi: Ja, viel cooler … hey, gefällt dir diese Jacke?
Ali: Ja, ich finde, sie sieht ganz gut aus. Anprobieren kostet ja nichts.

(he tries lots of clothes on)
Ali: Und, wie gefällt dir die Jeans?
Kathi: Ja, die Jeans finde ich gut, aber das T-Shirt …
Kathi: Oh ja … dieses T-Shirt gefällt mir besser …
Kathi: Schau mal, Ali. Der Pulli ist kürzer als das T-Shirt.
Ali: Ist das ein Problem? …
Ali: Und wie ist dieser Pulli?
Kathi: Ich weiß nicht … der Pulli ist schon länger, aber die Farbe ist nicht gut … ein bisschen zu knallig, finde ich …

Ali: Und?
Kathi: Oh ja! In dem Outfit siehst du viel cooler aus. Viel entspannter. Und auch ein bisschen älter, intelligenter …
Ali: Äh … Kathi … bin ich in diesem Outfit auch reicher?! …
Kathi: Dieses Hemd ist auch schön.
Ali: Einverstanden. Ich nehme es.

(later, outside the cinema)
Ali: Also, du ziehst vielleicht zurück nach Österreich – ich kann es nicht glauben.
Kathi: Ich kann es auch nicht glauben. Dabei liebe ich Berlin jetzt. Die Stadt ist super – sogar besser als Wien! … Ah … ich sehe sie schon.
Ali: Ich sehe Nico, aber wo ist Nina?
Nina: Äh …
Ali: Hi Nina.
Nina: Hi Ali.
Ali: Gehen wir rein?
Ali: Warte … lass mich die Tür öffnen …
Nina: Danke.

Sprachpunkt

Wie findest du das karierte Hemd?
Ich finde es schick.
Der Pullover ist sehr bequem. Ich mag ihn.
Wie gefällt dir die Jeans?
Der Pulli ist kürzer als das T-Shirt.

LLS 5.3, 5.5 Think

This skills box draws attention to one cognate (*die Jeans*) and one false friend (*die Hose*) in the clothing items (a–l). Ask students to identify other cognates and friends, first among the clothing items and then in the *Vokabular* lists at the end of each unit.

AT 1.1 / AT 3.1~2 1 Hör zu (1–12). Was ist die richtige Reihenfolge?

Students listen and match clothing items 1–12 to the pictures and captions a–l.
Point out the three compound nouns among the clothing items: *der Kapuzenpullover, die Lederjacke, die Sportschuhe*. Make sure students realise that each can be shortened to its final element: *der Pullover* – jumper, *die Jacke* – jacket, *die Schuhe* – shoes. Elicit the meanings of *die Kapuze* (hood) and *das Leder* (leather).

Answers: **1** e; **2** b; **3** l; **4** a; **5** h; **6** c; **7** g; **8** i; **9** f; **10** j; **11** d; **12** k

183

4A.1 Modestadt Berlin!

CD 2, track 50 — Seite 120, Übung 1

1 der Kapuzenpullover
2 der Pullover
3 die Shorts
4 der Rock
5 die Lederjacke
6 die Jeans
7 das Hemd
8 das T-Shirt
9 die Ballerinas
10 die Sportschuhe
11 das Kleid
12 die Stiefel

AT 3.1 — 2 Was passt zusammen?
Students match the German adjectives to their English equivalents.

Answers: *1 g; 2 i; 3 e; 4 b; 5 c; 6 j; 7 d; 8 h; 9 f; 10 a*

LLS 5.1 Follow-up
Point out that several words in ex. 2 end in *-isch*, *-ich* and *-ig*, and that these are common endings for German adjectives. Challenge students to suggest some others, e.g. *musikalisch, fantastisch, freundlich, sportlich, langweilig, lustig*.

This might be an appropriate point to work on the pronunciation focus of the unit (*isch, ich, ig*): see spread 4A.6 ex. 5–6.

KAL 4.3, 4.5 / LLS 5.3 — 3 Wähle das richtige Verb – *ist* oder *sind*?
Students fill in the missing verb (*ist* or *sind*) in each sentence.

Before they begin, read through the *Grammatik* box on page 121 on singular noun + singular verb (e.g. *der Rock ist* …) and plural noun + plural verb (*die Stiefel sind* …). Point out that *die Hose* and usually also *die Jeans* are singular in German, whereas in English they are treated as plural: *die Hose ist blau* – the trousers are blue. *Die Shorts* are usually plural, like in English: *die Shorts sind blau* – the shorts are blue.

Students may be interested to know that even among native German speakers opinion is divided on whether *Shorts* and *Jeans* should be singular or plural. In the case of words such as these that are borrowed from other languages, usage may vary. *Shorts*, for example, is a relatively young loan word, and although (in 2011) it is shown as a plural noun at its Duden dictionary entry and is widely used as a plural noun, this usage may change over time.

Answers: *a ist; b ist; c sind; d sind; e ist; f sind*

AT 2.2–3 — 4 Macht Sätze. Richtig oder falsch?
Students take turns to give true or false descriptions of clothes a–l on page 120. Their partner decides whether each description is true or false. Encourage them to use *sehr*, *ziemlich* and *total* to give more precise descriptions.

KAL 4.2, 4.4 — Think
Students are reminded of different ways to express opinions: *ich finde* … + *sehr / ziemlich / total* + adjective, *ich mag* … (*nicht*). Challenge them to suggest another expression, which they learned on spread 2B.1: *es gefällt mir* (*gut / nicht*). They are also encouraged to use linking words like *denn* and *aber* to add detail to their opinions. Point out that in German there must always be a comma before *denn* and *aber* (e.g. *Ich mag das Hemd, denn es ist modisch*), whereas in English the comma before "because" and "but" is generally optional, e.g. I like the shirt(,) because it's fashionable.

AT 3.3 — 5 Was ist die richtige Reihenfolge?
Students read the jumbled sentences expressing opinions of clothes. They copy them out with the words in the correct order. These sentences can be used as models for expressing opinions when students do the *Challenge* activity.

Answers: **a** *Ich finde die Lederjacke blöd, aber der Rock ist cool.* **b** *Ich mag die Stiefel nicht, denn sie sind unbequem.* **c** *Die Jeans ist schick, aber teuer.* **d** *Die Bluse ist unbequem, denn sie ist altmodisch.*

L&S 1.3, 1.4 — Follow-up
- Play the video clip again and challenge students to identify different ways to ask for and give opinions. Challenge them to work out the meaning of *es steht dir nicht* (it doesn't suit you) and *es geht* (it's OK / so-so). Focus on Kathi's facial expressions, body language and tone of voice – it's often possible to work out what she thinks from these alone, without understanding what she says.
- Students talk about the clothes in ex. 1, describing them and exchanging their opinions. Encourage them to speak with appropriate facial expression and tone of voice. For a variation on this, see the second plenary in the *Planner* above.

AT 4.3–4 / R&W 2.4, 2.5 — Challenge
Students imagine they are fashion journalists. They create a fashion scrapbook containing pictures of at least ten items of clothing, with a description of each one and their opinion. Encourage them to use dictionaries to research new language.

Encourage them to use a range of structures to express opinions, as in the *Think* activity and ex. 5.

4A.2 Modestadt Berlin!

4A.2 Coole Outfits

Seite 122–123

Planner

Objectives
- Vocabulary: say what you usually wear and what you would like to wear
- Grammar: the accusative case (*ich trage einen / eine / ein* + adjective + noun); present tense of *tragen*; *ich möchte* + infinitive
- Skills: identify language patterns; apply knowledge of grammar (the accusative) in a new context

Resources
- Student Book, pages 122–123
- CD 2, track 51
- Foundation and Higher Workbooks, page 65
- Copymasters 91 (ex. 2), 92
- Interactive OxBox, Unit 4A

Key language
Ich trage einen gelben Rock / eine blaue Bluse / ein grünes Top / schwarze Schuhe.
Ich möchte eine schicke Jeans tragen / kaufen / haben.
Ich möchte einkaufen gehen. Ich möchte (modisch / cool / schick / lässig) sein.
bunt
normalerweise

Framework references
R&W 2.4, 2.5; KAL 4.3, 4.4, 4.5; LLS 5.1, 5.8

Starters
- Before students begin ex. 1, set a time limit for them to identify in texts a–d two professions, eight clothing items, six colours and seven other adjectives. When the allocated time is up, check to see if anyone has managed to note down all the items requested.
- Give students a few moments to try to memorise the clothes and colours in the photos, then ask them to close their books. Name one of the people (or groups of people) and challenge the class to give you as much information as they can about what they are wearing, e.g.

Teacher: *Heidi Klum!*
Student A: *Sie trägt eine graue Jacke.*
Student B: *Sie trägt auch ein schwarz-weißes Top.*
Repeat with the other photos.
For a less challenging alternative, describe some of the clothes featured on this spread, giving a mixture of true and false information, and ask the class to spot what is false, e.g.
Teacher: *Der Fußballspieler Michael Ballack trägt ein schwarzes T-Shirt.*
Class: *Nein, das T-Shirt ist weiß und schwarz.*

Plenaries
- Students write a few gap-fill sentences to test their partner on adjective endings, e.g. *Ich trage ein_ blau_ Jeans und ein weiß_ Hemd. Sie trägt ein schick_ Kleid.* Tell them to prepare an answer sheet too. Students then swap sentences with their partner, fill in the missing endings and check against each other's answer sheet.
- Suggest the names of a few famous people or cartoon characters and challenge pairs to come up with a short text for one or two of them, saying what they usually wear and what they would like to wear. Try to suggest people (or cartoon characters) who are known for wearing a particular style of clothing, e.g. the prime minister or US president (smart but conventional), actors, musicians and models (chic and fashionable), so that students have the opportunity to suggest a complete contrast, e.g. *Ich heiße Victoria Beckham. Ich trage normalerweise ein kleines schwarzes Kleid … Ich möchte eine lässige Jeans und ein altes billiges T-Shirt tragen.* Invite pairs to read out their texts to the class: this should give them some ideas for *Challenge*.

Homework
- Students find photos of their favourite stars and write descriptions of their clothing.
- Student Book page 123, *Challenge!*

AT 3.3–4 **1 Sieh dir die Bilder an und lies die Texte. In jedem Text gibt es zwei Fehler.**
See the *Planner* above for a starter activity before students begin ex. 1. Students then read the descriptions of clothes worn by celebrities and compare them with the photos. They identify two false details (colours) in each description. As a follow-up activity, ask students to choose their favourite photo and translate the corresponding text into English.

Answers: **a** <u>blaue</u> Jeans, <u>gelbe</u> Hosen; **b** ein <u>grünes</u> T-Shirt, <u>grüne</u> Shorts; **c** eine <u>schwarz-weiße</u> Jacke, ein <u>blaues</u> T-Shirt; **d** ein <u>rot-weißes</u> Top, eine <u>gelbe</u> Jacke

4A.2 Modestadt Berlin!

KAL 4.3
LLS 5.1

Think

Students identify different forms of *ein* in texts a–d. They will find only two forms in the texts (*ein, eine*); elicit from them a third form that they've met before (*einen*).
Discuss the contexts in which students have met *einen / eine / ein*, e.g. talking about brothers, sisters and pets (unit 1A), saying what there is in your bedroom (unit 2B) or in your town (Unit 3B). Focus on the adjectives that follow *einen / eine / ein*, in the texts and in the language box at the bottom of the page. Elicit from students that the adjective endings are: masculine *-en*, feminine *-e*, neuter *-es*.

AT 2.3
KAL 4.3, 4.5

2 A beschreibt ein Bild. B gibt einen Punkt für jeden richtigen Satz.

Before students begin ex. 2, make sure they are comfortable with the adjective endings shown in the language box at the bottom of page 122. Point out that no matter how many adjectives there are before a noun, they all have the same ending, e.g. *Sie trägt einen langen schwarzen modischen Rock*. Refer them to the full present tense conjugation of *tragen* in the language box. Students then take turns to choose a photo and describe it. Their partner awards one point for each correct sentence. Emphasise that in order to be eligible for a point their sentences must be correct grammatically as well as in terms of colours, etc.

AT 4.3–4

3 Schreib Sätze.

Students choose one of the photos from ex. 2 and write a detailed description of what the person is wearing. Encourage them to use as many adjectives as they can and to express their opinions too.

AT 1.4–5

4 Hör zu. Was tragen Lena, Jimi und Heidi? Was möchten sie kaufen?

Students listen and identify what each person usually wears and what they would like to buy. Encourage them to note down the expressions of time and frequency for use in the *Follow-up* suggested below.

Answers: **Lena:** *usually wears comfortable jeans and a black T-shirt, would like to buy new trainers (at the weekend);* **Jimi:** *wears a casual hoodie and cheap trousers (every day), would like to buy a leather jacket (next weekend) because would like to look smart;* **Heidi:** *likes to wear a fashionable skirt, would like to buy a fashionable blouse (to go with her skirt)*

🎧 **CD 2, track 51**   Seite 123, Übung 4

Lena: In meiner Freizeit trage ich normalerweise bequeme Kleidung. Ich trage eine bequeme Jeans und ein schwarzes T-Shirt. Am Wochenende möchte ich neue Sportschuhe kaufen.

Jimi: Ich mag Kapuzenpullis. Ich trage jeden Tag einen lässigen Kapuzenpulli und eine billige Hose. Nächstes Wochenende möchte ich eine Lederjacke kaufen, denn ich möchte schick aussehen.

Heidi: Ich trage gern einen modischen Rock und ich möchte eine modische Bluse für meinen Rock kaufen.

KAL 4.4, 4.5
LLS 5.1

Think

Read through the *Think* box on *möchten* and point out the sentence structure in the key language box. Ask students what they notice about the position of the infinitives: they are at the end of the sentence. Play the ex. 4 recording again, focusing on the sentences that contain *ich möchte / möchte ich*, and ask students to raise their hand when they hear the infinitives at the end of the corresponding sentences.
Students then consider which other verbs they've met that have a similar effect on the infinitive (e.g. *Du sollst … essen / trinken, Willst du ins Kino gehen?, Man kann Rad fahren*).
For further practice of *ich möchte* + infinitive, set a time limit and challenge students to come up with as many sentences as they can in different contexts, e.g. *ich möchte … einen Hund haben / Fußball spielen / einen Hamburger essen / in einem Dorf wohnen*.

Follow-up

Challenge students to reconstruct the three texts from ex. 4, using their notes from the listening activity. Encourage them to include any time expressions they may have noted down, e.g. Lena: *Ich trage (normalerweise) eine bequeme Jeans und ein schwarzes T-Shirt. Ich möchte (am Wochenende) neue Sportschuhe kaufen*. Then play the recording again so that they can check their reconstructions against the originals.

AT 4.4–5
R&W 2.4, 2.5
LLS 5.8

Challenge

Students describe what three people usually wear and what they would like to wear in the future or for a special occasion. They are encouraged to illustrate their work with pictures, showing the people in their everyday clothing and in the clothing they would like to buy. See the *Planner* above for a plenary suggestion to give students some ideas for this.

4A.3 Modestadt Berlin!

Point out that this activity provides an opportunity to work towards level 5 in writing, because it asks students to refer to two different time frames (everyday experiences and future plans).

Discuss strategies for improving written work. Refer students to the *Think* box towards the end of spread 3B.1 and the advice in the skills section on spread 4A.6. See also the teaching notes for spread 3A.1 ex. 8.

4A.3 Wir gehen einkaufen! Seite 124–125

Planner

Objectives
- Vocabulary: go shopping for clothes; give opinions of clothes
- Grammar: the accusative case (*der* becomes *den*); object pronouns (*ihn, sie, es*)
- Skills: identify language patterns

Video
- Video clip 4A

Resources
- Student Book, pages 124–125
- CD 2, tracks 52–53
- Foundation and Higher Workbooks, page 66
- Workbook audio: CD 3 and 4, track 67
- Copymasters 89, 90 (ex. 1–3)
- Interactive OxBox, Unit 4A

Key language
Wie findest du (den karierten Rock / die blaue Hose / das gestreifte Hemd)?
Ich finde ihn / sie / es … (+ opinion adjectives).
(zu) teuer, (zu) groß, (zu) klein, (zu) altmodisch
Wie gefällt dir …? Wie ist …?
… gefällt mir (nicht). Ich mag ihn / sie / es (nicht).
Es steht dir nicht. Es geht.
Wie kann ich dir helfen? Ich möchte … anprobieren, bitte.
Natürlich. Die Kabine ist um die Ecke / hier links / hier rechts.
Ich kaufe ihn / sie / es nicht, danke. Ich möchte ihn / sie / es (nicht) kaufen.

Framework references
L&S 1.1, 1.4; KAL 4.2, 4.3; LLS 5.1, 5.6

Starters
- Before playing the video clip for ex. 1, ask students to spot the following in the script (page 124, ex. 1): four clothing items, one colour and seven other adjectives, three structures for expressing opinions (*Ich finde es …, Ich mag … (nicht), Ich denke …*). Challenge them to work out the meaning of *Es geht* (It's so-so / OK / nothing special).
- The grid on page 125 (ex. 3) can be used for other games as well as the suggested *Vier gewinnt*, e.g.
- Bingo. Students note down several grid coordinates and listen as you describe some of the items. They cross out the coordinates of any items you mention. The first person to cross out all their coordinates wins.
- Memory game. Student B has a few moments to memorise the location of items in the grid, then closes his / her book; A keeps the book open and tests B's memory, e.g.
A: *4, 2?*
B: *Äh … der karierte Rock? Ich möchte ihn kaufen.*
Make sure they swap roles so that they both have a turn at remembering.
- Battleships. In pairs, each student notes down a few coordinates (these represent the location of their "battleships"), keeping them hidden from their partner. They try to "sink" each other's ships by locating them, e.g. if B has noted down the coordinates 2, 1 and A says *Ich mag das karierte Hemd – ich möchte es kaufen*), B's ship is sunk. The first person to sink all their partner's ships is the winner. These games can be tailored to the ability of the class, e.g. for battleships and the memory game you could insist that able students produce one or more full sentences in order to win each square, including adjectives and object pronouns.

Plenaries
- Play the video clip from ex. 1 again (just the section where Kathi and Ali are in the market), with the sound turned down, and ask students to keep their books closed. Pause the clip at key moments and challenge students to suggest appropriate dialogue, e.g.
Ali: *Magst du das karierte Hemd?*
Kathi: *Nein, es ist total hässlich!*
Ali: *Wie findest du das gestreifte T-Shirt?*
Kathi: *Ich finde es …*
- See second starter activity: these games are suitable either as plenaries or starters.
- Student Book page 125, ex. 6. Alternatively, ask students to make up their own dialogue involving a customer who is very difficult to please, e.g. doesn't like the colour, finds the clothes either old-fashioned or too modern, too big or too small, etc.

Homework
- Student Book page 124, ex. 2.
- Student Book page 125, *Challenge*.

4A.3 Modestadt Berlin!

1 Sieh dir das Video an und lies den Dialog. Beantworte die Fragen.

AT 1.4
AT 3.4
LLS 5.6

Before playing the video clip, see the *Planner* above for a starter activity based on the script. Then play the section in which Kathi and Ali are browsing through clothes at the market. Students read the script and answer questions in English.

The video can be used for oral practice: students practise reading the script aloud, trying to keep in time with the video and aiming for authentic pronunciation and intonation. Turn down the sound and challenge pairs of confident students to speak on behalf of Ali and Kathi.

Answers: **1** it's smart; **2** it doesn't suit him; **3** it's ugly; **4** the jumper; **5** it's OK / comfortable but not cool

---

Video clip 4A
CD 2, track 52   Seite 124, Übung 1

Ali: Wie findest du das karierte Hemd? Ich finde es schick.
Kathi: Ich mag es nicht. Ich denke, es steht dir nicht.
Ali: Und das gestreifte T-Shirt? Wie findest du es?
Kathi: Ich finde es hässlich.
Ali: Wie findest du den grauen Pullover? Ich mag ihn.
Kathi: Ja … Du kannst ihn ja mal anprobieren. Ich passe auf deine Jacke auf.
Ali: Schau mal! Der Pullover ist sehr bequem. Ich mag ihn.
Kathi: *(doubtful)* Ja, es geht …
Ali: Und gar nicht teuer!
Kathi: Bequem, aber nicht cool!
Ali: Nicos Bruder, Ralf, sieht immer cool aus …
Kathi: Ja, er ist echt cool. Viel cooler als Nico …
Kathi: Ich denke, wir werden hier nichts finden. Ich zeige dir mal einen richtigen Laden.

---

2 Füll die Lücken aus: *ihn / sie / es* oder *sie*?

KAL 4.2, 4.3
LLS 5.1

Students fill in the missing object pronouns. Refer them to the *Grammatik* box on the accusative case and to the *Think* box on direct object pronouns.

As a follow-up, ask students to identify examples of direct object pronouns in the video script (ex. 1): there is no example of *sie*, so challenge students to make up their own, e.g. *Wie findest du die Jacke? Ich mag sie*.

Answers: **a** ihn; **b** sie; **c** es; **d** sie; **e** ihn; **f** sie

---

3 Ein Spiel. Vier gewinnt!

AT 2.4–5
L&S 1.4
KAL 4.3

Before students begin playing this game, point out the key language box below ex. 3, which provides a structure and model sentences to help them play the game. Emphasise that students must take care to use the correct form of the definite article (*den / die / das*), adjective endings and object pronouns (*ihn / sie / es*), as shown in the key language box.

Students will need eight counters each (these could just be small pieces of scrap paper). Student A chooses a couple of grid coordinates (e.g. *4, 2*) and asks B for his / her opinion. Encourage them to speak with appropriate tone of voice and facial expressions, e.g.
A: *Wie findest du (4, 2) den karierten Rock?*
B: (enthusiastically) *Ich finde ihn klasse! Ich möchte ihn kaufen!*
If B gives a grammatically correct answer, he / she may place a counter on the corresponding square. It is then B's turn to ask and A's turn to answer. The first person to place four counters in a row wins.

---

4 Hör zu. Wer kauft was? Warum (nicht)?

AT 1.4–5
L&S 1.1

Students listen to four conversations in a clothes shop. They note what each person is interested in and whether or not they buy it, including the reason why. Encourage them to note down as much information as they can on the first listening; play the recording again and ask them to fill in extra details.

Answers: **a Julia:** red skirt, doesn't buy it – too small; **b Jürgen:** white trousers, buys them – likes them very much / very comfortable; **c Michi:** striped shirt and red hoodie, buys the shirt – likes it / it's very smart / chic, doesn't buy the hoodie – doesn't like the colour; **d Doro:** striped jumper and yellow T-shirt, buys the T-shirt – very cool, doesn't buy the jumper – uncomfortable and old-fashioned

4A.4 Modestadt Berlin!

🎧 **CD 2, track 53** Seite 125, Übung 4

a Verkäuferin: Wie kann ich dir helfen?
Julia: Ich möchte den roten Rock anprobieren.
Verkäuferin: Bitte schön. Hier ist die Kabine. …
Verkäuferin: Wie findest du den Rock?
Julia: Er ist zu klein. Ich kaufe ihn nicht, danke.

b Verkäufer: Wie kann ich dir helfen?
Jürgen: Ich möchte die weiße Hose anprobieren.
Verkäufer: Ja, bitte schön. Die Kabine ist um die Ecke. …
Verkäufer: Und? Wie gefällt dir die Hose?
Jürgen: Sie gefällt mir sehr. Ich finde sie sehr bequem. Ich möchte sie kaufen.

c Verkäufer: Möchtest du das gestreifte Hemd anprobieren?
Michi: Ja, bitte. Und auch den roten Kapuzenpulli.
Verkäufer: Natürlich. Die Kabine ist hier links.
Michi: Danke schön. …
Verkäufer: Wie gefällt dir das Hemd?
Michi: Das Hemd gefällt mir gut – es ist sehr schick, aber ich mag den Kapuzenpulli nicht. Ich mag die Farbe nicht. Ich möchte das Hemd kaufen.

d Verkäuferin: Was darf es sein?
Doro: Ich möchte den gestreiften Pullover und das gelbe T-Shirt anprobieren, bitte.
Verkäuferin: Die Kabine ist rechts, da.
Doro: Okay, danke. …
Verkäuferin: Und? Wie findest du sie?
Doro: Ich möchte das T-Shirt kaufen – ich finde es sehr cool. Aber ich möchte den Pullover nicht – er ist nicht bequem und ich finde ihn zu altmodisch.

AT 3.3 **5 Was ist die richtige Reihenfolge?**
Students rearrange the sentences into the correct order to build a shopping dialogue.

Answers: c, b, f, a, e, d

AT 2.3–4 **6 👥 Macht Einkaufsdialoge mit den Bildern.**
Students make up shopping dialogues to match pictures a–c. Ex. 5 can be used as a basic model, but encourage students to expand it to include extra detail.

AT 4.4–5 **Challenge**
Students choose an outfit from one of the pictures in this unit (or they could find a picture in a magazine, clothing catalogue or on the internet). They describe the clothes, saying whether they like them or not and why, and whether they would like to buy them.
Remind students of strategies for improving written work. Refer them to the *Think* box towards the end of spread 3B.1 and the advice in the skills section on spread 4A.6. See also the teaching notes for spread 3A.1 ex. 8.

4A.4 Die Hose ist zu klein! Seite 126–127

Planner

Objectives
- Vocabulary: talk about problems with clothes and say what clothes you're going to buy
- Grammar: the future tense (*werden* + infinitive); the comparative (e.g. *kleiner als*)
- Skills: prepare for and evaluate language tasks

Video
- Video clip 4A

Resources
- Student Book, pages 126–127
- CD 2, track 54
- Foundation and Higher Workbooks, page 67
- Workbook audio: CD 3 and 4, track 68
- Copymasters 87 (ex. 3), 88 (ex. 3), 90 (ex. 4)
- Interactive OxBox, Unit 4A

Key language
Mein neuer Rock ist zu groß. Meine neue Hose ist zu klein. Mein Outfit ist zu alt.
Deshalb werde ich einkaufen gehen. Ich werde ihn / sie / es umtauschen. Ich werde ihn / sie / es eine Größe größer / kleiner kaufen. Ich werde ein neues Outfit kaufen. Ich möchte gut aussehen.
Die Bluse ist (viel) besser als das T-Shirt.

Framework references
R&W 2.4, 2.5; KAL 4.3, 4.4, 4.5; LLS 5.1, 5.3, 5.7, 5.8

4A.4 Modestadt Berlin!

Starters
- Copymaster 87, ex. 3.
- Before students attempt ex. 1, ask them to identify the following elements in the three texts: three items of clothing (*eine Hose, eine Bluse, mein Rock*), two days of the week (*Samstag, Freitag*), eight adjectives (*alt, neu, modisch, lässig, groß, schick, klein, gut*), one object pronoun (*ihn*), the name of a clothes shop (*Esprit*), two computer games (*Wii, Super Mario Galaxy*).
- Student Book page 127, ex. 3: students match the German adjectives to their comparative forms.

Plenaries
- Display some sentences in the present tense and challenge students to rewrite them in the future. Try to cover a range of contexts, e.g. *Ich spiele Gitarre, Wir essen Schokolade, Am Wochenende fahre ich Skateboard, Wir lernen Deutsch, Am Freitag gehe ich ins Kino, Ich trage eine neue Jeans*. If necessary, provide the infinitives for students to choose from. See also first homework suggestion.
- Student Book page 127, ex. 5.
- To encourage students to use the comparative with other topics, begin by brainstorming adjectives from a range of contexts (e.g. *langweilig, interessant, nett, sportlich, fleißig, faul, groß, lustig, nützlich, musikalisch*) and write them on the board, then call out the names of famous people, TV programmes and nouns from different topics (e.g. school subjects, places in town, hobbies, family members, pets) and ask students to compare them:
Teacher: *Meine Mutter und meine Schwester.*
Student A: *Meine Mutter ist fleißiger als meine Schwester!*
Teacher: *David und Victoria Beckham.*
Student B: *David ist sportlicher als Victoria.*

Homework
- Following on from the first plenary suggestion, challenge students to write a few sentences in the future tense about some or all of the following topics: sport, other hobbies or leisure activities, clothes, food and drink. They could do this from the point of view of their favourite sports personalities, actors, musicians, cartoon characters, etc., e.g. *Ich heiße Andy Murray: Am Wochenende werde ich Tennis spielen. Ich heiße Bart Simpson: Ich werde Skateboard fahren. Ich heiße Lisa Simpson: Ich werde lesen.*
- See third plenary suggestion: students continue this for homework. Provide a list of people or things to compare, or suggest broad categories, e.g. compare two sports, two hobbies, two school subjects, two family members, two sports personalities, two TV programmes, etc.
- Student Book page 127, *Challenge*.

AT 1.4–5
AT 3.4–5
KAL 4.4, 4.5
LLS 5.1

1 Hör zu und lies. Wer sagt was?
These texts about problems with clothes and shopping plans introduce the future tense: *werden* + infinitive. See the *Planner* above for a suggested starter activity to help students identify familiar language in the texts.
Read through the *Grammatik* box and ask students to identify examples of the future tense in the texts. Point out that if there is more than one clause in the sentence, the infinitive goes to the end of the clause rather than the end of the sentence, e.g. *Am besten werde ich Freitag in die Stadt fahren und ein neues Outfit kaufen.*
Elicit from students what other structures send the infinitive to the end of the sentence (or clause). They may suggest modal verbs (*können, wollen* and *sollen*) and should also spot *ich möchte gut aussehen* in Nico's text.
Students then read and listen to the texts and work out which person says each of English statements a–g.

Answers: **a** Nico; **b** Kathi; **c** Nico; **d** Kathi; **e** Nina; **f** Nico; **g** Kathi

CD 2, track 54   Seite 126, Übung 1

Nina: Ich habe am Samstag eine Party, aber es gibt ein Problem: mein Outfit ist zu alt. Am besten werde ich Freitag in die Stadt fahren und ein neues Outfit kaufen. Vielleicht werde ich eine modische Hose und eine lässige Bluse kaufen.

Kathi: Mein neuer Rock von Esprit ist zu groß. Ali und ich werden ihn umtauschen. Er ist total schick, aber ich werde ihn eine Größe kleiner kaufen.

Nico: Ich interessiere mich nicht für Mode, aber ich möchte gut aussehen. Deshalb werde ich einkaufen gehen. Dann werde ich Ali besuchen und wir werden Wii spielen. Super Mario Galaxy ist unser Lieblingsspiel.

Follow-up
To exploit the texts further, ask questions about the content, e.g.
1 When is Nina's party?
2 What is Nina's problem?
3 What is the best solution to her problem and when will she do this?
4 What does Nina plan to buy?
5 Which shop is Kathi's skirt from?
6 What do Kathi and Nico say about Ali?

4A.4 Modestadt Berlin!

Answers: **1** Saturday; **2** her outfit is too old; **3** go into town and buy a new outfit on Friday; **4** fashionable trousers and a casual blouse; **5** Esprit; **6** Kathi is going to go with Ali to exchange her skirt, Nico is going to go to Ali's house to play computer games

AT 2.4

2 👥 **Macht Dialoge. Was wirst du machen?**
Students imagine they are going to Nina's party on Saturday. They make up dialogues about shopping plans and what they're going to wear, to practise *werden* + infinitive.

LLS 5.7, 5.8

Think
Discuss with students what makes ex. 2 a level 4 activity rather than level 5, and how it could be developed to make it level 5. Point out that the conversation refers entirely to the future, whereas for level 5 there would usually need to be more than one time frame involved. There would also need to be more evidence of expressing and justifying opinions and producing extended responses. Elicit suggestions as to how this could be done, e.g. by mentioning an item of clothing that they already have and explaining their opinion of it:
A: *Was wirst du am Wochenende kaufen?*
B: *Ich werde einen schwarzen Rock kaufen. Ich habe einen schwarzen Rock, aber ich mag ihn nicht, denn er ist ziemlich lang und ich finde, er ist zu groß …*

KAL 4.3
LLS 5.3

3 Was passt zusammen?
Read through the *Grammatik* box on how to form the comparative in German. Point out that both English and German add *-er* to adjectives to form the comparative (*klein – kleiner*, small – smaller); but whereas with longer adjectives English usually puts the word "more" before the adjective instead of adding *-er*, German adds *-er* regardless of the length of the adjective (*altmodisch – altmodischer*, old-fashioned – more old-fashioned; *intelligent – intelligenter*, intelligent – more intelligent).
Students match the adjectives to their corresponding comparative forms. Ask them to translate the comparatives into English.

Answers: **1** d; **2** f; **3** g; **4** a; **5** e; **6** b; **7** c

4 Was ist der richtige Komparativ?
Students write the comparative form of some common adjectives.

Answers: **a** bequemer; **b** langweiliger; **c** schicker; **d** toller; **e** netter; **f** lauter

Follow-up
Play the section of video clip 4A set in the designer clothes shop. Challenge students to spot all the comparatives and translate them into English.

Answers: see underlining in transcript: *welches gefällt dir besser?* (which do you like best?); *das blaue ist netter* (the blue one is nicer); *T-Shirts sind cooler* (T-shirts are cooler); *viel cooler* (much cooler); *dieses T-Shirt gefällt mir besser* (I like this T-shirt better); *der Pulli ist kürzer als das T-Shirt* (the jumper is shorter than the T-shirt); *der Pulli ist schon länger* (the jumper is longer); *siehst du viel cooler aus* (you look much cooler); *viel entspannter* (much more relaxed); *ein bisschen älter, intelligenter* (a bit older, more intelligent); *bin ich in diesem Outfit auch reicher?!* (am I also richer in these clothes?!)

Video clip 4A (excerpt)

Kathi: Also, <u>welches gefällt dir besser?</u> Das weiße T-Shirt oder das blaue?
Ali: Äh … <u>das blaue ist netter</u>, finde ich.
Kathi: Möchtest du dieses Hemd anprobieren?
Ali: Ralf trägt nur T-Shirts … äh … ich meine … <u>T-Shirts sind cooler</u> …
Kathi: Ja, <u>viel cooler</u> … hey, gefällt dir diese Jacke?
Ali: Ja, ich finde, sie sieht ganz gut aus. Anprobieren kostet ja nichts.
(he tries lots of clothes on)
Ali: Und, wie gefällt dir die Jeans?
Kathi: Ja, die Jeans finde ich gut, aber das T-Shirt …
Kathi: Oh ja … <u>dieses T-Shirt gefällt mir besser</u> …
Kathi: Schau mal, Ali. <u>Der Pulli ist kürzer als das T-Shirt</u>.
Ali: Ist das ein Problem? …
Ali: Und wie ist dieser Pulli?
Kathi: Ich weiß nicht … <u>der Pulli ist schon länger</u>, aber die Farbe ist nicht gut … ein bisschen zu knallig, finde ich …
Ali: Und?
Kathi: Oh ja! In dem Outfit <u>siehst du viel cooler aus</u>. <u>Viel entspannter</u>. Und auch <u>ein bisschen älter, intelligenter</u> …
Ali: Äh … Kathi … <u>bin ich in diesem Outfit auch reicher?!</u> …
Kathi: Dieses Hemd ist auch schön.
Ali: Einverstanden. Ich nehme es.

At 4.3–4

5 Schreib Sätze.
Students compare the items of clothing shown, using *als* (see *Grammatik* box). Refer them to page 120 for a reminder of the clothes vocabulary, and encourage them to add their opinions.

191

4A.5 Modestadt Berlin!

AT 4.4–5
R&W 2.4, 2.5
LLS 5.7, 5.8

Challenge
Students imagine they have been invited to a party and have €100 to spend on new clothes. They write a text of at least 80 words in which they: explain who is having the party and when; say where they'll go shopping for clothes and what they'll buy; compare the new clothes to their old clothes, and give their opinion. Discuss with students the criteria for achieving level 4–5. Point out that the task instructions guide them towards level 5 by asking them to refer to two different time frames (present and future). Elicit from them two different ways to refer to the future: *ich werde* + infinitive, *ich möchte* + infinitive.
Remind students again of strategies for improving written work and refer them to the *Think* box towards the end of spread 3B.1 and the skills section on spread 4A.6. See also the teaching notes for spread 3A.1 ex. 8.

4A.5 Das trage ich!   Seite 128–129

Planner

Objectives
- Vocabulary: talk about designer clothing and school uniform
- Grammar: use the first, second and third person singular of some common verbs (*tragen, kaufen*); *ich möchte* + infinitive
- Skills: adapt and build texts

Video
- Video blog 4A

Resources
- Student Book, pages 128–129
- CD 2, track 55
- Foundation and Higher Workbooks, page 68
- Workbook audio (Higher only): CD 4, track 69
- Copymaster 88 (ex. 2)
- Interactive OxBox, Unit 4A

Key language
Was trägst du gern? Ich trage …
Wo kaufst du ein? Ich kaufe meine Kleidung bei …
Trägst du eine Schuluniform?
Was trägst du in der Schule? In der Schule trage ich …
Wie findest du die Schuluniform?
Was möchtest du tragen? Ich möchte … tragen.
die Krawatte, die Schuluniform, die Straßenkleidung

Framework references
L&S 1.1, 1.2, 1.4, 1.5; R&W 2.4, 2.5; IU 3.1, 3.2; LLS 5.7, 5.8

Starters
- Before watching Ali's video blog (ex. 1), ask students to predict the answers to a–e. Then play the video so that they can check their predictions.
- Before students begin ex. 4, ask them to identify key words and phrases in the texts: four colours (*grau, weiß, schwarz, hellblau*), one comparative adjective (*besser*), eight other adjectives (*blöd, unbequem, hässlich, langweilig, gut, praktisch, schick, modisch*), ten items of clothing (*ein Rock, ein Hemd, eine Krawatte, eine Jacke, Schuhe, eine Jeans, ein T-Shirt, ein Pulli, eine Hose*), the German words for "school uniform", "designer clothing" and "street clothing" (*Schuluniform, Designerkleidung, Straßenkleidung*), two time expressions (*jeden Tag, normalerweise*), three linking words (*und, denn, aber*), a structure that sends the infinitive to the end of the clause or sentence (*ich möchte … tragen*).

Plenaries
- Student Book page 128, ex. 3.
- Student Book page 129, ex. 5.
- Teacher versus the class. Ask students to close their books, then start talking about the three teenagers featured on this spread (Ali, Paula and Jan), giving a mixture of true and false information. Students win a point for each false detail they spot, and an extra point if they can correct it; the teacher wins a point for each error the class fail to spot:
Teacher: *Paula trägt in der Schule eine Jeans und einen Pulli …*
Student A: *Falsch … sie trägt eine Schuluniform.* (= 2 points)
Teacher: *Ali ist sehr modisch …*
Student B: *Nein, er ist nicht sehr modisch.* (= 2 points)

Homework
- Students research the German fashion scene and Berlin Fashion Week on the internet (see *Follow-up* to ex. 1). Sites that may be of interest:
  – Young Germany (www.young-germany.de)
  – UK-German Connection (www.ukgermanconnection.org)
  – the Goethe Institut's "Meet The Germans" (www.goethe.de/ins/gb/lp/prj/mtg/enindex.htm).
- Students write and record a video blog about their clothing preferences, similar to Alis blog.
- Student Book page 129, *Challenge*.

4A.5 Modestadt Berlin!

1 Sieh dir Alis Videoblog an. Was ist die richtige Antwort?

AT 1.4
L&S 1.1, 1.2

Students watch Ali's video blog about clothes. They choose the correct option to complete each sentence a–e.

Answers: **a** *many;* **b** *doesn't think;* **c** *Wolfgang Joop;* **d** *H&M;* **e** *his own clothes*

Video blog 4A
CD 2, track 55   Seite 128, Übung 1

Es gibt viele Designer in Berlin – Berlin ist eine tolle Stadt für Mode, aber ich bin nicht sehr modisch! Was trage ich gern? Am liebsten trage ich eine blaue Jeans und ein weißes T-Shirt. Ich trage auch immer meine alte Lederjacke von Wolfgang Joop.
Und du? Was trägst du gern?
Wo kaufe ich ein? Ich mag die kleinen Boutiquen, wie Wunderkind und Wolfgang Joop. Aber ich kaufe meine Kleidung bei H&M. Die Kleidung ist gut und nicht zu teuer. Wo kaufst du ein?
Was trage ich in der Schule? In Deutschland gibt es keine Schuluniform, deshalb trage ich mein normales Outfit: Jeans, T-Shirt und Pumas, natürlich!
Was trägst du? Gibt es in Großbritannien eine Schuluniform?

IU 3.1, 3.2

Follow-up
Focus on the unit title (*Modestadt Berlin!*) and Ali's first sentence: *Es gibt viele Designer in Berlin – Berlin ist eine tolle Stadt für Mode.* Ask students for their impressions: would they have associated Berlin (or Germany) with fashion? Do they know anything about the German fashion scene? How many German designers can they name? Have they heard of Berlin Fashion Week? Ask them to research the fashion scene in Germany: see first homework suggestion in the *Planner* above.

2 Macht eine Klassenumfrage mit Alis Fragen. Fragt drei Personen und macht Notizen.

AT 2.3–4
L&S 1.4

Students carry out a survey about clothes. They ask three people the questions from Ali's video blog and make a note of the answers.

3 Schreib die Antworten aus Übung 2 auf.

AT 4.4

Students report the survey results using the *er / sie* form of the verb: *Jake trägt am liebsten … Er kauft Kleidung bei … In der Schule trägt er …*

L&S 1.5

Follow-up
For homework, students could use their own answers to the survey questions as the basis for writing and recording their own video blog, similar to Ali's.

4 Lies die Texte von Paula und Jan und beantworte die Fragen.

AT 3.4–5
IU 3.2

Students read two accounts by an English teenager and a German teenager, describing what they wear to school and what they would like to wear. They answer questions in German. This activity provides another opportunity to practise the *er / sie* form of the verb.

Answers: **a** *Paula trägt eine Schuluniform.* **b** *Sie trägt einen grauen Rock, ein weißes Hemd, eine Krawatte, eine Jacke und schwarze Schuhe.* **c** *Sie findet den Rock hässlich und die Uniform langweilig (total blöd und unbequem).* **d** *Sie findet die Uniform gut / besser als Designerkleidung.* **e** *Er trägt eine Jeans und einen Pulli.* **f** *Er möchte eine Schuluniform tragen.* **g** *Seine Lieblingsuniform ist eine schwarze Hose, ein hellblaues Hemd, eine Krawatte, eine Jacke und schwarze, schicke Schuhe.*

Follow-up
Ask students to identify in the texts different ways to express likes, dislikes and opinions, e.g. *Ich finde das …, Ich mag … (nicht), Ich möchte …,* and opinion adjectives. Encourage them to note down any other words and phrases they could recycle in their own writing and speaking, e.g. *Meine Mutter sagt, es ist besser; Designerkleidung; Straßenkleidung.*

5 Macht ein Interview.

AT 2.4–5
L&S 1.4

Students interview each other about school uniform, using the questions and prompts provided.

AT 4.5
R&W 2.4, 2.5
LLS 5.7, 5.8

Challenge
Students imagine they have been asked by their head teacher to describe their school uniform, give their opinion of it, then design a uniform for the future. A framework of key phrases is provided to help them structure their text.
Look at the *Think* box, which points out that this task provides an opportunity to refer to the future. Elicit from two students two ways of doing this: *werden* + infinitive, *ich möchte* + infinitive. Challenge students to find a way to use both these structures in their text, e.g. *Ich möchte keine Schuluniform tragen. In der Zukunft werden wir keine Schuluniform tragen.*
Remind students again of strategies for improving written work and refer them to the *Think* activity towards the end of spread 3B.1 and the skills section on spread 4A.6. See also the teaching notes for spread 3A.1 ex. 8.

4A.6 Modestadt Berlin!

4A.6 Sprachlabor
Seite 130–131

Planner

Objectives
- Grammar: the accusative case; object pronouns (*ihn, sie, es*); the future tense
- Skills: evaluate and improve written work by checking for accuracy; pronounce *ich, ig* and *isch*

Resources
- Student Book, pages 130–131
- CD 2, track 56
- Foundation and Higher Workbooks, pages 69–70
- Copymasters 93, 94
- Interactive OxBox, Unit 4A

Framework references
KAL 4.1, 4.3, 4.4, 4.5; LLS 5.8

The accusative case

KAL 4.3 | **1 Underline the objects in the accusative case.**

Answers: **a** das Outfit, es; **b** den Blazer, ihn; **c** das T-Shirt, es; **d** die Schuluniform, sie; **e** den Pulli, ihn; **f** die Hose, sie; **g** neue Schuhe, sie

2 Fill in the gaps with *ihn, sie, es* and *sie* (plural).

Answers: **a** ihn; **b** sie; **c** es; **d** ihn

The future tense

KAL 4.4, 4.5 | **3 Fill in the gaps with the correct form of *werden* and underline the infinitive of the second verb.**

Answers: **a** wird, kaufen; **b** werden, spielen; **c** werde, gehen; **d** wird, tragen; **e** werdet, essen; **f** Wirst, einkaufen

Evaluating and improving your written work

LLS 5.8 Students are given tips on what to look for when checking written work for accuracy, e.g. verb forms, plural forms, word order. Ask them to suggest other things to check for, e.g. genders and the correct forms of the definite and indefinite article, adjective endings, spellings in general. Point out that when checking their work they should be prepared to use a range of resources, e.g. grammar reference materials, dictionaries, their own notes.

4 The text on the right has one mistake in every sentence. Write each sentence correctly, saying what type of mistake it is.

Answers: the corrected text is: Ich <u>trage</u> eine weiße Jeans und Sportschuhe. Ich finde <u>Ballerinas nicht gut</u>. Ich finde <u>Sportschuhe</u> besser als Ballerinas. <u>Es gibt</u> in meiner Stadt (or: In meiner Stadt gibt es) ein Einkaufszentrum. <u>Ich mag</u> es gern. Am Wochenende <u>werde</u> ich im Einkaufszentrum einkaufen.

Pronunciation of *ich, ig, isch*

KAL 4.1 | **5 Listen to the words and repeat them.**

🎧 CD 2, track 56   Seite 131, Übung 5

ich	launisch
dich	fantastisch
hässlich	billig
modisch	nervig
freundlich	traurig
altmodisch	

6 Now make sentences using the words in activity 5 and practise them with your partner.
Challenge students to include at least one example of each of the three letter strings in each sentence, e.g. *Ich finde die Jacke <u>altmodisch</u>, aber <u>billig</u>.*

4A.7 Modestadt Berlin!

4A.7 Extra Star
Seite 132

Planner

Objectives
- Vocabulary: detailed descriptions and opinions of clothes
- Grammar: comparative adjectives; adjective endings
- Skills: use knowledge of grammar and other strategies to understand texts

Resources
- Student Book, page 132
- Copymaster 95

AT 3.1 **1 Find the six comparatives in the word snake.**

Answers: besser, billiger, moderner, langweiliger, interessanter, launischer

AT 3.3–4 **2 Fill in the gaps using the words in the box below.**

Students choose from the words provided to complete the text about German film star Jimi Blue Ochsenknecht.

Make sure they realise that in order to fill in some of the gaps they will need to use their knowledge of grammar, e.g. the missing word in *eine __ Jeans* can only be an adjective with a feminine ending so it can't be *bequemen* – it must be *coole*; similarly, the missing word in *einen __ Kapuzenpulli* has to be an adjective with a masculine ending in the accusative case, so *bequemen* is the only option. Without a knowledge of German adjective endings, it would be impossible to work out which adjectives to put where.

To exploit the text further, set a few comprehension questions for students to answer, e.g. What does Jimi like to wear? What does Wilson wear? Where does Wilson buy his clothes and why doesn't he like H&M? What is Jimi going to wear to the party?

Answers: Ich bin Jimi Blue Ochsenknecht und ich <u>komme</u> aus Deutschland. Ich mache Filme und Musik. Ich <u>trage</u> sehr lässige Kleidung. Ich trage gern eine <u>coole</u> Jeans, einen <u>bequemen</u> Kapuzenpulli und schicke Sportschuhe. Mein Bruder Wilson Gonzalez trägt schickere Kleidung als ich. Seine Kleidung ist teuer, modisch und er kauft sie bei <u>Adidas</u> in Berlin. Er mag H&M nicht, denn die Kleidung ist zu billig.
Auf der Party am Samstag <u>werde</u> ich mein neues Outfit tragen. Ich werde eine Jeans, ein <u>rotes</u> T-Shirt und einen schwarzen Blazer tragen. Ich finde das Outfit <u>toll</u>.

AT 3.4 **3 Read the speech bubbles. True or false?**

Ask students to correct the false statements. Afterwards, ask them what strategies helped them to work out the answers, e.g. identifying familiar language / key words / cognates, using the visuals as clues, using logic / sensible guesses.

Answers: **a** true; **b** false (they are very comfortable and great for skateboarding); **c** true; **d** false (he thinks it makes him look like a gangster); **e** true; **f** false (she likes wearing a skirt); **g** false (motorcycling); **h** true; **i** true

4A.7 Extra Plus
Seite 133

Planner

Objectives
- Vocabulary: detailed descriptions and opinions of clothes
- Grammar: object pronouns
- Skills: use knowledge of grammar and other strategies to understand texts

Resources
- Student Book, page 133
- Copymaster 96

AT 3.4–5 **1 Lies den Dialog. Sind die Sätze unten richtig oder falsch?**

Students read a conversation about clothes and work out whether statements a–f are true or false.

Answers: **a** falsch; **b** falsch; **c** richtig; **d** falsch; **e** falsch; **f** richtig

195

4A.8 Modestadt Berlin!

AT 3,4–5 **2 Mach aus den falschen Sätzen oben richtige Sätze.**
Students correct the false statements from ex. 1.

Answers: **a** Tanja wants to buy a new outfit for her party. **b** Paul finds the new jeans, designed by H&M, stupid (or: Tanja finds the new jeans, designed by H&M, cool). **d** The skirt was a great success / wonderful. **e** The skirt costs 45 euros.

3 Lies den Dialog noch einmal. Was passt zusammen?
Students read the conversation again. They use their knowledge of German grammar to identify which clothing items are being referred to by the object pronouns in statements 1–4.

Answers: **1** b; **2** c; **3** d; **4** a

4A.8 Testseite

Seite 134

Planner

Resources
- Student Book, page 134
- CD 2, track 57
- Foundation and Higher Workbooks, page 71
- Copymasters 85, 86
- Assessments, Unit 4A

AT 1.2 **1 Listen (a–k) and look at the pictures. Who is speaking?**
Students identify which person is speaking in each clothing description.

Answers: **a** 3; **b** 3; **c** 1; **d** 1; **e** 2; **f** 2; **g** 3; **h** 2; **i** 3; **j** 1; **k** 3

🎧 **CD 2, track 57**   Seite 134, Übung 1

a Ich trage eine weiße Bluse.
b Ich trage eine blaue Jacke.
c Ich trage eine graue Jacke.
d Ich trage rot-weiße Sportschuhe.
e Ich trage graue Sportschuhe.
f Ich trage eine blaue Jeans.
g Ich trage blaue Ballerinas.
h Ich trage einen schwarzen Kapuzenpullover.
i Ich trage einen kurzen weißen Rock.
j Ich trage ein blaues Hemd.
k Ich trage einen roten Motorradhelm.

AT 3,4–5 **2 Read the email and answer the questions.**

Answers: **a** on Saturday; **b** he wants a new outfit for school because his clothes are old-fashioned and ugly; **c** fashionable jeans and a casual shirt; **d** he usually goes twice a month; **e** H&M, because the clothes are great yet they are cheaper than in designer shops

AT 2,3–5 **3 Discuss your clothing style with a partner.**
A list of questions are provided as prompts, to help students structure their discussion. Remind them of the criteria for achieving level 4–5, and point out that the questions guide them towards level 5 by prompting them to refer to different time frames (present and future) and use a range of structures.

AT 4,4–5 **4 Imagine you are Paul Pauli and you have to describe your clothing style.**
Referring to picture 2 in ex. 1, students describe what they usually wear, what they think of their outfit and why, and what they would like to wear. Remind students again of the criteria for achieving level 4–5 and point out the advice in the *Think* box: they are encouraged to use a range of structures, including adjectives, opinions, linking words, comparatives, *ich möchte* + infinitive and *ich werde* + infinitive.

4A Modestadt Berlin!

4A Lesen

Seite 159

> **Planner**
>
> **Resources**
> - Student Book, page 159
>
> **Framework references**
> R&W 2.1, 2.2, 2.4, 2.5; IU 3.1, 3.2

Deutsche Designer sind cool!

AT 3.4–5

1 Read the text. Choose the correct answer.
Students read the text about German fashion designers. They choose option 1 or 2 to complete each sentence.

Answers: *a* 1; *b* 2; *c* 2; *d* 1; *e* 2; *f* 1

2 Find the German words in the text above.
Students search the text for the German translations of some English words and phrases.

Answers: *a* weltweit; *b* berühmt; *c* Modedesigner; *d* sie repräsentieren; *e* Luxus; *f* Schönheit; *g* große Fans; *h* Sportmarke

3 Answer the questions in English.

Answers: *a* worldwide; *b* chic, fashionable, hip, very expensive; *c* Köln, München; *d* Regent Street in London; *e* Adidas and Puma; *f* David Beckham and Snoop Dogg

AT 4.4–5
R&W 2.4, 2.5

4 Research a German fashion designer and write a paragraph about him or her in German.
Illustrate your work with the type of fashion he or she designs.
Before students begin, encourage them to make a note of any words, phrases or structures from the *Deutsche Designer* text that they could use to add interest and variety to their own writing.

Follow-up
- Students visit the websites of German fashion designers, choose their favourite outfits and write descriptions of them. Encourage them to compare the styles of different designers, e.g. *Ich finde, Karl Lagerfeld ist cooler als …*

- Students write the commentary for a fashion show, e.g. *James trägt die neue Hose von Hugo Boss – sehr bequem, aber total schick! Er trägt auch ein weißes Hemd …* They could write it in the style of a blog or a photo report. If time permits, they could work in groups to stage their own fashion show.

4A Modestadt Berlin!

Foundation Workbook

4A.1 Die Jeans ist cool! (Seite 64)

AT 3.1 **1** Find ten words for clothes in the grid. They can be across, down or diagonal.

Answers:

J	L	B	A	L	L	E	R	I	N	A	S
H	E	M	D								P
	D	A									O
	E	N									R
	R		S								T
	J						S				S
	A	T	S	H	I	R	T				C
	C						I				H
	K	P	U	L	L	O	V	E	R		U
	E						F				H
				B	L	U	S	E			E
						K	L	E	I	D	

AT 1.1 **2** Listen to the adjectives and write in the letter of each one by the appropriate picture.

Answers: **1** c; **2** h; **3** g; **4** d; **5** a; **6** b; **7** e; **8** f

🎧 **CD 3, track 66**   Seite 64, Übung 2

- **a** schick
- **b** alt
- **c** hässlich
- **d** unbequem
- **e** bequem
- **f** altmodisch
- **g** billig
- **h** teuer

3 Choose *ist* or *sind*.

Answers: **a** ist; **b** ist; **c** sind; **d** sind; **e** ist; **f** sind

4A.2 Coole Outfits (Seite 65)

AT 3.2–3 **1** Read the article and work out who is who. Write the names in the blanks.

Answers: *left to right*: Aischa, Jennifer, Fatima, Maike

AT 3.2–3 **2** Read the article again and fill in the gaps in English.

Answers: **a** white, blue; **b** cool, fashionable; **c** black, red; **d** nice, yellow

3 Write in the correct endings.

Answers: **a** einen lässigen Rock; **b** eine bequeme Jeans; **c** ein billiges Hemd; **d** eine modische Jacke; **e** einen roten Pullover

4A.3 Wir gehen einkaufen! (Seite 66)

AT 1.2 **1** Listen to the conversation. Write numbers to show the order in which the items are mentioned. If the item isn't mentioned, leave it blank.

Answers: **1** shirt; **2** jumper; **3** T-shirt; **4** trousers; **5** jeans (the dress isn't mentioned)

🎧 **CD 3, track 67**   Seite 66, Übung 1

- Wie findest du das karierte Hemd?
- Ich finde es nicht so toll. Ich möchte den grünen Pulli anprobieren.
- So? Ich mag ihn nicht. Ich mag das bunte T-Shirt lieber.
- Hmm … Ich finde es nicht so schick. Ich möchte die graue Hose kaufen.
- Ich nicht. Ich möchte die schwarze Jeans kaufen. Sie ist cool.

AT 1.2–3 **2** Listen again and note down, in order, in English, a brief description of each item mentioned.

Answers: **a** checked shirt; **b** green jumper; **c** multicoloured T-shirt; **d** grey trousers; **e** black jeans

3 Circle the right word.

Answers: **a** sie; **b** ihn; **c** ihn; **d** es; **e** sie; **f** sie

AT 3.3 **4** Number each sentence to put them in the correct order to make a dialogue.

Answers: **1** Kann ich dir helfen? **2** Ich mag den roten Rock. **3** Möchtest du ihn anprobieren? **4** Ja, bitte. **5** Wie findest du ihn? **6** Ich finde ihn gut. **7** Möchtest du ihn kaufen? **8** Ja, ich kaufe ihn.

4A.4 Die Hose ist zu klein! (Seite 67)

AT 3.2 **1** Write in the comparative adjectives in these sentences.

Answers: **a** teurer, billiger; **b** größer, kleiner; **c** älter, neuer; **d** hässlicher, schöner

AT 4.2 **2** Fill in the gaps to make these sentences future.

Answers: **a** Ich werde nach Berlin fahren. **b** Wir werden zu H&M gehen. **c** Ali wird eine Jeans kaufen. **d** Wir werden Pommes essen. **e** Ich werde Tischtennis spielen.

4A Modestadt Berlin!

AT 1.2 **3 Listen to each sentence. Write 'P' if it is present and 'F' if it is future.**

Answers: *a* P; *b* F; *c* F; *d* P; *e* P; *f* F

🎧 **CD 3, track 68**   Seite 67, Übung 3

a Ich spiele oft am Computer.
b Wir werden schwimmen gehen.
c Ich werde Kaffee trinken.
d Olivia mag Musik.
e Wir essen gern Fleisch.
f Wiebke wird nach Italien fahren.

4A.5 Das trage ich!   (Seite 68)

AT 3.1 **1 Draw lines to link the German and English words.**

Answers: *interessanter – more interesting; alt – old; schön – nice; schöner – nicer; älter – older; billiger – cheaper; billig – cheap; moderner – more modern; langweilig – boring; hässlicher – uglier; modern – modern; langweiliger – more boring; hässlich – ugly; interessant – interesting*

AT 3.3–4 **2 Read the text and answer the questions.**

Answers: *a* on Saturday; *b* a nice jumper and a pair of black jeans; *c* it's cheaper and better than Esprit; *d* casual trousers and a smart/chic jacket; *e* fashionable clothing is expensive

4A.6A Sprachlabor   (Seite 69)

1 Circle the correct word.

Answers: *a* ihn; *b* es; *c* sie; *d* ihn; *e* ihn; *f* es; *g* sie; *h* es

2 Write in the correct endings.

Answers: *gelben, modische, lässiges, warmen, billige*

3 Draw lines to link the forms of the verb *werden*.

Answers: *ich werde, du wirst, er wird, wir werden, ihr werdet, sie werden*

4A.6B Think   (Seite 70)

1 These words look English but each has a different meaning in German. What are the meanings?

Answers: *a* skirt; *b* trousers; *c* red; *d* good; *e* eleven; *f* am; *g* has; *h* day; *i* like(s); *j* left

2 Although the English and German words look the same, they sound different. Read the words in Activity 1 aloud twice, once using the English pronunciation and once using the German.

3 Look carefully at these words and write C (Cognate) or NC (Near Cognate) by each word.

Answers: <u>Cognates</u>: *Pullover, Jeans, T-Shirt, Party, cool, intelligent, Sport;* <u>Near Cognates</u>: *Bluse, Musik, Elefant, Banane, braun, Spanisch, Mathe, Gitarre*

4A Modestadt Berlin!

Higher Workbook

4A.1 Die Jeans ist cool! (Seite 64)

AT 3.1
AT 4.1
1 Find ten words for clothes in the grid and write them below. They can be across, down or diagonal.

Answers: Ballerinas, Hemd, T-Shirt, Pullover, Bluse, Kleid, Lederjacke, Stiefel, Sportschuhe, Jeans (See wordsearch grid above for Foundation Workbook 4A.1, ex. 1.)

AT 1.2 **2** Listen to the adjectives and write in the letter of each one by the appropriate picture.

Answers: **1** c; **2** h; **3** g; **4** d; **5** a; **6** b; **7** e; **8** f

> **CD 4, track 66**   Seite 64, Übung 2
> **a** Mensch, ist die schick!
> **b** Mmm, es ist sehr alt.
> **c** Igitt, die ist vielleicht hässlich!
> **d** Die Schuhe sind sehr unbequem.
> **e** Hmmm, das ist schön bequem.
> **f** Die Kleidung ist altmodisch.
> **g** Toll, das ist billig!
> **h** Nein, das ist zu teuer.

3 Write in *ist* or *sind*.

Answers: **a** ist; **b** ist; **c** sind; **d** sind; **e** ist; **f** sind

4A.2 Coole Outfits (Seite 65)

AT 3.2–3 **1** Read the article and work out who is who. Write the names in the blanks.

Answers: left to right: Aischa, Jennifer, Fatima, Maike

AT 3.2–3 **2** Read the article again and describe in detail what each girl is wearing.

Answers: **a** Jennifer is wearing a white hoodie and blue shorts. **b** Maike is wearing cool trousers and a fashionable jacket. **c** Aischa is wearing black jeans and a red T-shirt. **d** Fatima is wearing a nice skirt and a yellow blouse.

AT 4.2 **3** Complete the sentences.

Answers: **a** einen lässigen Rock; **b** eine bequeme Jeans; **c** ein billiges Hemd; **d** eine modische Jacke; **e** einen roten Pullover

4A.3 Wir gehen einkaufen! (Seite 66)

AT 1.3–4 **1** Listen to the conversation and answer the questions in English.

Answers: **a** a shirt; **b** checked; **c** no, she doesn't think it's great; **d** try on the green jumper; **e** he doesn't like it; **f** the multicoloured T-shirt; **g** she doesn't think it's so chic/smart; **h** she'd like to buy the grey trousers; **i** he'd like to buy the black jeans; **j** they're cool

> **CD 4, track 67**   Seite 66, Übung 1
> – Wie findest du das karierte Hemd?
> – Ich finde es nicht so toll. Ich möchte den grünen Pulli anprobieren.
> – So? Ich mag ihn nicht. Ich mag das bunte T-Shirt lieber.
> – Hmm … Ich finde es nicht so schick. Ich möchte die graue Hose kaufen.
> – Ich nicht. Ich möchte die schwarze Jeans kaufen. Sie ist cool.

2 Write in *ihn*, *sie* or *es*.

Answers: **a** sie; **b** ihn; **c** ihn; **d** es; **e** sie; **f** sie

AT 4.2 **3** Translate these sentences to make a conversation in a clothes shop. Note: the shop assistant is an adult and the customer is a child.

Answers: **1** Kann ich dir helfen? **2** Ich mag den roten Rock. **3** Möchtest du ihn anprobieren? **4** Ja, bitte. **5** Wie findest du ihn? **6** Ich finde ihn gut. **7** Möchtest du ihn kaufen? **8** Ja, ich kaufe ihn.

4A.4 Die Hose ist zu klein! (Seite 67)

AT 4.2–3 **1** Write two sentences about each pair of pictures, using comparative adjectives.

Answers: **a** Die Stiefel sind teurer als die Schuhe. Die Schuhe sind billiger als die Stiefel. **b** Der Elefant ist größer als die Maus. Die Maus ist kleiner als der Elefant. **c** Das Auto ist älter als das Motorrad. Das Motorrad ist neuer als das Auto. **d** Das Monster ist hässlicher als die Königin. Die Königin ist schöner als das Monster.

AT 4.2 **2** Make these sentences future.

Answers: **a** Ich werde nach Berlin fahren. **b** Wir werden zu H&M gehen. **c** Ali wird eine Jeans kaufen. **d** Wir werden Pommes essen. **e** Ich werde Tischtennis spielen.

AT 1.2 **3** Listen to each sentence. Write 'P' if it is present and 'F' if it is future.

Answers: **a** P; **b** F; **c** F; **d** P; **e** P; **f** F

4A Modestadt Berlin!

🎧 **CD 4, track 68**   Seite 67, Übung 3

a Ich spiele oft am Computer.
b Wir werden schwimmen gehen.
c Ich werde Kaffee trinken.
d Olivia mag Musik.
e Wir essen gern Fleisch.
f Wiebke wird nach Italien fahren.

4A.5 Das trage ich! (Seite 68)

AT 4.1–2   **1 Translate these words.**

Answers: nice – schön; boring – langweilig; more boring – langweiliger; cheaper – billiger; uglier – hässlicher; nicer – schöner; more interesting – interessanter; cheap – billig; more modern – moderner; interesting – interessant; old – alt; modern – modern; ugly – hässlich; older – älter

AT 1.3–4   **2 Listen to Tanja and answer the questions.**

Answers: a on Saturday; b a nice jumper and a pair of black jeans; c it's cheaper and better than Esprit; d casual trousers and a smart/chic jacket; e fashionable clothing is expensive

🎧 **CD 4, track 69**   Seite 68, Übung 2

Wir werden am Samstag in die Stadt gehen und einkaufen. Ich werde einen schönen Pulli und eine schwarze Jeans kaufen. Ich werde zu H&M gehen. Ich finde, H&M ist billiger als Esprit, und auch besser. Meine Kleidung ist nicht mehr modisch. Ich möchte eine lässige Hose und eine schicke Jacke kaufen, aber modische Kleidung ist teuer.

4A.6A Sprachlabor (Seite 69)

1 Write in *ihn*, *sie* or *es*.

Answers: a ihn; b es; c sie; d ihn; e ihn; f es; g sie; h es

2 Write in the correct endings.

Answers: gelben, modische, lässiges, warmen, billige

3 Write in the correct form of the verb *werden*.

Answers: a werde; b Wirst; c wird; d werdet; e werden; f werden

4A.6B Think (Seite 70)

1 These words look English but each has a different meaning in German. What are the meanings?

Answers: a skirt; b trousers; c red; d good; e eleven; f am; g has; h day; i like(s); j left

2 Although the English and German words look the same, they sound different. Read the words in Activity 1 aloud twice, once using the English pronunciation and once using the German.

3 Look carefully at these words and write C (Cognate) or NC (Near Cognate) by each word.

Answers: <u>Cognates</u>: Pullover, Jeans, T-Shirt, Party, cool, intelligent, Sport; <u>Near Cognates</u>: Bluse, Musik, Elefant, Banane, braun, Spanisch, Mathe, Gitarre

4B Zu Besuch

Unit 4B Zu Besuch   Unit overview grid

Page reference	Objectives	Grammar	Skills and pronunciation	Key language	Framework	AT level
136–137 **4B.1 Die Ferien**	Talk about holidays	Prepositions *in* and *auf* followed by the dative case (*einem/einer*)	Language patterns; compound nouns	*Wohin fährst du in den Ferien? Ich fahre nach Frankreich/in die Türkei/an die Nordsee.* *Wie fährst du? Ich fahre mit dem Auto/Zug/Wohnwagen. Ich fliege.* *Wo wohnst du? Ich wohne in einem Hotel/in einem Wohnwagen/in einem Wohnmobil/in einem Ferienhaus/in einem Zelt/in einer Ferienwohnung/in einer Jugendherberge/auf einem Campingplatz.* *Wie lange bleibst du dort? Ich bleibe zwei Wochen/eine Woche dort.* *Ich freue mich darauf. Das finde ich langweilig.*	L&S 1.1, 1.2 KAL 4.2, 4.3 LLS 5.1, 5.3, 5.4, 5.7	1.1–2, 1.4 2.2–4, 3.1–3, 4.4
138–139 **4B.2 Wir fahren nach Wien!**	Talk about what you can do on holiday and what you're going to do	Modal verbs (*können, wollen*) The future tense (*werden* + infinitive)	Express opinions	*Was kann man/können wir in Wien machen?* *Es gibt viel zu machen. Man kann/Wir können einen Ausflug machen/in einen Freizeitpark gehen/den Dom besuchen/eine Stadtrundfahrt machen/ein Wiener Schnitzel essen/ins Museum gehen.* *Was werden wir machen? Wir werden Souvenirs kaufen/Pizza essen/ins Theater gehen/schwimmen/das Schloss besuchen/Freunde treffen.* *Willst du Rad fahren/Tennis spielen/ins Kino gehen?* *Das ist toll/super/schön/langweilig. Das gefällt mir (nicht).*	L&S 1.1, 1.2, 1.4 R&W 2.4, 2.5 KAL 4.3, 4.4, 4.5 LLS 5.1, 5.7, 5.8	1.2, 1.4, 2.3–4, 3.2–4, 4.3–5

Zu Besuch 4B

Page reference	Objectives	Grammar	Skills and pronunciation	Key language	Framework	AT level
140–141 **4B.3 Was hast du gemacht?**	Say what you did on holiday	The perfect tense (*haben* and *sein* + past participle)	Recycle familiar words and phrases in the perfect tense	*Was hast du gemacht? Ich habe/Wir haben Musik im Park gehört/Frisbee gespielt/Souvenirs gekauft/ einen Ausflug gemacht/in der Disco getanzt. Wohin bist du gefahren? Ich bin/Wir sind mit dem Zug/ Auto gefahren. Ich bin/Wir sind geflogen. Wo hast du gewohnt? Ich habe/Wir haben in einem Hotel/in einem Zelt/in einem Ferienhaus/in einer Ferienwohnung gewohnt.*	L&S 1.4 R&W 2.4, 2.5 KAL 4.3, 4.4, 4.5 LLS 5.1, 5.2, 5.8	1.2–3, 2.2–3, 3.2–3, 4.2–4
142–143 **4B.4 Im Prater**	Talk about a visit to an amusement park	Recognise and describe actions in the present, past and future	Recycle familiar words and phrases in a range of tenses	*Wohin bist du gestern gefahren? Wir sind mit dem Bus zum Prater gefahren. Was habt ihr dort gemacht? Wir sind Achterbahn gefahren. Wir haben einen Ausflug gemacht. Was macht ihr heute? Wir kaufen Souvenirs. Wir wollen mit dem Riesenrad fahren. Wir können im Wasserpark spielen. Was werdet ihr morgen machen? Wir werden ein Picknick machen. letztes Wochenende, gestern, heute, heute Abend, morgen, jeden Tag, zweimal in der Woche*	R&W 2.1, 2.2 IU 3.1, 3.2 KAL 4.2, 4.3, 4.4, 4.5, 4.6 LLS 5.1, 5.4, 5.5	1.2, 1.5–6, 3.2, 3.5–6, 4.3–5
144–145 **4B.5 Nicos Videoblog**	Talk about holiday experiences and future plans	Verbs in the past, present and future Modal verbs	Recognise and use a range of structures; apply previously learned language in new contexts	Recycle language from Unit 4B and other contexts	L&S 1.1, 1.2 R&W 2.1, 2.2, 2.4, 2.5 IU 3.1, 3.2 LLS 5.7, 5.8	1.5, 3.5, 4.4–6

4B Zu Besuch

Unit 4B: Week-by-week overview
(Three-Year KS3 Route: assuming six weeks' work or approximately 10–12.5 hours)
(Two-Year KS3 Route: assuming four weeks' work or approximately 6.5–8.5 hours)

About Unit 4B, *Zu Besuch*: In this unit, students work in the context of holidays: they discuss holiday plans, describe past holiday experiences and talk about what there is to see and do in different holiday destinations. They find out about some major cities and other places of interest in Germany, Austria and Switzerland.

Throughout the unit there is a strong focus on verbs and tenses: students are introduced to the perfect tense (with auxiliaries *haben* and *sein*), and they develop their use of the present tense, the future tense and modal verbs. They are encouraged to speak and write with increasing complexity, using a variety of structures and a range of tenses. They receive tips on improving their listening skills, and cope with increasingly challenging spoken and written texts.

The pronunciation focus is word endings: students are reminded that inflections (e.g. *einem, einer, eine,* etc.) convey information about gender and case, and can influence meaning, so it is important to pronounce them clearly.

Three-Year KS3 Route

Week	Resources	Objectives
1	4B.1 Die Ferien 4B.6 Sprachlabor ex. 5–7 *(if you wish to work on pronunciation at this point)*	Talk about holidays Prepositions *in* and *auf* followed by the dative case *(einem/einer)* Language patterns; compound nouns
2	4B.2 Wir fahren nach Wien! 4B.6 Sprachlabor: listening skills	Talk about what you can do on holiday and what you're going to do Modal verbs *(können, wollen)* The future tense *(werden* + infinitive) Express opinions
3	4B.3 Was hast du gemacht? 4B.6 Sprachlabor ex. 1–4	Say what you did on holiday The perfect tense *(haben* and *sein* + past participle) Recycle familiar words and phrases in the perfect tense
4	4B.4 Im Prater	Talk about a visit to an amusement park Recognise and describe actions in the present, past and future Recycle familiar words and phrases in a range of tenses

Two-Year KS3 Route

Week	Resources	Objectives
1	4B.1 Die Ferien *(Omit ex. 3)* 4B.6 Sprachlabor ex. 5–7 *(if you wish to work on pronunciation at this point)*	Talk about holidays Prepositions *in* and *auf* followed by the dative case *(einem/einer)* Language patterns; compound nouns
2	4B.2 Wir fahren nach Wien! *(Omit ex. 4)* 4B.6 Sprachlabor: listening skills	Talk about what you can do on holiday and what you're going to do Modal verbs *(können, wollen)* The future tense *(werden* + infinitive) Express opinions
3	4B.3 Was hast du gemacht? 4B.6 Sprachlabor ex. 1–4	Say what you did on holiday The perfect tense *(haben* and *sein* + past participle) Recycle familiar words and phrases in the perfect tense
4	4B.4 Im Prater *(Omit ex. 5)* 4B.8 Vokabular 4B.8 Testseite	Talk about a visit to an amusement park Recognise and describe actions in the present, past and future Recycle familiar words and phrases in a range of tenses Key vocabulary and learning checklist Assessment in all four skills

4B Zu Besuch

	Three-Year KS3 Route			Two-Year KS3 Route	
Week	Resources	Objectives	Week	Resources	Objectives
5	**4B.5 Nicos Videoblog**	Talk about holiday experiences and future plans Verbs in the past, present and future Modal verbs Recognise and use a range of structures Apply previously learned language in new contexts			
6	**4B.7 Extra (Star/Plus)** **4B.8 Vokabular** **4B.8 Testseite** **4B Lesen**	Reinforcement and extension of the language of the unit Key vocabulary and learning checklist Assessment in all four skills Further reading to explore the language of the unit and cultural themes			

4B.1 Zu Besuch

4B.1 Die Ferien
Seite 136–137

Planner

Objectives
- Vocabulary: talk about holidays
- Grammar: prepositions *in* and *auf* followed by the dative case (*einem / einer*)
- Skills: language patterns; compound nouns

Video
Video clip 4B

Resources
- Student Book, pages 136–137
- CD 2, track 58
- Foundation and Higher Workbooks, page 72
- Workbook audio: CD 3, track 69 (Foundation) CD 4, track 70 (Higher)
- Copymasters 99 (ex. 1–2), 100 (ex. 1), 103 (ex. 3–4)
- Interactive OxBox, Unit 4B

Key language
Wohin fährst du in den Ferien?
Ich fahre nach Frankreich / in die Türkei / an die Nordsee.
Wie fährst du?
Ich fahre mit dem Auto / Zug / Wohnwagen. Ich fliege.
Wo wohnst du?
Ich wohne in einem Hotel / in einem Wohnwagen / in einem Wohnmobil / in einem Ferienhaus / in einem Zelt / in einer Ferienwohnung / in einer Jugendherberge / auf einem Campingplatz.
Wie lange bleibst du dort?
Ich bleibe zwei Wochen / eine Woche dort.
Ich freue mich darauf. Das finde ich langweilig.

Framework references
L&S 1.1, 1.2; KAL 4.2, 4.3; LLS 5.1, 5.3, 5.4, 5.7

Starters
- Copymaster 99, ex. 1–2.
- Before students open their books at page 136, ask them to jot down (in English!) six different types of holiday accommodation, e.g. hotel, holiday cottage, etc. They then open their books and check against the pictures in ex. 1: how many did they guess? They match the pictures to the German captions a–f. (See also teaching notes for ex. 1.)
- As preparation for ex. 4 on Student Book page 137, ask students to note down what they consider to be the key words or phrases (to a maximum of five) in each paragraph a–c, e.g. in paragraph a: *Auto, Wohnwagen, Italien, drei Wochen*. This provides a focus for watching the video, and shows that it is not always necessary to understand every word.

Plenaries
- Student Book page 136, ex. 3: dice game practising types of holiday accommodation and *in* + dative.
- Student Book page 137, ex. 6: students use key language from the spread to build dialogues about holidays.

Homework
- After doing some work on the gender and plural of compound nouns (see *Follow-up* suggested on page 208), students carry out further research. Ask them to look back through the Student Book for examples of compound nouns and to list them in a grid as follows, showing their gender, plural, meaning and component parts:

Compound noun	Plural	Meaning	Components
die Schultasche	Schultaschen	school bag	Schule + Tasche
das Esszimmer	Esszimmer	dining room	Ess(en) + Zimmer

- Student Book page 137, ex. 5.
- Student Book page 137, *Challenge*.

Video clip 4B: Eine Schiffsfahrt!
Synopsis:
The four teenagers are discussing their holiday plans: Ali is going to Turkey to stay with his grandmother; Nico's family are going touring with their caravan to South Tyrol, via Weimar, Nuremberg and Munich; Nina and her mother will be spending two weeks in a holiday flat on the North Sea coast. Kathi seems quiet and preoccupied – she is still worried that her family might leave Berlin because of her father's job.

Nina suggests that all four of them could go away together on a cruise – she makes a phone call and it appears that she's making a booking with a travel agency … but it turns out to be a boat trip on the Spree!
Suddenly Kathi receives a text message – her father doesn't have to leave Berlin after all! Nico is overjoyed. Meanwhile, Nina asks Ali to stay in Berlin for the summer: she has forgotten all about Ralf. Nina and Ali walk off hand in hand.

4B.1 Zu Besuch

Play the video through a couple of times and ask questions to check that students understand the gist of it. Suggested focus:
- Can students identify any Berlin landmarks spotted in the clip? (If you pause the panorama at the start of the clip they may spot the TV Tower, Berlin Cathedral and the Marienkirche, then later we see the river Spree, the TV Tower again and the Bode Museum.)
- Which country is Ali going to? (Turkey)
- Name the places mentioned by Nico. (South Tyrol, Weimar, Nuremberg, Munich, Vienna)
- When Nina makes the phone call, what detail does she give first? What is the departure time? (her name – Neumann, three o'clock today)
- Can students explain what happens at the end of the clip (i) with Kathi? (ii) between Nina and Ali?
- Towards the end of work on this spread, play the clip again and ask students to note down as many details as possible about each person's holiday plans.

Video clip 4B

Nico: Und, Ali, was machst du in den Ferien? Fliegst du wieder in die Türkei?
Ali: Ja, wie jedes Jahr. Wir fliegen am sechsten Juli.
Nico: Und wohin?
Ali: Meine Großmutter hat ein Haus am Meer … in der Nähe von Izmir. Ich verbringe jeden Sommer bei ihr.
Nico: Ist das Haus groß?
Ali: Ja, ziemlich … es hat fünf Schlafzimmer und drei Bäder. Der Garten ist ziemlich klein, aber das Haus ist nur ein paar Meter vom Strand entfernt.
Nico: Da braucht man auch keinen großen Garten.
Ali: Eben.
Nico: Und fährst du gern jeden Sommer in die Türkei?
Ali: Bis jetzt schon … aber langsam … freue ich mich nicht mehr so sehr …
Nico: Wir fahren wieder mit dem Wohnwagen. Mein Vater will unbedingt nach Südtirol.
Ali: Und haltet ihr auch irgendwo unterwegs an?
Nico: Ja, jeder kann sich etwas aussuchen. Meine Mama ist Goethe-Fan und will unbedingt nach Weimar und sein Haus angucken. Ralf liebt alte Geschichte und mag sich die Nürnberger Burg angucken – und das Haus von Albrecht Dürer natürlich.
Ali: Na klar, das ist bestimmt interessant.
Nico: Ja, und Britta will die Bavaria Filmstudios in München sehen.
Ali: Cool. Und du?
Nico: Ich hoffe, wir schaffen es bis nach Wien …
Ali: Aber das liegt nicht ganz auf dem Weg nach Südtirol …?
Nico: Nein, liegt es nicht. Es ist ein Umweg … aber für Kathi tue ich alles …
Ali: Klar.
Nico: Und ihr, Nina?
Nina: Meine Mutter möchte eine Ferienwohnung an der Nordsee buchen.
Nico: Und das willst du nicht?
Nina: Kein Computer, keine Action. Nur Sand, Sonne, Meer, Fisch und das zwei Wochen lang. Nee, danke! …
Wisst ihr was? Warum fahren wir nicht zusammen weg? Was meint ihr?
Nico: Meinst du Campen? Oder eine Fahrradtour?
Nina: Nein, eine Schiffsreise!
Ali: Was? Das erlauben unsere Eltern doch nie …
Nina: Vielleicht doch …
Kathi: Ja!
Nico: Das ist fantastisch!
Ali: Das machen wir!

(Nina makes a phone call)
Nina: Guten Tag, Neumann ist mein Name. … Ich möchte gern vier Plätze reservieren. … Ja! Heute, wenn es möglich ist. … Super! Und wie viel kostet es pro Person? … So viel? Na gut, okay. Und wann fährt das Schiff heute? … Drei Uhr? Ja, das ist in Ordnung. Vielen Dank! Auf Wiederhören.
Nina: *(puts the phone down and speaks to the others)* Packt eure Sachen! Wir machen eine Schiffsreise!

(on a boat trip on the Spree)
Nina: Das ist der Fernsehturm, oder?
Ali: Es ist das zweitgrößte Gebäude Europas …
Nina: Und Ali, was das?
Ali: Das ist das Bode-Museum.
Nina: Und was kann man dort tun?
Ali: Dort finden Kunstausstellungen statt.

(Kathi receives a text message)
Nico: Alles okay, Kathi?
Kathi: *(nods and smiles)*
Nico: Dein Vater bleibt in Berlin!
Kathi: *(nods and smiles again)*
Nico: Das ist ja super! Das ist besser als super! Das ist fantastisch!

Nina: *(to Ali)* Geh nicht!
Ali: Was?
Nina: Bitte fahr nicht in die Türkei.
Ali: Aber ich komme doch im September wieder.
Nina: Bitte, fahr nicht!
Ali: Und Ralf?
Nina: Wer ist Ralf?

4B.1 Zu Besuch

Sprachpunkt
Was machst du in den Ferien?
Wir fahren wieder mit dem Wohnwagen.
Wir fliegen am sechsten Juli.
Meine Mutter möchte eine Ferienwohnung buchen.

AT 3.1–2 / LLS 5.4

1 Wo wohnst du in den Ferien? Was passt zusammen?
Students match pictures of holiday accommodation to the corresponding captions. Afterwards, discuss any clues that helped them to do this, e.g. cognates (*Hotel, Camping*), visuals, identifying familiar language in the component parts of compound nouns (e.g. *Haus, Wohnung*).

Answers: **a** 2; **b** 1; **c** 4; **d** 6; **e** 3; **f** 5

AT 1.1–2

2 Hör zu (1–6). Ist alles richtig?
Students listen to check their answers to ex. 1. Elicit the difference between *ich wohne* and *wir wohnen*.

CD 2, track 58 Seite 136, Übung 2

1 Ich wohne in einem Hotel.
2 Ich wohne in einer Ferienwohnung.
3 Ich wohne in einer Jugendherberge.
4 Wir wohnen in einem Wohnwagen.
5 Wir wohnen in einem Ferienhaus.
6 Ich wohne auf einem Campingplatz.

KAL 4.2, 4.3 / LLS 5.1

Think
Ask students to identify the odd one out in a–f in ex. 1: it's phrase d, because the preposition is *auf* instead of *in*.
Students then focus on the endings added to *ein* following each preposition. They try to identify the pattern: after *in* and *auf*, the word for "a" with masculine and neuter nouns becomes *einem*, and with feminine nouns it becomes *einer*. If necessary, before students begin, provide them with a clue by suggesting that they check the genders in a dictionary.
This might be an appropriate point at which to work on this unit's pronunciation focus: word endings. See spread 4B.6 ex. 5–7.

KAL 4.3 / LLS 5.4

Follow-up
Focus on the compound nouns in ex. 1. Ask students to look up the gender of the words *Wohnung, Wagen, Platz, Herberge* and *Haus,* and to compare with the gender of the compound nouns listed here. They should notice that each compound noun has the same gender as the final word of the compound. Point out that this always happens with German compound nouns, no matter how long the compound noun is. Point out, too, that the plural form of compound nouns is always the same as the plural of the final word of the compound, e.g. the plural of *Wohnung* is *Wohnungen*, so the plural of *Ferienwohnung* is *Ferienwohnungen*. Challenge students to work out the plural of each compound noun listed here.
Remind students that it is often possible to deduce the meaning of compound nouns by breaking them down into their component parts, e.g. *Wohn + Wagen* = a vehicle for living in = a caravan.
Ask students to look back through the Student Book for other familiar compound nouns, and to try out the gender rule on them. Can they work out their plural forms too? See also the *Planner* above for a homework suggestion.

AT 2.2

3 Macht Dialoge.
Students play a dice game to practise talking about holiday accommodation. The dots on the dice represent 1–6 in ex. 1. Students take turns to throw the dice and say a corresponding sentence, e.g.
A: *Wo wohnst du in den Ferien?* (throws a 4)
B: *Ich wohne in einem Wohnwagen.*
Encourage them to vary the person of the verb (*ich, wir*), as on the ex. 2 recording.

AT 1.4 / AT 3.3 / L&S 1.1, 1.2 / LLS 5.7

4 Sieh dir das Video an. Lies a–c. Wer ist das – Ali, Nico oder Nina?
Before watching the video, see the *Planner* above for a starter activity to help students prepare. Once you've done the starter, play the video: Ali, Nico and Nina talk about their holiday plans. Paragraphs a–c provide a summary of what each person says. Students work out which paragraph corresponds with each person.
You may wish to point out that although paragraph c uses the word *Oma*, which students should recognise from Unit 1A, a different word for "grandmother" is used on the video. Help students to work out what it might be: elicit the word for "grandparents", which students should remember from Unit 1A, and break it down into its component parts: *Großeltern = Groß + Eltern.*

208

4B.1 Zu Besuch

Based on this, challenge them to work out the words for "grandmother" and "grandfather": *Groß + Mutter = Großmutter*, *Groß + Vater = Großvater*. Elicit from students that these texts use the present tense to refer to future plans, and ask them to suggest another way to talk about the future: *werden* + infinitive, which they learned in Unit 4A. Challenge them to rewrite paragraphs a–c using *werden* + infinitive where appropriate.

Answers: **a** Nico; **b** Nina; **c** Ali

Video clip 4B (excerpt)
CD 2, track 59

See transcript on page 207.
Play the whole of the first section up to and including Nina's line: *Kein Computer, keine Action. Nur Sand, Sonne, Meer, Fisch und das zwei Wochen lang. Nee, danke!* …

AT 3.3 **5 Lies den Text in Übung 4 noch einmal. Was passt zusammen?**
Students read paragraphs a–c in ex. 4 again. They work out which pictures (1–10) represent each paragraph.

Answers: **a** 1, 6, 9, 10; **b** 3, 5, 7; **c** 2, 4, 8

KAL 4.2 **Follow-up**
LLS 5.3 Ask students to identify four prepositions in texts a–c in ex. 4 (*mit, nach, an / am, in*) and consider how to translate them into English. This is an opportunity to focus on non-literal translations and words that are translated differently in different contexts. Begin with *mit*, and elicit its meaning in the phrase *Pommes mit Ketchup*: "with". Point out that here, in the context of transport (*mit dem Zug, mit dem Auto*), it can't be translated as "with" because in English we don't talk about travelling "with the train" or "with the car" – we say "by train", "by car".
Look at *nach* in the texts and point out that it too is translated differently in different contexts, e.g. *Viertel nach elf* – quarter <u>past</u> eleven / quarter <u>after</u> eleven, *Komm nach Berlin* – come <u>to</u> Berlin.
Ask students how they would translate *in* (paragraph c). Here, it means "to" (i.e. it has the same meaning as *nach*), but in other contexts it can mean "in". Ask them how they would translate *an* and *am*: in paragraph 2, *an die Nordsee* means "to the North Sea", but in paragraph 3, *am* (or *an dem*) *Meer* means "<u>by</u> the sea" or "<u>at</u> the seaside".

AT 2.3–4 **6 Macht Dialoge.**
Students make up dialogues about holiday plans in response to the picture prompts. They ask and answer questions about destination, means of travel, length of stay and accommodation. Support is provided in the key language box.

AT 4.4 **Challenge**
Students imagine they are about to go on their dream holiday. They write a text explaining where they're going, how they're travelling, what type of accommodation they'll be staying in and the length of their stay. They are reminded to express their opinions too.

4B.2 Zu Besuch

4B.2 Wir fahren nach Wien!

Seite 138–139

Planner

Objectives
- Vocabulary: talk about what you can do on holiday and what you're going to do
- Grammar: modal verbs (*können, wollen*); the future tense (*werden* + infinitive)
- Skills: express opinions

Resources
- Student Book, pages 138–139
- CD 2, tracks 60–61
- Foundation and Higher Workbooks, page 73
- Workbook audio: CD 3, track 70 (Foundation), CD 4, track 71 (Higher)
- Copymasters 100 (ex. 2), 101 (ex. 2–3), 102 (ex. 1)
- Interactive OxBox, Unit 4B

Key language
Was kann man / können wir in Wien machen?
Es gibt viel zu machen. Man kann / Wir können … einen Ausflug machen / in einen Freizeitpark gehen / den Dom besuchen / eine Stadtrundfahrt machen / ein Wiener Schnitzel essen / ins Museum gehen.
Was werden wir machen?
Wir werden … Souvenirs kaufen / Pizza essen / ins Theater gehen / schwimmen / das Schloss besuchen / Freunde treffen.
Willst du Rad fahren / Tennis spielen / ins Kino gehen?
Das ist toll / super / schön / langweilig. Das gefällt mir (nicht).

Framework references
L&S 1.1, 1.2, 1.4; R&W 2.4, 2.5; KAL 4.3, 4.4, 4.5; LLS 5.1, 5.7, 5.8

Starters
- Student Book page 138, ex. 1. Before doing the listening activity, make sure students understand what the six photos represent: display the English equivalents of phrases a–f and give students a few moments to match them up. Talk about Vienna and Austria: has anyone in the class been there?
- Before beginning work on page 139, remind students of the future tense (taught in Unit 4A). Display two sentences, one with a modal verb and one with *werden* + infinitive, e.g. *Wir können einen Ausflug machen* and *Wir werden einen Ausflug machen*. Elicit from students the difference between them, then challenge them to rewrite ex. 4 from page 138 in the future tense, using the *wir* form of the verb throughout.

Plenaries
- Divide the class into teams. Call out a series of nouns or noun phrases; the teams take turns to put them into a sentence with a modal verb, e.g.
Teacher: *Fußball!*
Team A: *Wir können Fußball spielen.*
Teacher: *In einem Zelt!*
Team B: *Man kann in einem Zelt wohnen.*
Try to cover a range of contexts, and encourage students to vary the modals, e.g. *Man kann, Wir können, Willst du …?* You could also remind them of *Man soll* (from Unit 3A). Teams win a point per correct sentence.
- Repeat the first plenary, using the future tense instead of modal verbs. Alternatively, call out sentences in the present tense and ask teams to put them into the future.

Homework
- Student Book page 138, ex. 4.
- Student Book page 139, ex. 8.
- Student Book page 139, *Challenge*.

AT 1.4
L&S 1.1, 1.2
LLS 5.7, 5.8

1 Hör zu. Was ist die richtige Reihenfolge? Meinung: gut (✓) oder schlecht (✗)?
See *Planner* above for a starter activity before students listen to the recording. Before listening, students might also find it useful to read through the section on improving listening skills on Student Book spread 4B.6.
Play the recording: Kathi, Nina, Nico and Ali are going to Vienna for the weekend, and are discussing what there is to see and do there. Students listen and note the order in which Kathi mentions a–f, and whether each suggestion is met with a positive or negative comment.

Although this is a challenging script, support is provided by the photos and captions, so students can complete the activity by focusing on key words and phrases. They can work out the gist of the opinions by listening for tone of voice and familiar words (e.g. *Toll! Fantastisch!*). See *Follow-up* below for suggestions to exploit the script further.

Answers: b ✓, f ✗, d ✓, e ✗, c ✗, a ✓

4B.2 Zu Besuch

CD 2, track 60 Seite 138, Übung 1

Kathi: Schaut mal – wir machen eine Reise nach Wien! Meine Oma hat vier Fahrkarten gekauft – wir fahren mit dem Zug!
Ali: Super! Und wann fahren wir?
Kathi: Wir fahren am Wochenende – am Freitagabend, und wir kommen am Sonntagabend wieder zurück!
Nina: Toll! Aber wo wohnen wir?
Kathi: Kein Problem – wir können bei meiner Oma wohnen. Sie hat ein Haus in der Stadt.
Nico: Fantastisch! Und was können wir in Wien machen?
Kathi: Es gibt in Wien viel zu machen! Wir können in den Prater gehen.
Nico: Der Prater – was ist das?
Kathi: Das ist ein Freizeitpark.
Ali: Ja, toll!
Kathi: Oder wir können ins Museum gehen …
Nina: Nein, das gefällt mir nicht. Aber können wir eine Stadtrundfahrt machen?
Nico: Ja, super Idee!!
Kathi: Und danach können wir Wiener Schnitzel mit Pommes essen!
Ali: Nein, ich esse kein Fleisch!
Nina: Und was kann man noch in Wien machen?
Kathi: Wir können den Stephansdom besichtigen – das ist eine Kirche.
Nico: Nein, das ist langweilig!
Ali: Kann man in Wien auch einen Ausflug machen? Gibt es zum Beispiel einen Park?
Kathi: Ja, wir können einen Ausflug in den Wienerwald machen!
Nina: Schön!

Follow-up
Play the beginning of the recording again and challenge students to note the following details: How are they travelling to Vienna? (by train); When are they going and coming back? (they're going on Friday evening and returning on Sunday evening); Where will they stay? (with Kathi's grandmother).
For a reminder of different ways to express likes, dislikes and opinions, play the recording again and ask students to make a note of the comments made about a–f. This will help to prepare them for ex. 2.
Ask them to identify in the recording two ways to say "we can" (*wir können, man kann*).

2 Macht Dialoge. Was können wir in Wien machen?
Students take turns to suggest activities in Vienna (referring to a–f in ex. 1) and express opinions about them, e.g.
A: *Was können wir in Wien machen?*
B: *Wir können ins Museum gehen.*
A: *Nein, das gefällt mir nicht – das Museum ist langweilig.*

3 Lies den Text und füll die Lücken aus.
Students read a short text about what there is for young people to do in Vienna. They use their knowledge of grammar patterns to work out the correct position in the text for each modal verb and infinitive. Ask them to translate the text into English.

Answers: Hallo Jan! Ich freue mich auf deinen Besuch! Es gibt viel zu machen für Teenager in Wien. Wir können *im Markt-Café Kaffee* trinken. *Wir können auch in den Zoo* gehen. *Und man* kann *in den Park gehen – wir können dort Rad* fahren. *Willst du auch Tennis* spielen? *Oder* willst *du ins Kino gehen?*

4 Was kann man in Bremen machen? Schreib einen Text.
Students build a text based on the pictures provided, describing what there is to see and do in Bremen.

Example answer: Man kann ein Eis essen und einen Kaffee trinken, und man kann eine Stadtrundfahrt machen. Man kann auch Fußball spielen. Man kann Skateboard fahren und in den Freizeitpark gehen. Man kann auch in den Park gehen / einen Ausflug machen.

5 Was passt zusammen?
This activity and the *Grammatik* box remind students of the future tense (*werden* + infinitive), which was taught in Unit 4A. Students match activities a–f to pictures 1–6.

Answers: **a** 3; **b** 6; **c** 4; **d** 1; **e** 2; **f** 5

6 Hör zu (1–6). Ist alles richtig?
Students listen to check their answers to ex. 5.

4B.2 Zu Besuch

CD 2, track 61 Seite 139, Übung 6

Also, was werden wir am Sonntag alles machen?
1. Wir werden schwimmen – im Schwimmbad.
2. Wir werden das Schloss Schönbrunn besuchen.
3. Wir werden Souvenirs kaufen.
4. Wir werden Pizza essen.
5. Wir werden meine Freunde treffen.
6. Wir werden ins Theater gehen.

AT 2.3–4
L&S 1.4

7 Macht Dialoge.
Students take turns to suggest a different activity for each day of the week, using *werden* + infinitive. Encourage them to add a comment or opinion about each activity. If one of them makes a negative comment about an activity, they must negotiate an alternative for that day, e.g.
A: *Was werden wir am Montag machen?*
B: *Wir werden das Schloss besuchen. Das ist ziemlich interessant, oder?*
A: *Nein, das Schloss ist langweilig! Wir werden Eis essen!*
B: *Lecker! Und was werden wir am Dienstag machen?*
A: *Wir werden …*

AT 4.3
KAL 4.3, 4.4, 4.5

8 Schreib die Sätze im Futur auf.
Students rewrite sentences a–f using *werden* + infinitive. As a follow-up, ask them to rewrite the sentences again using modal verbs, e.g. *Man kann eine Stadtrundfahrt machen*, *Willst du ein Eis essen?*, *Wir können ins Museum gehen*, etc.

Answers: **a** Wir werden eine Stadtrundfahrt machen. **b** Ich werde ein Eis essen. **c** Wir werden ins Museum gehen. **d** Ich werde in der Disco tanzen. **e** Ich werde meine Oma besuchen. **f** Ich werde ins Schwimmbad gehen.

AT 4.4–5
R&W 2.4, 2.5
LLS 5.7, 5.8

Challenge
Students imagine that Kathi, Nico, Nina and Ali are coming to visit their town next week. They write out a schedule for a week's activities, giving their opinion of each suggestion.
Encourage them to explain their opinions using *denn*, and to include a range of structures: the present tense, the future, modal verbs, different persons of the verb (*ich, du, man, wir*), e.g. *Am Montag werden wir das Schloss besuchen. Das gefällt mir, denn es ist sehr interessant. Magst du Tennis? Man kann am Dienstag Tennis spielen, denn ich bin ziemlich sportlich und ich spiele sehr gern Tennis!*
Remind students of the criteria for achieving level 5, which you may have discussed in Unit 4A (see teaching notes for spread 4A.4 *Think* and *Challenge* on pages 191–192 of this book). For tips on evaluating and improving written work, refer them to the *Think* box towards the end of spread 3B.1 and the skills section on spread 4A.6.

4B.3 Zu Besuch

4B.3 Was hast du gemacht?

Seite 140–141

Planner

Objectives
- Vocabulary: say what you did on holiday
- Grammar: the perfect tense (*haben* and *sein* + past participle)
- Skills: recycle familiar words and phrases in the perfect tense

Resources
- Student Book, pages 140–141
- CD 2, tracks 62–63
- Foundation and Higher Workbooks, page 74
- Workbook audio: CD 3, track 71 (Foundation), CD 4, track 72 (Higher)
- Copymasters 101 (ex. 1), 102 (ex. 2–3)
- Interactive OxBox, Unit 4B

Key language
Was hast du gemacht?
Ich habe / Wir haben … Musik im Park gehört / Frisbee gespielt / Souvenirs gekauft / einen Ausflug gemacht / in der Disco getanzt.
Wohin bist du gefahren?
Ich bin / Wir sind … mit dem Zug / Auto gefahren.
Ich bin / Wir sind geflogen.
Wo hast du gewohnt?
Ich habe / Wir haben … in einem Hotel / in einem Zelt / in einem Ferienhaus / in einer Ferienwohnung gewohnt.

Framework references
L&S 1.4; R&W 2.4, 2.5; KAL 4.3, 4.4, 4.5; LLS 5.1, 5.2, 5.8

Starters
- Before beginning work on page 140, set students a puzzle on tenses. Display a jumble of past, present and future tense sentences, using the perfect tense sentences from a–e in ex. 1 together with the present and future tense versions of the same sentences: *Wir haben Musik im Park gehört, Wir hören Musik im Park, Wir werden Musik im Park hören, Wir haben Frisbee gespielt, Wir spielen Frisbee, Wir werden Frisbee spielen,* etc. Display a grid as follows with a question mark at the top of the left-hand column, the first row filled in as an example and four blank rows:

?	Present tense	Future tense
Wir haben Musik im Park gehört.	Wir hören Musik im Park.	Wir werden Musik im Park hören.
Wir …	Wir …	Wir …

Challenge students to copy out the grid and fill in the blanks with the jumbled sentences. Once they've identified the present tense and the future tense, everything else must go in the mystery column. Talk through the answers and ask students to guess what the mystery heading might be (Past tense). Elicit the English translations of the sentences and make sure students understand that different time frames are involved.
- Students play a dice game in pairs to practise the perfect tense with *haben*. The persons of the verb are numbered 1–6 to correspond with the dots on the dice: 1 = *ich habe gespielt*, 2 = *du hast gespielt*, 3 = *er / sie hat gespielt*, 4 = *wir haben gespielt*, 5 = *ihr habt gespielt*, 6 = *sie / Sie haben gespielt*. Students take turns to throw the dice and say the corresponding phrase. The first person to say all parts of the verb is the winner. To increase the challenge, ask them to say a full sentence (e.g. *Ich habe Frisbee gespielt*) or to vary the past participles (e.g. *Du hast ein Eis gekauft*).
- Repeat the previous starter using *sein*.

Plenaries
- Past–Present–Future duel. Two students stand up. Call out a sentence in the perfect tense, the present or the future. The two students compete to identify the tense, e.g.
Teacher: *Ich werde Souvenirs kaufen.*
Student A: Future!
The fastest student remains standing. The loser sits down and is replaced by another challenger. Continue around the class.
- Divide the class into teams. Call out a series of words or phrases; the teams take turns to put them into sentences using the perfect tense, e.g.
Teacher: *Rugby!*
Team A: *Ich habe Rugby gespielt.*
Teacher: *Skateboard!*
Team B: *Ich bin Skateboard gefahren.*
Be careful to choose only words or phrases that work with the past participles learned on this spread. Teams win a point per correct sentence.

Homework
- Student Book page 140, ex. 3.
- Student Book page 141, ex. 6 and / or *Challenge*.

4B.3 Zu Besuch

AT 1.2
AT 3.2
KAL 4.4, 4.5

1 Was passt zusammen? Ist alles richtig? Hör zu.
Before listening, make sure students understand what pictures 1–5 represent: ask them to match the phrases in the language box to the corresponding pictures. See the *Planner* above for a starter to introduce the perfect tense and revise the present and future.
Students then listen to check their answers.

Answers: **1** c; **2** e; **3** b; **4** d; **5** a

🎧 **CD 2, track 62** Seite 140, Übung 1
1 Wir haben einen Ausflug gemacht.
2 Wir haben Souvenirs gekauft.
3 Wir haben Frisbee gespielt.
4 Wir haben Musik im Park gehört.
5 Wir haben in der Disco getanzt

AT 2.2
LLS 5.2

2 Welcher Satz passt?
Students test each other on the perfect tense sentences from ex. 1. Student A gives the number of a picture; B responds by saying the corresponding sentence:
A: *Foto 4!*
B: *Wir haben Musik im Park gehört.*
Encourage students to progress to saying the sentences from memory, without reading from the language box.

KAL 4.3, 4.4, 4.5
LLS 5.1

Think
After reading through the *Grammatik* box, students work out how to build other phrases in the perfect tense: We played football – *Wir haben Fußball gespielt*, What did you do? – *Was habt ihr gemacht?*
Challenge them to make as many sentences as they can by replacing the noun *Frisbee* in the sentence *Wir haben Frisbee gespielt* with different sports or games, e.g. *Wir haben Rugby / Hockey / Klavier / Gitarre*, etc. *gespielt*. Do the same with other past participles, e.g. *Wir haben Souvenirs / Pommes / eine Jeans / einen Liter Milch*, etc. *gekauft*.

AT 4.2–3

3 Schreib Sätze im Perfekt mit *Ich habe* …
Students build sentences in the perfect tense.

Answers: **a** Ich habe einen Hamburger gekauft. **b** Ich habe Computerspiele gespielt. **c** Ich habe CDs gehört. **d** Ich habe eine Stadtrundfahrt gemacht. **e** Ich habe ein T-Shirt gekauft. **f** Ich habe Tennis gespielt.

AT 2.2–3
L&S 1.4
LLS 5.8

Follow-up
Ask students to compare their sentences for ex. 3. Do they agree? Can they identify and explain any mistakes? This provides an opportunity for peer assessment. Challenge students to do the activity entirely in German, e.g.
A: *Hast du „Ich habe ein Hamburger gekauft"?*
B: *Nein, a ist „einen Hamburger" – „Ich habe einen Hamburger gekauft."*
A: *Ach ja, richtig. Und b ist …*

AT 1.2–3
AT 3.2–3
KAL 4.4, 4.5

4 Was passt zusammen? Hör zu und lies.
Students read and listen to the texts, in which Nina, Kathi, Ali and Nico explain where they went on holiday last year, how they travelled and what type of accommodation they stayed in. Students choose two pictures to represent each person's holiday.
This activity recycles familiar vocabulary with a new grammar point (the perfect tense). The texts introduce another regular past participle (*gewohnt*) and two verbs that form their perfect tense with *sein* instead of *haben*: *wir sind gefahren, wir sind geflogen*. Read through the *Grammatik* box on the perfect tense with *sein*.

Answers: Nina: 2 d; Kathi: 4 c; Ali: 1 a; Nico: 3 b

🎧 **CD 2, track 63** Seite 141, Übung 4
Nina: Wir sind mit dem Zug nach Griechenland gefahren. Wir haben in einem Ferienhaus gewohnt.
Kathi: Wir sind nach Spanien geflogen. Wir haben in einem Hotel gewohnt.
Ali: Wir sind mit dem Auto nach Istanbul gefahren. Wir haben in einer Wohnung gewohnt.
Nico: Wir sind mit dem Wohnwagen nach Frankreich gefahren. Wir haben auf einem Campingplatz gewohnt.

AT 3.3

5 Lies den Brief und füll die Lücken aus.
Students read a letter about a past holiday. They fill in the missing past participles and auxiliary verbs, choosing from the words provided.

Answers: Wir <u>sind</u> im Sommer nach Österreich gefahren. Wir sind mit dem Auto <u>gefahren</u>, und wir <u>haben</u> in einer Ferienwohnung gewohnt. Wir haben ein Picknick im Park <u>gemacht</u>. Ich <u>habe</u> auch Souvenirs <u>gekauft</u>. Und ich habe in der Disco <u>getanzt</u>!

4B.3 Zu Besuch

AT 4.2–3
KAL 4.3, 4.4, 4.5

6 Schreib Sätze.
Students write sentences in the perfect tense to correspond with pictures a–d.

Answers: **a** *Ich bin mit dem Auto nach Italien gefahren. Ich habe in einem Hotel gewohnt.* **b** *Ich bin mit dem Zug nach Spanien gefahren. Ich habe in einer Ferienwohnung gewohnt.* **c** *Ich bin nach Österreich mit dem Rad gefahren. Ich habe in einem Zelt gewohnt.* **d** *Ich bin nach Griechenland geflogen. Ich habe in einem Hotel gewohnt.*

AT 4.4
R&W 2.4, 2.5

Challenge
Students write their own short account of a past holiday, using ex. 5 as a model. Questions are provided as prompts: Where did they go? How did they travel? Where did they stay? What did they do?

4B.4 Zu Besuch

4B.4 Im Prater
Seite 142–143

Planner

Objectives
- Vocabulary: talk about a visit to an amusement park
- Grammar: recognise and describe actions in the present, past and future
- Skills: recycle familiar words and phrases in a range of tenses

Resources
- Student Book, pages 142–143
- CD 2, tracks 64–65
- Foundation and Higher Workbooks, page 75
- Workbook audio: CD 3, track 72 (Foundation), CD 4, track 73 (Higher)
- Copymasters 100 (ex. 3), 103 (ex. 1–2), 104
- Interactive OxBox, Unit 4B

Key language
Wohin bist du gestern gefahren? Wir sind mit dem Bus zum Prater gefahren.
Was habt ihr dort gemacht? Wir sind Achterbahn gefahren. Wir haben einen Ausflug gemacht.
Was macht ihr heute? Wir kaufen Souvenirs. Wir wollen mit dem Riesenrad fahren. Wir können im Wasserpark spielen.
Was werdet ihr morgen machen? Wir werden ein Picknick machen.
letztes Wochenende, gestern, heute, heute Abend, morgen, jeden Tag, zweimal in der Woche

Framework references
R&W 2.1, 2.2; IU 3.1, 3.2; KAL 4.2, 4.3, 4.4, 4.5, 4.6; LLS 5.1, 5.4, 5.5

Starters
- Student Book page 142, *Think*. This activity revises time expressions in preparation for the work on tenses on this spread.
- Set students a sudoku-style puzzle. Display a four-by-four grid, with *ich fahre nach Berlin, ich habe eine Jacke gekauft, ich werde Tennis spielen* and *man kann Musik hören* filled in as shown in bold in the following answer grid and the rest of the squares blank. Display the other sentences (shown in non-bold in the solution) jumbled up alongside the grid. Challenge students to copy out the grid and fill in the blank squares using the sentences provided, so that each row and each column contains one example each of the perfect tense, the present tense, the future and a modal verb. Finally, ask students to translate the completed grid into English. Possible solution:

ich fahre nach Berlin	ich werde Kaffee trinken	man kann Rad fahren	ich habe in der Disco getanzt
man kann in den Zoo gehen	**ich habe eine Jacke gekauft**	ich wohne in einem Hotel	ich werde schwimmen
ich habe Fußball gespielt	man kann ein Eis essen	**ich werde Tennis spielen**	ich fahre mit dem Zug
ich werde ins Kino gehen	ich mache einen Ausflug	ich bin nach Wien geflogen	**man kann Musik hören**

Plenaries
- Teacher versus the class. Ask students to close their books, then begin to talk about Kathi's trip to the Prater, giving a mixture of true and false information. Challenge students to identify what is false. They win a point for each error they spot and an extra point if they can correct it; the teacher wins a point for each error students fail to spot:
Teacher: *Wir sind mit dem Zug zum Prater gefahren.*
Class: *Falsch! Mit dem Bus!* (2 points to the class)
Teacher: *Morgen werden wir mit dem Riesenrad fahren.*
Class: *Falsch! Wir sind gestern mit dem Riesenrad gefahren.* (2 points to the class)
- Divide the class into teams. Call out a series of time expressions; the teams take turns to put them into sentences (in any context) using an appropriate tense, e.g.
Teacher: *Morgen!*
Team A: *Ich werde morgen Pizza essen.*
Teacher: *Letztes Wochenende!*
Team B: *Ich bin letztes Wochenende nach Deutschland gefahren.*
Teams win a point for each correct sentence.

Homework
- Ask students to research some of the attractions mentioned in the ex. 1 text, e.g. the Prater and the Riesenrad (www.praterservice.at, www.wienerriesenrad.com). If they were planning a trip to Vienna, which places would they want to visit?
- Student Book page 142, ex. 2.
- Student Book page 143: ex. 4, 5 and *Challenge* are all suitable homework tasks. Alternatively, ask students to rewrite a–g from ex. 3 using modal verbs, e.g. *Willst du einen Ausflug zum Prater machen? Man kann mit der U-Bahn fahren. Wir können …*

4B.4 Zu Besuch

KAL 4.2
LLS 5.4

Think
Before doing ex. 1, look at the *Think* box. Students consider a set of time expressions and work out which ones relate to the past, which to the present and which to the future. Explain that while some of them relate to one time frame only (e.g. *gestern* and *letztes Wochenende* can only relate to the past, *morgen* can only relate to the future), others may relate to several time frames (e.g. *ich spiele jeden Tag Fußball, ich werde jeden Tag Fußball spielen*).
Point out that time phrases can provide clues to help work out meaning, e.g. if you aren't able to understand the tenses in a text, it is still possible to work out references to the past, present and future by using the time phrases as signals.
Ask students to identify which of the time expressions listed in the *Think* box come up in the ex. 1 text (*gestern, heute, morgen*) and to spot one more in the text (*heute Abend*). Challenge them to come up with further time expressions.

AT 1.5–6
AT 3.5–6
KAL 4.3, 4.4, 4.5, 4.6
LLS 5.1

1 Hör zu und lies. Welche Sätze sind im Präsens (Pr), im Perfekt (Pe) und im Futur (F) – und welche enthalten Modalverben (M)?
Students read and listen to a conversation about sightseeing in Vienna. They identify verbs in the present, past and future, and modal verbs. Explain that being able to distinguish between present, past and future events is one of the features of level 6 reading and listening. Point out the question forms in the past, present and future in the ex. 1 text.

Answers: see transcript

🎧 **CD 2, track 64**   Seite 142, Übung 1

Susi: Wohin <u>bist</u> du gestern <u>gefahren</u> (*Pe*), Kathi?
Kathi: Wir <u>sind</u> mit dem Bus zum Prater <u>gefahren</u> (*Pe*). Der Prater <u>liegt</u> (*Pr*) in einem großen Park in der Stadtmitte.
Susi: Und was <u>habt</u> ihr dort <u>gemacht</u>? (*Pe*)
Kathi: Im Prater <u>gibt</u> es (*Pr*) viel zu machen: Wir <u>sind</u> Achterbahn und mit dem Riesenrad <u>gefahren</u> (*Pe*), und wir <u>haben</u> im Wasserpark <u>gespielt</u> (*Pe*). Wir <u>haben</u> auch in der Open-Air-Disco <u>getanzt</u>! (*Pe*)
Susi: Und was <u>macht</u> ihr (*Pr*) heute?

Kathi: Wir <u>machen</u> (*Pr*) heute eine Stadtrundfahrt, und wir <u>besichtigen</u> (*Pr*) den Stephansdom. Und wir <u>wollen</u> (*M*) ins Mozart-Museum gehen. Und heute Abend <u>können</u> wir (*M*) in ein Konzert gehen – an der Donau.
Susi: Was <u>werdet</u> ihr morgen <u>machen</u>? (*F*)
Kathi: Wir <u>werden</u> einen Ausflug in den Wienerwald <u>machen</u> (*F*) – man <u>kann</u> (*M*) dort gut ein Picknick machen. Das <u>macht</u> (*Pr*) Spaß! Meine Oma <u>hat</u> Salat <u>gemacht</u> (*Pe*), und Nina und ich <u>werden</u> Pizza machen (*F*).

AT 3.5–6
R&W 2.1, 2.2
IU 3.1, 3.2

2 Richtig (R) oder falsch (F)?
Students read the ex. 1 conversation again and work out whether statements a–f are true or false. To exploit the range of tenses in the text, ask students to note down as much detail as possible in English, identifying which activities took place yesterday, which are happening today and which will take place tomorrow.
The text mentions a number of attractions in Vienna. Ask students to research some of them: see first homework suggestion in the *Planner* above.

Answers: **a** F (they went by bus); **b** R; **c** R; **d** F (they can go to a concert on the Danube); **e** R; **f** F (Kathi's grandmother has made a salad, and Kathi and Nina are going to make a pizza)

AT 1.2
AT 3.2

3 Hör zu und lies. Was passt zusammen?
Students read and listen to the schedule for a day's activities. They choose a picture to represent each sentence.

Answers: **a** 7; **b** 3; **c** 5; **d** 1; **e** 4; **f** 2; **g** 6

🎧 **CD 2, track 65**   Seite 143, Übung 3

 9 Uhr: Wir machen einen Ausflug zum Prater!
10 Uhr: Wir fahren mit der U-Bahn.
11 Uhr: Wir kaufen ein Programm für den Prater.
12 Uhr: Wir machen eine Fahrt mit dem Karussell.
13 Uhr: Wir spielen im Wasserpark.
14 Uhr: Wir hören tolle Musik.
15 Uhr: Wir tanzen in der Open-Air-Disco.

4B.4 Zu Besuch

AT 4.3 / KAL 4.4, 4.5

4 Schreib die Sätze von Übung 3 im Perfekt auf.
Students rewrite each sentence from ex. 3 in the perfect tense.

Answers: **a** Wir haben um neun Uhr einen Ausflug zum Prater gemacht. **b** Wir sind um zehn Uhr mit der U-Bahn gefahren. **c** Wir haben um elf Uhr ein Programm für den Prater gekauft. **d** Wir haben um zwölf Uhr eine Fahrt mit dem Karussell gemacht. **e** Wir haben um dreizehn Uhr im Wasserpark gespielt. **f** Wir haben um vierzehn Uhr tolle Musik gehört. **g** Wir haben um fünfzehn Uhr in der Open-Air-Disco getanzt.

AT 4.3 / KAL 4.4, 4.5

5 Was werden sie morgen machen? Jetzt schreib die Sätze im Futur auf!
Students rewrite each sentence from ex. 3 in the future tense, replacing the clock times with *morgen*.

Answers: **a** Wir werden morgen einen Ausflug zum Prater machen. **b** Wir werden morgen mit der U-Bahn fahren. **c** Wir werden morgen ein Programm für den Prater kaufen. **d** Wir werden morgen eine Fahrt mit dem Karussell machen. **e** Wir werden morgen im Wasserpark spielen. **f** Wir werden morgen tolle Musik hören. **g** Wir werden morgen in der Open-Air-Disco tanzen.

AT 4.4–5 / KAL 4.4, 4.5 / LLS 5.5

Challenge
Students write three sentences for each picture, one in the perfect tense, one in the present and one in the future. Encourage them to make up additional sentences using their own ideas and to check the past participles in the verb list on page 166 of the Student Book.

Answers: Wir haben einen Hamburger gegessen. Wir essen einen Hamburger. Wir werden einen Hamburger essen.
Wir sind ins Kino gegangen. Wir gehen ins Kino. Wir werden ins Kino gehen.
Wir haben in der Disco getanzt. Wir tanzen in der Disco. Wir werden in der Disco tanzen.
Wir haben eine Stadtrundfahrt gemacht. Wir machen eine Stadtrundfahrt. Wir werden eine Stadtrundfahrt machen.
Wir haben eine CD gekauft. Wir kaufen eine CD. Wir werden eine CD kaufen.
Wir haben Cola getrunken. Wir trinken Cola. Wir werden Cola trinken.

4B.5 Zu Besuch

4B.5 Nicos Videoblog

Seite 144–145

Planner

Objectives
- Vocabulary: talk about holiday experiences and holiday plans
- Grammar: verbs in the past, present and future; modal verbs
- Skills: recognise and use a range of structures; apply previously learned language in new contexts

Video
- Video blog 4B

Resources
- Student Book, pages 144–145
- CD 2, track 66
- Foundation and Higher Workbooks, page 76
- Workbook audio: CD 3, track 73 (Foundation), CD 4, track 74 (Higher)
- Interactive OxBox, Unit 4B

Key language
Recycle language from Unit 4B and other contexts

Framework references
L&S 1.1, 1.2; R&W 2.1, 2.2, 2.4, 2.5; IU 3.1, 3.2; LLS 5.7, 5.8

Starters
- Before watching Nico's video blog, display a–h from ex. 1 and tell students to keep their books closed. Challenge them to predict the correct answers. (Alternatively, if you feel you can trust them not to look at Nico's text, allow them to work from a–h on page 144, keeping Nico's text covered!) Students should be able to work out a lot of the answers using a combination of logic, guesswork and what they already know about Vienna.
- Before beginning work on Bernd's text in ex. 2, ask students to keep their books closed and tell them they are about to read about a German boy's future visit to Edinburgh to stay with his penfriend. Display a list of key words and phrases from the text (e.g. *Schottland, Edinburgh, in den Sommerferien, zwei Wochen, langweilig, Nintendo*, means of transport, family members, places in Edinburgh) together with others that aren't in the text but seem plausible (e.g. *Schottisch, Haggis, Dom, Schloss, Museum, einkaufen, Altstadt*). Tell students how many of the words appear in the text (e.g. try to make it roughly between ten and fifteen), and challenge them to predict which they are. Students then check against Bernd's text.

Plenaries
- Read out Nico's blog but introduce some errors and challenge the class to spot them, e.g.
  Teacher: *In den Sommerferien fahren wir nach Wien …*
  Class: *Nein, nicht in den Sommerferien … am Wochenende!*
  Teacher: *Okay, am Wochenende fahren wir nach Wien – das wird bestimmt super! Wir fahren mit dem Bus von Berlin …*
  Class: *Nein, wir fahren mit dem Zug, nicht mit dem Bus!*
- Working in pairs, students tell each other what they feel are the most important and / or interesting things they have learned in Unit 4B, in terms of grammar, vocabulary, cultural information or skills. What do they feel they did well? What did they find most difficult? Allow time for whole-class feedback and discussion.
- See second homework suggestion: students exchange their questions with a partner, or you could collect them in for a class quiz.

Homework
- Ask students to find out about Viennese café culture and the tradition of *Kaffee und Kuchen* (mentioned by Nico in his video blog). Alternatively, they could research some of the other Viennese attractions and report back to the class in a following lesson.
- Students write five questions to test their partner's knowledge of Unit 4B (vocabulary, grammar and culture) and compile a separate answer sheet. They exchange their questions with their partner in a following lesson. Alternatively, collect in everyone's questions and use them in a class quiz.
- Student Book page 145, ex. 3 or *Challenge*.

---

1 Sieh dir das Video an. Wähle die passenden Antworten.

AT 1.5
AT 3.5
L&S 1.1, 1.2
IU 3.1, 3.2
LLS 5.7, 5.8

Nico talks about the four teenagers' plans for their trip to Vienna. Students choose option 1 or 2 to complete each sentence a–h. Point out that they can probably predict some of the answers in advance, based on sensible guesswork and what they already know. Refer them to the listening strategies on spread 4B.6.

The full text of Nico's blog appears in the Student Book, so the activity could be done as a reading exercise. Alternatively, students could watch the video blog and try to complete as much of a–h before reading the text, then refer to the text for any details they were unable to spot. For an additional challenge, ask students to note down as much extra detail as they can.

219

4B.5 Zu Besuch

Nico refers to a number of things to see and do in Vienna, including Viennese café culture and the tradition of *Kaffee und Kuchen*. Encourage students to do further research online: see first homework suggestion in the *Planner* above.

Answers: **a** 1; **b** 2; **c** 1; **d** 1; **e** 2; **f** 1; **g** 2; **h** 1

Video clip 4B
CD 2, track 66 Seite 144, Übung 1

Am Wochenende fahren wir nach Wien! Das wird bestimmt super! Wir fahren mit dem Zug von Berlin aus. Wien ist sehr groß – dort leben fast zwei Millionen Menschen. Und im Sommer ist es dort sehr sehr heiß und sonnig, natürlich auch. Aber im Winter ist es dort kalt und es schneit oft, sagt Kathi.
In Wien ist auch ein Fluss: die Donau. Da kann man Schiffsfahrten darauf machen. Und es gibt auch ein Schloss: Schloss Schönbrunn. Das ist sehr alt und ziemlich berühmt.
Und was kann man dann noch in Wien machen? Wir können auch in ein Kaffeehaus gehen, denn die Wiener essen gern Kuchen und trinken viel Kaffee. Das wollen wir natürlich auch machen!
Und wir wollen auch eine Stadtrundfahrt machen, und Souvenirs für meine Eltern kaufen. Das wird bestimmt total toll!

2 Lies den Text und beantworte die Fragen.
Students read about Bernd's holiday plans and answer questions in English. Encourage them to note down as much detail as they can in answer to each question.

Answers: **a** to Edinburgh for two weeks; **b** by bus, ferry and train; **c** it's a 12-hour journey so it will be boring, but he'll take his Nintendo and iPod for something to do; **d** with his penfriend Joseph and family (sister Sandra is 11, brother William is 16, parents are called Penny and Angus); **e** he'll have to speak English all the time because Joseph's family don't speak German; **f** youth club, cinema, disco, football match, swimming pool, skateboarding

3 Schreib einen neuen Brief – im Perfekt oder im Futur.
Students write a letter about a past holiday or their plans for a future holiday.
Although they can use Bernd's letter as a model and a source of language / ideas, they will need to make sure they use the correct tenses depending on whether they choose to describe a past or a future holiday.
Point out that even though they are writing about the past or the future, their text should still include some examples of the present tense, e.g. descriptions (*es gibt …*) and opinions, modal verbs (*man kann …*).
Instead of doing this in letter format, students could write and record a video blog, similar to Nico's.

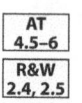

Challenge
Students write a letter to a German penfriend, inviting him or her to visit them. Prompts and key phrases are provided. Point out the tip about level 6, and encourage students to look for an opportunity to use the perfect tense in their letter as well as the present and the future, e.g. by referring to past experiences, e.g. *Wir können einkaufen gehen, denn es gibt hier tolle Geschäfte. Letztes Wochenende habe ich eine neue Jeans gekauft! Teuer, aber schick! …*
For tips on evaluating and improving their written work, refer students to the *Think* box towards the end of spread 3B.1 and the skills section on spread 4A.6.

4B.6 Zu Besuch

4B.6 Sprachlabor
Seite 146–147

> **Planner**
>
> **Objectives**
> - Grammar: the perfect tense with *haben* and *sein*
> - Skills: improve listening skills; pronounce word endings
>
> **Resources**
> - Student Book, pages 146–147
> - CD 2, tracks 67–68
>
> - Foundation and Higher Workbooks, pages 77–78
> - Copymasters 105, 106
> - Interactive OxBox, Unit 4B
>
> **Framework references**
> KAL 4.1, 4.3, 4.4, 4.5; LLS 5.1, 5.7, 5.8

The perfect tense with *haben*

KAL 4.3, 4.4, 4.5 / LLS 5.1 1 Unscramble the word order in these sentences.

Answers: **a** Wir haben in einem Ferienhaus gewohnt. **b** Ich habe Kuchen gekauft. **c** Ich habe ein Poster gemacht. **d** Ich habe in einem Wohnwagen gewohnt. **e** Wir haben eine Stadtrundfahrt gemacht. **f** Ich habe viele Souvenirs gekauft.

The perfect tense with *sein*

KAL 4.3, 4.4, 4.5 / LLS 5.1 2 Fill in the gaps with the correct form of *sein* or *haben*.

Answers: **a** bin; **b** haben; **c** haben; **d** bin; **e** haben; **f** sind

3 Fill in the missing past participles.

Answers: **a** gewohnt; **b** gefahren; **c** gespielt; **d** gehört; **e** gefahren

4 Write the sentences in the perfect tense.

Answers: **a** Wir sind nach Spanien geflogen. **b** Ich habe Souvenirs gekauft. **c** Wir haben Schokoladeneis gegessen. **d** Ich bin nach Berlin gefahren. **e** Ich habe in der Disco getanzt. **f** Ich habe eine Stadtrundfahrt gemacht.

Improving your listening skills

LLS 5.7, 5.8 This section focuses on listening strategies:
- Prepare for listening by looking carefully at pictures and headings: they often provide clues to help you predict the context.
- Read the questions carefully in advance: they sometimes help you to anticipate what the answers are likely to be and what sort of language might come up.
- While listening, focus on the speakers' tone of voice: do they sound happy, surprised, angry, etc.? Are they asking questions or making statements?
- Instead of trying to understand everything, focus on identifying key words / phrases and ignore anything irrelevant.

Point out that if you're watching a video or having a face-to-face conversation with someone, you can use visuals as clues too, including people's facial expressions and gestures.

Word endings

KAL 4.1 This section highlights the importance of pronouncing word endings clearly (and identifying them when listening), because the endings provide grammar information which can affect meaning.

5 Listen carefully: *einen*, *einer* or *einem*? (a–h)

Answers: see underlining in transcript

4B.7 Zu Besuch

CD 2, track 67   Seite 147, Übung 5 und 6

a Ich wohne in <u>einem</u> Wohnwagen.
b Ich habe <u>einen</u> Hund.
c Ich wohne in <u>einer</u> Stadt.
d Ich habe <u>einen</u> Bruder.
e Ich trage <u>einen</u> Rock.
f Ich wohne in <u>einem</u> Haus.
g Ich wohne in <u>einer</u> Wohnung.
h Ich wohne in <u>einem</u> Zelt.

6 Listen again to check your answers.
When checking the answers, ask students what sort of information is provided by each word ending, e.g. *einem* shows that the noun is masculine and in the dative case, *einen* shows that the noun is masculine and in the accusative case.

7 Now practise pronouncing a–h. Be careful to say the word endings clearly!
This recording is identical to ex. 5, except that here there is a pause after each sentence to give students time to repeat it.

CD 2, track 68   Seite 147, Übung 7

a Ich wohne in einem Wohnwagen.
b Ich habe einen Hund.
c Ich wohne in einer Stadt.
d Ich habe einen Bruder.
e Ich trage einen Rock.
f Ich wohne in einem Haus.
g Ich wohne in einer Wohnung.
h Ich wohne in einem Zelt.

4B.7 Extra Star   Seite 148

Planner

Objectives
- Vocabulary: talk about holidays
- Grammar: prepositions followed by the dative case (*mit, in*); verbs in the past, present and future
- Skills: identify language patterns and use knowledge of grammar to work out meaning

Resources
- Student Book, page 148
- Copymaster 107

AT 4.2 **1 Fill in the gaps.**
Students complete each phrase with the correct form of the definite or indefinite article and mode of transport.

Answers: **a** mit dem Wohnwagen; **b** in einem Zelt; **c** mit dem Auto; **d** in einer Ferienwohnung; **e** mit dem Zug; **f** in einem Hotel

AT 3.2 **2 Find the correct pictures.**
Students choose a picture to represent each sentence about future holiday activities.

Answers: **a** 3; **b** 4; **c** 2; **d** 6; **e** 1; **f** 5

AT 3.2 **3 Match up the sentences.**
Students match the German sentences to their English translations.

Answers: **a** 3; **b** 5; **c** 1; **d** 6; **e** 4; **f** 2

AT 3.3 **4 Fill in the gaps using the words below.**
Students need to use their knowledge of language patterns to complete this activity, since the missing words are a mixture of past participles, auxiliary verbs and present tense verbs. Once they've filled in the missing words, ask them to translate the sentences into English.

Answers: **a** bin; **b** gewohnt; **c** machen; **d** gehe; **e** werden; **f** kaufen

4B.7 Zu Besuch

4B.7 Extra Plus

Seite 149

Planner

Objectives
- Vocabulary: talk about holidays
- Grammar: verbs in the past, present and future; modal verbs (*können*)
- Skills: identify language patterns and use knowledge of grammar to work out meaning

Resources
- Student Book, page 149
- Copymaster 108

AT 3.2–3

1 Was ist die richtige Reihenfolge?
Students rewrite the sentences using correct word order. Structures include the perfect tense, the future tense, the present tense and modal verbs. Ask students to translate the sentences into English.

Answers: **a** Wir haben in einem Zelt geschlafen. **b** Wir können ein Eis essen. **c** Ich fahre am Wochenende nach Berlin. **d** Wir werden den Stephansdom besichtigen. **e** Man kann einen Ausflug in Wien machen. **f** Ich bin nach Spanien geflogen.

AT 4.4–6

2 Beantworte diese Fragen.
Students give written responses to questions about a past holiday, what there is to do in their town, what they're doing today and what they're going to do tomorrow. They follow the picture prompts provided.
Challenge able students to expand their answers to produce a longer, more detailed text instead of just writing a list of sentences. Discuss with them the criteria for level 4, 5 and 6.

AT 3.5–6

3 Richtig (R) oder falsch (F)?
Students read about a holiday in Switzerland and work out whether statements a–h are true or false. Ask them to correct the false statements.

Students who give the correct response to statement b show that they are beginning to work towards level 6, because one of the features of level 6 reading is the ability to distinguish between past, present and future events.

Answers: **a** R; **b** F (he's already been on a sightseeing tour); **c** F (he bought a watch); **d** R; **e** F (there are restaurants at the amusement park); **f** R; **g** F (he says he'll dance in the disco); **h** R

AT 3.3–4

4 Füll die Lücken aus.
Students need to use their knowledge of language patterns to complete this activity, since the missing words are a mixture of past participles, auxiliary verbs and present tense verbs. Once they've filled in the missing words, ask them to translate the text into English.

Answers: Ich <u>bin</u> am Sonntag nach Paris <u>gefahren</u>. Ich <u>habe</u> in einem Hotel <u>gewohnt</u>. Wir <u>besuchen</u> heute den Eiffelturm. Wir können auch den Louvre <u>besichtigen</u>. Wir <u>werden</u> morgen nach Versailles fahren, und ich werde dort Souvenirs <u>kaufen</u>.

4B.8 Zu Besuch

4B.8 Testseite

Seite 150

Planner

Resources
- Student Book, page 150
- CD x, track xx
- Foundation and Higher Workbooks, page 79
- Copymasters 97, 98
- Assessment, Unit 4B

AT 1.5 **1 Listen and answer the questions.**
Encourage students to note down as much additional detail as possible. If they are able to work out that Jan's family usually goes to Austria but this year went to Greece, it shows they are able to distinguish between different tenses.

Answers: a Greece (usually goes to Austria but this summer he and his parents went to Greece); b he flew; c in a hotel (by the sea); d went on an excursion, bought (lots of) souvenirs, swam in the sea (every day); e ate fish (every day), drank cola; f (sometimes) danced in the disco (he likes dancing)

🎧 **CD 2, track 69** Seite 150, Übung 1

– Jan, wohin bist du in den Ferien gefahren?
– Also, wir fahren normalerweise in den Ferien nach Österreich, aber diesen Sommer bin ich mit meinen Eltern nach Griechenland geflogen. Griechenland ist sehr schön, aber es ist dort sehr heiß.
– Und wo hast du gewohnt?
– Wir haben in einem Hotel direkt am Meer gewohnt.
– Und was hast du dort alles gemacht?
– Man kann in Griechenland viel machen! Wir haben einen Ausflug gemacht, und ich habe viele Souvenirs gekauft. Man kann auch im Meer schwimmen – das habe ich jeden Tag gemacht.
– Und was hast du in Griechenland gegessen?
– Also, das Essen in Griechenland ist super – wir haben jeden Tag Fisch gegessen, und ich habe Cola getrunken.
– Und was hast du abends gemacht?
– Abends bin ich manchmal in die Disco gegangen. Ich tanze sehr gern!

AT 3.5 **2 Read Maja's message and answer the questions below in English.**
Encourage students to note down as much extra detail as possible.

Answers: a to Spain (with her mother); b by train, stayed in a holiday flat; c to Munich (with her father); d by car, will stay with grandparents; e to Zurich (with her school, by bus, will stay for a week); f go skiing (because it often snows in the winter)

AT 2.3–5 **3 Describe your holiday plans. Make a mini-presentation if you can, using the following points.**
Students give a presentation about their holiday plans, following the prompts provided.
Point out the tip about aiming for level 5, and suggest how students might create an opportunity to use another tense, e.g. by comparing a past holiday with their plans for this year: *Letztes Jahr bin ich nach Frankreich gefahren. Ich habe in einem Zelt gewohnt – billig, aber unbequem! Dieses Jahr werde ich nicht in einem Zelt wohnen. Ich möchte in einem Hotel wohnen, denn ein Hotel ist bequemer als ein Zelt!*
Remind students to express and justify their opinions, and to use a variety of structures.

AT 4.4–6 **4 Write at least five sentences about a recent holiday. Include the details below.**
Students describe a recent holiday (real or imaginary). Emphasise that in activities like this where they are specifically asked to include certain details, they must be sure to cover all the points or they will risk losing marks. Point out the tip about aiming for level 6, and remind them of the criteria for level 4, 5 and 6.

4B Zu Besuch

4B Lesen

Seite 160

Planner

Resources
- Student Book, page 160

Framework references
R&W 2.1, 2.2; IU 3.1, 3.2

Ferienländer: die Top 10 der Deutschen!

AT 3.3–4

1 Look at the list of German holiday destinations at the top of the page. True or false?
Students read the percentages about favourite holiday destinations and work out whether statements a–d are true or false.

Answers: **a** true; **b** false; **c** true; **d** false

AT 3.5–6

2 Answer the questions in English.
Students answer questions about Zurich.

Answers: **a** in north-east Switzerland; **b** 1.1 million people live there, 9 million people visit each year; **c** opera, lots of theatres, more than 50 museums (including a doll museum); **d** the Bahnhofstraße is very famous as a shopping street because it has big department stores, expensive fashion shops, modern boutiques, lots of shops selling clocks / watches, and you can buy the famous Swiss chocolate there; **e** you can go on a lake cruise, swim, go sailing or go for a walk; **f** go skiing

Follow-up

- Students do a survey to find the Top Ten holiday destinations of their classmates, then compare with the German results.

- Student B has a few moments to memorise the order of the holiday destinations before closing his / her book. A then tests B's memory with some true / false statements:
  A: *Polen ist beliebter als Frankreich.*
  B: *Nein, das ist falsch.*
  A: *Griechenland ist Nummer sechs.*
  B: *Falsch?*
  A: *Nein, das ist richtig!*
  Make sure they reverse roles so that they both have a turn at asking and answering.

- Students look online for some of the places in Zurich mentioned in the text. Ask them to choose one aspect of Zurich (e.g. culture, shopping, outdoor activities) and to find out something about it. They tell the class about it in a following lesson.

- Students imagine they can choose an all-expenses-paid holiday to any area of Germany, Austria or Switzerland. They find out as much as they can about their chosen destination and build a schedule of activities (either in English or German). They give a presentation about it or produce a classroom display.

4B Zu Besuch

Foundation Workbook

4B.1 Die Ferien (Seite 72)

AT 1.3 **1** Listen to the conversation and circle the right information.

Answers: **a** Spain; **b** plane; **c** apartment; **d** two weeks; **e** always sunny; **f** with other people

🎧 **CD 3, track 69** Seite 72, Übung 1

- Hey Olaf, wohin fährst du in den Ferien?
- Ach, wir fahren nach Spanien, wie immer.
- Wo denn in Spanien?
- Wir fliegen nach Mallorca. Da ist es immer sonnig.
- Wo wohnt ihr?
- Wir wohnen in einer Ferienwohnung direkt am Meer. Es ist echt toll da.
- Schön! Wie lange bleibt ihr?
- Wir bleiben zwei Wochen.

2 Choose *einer* or *einem*.

Answers: **a** einem; **b** einer; **c** einem; **d** einem; **e** einer; **f** einem

AT 3.2 **3** Fill in the grid in English.

Answers: **a** car, Italy; **b** train, Austria; **c** plane, Turkey; **d** camper van, France

4B.2 Wir fahren nach Wien! (Seite 73)

AT 3.2 **1** Complete the sentences in the same order as the places are mentioned in the brochure.

Answers: **a** eine Hafenrundfahrt machen; **b** auf dem Markt einkaufen; **c** Fisch essen; **d** zum Zoo gehen; **e** Karussell fahren; **f** ins Museum gehen

AT 1.3 **2** Listen to these people planning a day out in Hamburg. Put a tick by the things they plan to do and a cross by those they don't.

Answers: **a** ✓; **b** ✗; **c** ✗; **d** ✓; **e** ✗; **f** ✗; **g** ✓

🎧 **CD 3, track 70** Seite 73, Übung 2

- Was werden wir heute machen?
- Wir werden zuerst auf den Markt gehen und einkaufen.
- Toll. Und dann?
- Wir werden zum Dom gehen und Karussell fahren.
- Wollen wir ins Museum gehen?
- Nee, das finde ich langweilig.
- Werden wir zum Zoo gehen?
- Ja. Hagenbecks Tierpark ist super. Und dann werden wir zum Fischrestaurant gehen.
- Ach nee, bitte nicht. Fisch mag ich nicht.

4B.3 Was hast du gemacht? (Seite 74)

AT 1.2-3 **1** Listen to these people talking. Circle Past, Present or Future.

For an additional challenge, play the recording again and ask students to identify the activities.

Answers: **a** future (will go for a meal); **b** past (bought souvenirs); **c** present (play football); **d** past (ate salad); **e** future (will go to France); **f** present (go to the cinema); **g** future (will stay in a tent); **h** past (went on a tour of the town)

🎧 **CD 3, track 71** Seite 74, Übung 1

a Wir werden essen gehen.
b Wir haben Souvenirs gekauft.
c Wir spielen oft Fußball.
d Ich habe Salat gegessen.
e Wir werden nach Frankreich fahren.
f Ich gehe ins Kino.
g Ich werde in einem Zelt wohnen.
h Wir haben eine Stadtrundfahrt gemacht.

2 Circle the correct form.

Answers: **a** haben; **b** bin; **c** sind; **d** habe; **e** sind; **f** haben

AT 3.2 **3** Complete the sentences with the correct past participle.

Answers: **a** gekauft; **b** gespielt; **c** gemacht; **d** gehört

4B.4 Im Prater (Seite 75)

AT 3.2 **1** Write in the correct words.

Answers: **a** letztes Wochenende; **b** morgen; **c** heute; **d** jeden Tag; **e** zweimal in der Woche; **f** gestern

AT 1.4-5 **2** Listen to the phone conversation and circle Past, Present or Future.

Answers: **a** past; **b** present; **c** past; **d** future; **e** past; **f** present

4B Zu Besuch

🎧 **CD 3, track 72**   Seite 75, Übung 2

- Hallo Mama!
- Hey, hallo Vanessa. Na, wie ist es in Wien?
- Hier ist es echt super. Gestern sind wir zum Prater gegangen. Wir sind mit der U-Bahn gefahren. Wir sind Karussell gefahren und haben tolle Musik gehört.
- Toll! Und heute?
- Also heute bleiben wir im Hotel und spielen Karten. Mensch, ist das doof. Es regnet ganz furchtbar!
- Wie schade.
- Ja, aber morgen werden wir ins Kino gehen.
- Na dann, viel Spaß!

4B.5 Nicos Videoblog (Seite 76)

AT 1.4–5 **1 Listen to these people talking about holidays and write in the information in English.**

Answers: **a** went to England, will go to France; **b** went swimming, will play basketball; **c** went to Hamburg, will go to school; **d** ate cornflakes for breakfast, will eat pizza

🎧 **CD 3, track 73**   Seite 76, Übung 1

a Wir werden nächstes Jahr nach Frankreich fahren. Wir waren letztes Jahr in England.
b Gestern bin ich schwimmen gegangen. Morgen werde ich Basketball spielen.
c Letztes Wochenende bin ich nach Hamburg gefahren. Nächste Woche werde ich in die Schule gehen.
d Wir werden heute Abend Pizza essen. Heute Morgen haben wir zum Frühstück Cornflakes gegessen.

AT 3.4–5 **2 Read the sentences and write F (*falsch* = wrong) or R (*richtig* = right).**

Answers: **a** F; **b** F; **c** R; **d** R; **e** R; **f** F; **g** F; **h** F; **i** R; **j** F

4B.6A Sprachlabor (Seite 77)

1 Circle the correct form of *haben* or *sein*.

Answers: **a** haben; **b** habe; **c** haben; **d** habe; **e** sind; **f** bin; **g** sind; **h** bin

2 Fill in the gaps. Look back through this unit to find the information.

Answers: <u>machen</u>, gemacht, haben; <u>hören</u>, gehört, haben; <u>fahren</u>, gefahren, sein; <u>tanzen</u>, getanzt, haben; <u>gehen</u>, gegangen, sein; <u>essen</u>, gegessen, haben; <u>fliegen</u>, geflogen, sein; <u>kaufen</u>, gekauft, haben; <u>wohnen</u>, gewohnt, haben

3 Fill in the gaps with *einem* or *einer*.

Answers: **a** einem; **b** einem; **c** einer; **d** einer; **e** einem; **f** einem

4B.6B Think (Seite 78)

1 Find compound nouns meaning …

Answers: **a** Jugendherberge; **b** Ferienhaus; **c** Campingplatz; **d** Wohnwagen; **e** Freizeitpark; **f** Stadtrundfahrt; **g** Schwimmbad; **h** Riesenrad; **i** Kleiderschrank; **j** Schokoladeneis

2 Write P (positive) or N (negative) next to these opinions.

Answers: **a** P; **b** N; **c** P; **d** P; **e** N; **f** P; **g** P; **h** N

4B Zu Besuch

Higher Workbook

4B.1 Die Ferien (Seite 72)

AT 1.3 **1 Listen to the conversation and answer the questions in English.**

Answers: **a** Spain; **b** by plane; **c** apartment; **d** two weeks; **e** always sunny; **f** no, with other people

🎧 **CD 4, track 70** Seite 72, Übung 1

- Hey Olaf, wohin fährst du in den Ferien?
- Ach, wir fahren nach Spanien, wie immer.
- Wo denn in Spanien?
- Wir fliegen nach Mallorca. Da ist es immer sonnig.
- Wo wohnt ihr?
- Wir wohnen in einer Ferienwohnung direkt am Meer. Es ist echt toll da.
- Schön! Wie lange bleibt ihr?
- Wir bleiben zwei Wochen.

2 Write einer or einem.

Answers: **a** einem; **b** einer; **c** einem; **d** einem; **e** einer; **f** einem

AT 3.2 **3 Fill in the grid in English.**

Answers: **a** car, Italy; **b** train, Austria; **c** plane, Turkey; **d** camper van, France

4B.2 Wir fahren nach Wien! (Seite 73)

AT 3.2 **1 Complete the sentences in the same order as the places are mentioned in the brochure.**

Answers: **a** eine Hafenrundfahrt machen; **b** auf dem Markt einkaufen; **c** Fisch essen; **d** zum Zoo gehen; **e** Karussell fahren; **f** ins Museum gehen

AT 1.3 **2 Listen to these people planning a day out in Hamburg. Write down, in English: a) three things the people will do; b) two things they won't do, and why.**

Answers: **a** go shopping at the market, go to the fairground at the cathedral, go to the zoo; **b** they won't go to the museum because it's boring, they won't go to the fish restaurant because one of them doesn't like fish

🎧 **CD 4, track 71** Seite 73, Übung 2

- Was werden wir heute machen?
- Wir werden zuerst auf den Markt gehen und einkaufen.
- Toll. Und dann?
- Wir werden zum Dom gehen und Karussell fahren.
- Wollen wir ins Museum gehen?
- Nee, das finde ich langweilig.
- Werden wir zum Zoo gehen?
- Ja. Hagenbecks Tierpark ist super. Und dann werden wir zum Fischrestaurant gehen.
- Ach nee, bitte nicht. Fisch mag ich nicht.

4B.3 Was hast du gemacht? (Seite 74)

AT 1.2–3 **1 Listen to these people talking. Write Past, Present or Future and exactly where or when.** For an additional challenge, ask students to identify the activities.

Answers: **a** future, tomorrow (will go for a meal); **b** past, in Paris (bought souvenirs); **c** present, often (play football); **d** past, in the restaurant (ate salad); **e** future, next year (will go to France); **f** future (present tense with future time expression), this evening (will go to the cinema); **g** future, in the holidays (will stay in a tent); **h** past, in London (went on a tour of the town)

🎧 **CD 4, track 72** Seite 74, Übung 1

a Wir werden morgen essen gehen.
b Wir haben in Paris Souvenirs gekauft.
c Wir spielen oft Fußball.
d Ich habe im Restaurant Salat gegessen.
e Wir werden nächstes Jahr nach Frankreich fahren.
f Ich gehe heute Abend ins Kino.
g Ich werde in den Ferien in einem Zelt wohnen.
h Wir haben in London eine Stadtrundfahrt gemacht.

2 Write in the correct form of haben or sein.

Answers: **a** haben; **b** bin; **c** sind; **d** habe; **e** sind; **f** haben

AT 3.2 **3 Complete the sentences with the correct form of haben and the correct past participle.**

Answers: **a** habe, gekauft; **b** haben, gespielt; **c** haben, gemacht; **d** habe, gehört

4B.4 Im Prater (Seite 75)

AT 3.2 **1 Write in the correct words.**

Answers: **a** letztes Wochenende; **b** morgen; **c** heute; **d** jeden Tag; **e** zweimal in der Woche; **f** gestern

4B Zu Besuch

2 Listen to the phone conversation. Write Past, Present or Future, and exactly when.

Answers: **a** past, yesterday; **b** present, today; **c** past, yesterday; **d** future, tomorrow; **e** past, yesterday; **f** present, today

> 🎧 CD 4, track 73   Seite 75, Übung 2
>
> – Hallo Mama!
> – Hey, hallo Vanessa. Na, wie ist es in Wien?
> – Hier ist es echt super. Gestern sind wir zum Prater gegangen. Wir sind mit der U-Bahn gefahren. Wir sind Karussell gefahren und haben tolle Musik gehört.
> – Toll! Und heute?
> – Also heute bleiben wir im Hotel und spielen Karten. Mensch, ist das doof. Es regnet ganz furchtbar!
> – Wie schade.
> – Ja, aber morgen werden wir ins Kino gehen.
> – Na dann, viel Spaß!

4B.5 Nicos Videoblog (Seite 76)

1 Listen to these people talking about holidays. For each speaker, note down one thing they did in the past and one thing they will do in the future.

Answers: **a** went to England, will go to France; **b** went swimming, will play basketball; **c** went to Hamburg, will go to school; **d** ate cornflakes for breakfast, will eat pizza

> 🎧 CD 4, track 74   Seite 76, Übung 1
>
> **a** Wir werden nächstes Jahr nach Frankreich fahren. Wir waren letztes Jahr in England.
> **b** Gestern bin ich schwimmen gegangen. Morgen werde ich Basketball spielen.
> **c** Letztes Wochenende bin ich nach Hamburg gefahren. Nächste Woche werde ich in die Schule gehen.
> **d** Wir werden heute Abend Pizza essen. Heute Morgen haben wir zum Frühstück Cornflakes gegessen.

2 Read the text. Write down, in English: three things Joachim has already done; three things he will do; at least four general facts (mentioned in the present tense).

Answers: three things he has done: went to Munich last week with his family, they went on a sightseeing tour of the city, he bought a new T-shirt; three things he will do: next week they are going to Innsbruck, they will go skiing, they will go snowboarding, four general facts: Munich is a great city, you can eat and drink well there, the beer is cheap but he is still too young to drink beer, Innsbruck is in Austria, the weather in Austria is cold in winter

4B.6A Sprachlabor (Seite 77)

1 Write in the correct form of haben or sein plus the correct past participle.

Answers: **a** haben, gegessen; **b** habe, gekauft; **c** haben, gewohnt; **d** habe, gespielt; **e** sind, gegangen; **f** bin, gefahren; **g** sind, geflogen; **h** bin, gegangen

2 Fill in the gaps. Look back through this unit to find the information.

Answers: machen, gemacht, haben; hören, gehört, haben; fahren, gefahren, sein; tanzen, getanzt, haben; gehen, gegangen, sein; essen, gegessen, haben; fliegen, geflogen, sein; kaufen, gekauft, haben; wohnen, gewohnt, haben

3 Fill in the gaps with einem or einer.

Answers: **a** einem; **b** einem; **c** einer; **d** einer; **e** einem; **f** einem

4B.6B Think (Seite 78)

1 Find compound nouns meaning …

Answers: **a** Jugendherberge; **b** Ferienhaus; **c** Campingplatz; **d** Wohnwagen; **e** Freizeitpark; **f** Stadtrundfahrt; **g** Schwimmbad; **h** Riesenrad; **i** Kleiderschrank; **j** Schokoladeneis

2 Translate these opinions into German.

Answers: **a** Ich freue mich darauf. **b** Das finde ich langweilig. **c** Das finde ich nicht langweilig. **d** Das ist toll. **e** Ich freue mich nicht darauf. **f** Das gefällt mir. **g** Das macht Spaß! **h** Das gefällt mir nicht.